WITHDRAWN

Urban Life and Urban Landscape
Zane L. Miller, Series Editor

A Fatal Drifting Apart

Democratic Social Knowledge and Chicago Reform

Laura M. Westhoff

The Ohio State University Press
Columbus

Library of Congress Cataloging-in-Publication Data
Westhoff, Laura M.
 A fatal drifting apart : democratic social knowledge and Chicago reform / Laura M.
Westhoff. — 1st. ed.
    p. cm. — (Urban life and urban landscape)
 Includes bibliographical references and index.
 ISBN-13: 978-0-8142-1058-1 (cloth : alk. paper)
 ISBN-10: 0-8142-1058-9 (cloth : alk. paper)
 ISBN-13: 978-0-8142-9137-5 (cd-rom)
 ISBN-10: 0-8142-9137-6 (cd-rom)
    1. Social reformers—Chicago—Illinois—History. 2. Social ethics—Chicago—
Illinois—History. 3. Chicago (Ill.)—Social conditions. 4. United States—Social
conditions—1865–1918. I. Title.
 HN80.C5W47 2007
 303.48'40977311—dc22
              2006100374

Cover design by Laurence J. Nozik
Type set in Minion
Printed by Thomson-Shore

To Darel, Henry, and Jacob

Contents

Preface

American democracy was in question in the 1890s. The pressures of industrial capitalism, the anonymity of urban life, the social dislocations of migration and immigration, the corruption of business and politics, the promises of the new social sciences led reformers to ponder the nature of democracy and work toward new means of fostering it in America's cities. This book examines the democratic aspirations of Chicago reformers at the turn of the twentieth century. It focuses on a particular vision of democracy as a set of social practices and epistemological commitments that emphasized deliberation, interaction, proximity, sympathetic understanding, and mutual relationships. Together these composed a democratic social knowledge that was inclusive, socially mediated, and offered a methodology for social action. Though its proponents believed it would revitalize political practices such as voting, such democracy extended beyond procedural, formal politics into the realm of everyday practice.

My work on this project began as my friend Annjie moved into Karen House, a Catholic Worker project in North St. Louis. Through her, I learned of the Worker Movement which since the 1930s has offered hospitality to the poor, not as a welfare agency or connected to any church, but as a home shared by our society's neediest people and those who choose to live their lives in relationships with them, in witness to their struggles. Though many of the culturally middle-class people like Annjie who move into Worker houses are activists, this is not the primary vision of the movement. Instead, it focuses on the radical transformations that accompany a life committed to fostering close and equitable relationships with and recognizing the dignity of every individual who comes through the door—even those our society rejects: the drug abusers, mentally ill, and chronically homeless people, who are frequent guests at Karen House. Annjie's reasons for moving into Karen House are her story to tell, but in the twelve years that she has lived there—twelve years during which I have been an observer and occasional interloper into the community while writing this book—I have been struck by parallels between the democratic practices of the reformers whose stories I tell here and the life my friend lives. In important ways it has helped me to understand the similarities and differences in past struggles for social justice and those of the present, the possibilities and limitations of radical democratic social relationships, and the ways that we have in the past and continue in the present to award (or deny) political and epistemological legitimacy to certain people, viewpoints, and groups. My friend's struggles to share in the lives of people so different from her and to take seriously their ideas and the lessons these marginalized people's experiences offer us about our society, echo an earlier commitment to a vision of democracy. This vision was one of mutual relationships in which shared experiences and engagement with community problems rendered a new form of democratic social knowledge that included a wide variety of experiences and perspectives and helped shape political discussions.

As I finish this project, we seem to take the meaning of democracy for granted, and it is a very different conception from the one outlined here. Pressure for elections in other parts of the Middle East receive a great deal of attention as evidence of growing democratic commitments in nations usually characterized as undemocratic. Elected government appears synonymous with democracy, though even dictators have held elections from time to time. This view is not entirely without precedent. The right to vote has been sacred in this country and much sought after by those to whom it was denied. One need only study the women's suffrage movement or learn how African Americans put their lives in jeopardy throughout the nineteenth and much of the twentieth centuries to cast a ballot to recognize that participating in elections holds great meaning for Americans. But during the Progressive Era, Chicago reformers worked toward a vision of democracy that encompassed much more than voting rights.

Several types of democratic thought emerged by the 1890s. Not surprisingly, one focused primarily on voting—expanding suffrage to women and disfranchised African Americans, revising voting and party practices, wielding direct, as opposed to representative, democracy. Another focused on shaping a new liberal regulatory state capable of providing a modicum of social welfare. Still another was more reactionary; believing that the ills of American democracy were rooted in the immigrant political machines and the votes of newly emancipated African Americans, nativists and racists sought to limit their political participation. Another looked to a framework of participatory democracy that foregrounded deliberation in the public sphere and engaged interaction in voluntary associations as a way to enact democracy. Each of these, tied as they were to Progressive reform, was intertwined with the others and responded to the social, economic, and intellectual problems that attended a nation in rapid transformation. We know the outcome of that transformation: By the 1920s women had gained the suffrage, some states had passed direct democracy laws, and many more had expanded the regulatory role of a new liberal administrative state working in concert with bureaucratic experts. However, in the early 1890s the direction of American democracy was yet unknown. It was a moment of great possibility.

This book explores that possibility from the vantage point of a group of Chicago social reformers who took the city as their laboratory for democracy. Though many varieties of democratic thought pervaded their efforts, it focuses on the specifically social and interactive ways they envisioned democracy. The democratic ideals they espoused were a set of practices, habits of mind that encouraged mutual relationships built on knowledge and sympathetic understanding of one's neighbors—be they the people next door or in the imagined civic community that made up the city—and on deliberation among people positioned differently throughout the city. Process, rather than outcome, was their primary concern, for they believed that through democratic praxis—of discussion, of interaction with people very different from one's self, of shared experiences—one learned to regard others as equals and to work for a public good that was collectively defined. Democracy, then, was social, cultural, and psychological, as well as procedural.

Key to their vision of democracy was the development of a democratic social knowledge. By social knowledge I mean the ideas, beliefs, information, and observations communities use to describe, explain, and understand social reality and shape social institutions. Social knowledge structures the collective narratives we tell about our lives. Though they did not describe it in such terms, reformers sought a democratic epistemology (theory of knowledge and how we know) as the basis of the social knowledge they created. Seeking to understand the problems of their society and formulate solutions, reformers tried ways of including a variety of perspectives and experiences of community members as they forged new social explanations and cultural meanings. This book thus looks to the efforts of Chicago reformers to better understand the nature of processes to build democratic social knowledge—how this knowledge was created; the frameworks of meaning it provided; its potential to offer recognition and epistemological status to community members on the margins; its ability to reshape dominant social narratives and thus inspire political and social change—and its limitations.

Since reformers worked out their ideas about democratic praxis (defined as the intersection of theory and everyday practices) in the context of reform, they also engaged with prevailing collective narratives that functioned as a type of social knowledge to order institutions, policies, and cultural meaning and status. Because the United States was in the midst of tumultuous change, these narratives—about the economy, about responsibilities of the state, about class, gender, race, and ethnic relations—were fragile, and much of the struggle over social reform was not just about creating social welfare institutions but also about determining the cultural authority to interpret, explain, and shape the dominant narrative. Thus the book not only explores social knowledge as a *process;* it also examines its *content*—the explanations and cultural meanings and values of multiple narratives—that gave rise to reform impulses in the first place. Competing and contesting forms of social knowledge—as both process and content—at times were at odds, suggesting that one of the fundamental challenges was (and remains) confronting questions of epistemological authority and status. In a democracy, who has the power to define social problems and offer solutions? Whose experience and knowledge are legitimate?

While I did not set out to write a book that offers a past usable in the present—indeed, there is far too much that is different between the world of the Progressives and our own circumstances to think we can find in the past easy solutions to the challenges democracy faces today—I have been repeatedly struck by the continued traces of issues revealed by the analytical lens of democratic social knowledge I employ. I hope that its small contribution to a larger and still growing body of writing on the democratic aspirations found in the Progressive Era will help us think about the meaning of democracy in our own day.

Acknowledgments

The support and encouragement of many teachers, colleagues, friends, and family have made this book possible. This project grew out of my interest in the Progressive Era and changing meanings of democracy, nourished long ago as an undergraduate student in Bob Wiebe's history classes at Northwestern University. Bob's generous oversight of an independent study my senior year set me down the path that has led to this book. As a graduate student at Washington University, I had the privilege of working with two wonderful advisors, Iver Bernstein and Mary Ann Dzuback. Iver helped me to understand nineteenth-century cultural history, which ultimately proved so important in my interpretation of the Progressive Era, and ever pushed me to find just the right word or phrase. Mary Ann encouraged my early interest in the social production of knowledge and my very broad understanding of the history of education. I am grateful for the mentoring and friendship both have offered through the years. Other members of my dissertation committee were invaluable. Howard Brick asked the kind of difficult questions that help turn a dissertation into a book. Andrea Friedman's insight and support of the project proved immensely helpful when the dissertation was in its home stretch and I began working in earnest on the book manuscript.

I appreciate the colleagues who have read all or parts of the manuscript and agreed, disagreed, deliberated, and argued with me over the years. Some simply took the time to answer my questions or listen to me think out loud. Thanks to Robin Bachin, Susan Porter Benson, Victoria Bissell Brown, Ben Cawthra, Kevin Fernlund, Marilyn Fischer, Indira Falk Gesink, Minsoo Kang, Kimberly Little, Elisabeth Israels Perry, Gerda Ray, and Sharra Vostral. I am grateful to the anonymous reviewers who read the manuscript and offered suggestions for its improvement. A special thanks to Robert Johnston, whose support for this project moved it toward publication and whose personal example of collegiality has been a model for me. I would never have finished this book had it not been for the diligent reading, draconian schedules, and enthusiastic encouragement of the Learned Sisters Club. My fellow club members, Lessie Jo Frazier and Deborah Cohen, deserve much credit for pushing me toward its completion. Despite the help of these intellectually and personally generous friends, I am responsible for the book's final form.

I received financial support for the research and writing of this book from Washington University's Mellon Dissertation Fellowship, a Newberry Library Short-term Fellowship, a University of Missouri-St. Louis Small Grant, and a University of Missouri Research Board Award. For diligent, timely, and resourceful research assistance, I am grateful to Mike Gavin and Gary Fishgall. My thanks to the library and research staffs at the Chicago Historical Society, the Richard J. Daly Library at the University of Illinois-Chicago, Special Collections and University Archives, the University of Chicago Regenstein Library Special Collections and Research Center, Wiggin Library at Meadville-Lombard Theological School, New York Public Library, Inter-library Loan at University of Missouri-St. Louis, Thomas Jefferson Library. Thanks to Kathy and Chuck Ripp and Marty Swatek for their hospitality during my many research trips to Chicago, and to Chris Murphy and Amy Rountree for their friendly accommodations during several visits to Madison.

At The Ohio State University Press, Heather Lee Miller first expressed interest in the manuscript and saw it through the early stages of the review process. Sandy Crooms took up the project and saw it through to completion. I am grateful to series editor Zane Miller for his interest and for his expert critiques and editorial suggestions. In the final stages of this project I received prompt and professional editorial help from Eugene O'Connor. It has been a pleasure to work with the entire staff, who have patiently answered my questions and accommodated my requests.

I am grateful to my dear friends Annjie Schiefelbein, Lisa Moscoso, and Sheena Backman for conversations over many morning coffees, lunches, and dinners. I'm not sure how this nurse practitioner, pediatrician, and businesswoman/stay-at-home mom put up with my musings and tirades about history, but I am glad they kept asking me about my work. I am even more glad about our many other conversations and their unquestioning support in many difficult times. Terry Quinn has been a constant friend and companion in my journey as an author, sharing delight (and misery) in the freedom of writing and the occasional escape into the aesthetics of fine wine, beautiful food, and tango. The staff at La Dolce Via kept me well fed while I rewrote and edited the manuscript.

Philip and Diane Shelton have offered moral support, understanding, and generosity over the years. During the years in which I wrote this book, my siblings Dan Westhoff, Julie Ashmun, and Kate Westhoff, have done what they've done best throughout our lives: reminded me to have fun and not take myself so seriously. Many thanks to them, and to my sister-in-law, Melissa Westhoff, and brother-in-law, Mark Ashmun, for not asking me too often "how's the book coming?" I cannot begin to thank my parents, Herb and Mary Beth Westhoff, enough for all of their support throughout the years. They nurtured my intellectual curiosity, were committed to my education at sacrifice to themselves, and offered me their unfailing confidence. They have made my family's life easier in so many concrete ways—offering a hand to clean the house, cook a meal, watch a sick child when I had to teach, go to a meeting, or had a deadline. Without their help from the very outset, this book would have remained only a dream. I am grateful that they are able to offer my children the example of love and support they have given to me.

This book is dedicated to my boys, Hank and Jake Shelton, and my husband, Darel Shelton. Hank inspires me every day. Diagnosed with autism six years ago, he struggles daily to make sense of his world and to communicate with us. His courage, hard work, and frustrations in expressing even his most basic desires have helped me keep my bouts of writer's block in perspective. Jake's creativity and enthusiasm are infectious, as is his excitement about pirates, superheroes, and guitars. He makes me laugh and reminds me to look for lightning bugs. Both boys are a reminder of why finishing this book mattered so much to me. Perhaps some day they'll ask me about it. My husband likes to tell people that I've been working on this project longer than he's known me (which is almost fifteen years now!). His patience with me is the ultimate reason this book is done. His sacrifice, his willingness to let me work far too many evenings, weekends, and vacations, to do more than his share of housework and child care, have afforded me the opportunity to finally finish this book. Only he knows what it has cost, and it is a debt I can never repay. For this and for so many other reasons, he is the love of my life.

Introduction

On December 3, 1891, two years after Jane Addams and Ellen Gates Starr opened Hull House social settlement on the near west side of Chicago, Addams spoke to fellow members of the Chicago Woman's Club. She was gaining local notoriety for her work with the city's poor and ethnic populations, and her talk that day highlighted the maladies accompanying late nineteenth-century urbanization. Citing the political corruption, economic inequities, and moral malaise that gripped the modern city, Addams asserted that "the social organization has been broken down." Residents "live for the moment side by side, many of them without knowledge of each other, without fellowship, without local tradition, or public spirit." Addams identified the problem as one of democratic social knowledge—understanding of social organizations and relations enacted in fellowship, commonalities, and engagement—in short, democratic practices. She feared a "fatal drifting apart, the dividing of a city between the rich and poor," and, given her experience in settlement work, she might well have added immigrant and native-born men and women, black and white.[1]

The "fatal drifting apart" that Addams described is an apt metaphor for understanding the anxieties and motivations of Chicago reformers in the 1890s. It captured the cultural and psychological fragmentation that historians recognize as a significant aspect of late nineteenth-century American life.[2] It also pointed out the dangers to democracy posed by the major economic transformation from proprietary to corporate capitalism, by the circumscribed racial, ethnic, and gendered boundaries around full citizenship, and by the political corruption that plagued U.S. cities. These dangers left reformers struggling over the shifting meanings and practices of democracy. This book explores their contributions to the Progressive Era battle over democracy as the intersection of social knowledge and democratic practices.

1. Though she spoke specifically of London's East End, she did so to illustrate Chicago's problems. Jane Addams, "Outgrowths of Toynbee Hall," 3, Jane Addams Papers, Swarthmore College Peace Collection, Reel 47 (hereafter cited as JAP).

2. T. J. Jackson Lears, *No Place of Grace: Antimodernism and the Transformation of American Culture, 1880–1920* (Chicago: University of Chicago Press, 1981); Casey Nelson Blake, *Beloved Community: The Cultural Criticism of Randolph Bourne, Van Wyck Brooks, Waldo Frank, and Lewis Mumford* (Chapel Hill: University of North Carolina Press, 1991); Alan Trachtenberg, *The Incorporation of America: Culture and Society in the Gilded Age* (New York: Hill and Wang, 1982); Christopher Lasch, *The New Radicalism in America, 1889–1963: The Intellectual as a Social Type* (New York: Knopf, 1965).

As Addams surveyed Chicago, she found ample evidence of a drifting apart. Ethnic and class tension had exploded in the Haymarket Affair five years earlier, and violent skirmishes were typical between striking workers and police. Neighborhoods increasingly separated by class, race, and ethnicity were built in the wake of the Great Fire of 1871. The boundaries defined the city's cultural geography as well, leaving residents not only spatially but also psychologically distanced from one another. As one observer remarked, "We are getting to be a community of strangers. No one expects to know . . . half the audience at the church or theater, and, as to knowing one's neighbors, that has become a lost art."[3]

This observation of the lost art of knowing others was not just a lament about the passing of small town America into an industrialized, urban nation. It also suggested a significant political and social problem for a nation in which the democratic ethos depended not only on the freedom occasioned by proprietary capitalism, in which individual ownership of productive resources was a prerequisite for political independence, but also on the ability to forge sympathetic bonds with others.[4] Indeed a moral language of sentiment and sympathy had pervaded the work of Scottish Enlightenment theorists, early American novelists, Romantic thinkers, and political leaders as prominent as Thomas Jefferson.[5] Adam Smith suggested that sympathy provided the affective tie that held society together and created the boundaries of an imagined ethical and political community.[6] In his 1801 inaugural address, Thomas Jefferson urged Americans to put aside a decade of conflict. "Liberty and even life itself are but dreary things," he wrote, without "harmony and affection" undergirding the political community.[7] Horace Bushnell, the Romantic minister, wrote in an 1846 sermon, "beholding, as in a glass, the feelings of our neighbor, we are changed into the

---

3. *Chicago Tribune,* March 30, 1873, quoted in Bessie Louis Pierce, *A History of Chicago,* vol. 3, *The Rise of a Modern City, 1871–1893* (New York: Knopf), 1947.

4. Jeff Sklansky, *The Soul's Economy: Market Society and Selfhood in American Thought, 1820–1920* (Chapel Hill: University of North Carolina Press, 2002), discusses proprietary capitalism in the early republic. He argues that proprietary capitalism, with its emphasis on the autonomous, free individual, declined in the nineteenth century and that the advent of industrial capitalism and emphasis on the social self has limited discussion of the economic inequality arising from corporate capitalism. For an alternative interpretation of corporate capitalism that sees it as rendering the possibility for new subjectivities and new forms of politics, see James Livingston, *Pragmatism and the Political Economy of Cultural Revolution, 1850–1940* (Chapel Hill: University of North Carolina Press, 1994).

5. On the civic role of sympathy in the early United States, see Elizabeth Barnes, *States of Sympathy: Seduction and Democracy in the American Novel* (New York: Columbia University Press, 1997), 1–18; Andrew Burstein, *Sentimental Democracy: The Evolution of America's Romantic Self-Image* (New York: Hill and Wang, 1999); and Sklansky, *Soul's Economy.*

6. Adam Smith, *The Theory of Moral Sentiments,* ed. D. D. Raphael and A. L. Macfie (Oxford: Clarendon, 1976). Also Benedict Anderson, *Imagined Communities: Reflections on the Origin and Spread of Nationalism* (London: Verso, 1991).

7. Quoted in Burstein, *Sentimental Democracy,* 3–4.

same image, by the assimilating power of sensibility and fellow-feeling."[8] Democratic society, then, seemed predicated on a way of knowing others that was relational and that emphasized familiarity and sympathy. Conversely, without social understanding, sympathetic identification was rendered impossible and civic bonds threatened—a fear that haunted many reformers. By century's end, finding a basis for democratic social relations seemed increasingly urgent as classical political economy and republican government had clearly failed to bring about the harmony of interests that Jefferson's generation anticipated.

During the 1890s the eyes of the world turned frequently to Chicago as it struggled with the promises and challenges of urban democracy. Local government was limited in its ability to meet the problems of sanitation, housing, and transportation. Its relationship to county government, which also provided some services to city residents, was complicated, and its ability to raise revenue, either through taxes or bond issues, was strictly constrained by state law. Plagued by extensive corruption and antipathy from downstate legislators, city government was ill equipped to meet the needs of a rapidly expanding city as the population doubled to one million between 1880 and 1890; ten years later it had grown to 1.7 million.

Annexation of surrounding townships and immigration primarily from Germany, Ireland, Italy, Russia, and other Eastern European countries accounted for the growth. Between 1887 and 1893 the city annexed several townships, expanding its area from 35 to 190 square miles. Three-quarters of the residents in this metropolis were foreign born or the children of immigrants, drawn by the city's rapidly expanding economy. Industrial, craft, and commercial economies comprising the Pullman Palace Car Company, Illinois Steel, McCormick Reaper Works, meat-packing companies such as Swift and Armour, garment and building industries, and retail companies such as Montgomery Ward, Sears and Roebuck, and Marshall Field and Company provided a robust economic infrastructure. Along with immigration and economic expansion came the growth of a strong and frequently radical labor movement, as unions enjoyed strong support in the city.[9] Events like the Haymarket Affair and the subsequent execution of anarchists blamed for the deaths of several policemen, as well as the Pullman strike and boycott that spread across the United States—and the government injunction used to break the strike—were not just national but indeed

8. Horace Bushnell, "Unconscious Influence" (1846), in Horace Bushnell, *Sermons for the New Life,* rev. ed. , 192–93 (New York: Charles Scribner's Sons, 1886). Quoted in Sklansky, *Soul's Economy,* 58.

9. Richard Schneirov, *Labor and Urban Politics: Class Conflict and the Origins of Modern Liberalism in Chicago, 1864–1897* (Urbana: University of Illinois Press, 1998); Bruce Nelson, *Beyond the Martyrs: A Social History of Chicago's Anarchists, 1870–1900* (New Brunswick, NJ: Rutgers University Press, 1988).

worldwide symbols of industrial class conflict and the growing alliances between capital and the state.[10] Indeed, the city was a hotbed of social activism.

These challenges made Chicago emblematic of the difficulties confronting other cities undergoing rapid urbanization and industrialization. Its symbolic importance, standing between the commercial, "civilized" East and the wilderness of the West and encapsulating all of the problems of urbanization and industrialization—and all of the aspirations and opportunities of innovative technological and economic growth—captures historical attention. It offers us a vantage point from which to explore the struggle to define the future of American democracy. The backdrop of industrialization, emerging classes, and ethnic and racial pluralism set the stage on which Chicago reformers took up the seemingly impossible challenge of enacting democracy.

This book examines the efforts of local reformers as they collectively experimented with ways to foster democracy built on mutual respect, trust, and sympathetic understanding—traits that were important components for political deliberation and social cohesion and ultimately activism.[11] This was no small undertaking in a city that comprised primarily foreign immigrants and migrants from other parts of the United States and increasingly riven by class conflict. They tried to overcome these barriers and to know one another and negotiate ways to explain their city's problems and shape its future. *A Fatal Drifting Apart* examines the Chicago reform community as it wrestled with the meaning of democracy and forms of democratic practice in the urban environment.

The book argues that Chicago reformers offered a democratic social knowledge that helped transform American liberal democracy and political culture at the turn of the twentieth century and beyond. By "democratic social knowledge" I mean a way of knowing that privileges experience, proximity, interaction, and sympathetic understanding and that encourages negotiation of multiple perspectives and community participation in defining the narratives and various types of knowledge that shaped widely accepted social meanings.[12] In contrast

10. For example, Lessie Jo Frazier notes that, as late as the 1990s, labor activists in northern Chile still celebrated as martyrs the men executed in connection with the Haymarket Affair. See Lessie Jo Frazier, *Salt in the Sand,* forthcoming, Duke University Press.

11. I use the terms "reformer" and "reform community" throughout this work to refer to people who sought change in the existing conditions of the city. While this definition at times makes strange bedfellows of conservative, moderate, and more radical men and women, it speaks to the fact that this period witnessed a great deal of conversation and cooperation among them. It also highlights the difficulty of categorizing reformers during the Progressive Era. For example, Maureen Flanagan has demonstrated the difficulty of the term "reformer" by illustrating how the designation was appropriated by businessmen as a strategy to marginalize the working classes and ethnic societies who offered different visions of urban reform. Maureen Flanagan, *Charter Reform in Chicago* (Carbondale: Southern Illinois University Press, 1987), ix–x.

12. My use of "proximate" as an aspect of democratic social knowledge builds on the work of

to earlier a priori formal knowledge and emerging academic expertise, such ways of knowing become a form of democratic induction in which experience and observation were shared and mediated in public and used to challenge and redefine prevailing cultural assumptions. Efforts to promote democratic social knowledge could be found in a wide variety of reform efforts and communities such as social settlements, cross-class civic organizations, cross-race alliances, labor arbitration, the narrative styles of reform literature, and the visual culture of media forms like public expositions and movies. Reformers' emphasis on interactive ways of knowing further offered a democratic praxis (theory and action) that promoted mutuality, trust, and respect in order to invigorate public engagement and to overcome the tendency toward a "fatal drifting apart."

The reformers who promoted such practices eschewed the atomistic and abstract natural laws of classical political economy; they sought to expand the democratic polity by extending sympathetic understanding built on recognition of common humanity. They frequently wrestled with the role of government, envisioning it as an agent of redistributive justice whose priority was to meet social needs and not just to fulfill a limited social contract in which the state's primary function was the defense of private property.

As we see in chapter 1, a liberal republicanism built on classical political economy served as a powerful narrative emphasizing a unity of interests that had grown up along with the city and as a natural and divine justice operating through the free market. It described as universal a style of rationality that privileged calculated exchange, self-interest, and formal laws of nineteenth-century economic and legal systems. As civic elites extolled the economic opportunities available in Chicago and argued for the supremacy of free labor as the source of discipline necessary to maintain social order, they rendered suspect those who did not share in Chicago's material success or who held conflicting ideas. The conception of rationality found in classical economic and free labor paradigms thus functioned as a measure of legitimacy in public debate. In this chapter we see the power of dominant narratives of social knowledge to frame public debate and social institutions. But by the 1890s the liberal republican narrative was under extraordinary strain, and, as we see in subsequent chapters, reformers outlined an alternative way—in the form of democratic social knowledge—to conceive of the democratic polity and the practice of democracy by drawing on Chicago residents' experiences and ideas.

Shannon Jackson, who describes a "proximate epistemology" as the basis of "participatory fieldwork in the early stages of American sociology, social work, and social reform." She emphasizes its roots in domestic discourse and its similarities to pragmatism. Proximate epistemology, as it was practiced at Hull House, drew primarily from the discourse of domesticity, privileging women as interpreters of experiences of private and ordinary routines of living. Shannon Jackson, *Lines of Activity: Performance, Historiography, Hull-House Domesticity* (Ann Arbor: University of Michigan Press, 2000), 6.

To understand how reformers promoted democratic social knowledge, its possibilities and limitations, and its implications for the practice of democracy and the role of the state, the book examines select individuals, groups, and events prominent in Chicago's social and political reform movements in the period between 1890 and 1919. In chapter 2 we explore the Civic Federation of Chicago (CFC), which comprised a diverse group of businessmen, unionists, middle-class and elite women, social scientists, and religious leaders. The organization was at the forefront of political reform for fifteen years, spearheading efforts to create a new city charter. It espoused the idea that social knowledge was the result of constant negotiation among multiple perspectives, and it brought residents from different sectors together to facilitate that debate, search for common solutions to social problems, and promote political action. However, early on the CFC was torn between its hope that a more open-ended and inclusive process of creating this knowledge would reconcile division and its anticipation that the group's promotion of social science expertise would serve as a means of bringing order and rationality to the city. While these processes were not necessarily mutually exclusive, they became so as many members increasingly privileged an elitist model of expertise based on social science. Competing views of reason and justice manifested in debates over poor relief, gambling, and school reform were constituent with these tensions and resulted in a gender and class split within the organization. This chapter thus illustrates competing ideas about democratic social knowledge and foreshadows their struggle in the arena of formal politics.

In chapter 3 we journey to Hull House social settlement, where Jane Addams and female residents laid out a framework of democratic social knowledge different from that which ultimately shaped the CFC. It emphasized proximity and experience, mutuality, public deliberation, sympathetic understanding, and aesthetic knowing while offering a (gendered) activist social science that sought to wed new forms of expertise with local participation. They built on the personal relationships they had developed living in their multiethnic, working-class neighborhood to turn their settlement house into an arena for public deliberation, social inquiry, and political and social experimentation. Addams's work in the settlement, which pushed her into a multitude of reform endeavors throughout the city, suggests the potential of interaction across class and ethnic lines to yield a fuller social understanding and redefine the boundaries of the state to promote social justice. The chapter further shows the centrality of everyday interactions in the formation and practice of democratic social knowledge.

Chapter 4 uses the Pullman strike and debates over labor arbitration to more closely examine the class dilemmas confronting democratic social knowledge. In an environment where class and urban boundaries meant that workers and owners were largely unknown to one another and where industrial capitalist economic transformation bred class hostility, some reformers looked to arbitration to encourage democratic character traits among both capitalists and workers. Many reformers believed arbitration served simultaneously as a deliberative forum for resolving disputes in a way that built mutual recognition and respect, trust, and understanding. It also served as a process that promoted the formation of democratic social knowledge built on the collective knowledge of the work process held by workers and businessmen alike. Following these issues into the Hart, Shaffner, and Marx trade agreements and joint arbitration boards in the 1910s, we see a transformation in the attitudes of a few capitalist elites toward labor arbitration. Similarly we find a new willingness among Chicago's labor leaders to use the state to advance and protect their agendas; hence we see the foreshadowing of an expanded role for the state as the arbitrator of conflicting concepts of social claims and economic justice.

Further testing the possibilities and limits of democratic social knowledge to mediate social justice claims and secure cultural agency, chapter 5 investigates instances and strategies that African Americans and their white allies employed to bring the races together.[13] Believing that interaction between and proximity of the races would help overcome racial division, race reformers built the Frederick Douglass Club, an interracial social settlement, and encouraged interracial cooperation on a variety of reform measures. Using an embodied knowledge, one that posited social knowledge in public representations of themselves as respectable, hard-working, and worthy citizens, African Americans pressed their cultural agency, countering popular and social scientific racism in antilynching texts, social interactions, and public displays of an alternative (middle-class) black body legible to (middle-class) white Americans. Yet we also see in this chapter the racialized limitations of democratic social knowledge, limitations that suggested a larger tension between democratic social knowledge and the conflation of prejudice and subjective viewpoints with knowledge.

The book concludes in chapter 6 with a brief examination of the struggle over democratic social knowledge in the arena of formal politics. As was apparent in the charter campaign of 1906–7 and in debates over direct democracy in

---

13. I use the term "race" herein as a historically contingent category that was in flux. See, for example, David R. Roediger, *Wages of Whiteness: Race and the Making of the American Working Class* (London: Verso, 1991); Mae Ngai, "The Architecture of Race in American Immigration Law: A Reexamination of the Immigration Act of 1924," *Journal of American History* 86, no. 1 (June 1999): 67–93; Thomas A. Guglielmo, *White on Arrival: Italians, Race, Color, and Power in Chicago, 1890–1945* (New York: Oxford University Press, 2003). Similarly, I recognize distinctions within other categories such as "women" or "businessmen." See, for example, Nan Enstad, *Ladies of Labor, Girls of Adventure: Working Women, Popular Culture, and Labor Politics at the Turn of the Twentieth Century* (New York: Columbia University Press, 1999); Howell John Harris, "The Making of a 'Business Community,' 1880–1930: Definitions and Ingredients of a Collective Identity," in *Federalism, Citizenship, and Collective Identities in U.S. History*, ed. Cornelius A. van Minnen and Sylvia L. Hilton, 123–40 (Amsterdam: Vu University Press, 2000).

the years following, the ultimate failure of reformers to reach a new consensus about democratic social knowledge would have significant consequences for the course of liberal democracy in the twentieth century. Desires for legitimization of experience and viewpoint, not only self-interest defined by a market model of exchange in economics, motivated women's organizations, ethnic societies, and labor organizations to oppose the charter. Holding fast to a classical political economic view of the autonomous individual as the universal political and economic actor, the conservative members of the CFC and business elites were outraged at the stance of what they called interest groups, whose activism ultimately defeated the charter. Some were further disheartened that citizens rejected the expertise of the businessmen, political scientists, and legal scholars who helped write and stump for the charter. Here we will see the resilience of liberal republicanism and its consequences for constraining the possibilities of democratic social knowledge.

These key examples of democratic social knowledge in formation—Jane Addams and Hull House, the Civic Federation, labor arbitration, interracial activism, and charter reform—together point to three fronts on which democratic social knowledge battled. The first front was the emerging discourse of reason and expertise, which businessmen and social scientists sought to claim for themselves. Yet we also see that the language of expertise was flexible; it was employed by people like Jane Addams and Ida Wells-Barnett and by unionists seeking to secure a voice in industry, who all claimed their experience with and proximity to social problems as a basis for their own logic and authority in matters of reform.[14]

The cultural terrain served as a second front, as reformers noted that social knowledge was shaped by and through drama, reform literature, public expositions, and movies. Efforts by African Americans to exercise cultural agency, for example, were important means to ensure that the input into social knowledge about race was more inclusive. Finally, democratic social knowledge battled on

14. For example, Robin Bachin explains that "emerging faith in the power of experts and social science to transform knowledge and shape urban growth forced a reexamination of the power of religious leaders, genteel elites, and ward bosses," while, at the same time, a language of expertise was used by a variety of groups. She juxtaposes the epistemological concerns of the University of Chicago and the University of Chicago Settlement to illustrate the differences between the distanced, formal epistemology represented in the former and the interactive social inquiry encouraged by the latter. Similarly, historians have demonstrated that female reformers appropriated the rhetoric of expertise to expand women's role in public life. Robin F. Bachin, *Building the South Side: Urban Space and Civic Culture in Chicago, 1890–1919* (Chicago: University of Chicago Press, 2004), 7. Kathryn Kish Sklar, *Florence Kelley and the Nation's Work: The Rise of Women's Political Culture, 1830–1900* (New Haven: Yale University Press, 1995); Camilla Stivers, *Bureau Men, Settlement Women: Constructing Public Administration in the Progressive Era* (Lawrence: University of Kansas Press, 2000); Robyn Muncy, *Creating a Female Dominion in American Reform, 1890–1935* (New York: Oxford University Press, 1991).

the terrain of formal politics, particularly in the form of struggles over political knowledge—that is, knowledge of how to make the political process work. For example, in debates over the charter campaign, we see competing ideas about the nature, responsibilities, and mechanisms of city government.

Taken together, these examples of democratic social knowledge in formation and the fronts on which they battled illustrate the extent to which public debates over social and political reform reflected widespread tension over pluralist conceptions of knowledge. Such pluralism served to challenge a nineteenth-century republican paradigm of a singular public good and classical liberal political economy's privileging of self-interested economic behavior.[15] The examples of democratic social knowledge thus offer new ways to think about the goals and practices of democracy and the purposes of the liberal democratic state. By the end of the book, we see that the democratic praxis—the intersection of knowledge and everyday practices—emerging from the lessons of Chicago reform requires democratic social knowledge in a dual sense. It is both inclusive processes of input into shaping pervasive cultural, social, and political attitudes and institutions and the framework of knowledge that result from those processes.

The men, women, and their organizations that constituted the Chicago reform community played important roles as mediators of democratic social knowledge. Primarily members of a civic elite and an expanding and fluid middle class that included petite bourgeois proprietors, union leaders, college-educated women, as well as professionals, these reformers found that they occupied strategic positions within Chicago's social, moral, and political economies.[16]

15. Philip Ethington has suggested the importance of the role of pluralist conceptions of knowledge in the modern city. See, for example, Philip J. Ethington, *The Public City: The Political Construction of Urban Life in San Francisco, 1850–1900* (New York: Cambridge University Press, 1994), and "The Metropolis and Multicultural Ethics: Direct Democracy versus Deliberative Democracy in the Progressive Era," in *Progressivism and the New Democracy,* ed. Sidney M. Milkis and Jerome M. Mileur, 192–225 (Amherst: University of Massachusetts Press, 1999).

16. Burton J. Bledstein, *The Culture of Professionalism: The Middle Class and the Development of Higher Education* (New York: Norton, 1976); Stuart Blumin, *The Emergence of the Middle Class: Social Experience in the American City, 1760–1900* (New York: Cambridge University Press, 1989). Historians have struggled to identify the "middle class" with much precision. See, for example, Burton J. Bledstein, "Introduction: Storytellers to the Middle Class"; Sven Beckert, "Propertied of a Different Kind: Bourgeoisie and Lower Middle Class in the Nineteenth-century United States"; and Robert D. Johnston, "Conclusion: Historians and the Middle Class," all in *The Middling Sorts: Explorations in the History of the American Middle Class,* ed. Burton J. Bledstein and Robert D. Johnston (New York: Routledge, 2001). See also Robert D. Johnston, *The Radical Middle Class: Populist Democracy and the Question of Capitalism in Progressive-era Portland, Oregon* (Princeton, NJ: Princeton University Press, 2003). Johnston argues that historians should more carefully attend to the contributions of the middle classes to American political culture. Though it is not the purpose of this book to engage a thorough analysis of class and class formation, I have found Johnston's suggestion valuable in helping to identify the ways that Chicago reformers were instrumental in promoting political engagement that not only was shaped by but also transcended class identity. In understanding the role of reformers as mediators, I suggest that they were engaged in a process of

Aligning with more marginalized members of Chicago society—workers, poor people, recent immigrants—they were able to use their newfound social capital to bring their allies' concerns into important conversations about the democratic polity and the role of the state. Moreover, they were able to create counter public spheres in which to freely deliberate alternative social narratives.[17] Seeking to broker greater understanding among Chicago's disparate sectors and more extensive knowledge about Chicago's problems, their reform efforts were not simply calculated to secure the status quo, which increasingly privileged a middle class cohered around proprietary ownership, professional occupations and expertise, and a cultural rhetoric of respectability. As they translated the experiences and perspectives of different groups, they also offered a model of the middle-class mediator as one able to take different perspectives, negotiate among various interests, and form alliances with those below to put pressure on those above.[18] Given the cultural expectations of the time, the people with whom one interacted and built relationships was indeed political.

These mediators were able to exercise significant influence in reform debates since government at the local, state, and national levels did not yet play an active role in matters of social welfare or economic regulation. Reformers stepped into the vacuum created by the weak state, and indeed many of them, women and African Americans in particular, were disfranchised. Closed off from access to formal political power, they responded creatively to the social needs around them, sometimes by forming voluntary associations to address those needs and sometimes by pressing social claims on the state to take more

---

forging relationships across class that did not simply seek social control. Rather, their efforts suggest a deeper commitment, shared with people across the class spectrum, to engaging issues of justice and the responsibilities of individuals and the democratic state. For Johnston's discussion of the political role of class in modern politics, see *Radical Middle Class,* 257–78. For an articulation of the political potential of viewing the social agent as encompassing *multiple* political identities, not just single or totalizing interests defined in terms of gender or class, see Chantal Mouffe, "Feminism, Citizenship, and Radical Democratic Politics," in *Feminists Theorize the Political,* ed. Judith Butler and Joan W. Scott, 369–84 (New York: Routledge, 1992).

17. Jackson, *Lines of Activity,* 73; Nancy Fraser, "Rethinking the Public Sphere: A Contribution to the Critique of Actually Existing Democracy," in *Habermas and the Public Sphere,* ed. Craig Calhoun, 109-42 (Cambridge, MA: MIT Press, 1992).

18. For an alternative view of Progressive reformers, one that argues they ignored real class divisions in claiming to speak for a broader "public," see Shelton Stromquist, *Reinventing "The People": The Progressive Movement, the Class Problem, and the Origins of Modern Liberalism* (Urbana: University of Illinois Press, 2005). Similar to my argument that reformers sought to prevent a drifting apart, Stromquist emphasizes their efforts to promote social harmony, though he emphasizes the ways that their reform language masked class divisions and ultimately undermined labor Progressives. His analysis clarifies one of the limitations of Progressivism, though my concern with democratic social knowledge emphasizes something different—an intersection of democracy, knowledge, and politics—which, as we will see in chapter 4, also had class limitations.

responsibility for ensuring the public welfare.[19] Nevertheless, although their role in state building is well documented, some reformers who acted as mediators also offer us an alternative way to think about democracy as relational. As these historical actors formed relationships that were mutually educative and transformative, they sought to understand and explain various worldviews and to legitimate perspectives in the hope that a democratic social knowledge would help equalize power both in formal politics and in a broader, informal negotiation of cultural politics.

The individuals, groups, and reform issues in this book are all familiar to students of Chicago history and of those years between 1890 and 1920 known as the Progressive Era, but they appear here through a new analytical lens that helps us see democratic social knowledge and its possibilities and limitations. Well known for its Progressive Era social reform and the activism of its intellectuals, Chicago has been the subject of several studies of new methods of social inquiry and their connection to the nascent field of social work and to the welfare state, as well as their effect on the emergence of the modern university and its role in the city.[20] Such studies have contributed to interpretations of the Progressive Era that emphasize a burgeoning middle-class culture of bureaucracy, professionalism, and efficiency, as well as an intellectual reorientation toward scientism and expertise. In contrast, by placing them side by side here, I offer a different window onto conflicts of the period through which we see multiple arenas of reform in which local residents wrestled with the intersection of epistemology (theory of knowledge and how we know) and democratic politics (conceived not just in procedural terms, such as the working of government mechanisms or formal political acts such as voting, but also as negotiations over cultural meanings and everyday practices). The democratic praxis this intersection inspired offered a methodology for social action, where the primacy of personal interactions and

19. Kathryn Kish Sklar, "Hull House in the 1890s: A Community of Women Reformers," *Signs* 10, no. 4 (1985): 658–77; Muncy, *Creating a Female Dominion;* Allan Davis, *Spearheads of Reform* (New York: Oxford University Press, 1967); Elisabeth Clemens, *The People's Lobby: Organizational Innovation and the Rise of Interest-group Politics in the United States, 1890–1925* (Chicago: University of Chicago Press, 1997).

20. Steven J. Diner, *A City and Its Universities: Public Policy in Chicago 1892–1919* (Chapel Hill: University of North Carolina Press, 1980); Andrew Feffer, *The Chicago Pragmatists and American Progressivism* (Ithaca, NY: Cornell University Press, 1993); Ellen Fitzpatrick, *Endless Crusade: Women Social Scientists and Progressive Reform* (New York: Oxford University Press, 1990); Robert Westbrook, *John Dewey and American Democracy* (Ithaca, NY: Cornell University Press, 1991); Mary O. Furner, *Advocacy and Objectivity: A Crisis in the Professionalization of American Social Science, 1865–1905* (Lexington: University Press of Kentucky, 1975); Jackson, *Lines of Activity;* Muncy, *Creating a Female Dominion;* Bachin, *Building the South Side.*

shared experiences served as a basis for mutual understanding, for social explanations that incorporated multiple perspectives, and for political engagement. This praxis, reformers hoped, would lead to an inclusive and just democracy.

Chicago reformers were wrestling with one of the enduring difficulties of democratic government—balancing group interests and individual rights against an idea of the public good, which was increasingly identified with social order. The narrative of liberal republicanism that shaped stories of Chicago's phenomenal growth and the responsibilities of its government was one response to this conundrum. It posited a myth of civic harmony in the pursuit of city building, a myth that, not incidentally, secured the cultural position of the capitalist elite. This civic myth used the grammar of natural or universal rights and reason growing out of liberalism to mask its underlying contentiousness. Indeed, as scholar Wai Chee Dimock has argued, the "triumph of rights is, above all, an epistemological triumph, one that confers reality on one claim, one body of evidence and lone lines of reasoning, over that of its opponents."[21] Thus, the triumph of the right holder must never appear as anything other than the triumph of sole and objective truth. Taking Dimock's argument further, we can see that the winners in such arguments must make such claims to an absolute, objective, and neutral reason since to do otherwise would be to admit their assertion of power over others—an assertion that is odious in a democracy that professes equality. As communications theorist David Allen has argued, the problem with such an approach to politics and epistemology is that it undermines the deliberative dimension of democracy as a process. Instead, the liberal marketplace of ideas becomes a place not for forging understanding "where ideas are exchanged for the sake of deliberation but a way to assure that an idea becomes dominant."[22]

However, reformers engaged in promoting democratic social knowledge sought different ways to resolve this tension. When we begin in 1890 with chapter 1, political economy had long since rendered market exchange a natural and impersonal process, ostensibly devoid of meaning and feeling. Furthermore, rational, self-interested market exchange suggested that economic gain could "be attained only by an attitude involving a distinctive antagonistic relationship between the partners."[23] As the fear of a social harmony permanently disrupted

---

21. Wai Chee Dimock, *Residues of Justice: Literature, Law, Philosophy*, 197, 188 (Berkeley: University of California Press, 1996). Similarly, Oliver Wendell Holmes explained that the "best test of truth is the power of the thought to get itself accepted in the competition of the market." Oliver Wendell Holmes, in *Abrams v. United States*, 250 U.S. 616 (1919), 22, quoted in David S. Allen, *Democracy, Inc.: The Press and Law in the Corporate Rationalization of the Public Sphere*, 38 (Urbana: University of Illinois Press, 2005).

22. Allen, *Democracy, Inc.*, 38.

23. Karl Polyani, quoted in Jean-Christophe Agnew, *Worlds Apart: The Market and the Theater in Anglo-American Thought, 1550–1750*, 3 (New York: Cambridge University Press).

by class, ethnic, and racial conflict haunted Chicago reformers, their lens of democratic social knowledge encouraged identification with—not advantage over—others. Such an imaginative exchange was personal and intimate, as it was often located in the physical and emotional experiences of individuals and groups, but it had consequences for democratic politics. In trying to "add the social function to democracy," as Jane Addams put it, Chicago reformers argued for a broader idea of democracy than that simply of the suffrage. While some historians have noted that the culture of consumerism attendant to the transformation to corporate capitalism opened up new ways of thinking about democracy as a mode of freedom in creating one's subjectivities and identities, the Chicago reformers herein experimented with methods and spaces outside those of the market to enact democracy, to recognize others' similarities, and to resolve the implicit contentiousness of reason and rights.[24] By reformers' standards, the measure of democratic practice lay not only in voting and political participation but also in the degree to which their community fostered the means to overcome barriers and connect individuals in a common pursuit of the public good. They saw the multiple perspectives of various communities as resources to be recognized and incorporated into public life.

The democracy that many reformers envisioned was thus rooted in praxis and had important implications for the formal political arena. They hoped that by bringing diverse groups together for the purposes of discussion of shared experiences and relationships, city residents could more easily move beyond their personal and group perspectives to understand others and pursue an inclusive vision of democracy based on social justice. Many Chicago reformers assumed that the ability to cultivate sympathy for others' experiences offered a way to overcome an epistemological divide often caused by disparate cultural experience and to build the foundation for collective social and political action. They believed that the intermixing of classes, races, and ethnic groups would help break down social division while generating a broader knowledge of their community and its problems. The purpose of such civic interaction was not only to impose social control (though this, for some, was clearly a factor) but also to better create democratic social knowledge and, in the process, foster a firmer basis for democratic praxis.

While at times reformers met with success, their ultimate effectiveness was limited by problems of power and prejudice (especially regarding class and race) and by epistemological differences that worked to privilege their different ideological positions.[25] But far from contributing to a simple reorientation of knowledge

24. Livingston discusses the culture of consumerism and corporate capitalism in *Pragmatism and the Political Economy of Cultural Revolution*.

25. My use of the term "epistemology" is informed by social theory that recognizes the socially constructed nature of knowledge. As such, what counts as knowledge and legitimate ways of

that ushered in a culture of expertise, Chicago's reform struggles emphasized the fluid nature and significant intersections between democratic social knowledge and the practice of democracy. Exploring them on such terms helps deepen our understanding of the ways in which individuals and urban communities struggle over knowledge and the meaning and practice of democracy.

Democracy and the Politics of Knowledge

This story of democratic social knowledge draws our attention to a broader politics of knowledge played out in the Progressive Era, its connection to the practice of democracy, and its treatment in the historiography. In this section I situate my book within those discussions, but first let me further explain my use of the term "social knowledge."

The term "social knowledge" came into usage in the late 1800s, during the professionalization of the social sciences. Though today the term primarily describes the product of academic and professional social science investigations, in the nineteenth century it referred to collective practices that ordinary individuals and communities used to describe, explain, and understand social reality. Reacting against formal, a priori knowledge and seeking to illuminate the social

---

knowing—epistemology—is closely tied to matters of power. I mean to explore these issues without suggesting that the rationale for any historical actor's particular claim to knowledge (that person's epistemology) was the "correct" one. Rather, they offer us important ways to think about knowledge and democracy. I find it important, however, to recognize that historical actors have an epistemology, even if they themselves do not characterize it as such. Despite the wide body of literature supporting this use, some scholars will find it problematic and prefer to maintain stricter boundaries around what constitutes epistemology and epistemological claims and to reserve the term to denote a branch of philosophy. These differences have important implications for historical interpretation and methodology, in that the latter reserves epistemology to elite social actors and intellectuals, thus rendering non-elite social actors less visible and denying their intellectual agency and the framework of logic and rationality undergirding their ideological positions. Much of this debate comes down to a question of which social actors can have overarching worldviews and political projects. Works in cultural studies and feminist theory contend that subaltern actors have larger political projects and visions and that these are informed by epistemological frameworks different from, not just in reaction to, those of elite intellectual and political actors. My work speaks directly to these issues, in that it explores the ways that non-elite actors offered political projects built on alternative frameworks of knowing. See, for example, Michel Foucault, *The Archeology of Knowledge,* trans. A. M. Sheridan Smith (New York: Pantheon, 1972), *Power/Knowledge: Selected Interviews and Other Writings, 1972–1977,* ed. and trans. Colin Gordon (New York: Pantheon, 1980), *The Order of Things: An Archaeology of the Human Sciences* (New York: Pantheon Books, 1970), and *Discipline and Punish: The Birth of the Prison,* trans. Alan Sheridan (New York: Pantheon Books, 1977); Joan Wallach Scott, "The Evidence of Experience," *Critical Inquiry* 17 (Summer 1991): 773–97; Judith Butler and Joan W. Scott, eds., *Feminists Theorize the Political* (New York: Routledge, 1992); James C. Scott, *Weapons of the Weak: Everyday Forms of Peasant Resistance* (New Haven: Yale University Press, 1985). For discussion of debates over knowledge and historical methodology, see Joyce Appleby, Lynn Hunt, and Margaret Jacob, *Telling the Truth about History* (New York: Norton, 1994).

bases of knowledge, Progressive Era social theorists offered a nascent articulation of social knowledge as a theoretical term, pointing to the social processes by which widely shared ideas, beliefs, and values shaping common explanations of society are forged.

In *Democracy and Education* (1916), John Dewey suggests that individuals incorporate a variety of frameworks of meaning into their everyday lives. These include the more familiar scientific or rationalized knowledge, but some frameworks might be called commonsense or second-hand knowledge. He contrasted "empirical knowing," which "is connected with everyday affairs, [and] serves the purposes of the ordinary individual who has no specialized intellectual pursuit," with "rational knowledge," which "touches reality in ultimate, intellectual fashion . . . [and is] not debased by application in behavior. Socially the distinction corresponds to that of the intelligence used by the working classes and that used by a learned class remote from concern with the means of living."[26] In characteristic pragmatic fashion, he rejected this dualism, seeing all knowledge as a combination of sensation, emotion, and thought.

In a similar vein, William Graham Sumner, the widely read Yale professor of social and political sciences, described "folkways," the "habits of the individual," the "customs of society," and "mores" as "simply folkways with the added sanction of ethical value and an added imperative to obey" that normatively structured society.[27] Albion Small, a University of Chicago sociologist considered to be the founder of American academic sociology, sought to provide a foundation upon which to study such frameworks. "Social knowledge," Small wrote in his 1894 textbook, was "something other than the mere addition of the impressions of individuals; . . . the standards of conduct of a given community are peculiar combinations of personal codes, which may vary widely from the former." Together they function to shape norms and social institutions.[28]

More recently, scholars have defined categories of social knowledge. Mary Furner and Michael Lacey articulate at least three different kinds of knowledge, all useful for helping us understand it as a theoretical term: "(1) disciplinary and professional knowledge; (2) informed opinion of the sort necessarily possessed by elites in politics, government, the media, and active interest groups; and (3) those general forms of cultural beliefs and values, widely shared, that shape civic culture, providing a sense of propriety and impropriety that is called on

26. John Dewey, *Democracy and Education* (New York: Free Press, 1966), 334.

27. Sklansky, *Soul's Economy*, 134. This discussion of Sumner follows from ibid., 132–34. The quote is from William Graham Sumner, *Folkways: A Study of the Sociological Importance of Usages, Manners, Customs, Mores, and Morals* (Boston, Ginn: 1907), 77.

28. Albion Small and George E. Vincent, *An Introduction to the Study of Society* (New York: American Book, 1894), 306–8.

in evaluating the nature of social problems and proposed remedies to them."[29] Each of these comprises assumptions about human nature, economics, religion, family, race, gender, politics, and the state that shape social institutions, although the third form calls attention to the way in which social knowledge is hegemonic and consequently barely recognized as a social construct. Feminist theorists, anthropologists, and sociologists of knowledge further point out that everyday, embodied experience, common sense, and sympathetic understanding often provide the fabric of meanings that constitute social explanation.[30]

My use of social knowledge is thus emergent from the Progressive Era itself—a period during which social scientists were preoccupied with and contested the methods used to understand society—while also drawing from more recent articulations. Although the term was not widely used outside of academic circles during the era, we find an attentiveness among social reformers and activists to what we would today call the intersection of knowledge and power, as well as its implications for democracy. In this book I theorize social knowledge and use it as an analytical lens to explore a variety of deeply rooted coexistent and competing frameworks that gave meaning to individual and collective experiences. Here it reflects frameworks of meaning—the content of civic narratives such as liberal republicanism or democracy—as well as processes through which those frameworks of meaning developed and competed.[31]

Social knowledge, as some have cast it and as I use it here, has few of the standards or strictures of formal definitions of knowledge that emerged within social scientific communities. It is different from academic knowledge in that it is primary and accessible to all members of a society and emerges from their experiences; it is taken for granted, not theoretical nor distanced from the experience of ordinary individuals.

Social knowledge, whether the distanced, academic version or a more informal sort, entails the exercise of power to include or exclude and to distribute

29. Mary O. Furner and Michael J. Lacy, "Social Investigation, Social Knowledge, and the State: An Introduction," in *The State and Social Investigation in Britain and the United States,* ed. Mary O. Furner and Michael Lacey, 3–62 (Washington, D.C.: Woodrow Wilson Center Press, 1993), and Clifford Geertz, *Local Knowledge: Further Essays in Interpretive Anthropology* (New York: Basic Books, 1983) for elaboration of the third type of knowledge Furner and Lacy describe.

30. For discussion of the sociology of knowledge at the grassroots level, see Peter L. Berger and Thomas Luckmann, *The Social Construction of Reality: A Treatise in the Sociology of Knowledge* (New York: Doubleday, 1966). Also Peter Burke, *A Social History of Knowledge: From Gutenberg to Diderot* (Cambridge, MA: Blackwell, 2000); Clifford Geertz, *The Interpretation of Cultures* (New York: Basic Books, 1973); Geertz, *Local Knowledge;* Joan Wallach Scott, *Gender and the Politics of History* (New York: Columbia University Press, 1988), and "Evidence of Experience."

31. See Margaret R. Somers and Gloria D. Gibson, "Reclaiming the 'Other': Narrative and the Social Constitution of Identity," in *Social Theory and the Politics of Identity,* ed. Craig Calhoun, 37–99 (Cambridge, MA: Blackwell, 1994), on the role of narrative as a social epistemology that helps us "know, understand, and make sense of the social world" (59).

the community's material resources and psychological censure or support. As such, in times of social upheaval and change, it is highly contested as reformers seek to expose and challenge its assumptions and effects and to expose its power dynamics and reshape its political consequences.

Several sometimes contradictory frameworks of meaning were available to Chicago residents, and these structures shaped the boundaries and terms of public debates. In addition to the liberal republicanism I discuss in the first chapter, reformers drew from Romanticism, a discourse of domesticity, social gospelism, socialism, and pragmatism and social psychology. These offered different ways to think about the democratic polity, social justice, and the basis of expertise. While details of these discourses varied, they shared an underlying framework of sympathy and proximity. As commitment to cooperation and sympathetic identification developed in these multiple discourses, they undermined the liberal narrative of self-interested Economic Man. As epistemological and political commitments, sympathetic understanding and interaction offered an important transformation in nineteenth-century society. Collapsing the divide between self and others, sympathy for others' physical, emotional, or material situations offered a basis for understanding, inquiry, and knowledge. Sympathy rendered not just psychic comfort for the suffering but also a starting point from which to mobilize political action to bring about material changes in the circumstances of others.[32]

Furthermore, proximity was a related critical factor within several of these epistemological frameworks. As a way of knowing, proximity privileges nearness to and even engagement with experience. Reformers who were promoting processes of democratic social knowledge thus assumed that the nature of one's experience and knowledge was contingent on one's location in the social order, the geography of the city, and one's relationship to the market and industrial production. Democratic social knowledge thus had to draw upon the diverse experiences of different members of society to reconcile multiple perspectives in a fuller knowledge of society.

Of course, Chicago reformers who were engaged in practical work rarely invoked specific frameworks of knowledge directly. But such frameworks were implicit in their activities, strategies, and rationales. For example, the Civic Federation, Jane Addams and the women at Hull House, and Ida Wells-Barnett

32. David Marshall, *The Surprising Effects of Sympathy: Marivaux, Diderot, Rousseau, and Mary Shelley* (Chicago: University of Chicago Press, 1988); Elizabeth Clarke, "'Sacred Rights of the Weak': Pain, Sympathy, and the Culture of Individual Rights in Antebellum America," *Journal of American History* 82 (1995): 463–93; Karen Ruth Smith, "'Pain into Sympathy': Ethical Realism and the Conversion of Feeling in Eliot, Tolstoy, and Stowe" (PhD diss., University of Michigan, 1992). The political implications of women's sentimental fiction have received much attention among literary historians. See Shirley Samuels, ed., *The Culture of Sentiment: Race, Gender, and Sentimentality in Nineteenth-century America* (New York: Oxford University Press, 1992).

drew from social science methods to legitimize their methods of inquiry. However, they all also argued for the importance of shared experience, cooperative action, and proximity to justify their expertise on reform matters. As historian Dorothy Ross demonstrates, Addams drew from an ideology of domesticity, as well as pragmatist and Romantic thought, in forging an alternative version of sociology.[33] Wells-Barnett also employed sympathetic strategies and proximal justifications to argue for the psychological and political dangers of lynching. Workers claimed their experience in the production process and their social location as a basis for specialized knowledge of the effects of laissez-faire economics. Reminiscent of pragmatic explanations of experience as the basis of knowledge, workers asserted that their experience awarded them epistemological status in the community. Such a position, which argued for the importance of incorporating multiple perspectives in social debate, upset the usual hierarchy of reform, in which the working classes and poor people were the objects—not the agents—of social change. In a culture increasingly marked by social scientific expertise, the reformers' position constituted an important strand in Progressive Era democratization.

Though it speaks to intellectual historians and historians of education concerned with the genealogy of ideas and the transmission of culture, as well as to urban historians interested in the way cultural ideas and social and political reform shape cities, this book is primarily about politics as a vision of democratic praxis. In this work I use the term "politics" in an expansive way to include both the negotiations and actors in the formal political arena and the formal political practice of voting, as well as the struggle over cultural meanings and everyday practices and relationships—and the actors, both group and individual—who engage in them. Even though we may not recognize the efforts of reformers as political in a traditional sense, the ways that they struggled over intersecting and overlapping frameworks of understanding suggest that their work reflected competition over power to define what counts as knowledge.[34]

33. Dorothy Ross, "Gendered Social Knowledge: Domestic Discourse, Jane Addams, and the Possibilities of Social Science," in Gender and American Social Science, ed. Helene Silverberg, 235–64 (Princeton, NJ: Princeton University Press, 1998).

34. The book is ultimately about politics conceived broadly as encompassing power dynamics present in everyday practices. In his now classic formulation of power and knowledge, Michel Foucault reminds us that power is dispersed in the modern world; it involves not just outright demonstrations of might but also the shaping of people's ideas and values. As Antonio Gramsci explains in his formulation of hegemony, power operates at a cultural level but is also inscribed into formal institutional structures as ideas and values shape the practices of those structures, which in turn act on individuals and whole sectors of society. Second-wave feminists have thus further pointed out that the personal is political, meaning that private matters are frequently construed as matters of state concern and cultural contest. Thus, politics means not only formal practices associated with the mechanisms of government but also the way that everyday practices shape power dynamics in the lives of both individuals and collectives. In this book we see that social knowledge is intricately

Indeed, social knowledge is not only marked by wide consensus; because it also embodies values, moral assumptions, and various cultural frames of reference, it also connotes a sense of struggle as various groups compete and compromise to have their versions of social reality inform collective narratives, as well as social and governmental institutions and policies.

Let me turn now to the broader context in which this politics of knowledge was played out. The last decades of the nineteenth century bequeathed a growing interest in knowledge of others (and the Other) and new methods for creating such knowledge. Across the nation, study clubs and amateur social science organizations attracted thousands of members. Formal social science disciplines emerged as university departments and professional organizations defined economics, political science, anthropology, sociology, and history as distinct branches of knowledge. Literary realism attempted to capture unadorned the raw experience and details of life; in so doing, it influenced investigative journalism, produced a new genre of fiction, and highlighted narrative ways of knowing that used stories to raise consciousness and spark action. Social surveys, statistics, and the investigations of governmental bureaus reflected the cultural hunger for new ways to understand unfamiliar social groups and urban problems. Popular interest in these new forms of inquiry suggested widespread hope that they—and with them, the disinterested, objective knowledge of experts—would provide the antidote to problems of social and political alienation.[35]

---

connected to this formulation of politics. Foucault, *The Archeology of Knowledge* and *Power/Knowledge;* Antonio Gramsci, *Selections from the Prison Notebooks of Antonio Gramsci,* ed. and trans. Quintin Hoare and Geoffrey Nowell Smith (New York: International Publishers, 1972).

35. Thomas Haskell, *The Emergence of Professional Social Science: The American Social Science Association and the Nineteenth-century Crisis of Authority* (Urbana: University of Illinois Press, 1977); Thomas Haskell, ed., *The Authority of Experts: Studies in History and Theory* (Bloomington: Indiana University Press, 1984); Mary O. Furner, *Advocacy and Objectivity: A Crisis of Professionalization of American Social Science, 1865–1905* (Lexington: University of Kentucky Press, 1975); Alexandra Oleson and John Voss, *The Organization of Knowledge in Modern America* (Baltimore: Johns Hopkins University Press, 1979); Dorothy Ross, *The Origins of American Social Science* (New York: Cambridge University Press, 1991); Ellsworth R. Fuhrman, *The Sociology of Knowledge in America, 1883–1915* (Charlottesville: University Press of Virginia, 1980); Daniel Rodgers, *Contested Truths: Keywords in American Politics since Independence* (New York: Basic Books, 1987), 156–211, on political science. On realism, see Amy Kaplan, *The Social Construction of American Realism* (Chicago: University of Chicago Press, 1988); Daniel H. Borus, *Writing Realism: Howells, James, and Norris in the Mass Market* (Chapel Hill: University of North Carolina Press, 1989), 139–82; David E. Shi, *Facing Facts: Realism in American Thought and Culture, 1850–1920* (New York: Oxford University Press, 1995); Philip Fisher, *Hard Facts: Setting and Form in the American Novel* (New York: Oxford University Press, 1985). On the use of the social survey and maps, see Martin Bulmer, Kevin Bales, and Kathryn Kish

However, while the amateur and professional social sciences provided some research methods, mixed in with these increasingly popular modes of knowing were even less formal means of interaction and inquiry. Women's groups read novels along with social science studies; settlements brought social classes and ethnic groups together to provide firsthand experience of others' lives and engage in political action; social gospelists emphasized Christian sympathy along with social science as a basis for knowledge of social ills and remedies. Labor organizations published newspapers and journals, and workers met to discuss both regular union business and strike-related matters. The forms of inquiry that mobilized reform-minded citizens thus ranged from social science methods and distanced observation to participatory social inquiry, informal and personal interaction, intuition, and sympathy.

In this milieu, growing numbers of reform-minded men and women, social scientists, and civic and labor leaders in Chicago worked toward greater understanding of the problems their communities faced. These reform communities were not ones engaged in the formal processes of verification required of empirical knowledge. Rather, they were civic actors whose frameworks of knowledge were often rooted in firsthand experience and local traditions and who sought verification through political and social reform processes.[36] While many historians depict the decades surrounding the turn of the twentieth century as marked by a steady growth of scientism and bureaucracy, the cultural and political significance and the range of reform communities involved in this process suggest that multiple forms of local knowledge coexisted, competing and colliding with one another as they gave rich texture to reform endeavors and political debate. By framing these conflicts as a struggle over democratic social knowledge and thus the practice of democracy, I suggest that epistemological dimensions of reform projects can serve as a way to understand political conflict both in the Progressive Era and in our own day.

Sklar, eds., *The Social Survey in Historical Perspective, 1880–1940* (New York: Cambridge University Press, 1991), and Jackson, *Lines of Activity*, 271–82.

36. John Dewey suggested that a community of inquiry need not be exclusively scientific but could be a democratic public itself. John Dewey, *The Public and Its Problems* (New York: Holt, 1927); David Hollinger, "William James and the Culture of Inquiry," 3–222 and "Science and Anarchy: Walter Lippmann's *Drift and Mastery*," 44–55, in In the American Province: Studies in the History and Historiography of Ideas (Bloomington: Indiana University Press, 1985); James Kloppenberg, *Uncertain Victory: Social Democracy and Progressivism in European and American Thought, 1870–1920* (New York: Oxford University Press, 1986); Westbrook, *John Dewey and American Democracy*. For more critical views of the Progressives emphasizing elitism over democratic tendencies, see R. Jeffrey Lustig, *Corporate Liberalism: The Origins of Modern American Political Theory, 1890–1920* (Berkeley: University of California Press, 1982), particularly chapter 6, "Pragmatism, Science, and the Politics of Administration"; James Weinstein, *The Corporate Idea in the Liberal State, 1900–1918* (Boston: Beacon, 1968); and Patrick Diggins, *The Promise of Pragmatism: Modernism and the Crisis of Knowledge and Authority* (Chicago: University of Chicago Press, 1994). For a classic on the Progressives, see Richard Hofstadter, *The Age of Reform, from Bryan to F. D. R.* (New York: Knopf, 1955).

My focus on "democratic" social knowledge complicates the usual story of the Progressive Era as the period in which rational and objective social science emerged as the dominant or privileged method of knowing about society.[37] A number of scholars of the Progressive Era have explored the political implications of the shift in intellectual life when social science disciplines, universities, and state bureaucracy emerged as the privileged locations of knowledge production. During the 1870s and accelerating through the 1880s and 1890s, the social science disciplines and their professional organizations claimed as their own the task of exploring social questions and argued that their methods, standards, and disinterested expertise justified their authority. The model of social understanding they advanced emphasized empirical methods that distanced the investigator from the object of study. It emphasized that theoretical assertions could be verified by a community of inquirers. And the process of professionalization narrowed that community to a body of experts who shared commitments to scientific methods and disinterested objectivity. As the social sciences emphasized that truths were empirically observed and discovered rather than revealed, religion as an explanatory tool was displaced. Other claims one might make to knowledge, such as literary insight, common sense, emotion, or personal, practical, everyday experience were similarly disregarded as subjective and thus illegitimate forms of social understanding.[38] Scientism, marked by an effort to establish prediction and control of human behavior and social institutions, took center stage in American intellectual life and was connected to the logic of liberalism.[39]

In these familiar stories of Progressive Era reform, an increasingly positivist social science was variously used to promote humanitarian goals and social control of immigrants and the working classes and to provide a new organizational basis for American life.[40] In corporate liberal models of reform, bureaucratic experts drawn from businesses and universities provided orderly and rational social

37. Ross, *Origins of American Social Science,* and Haskell, *Emergence of American Social Science.*

38. David Hollinger, "The Knower and the Artificer, with Postscript 1993," in *Modernist Impulses in the Human Sciences,* ed. Dorothy Ross, 33 (Baltimore: Johns Hopkins University Press, 1994). For discussion of the tensions and overlap between the sciences and the humanities during this era, see Julie Rueben, *The Making of the Modern University: Intellectual Transformation and the Marginalization of Morality* (Chicago: University of Chicago Press, 1996).

39. *Origins of American Social Science;* Ross, 472; Mark Smith, *Social Science in the Crucible: The American Debate over Objectivity and Purpose, 1918–1941* (Durham, NC: Duke University Press, 1994). Lustig exemplifies such a position in his *Corporate Liberalism,* explaining that "the knower began to be seen as a person guided in his or her judgments by the verdicts of institutional experimental procedures" (173). For a similar interpretation, see Allen, *Democracy, Inc.* As I argue throughout, such interpretations neglect other democratizing strands of Progressive Era social thought.

40. For these varieties of Progressive reform see Robert Wiebe, *The Search for Order, 1877–1920* (New York: Hill and Wang, 1967); John D. Buenker, John C. Burnham, and Robert M. Crunden, *Progressivism* (Cambridge, MA: Harvard University Press, 1977); Daniel Rodgers, "In Search of Progressivism," *Reviews in American History* 10, no. 4 (December 1982): 113–32.

planning that modernized city government and addressed the worst effects of industrial capitalism.[41] These versions of social reform helped refashion a negative, laissez-faire conception of liberalism into a positive, "new" liberalism that buttressed the creation of the capitalist welfare state.[42] The state, along with universities and social science professional organizations, became an important source of social knowledge through sponsorship of investigative and regulatory agencies and legislative inquiries.[43] Women's historians have used a gendered lens of analysis to move beyond implicit associations of state-sponsored reform as a masculine domain, yet their work has continued to focus primarily on expert rationalization and the state's role in social reform.[44] By World War I, these histories of social reform suggest that a burgeoning culture of expertise offered a new form of authority to replace older religious and economic orthodoxy. In this view of the reorientation of knowledge, politics as a process for exploring and reaching consensus on social knowledge and public policy was de-emphasized or was replaced with elite experts working within the insulated confines of government bureaucracy and academic institutions without connection to the polity.[45]

41. Diner, *A City and Its Universities;* Kenneth Finegold, *Experts and Politicians: Reform Challenges to Machine Politics in New York, Cleveland, and Chicago* (Princeton, NJ: Princeton University Press, 1995); Martin Schiesl, *Politics of Efficiency: Municipal Administration and Reform in America, 1800–1920* (Berkeley: University of California Press, 1977); David Tyack, *The One Best System: A History of American Urban Education* (Cambridge, MA: Harvard University Press, 1974); Thomas Pegram, *Partisans and Progressives: Private Interest and Public Policy in Illinois, 1870–1922* (Urbana: University of Illinois Press, 1992.

42. On new liberalism in American thought, see Kloppenberg, *Uncertain Victory;* Furner, "The Republican Tradition and the New Liberalism: Social Investigation, State Building, and Social Leaning in the Gilded Age," in *The State and Social Investigation in Britain and the United States,* ed. Lacey and Furner, 171-242; Schneirov, *Labor and Urban Politics;* Nancy Cohen, *The Reconstruction of American Liberalism, 1865–1914* (Chapel Hill: University of North Carolina Press, 2002).

43. *The State and Social Investigation in Britain and the United States,* Furner and Lacey, eds.

44. Ellen Fitzpatrick, *Endless Crusade: Women Social Scientists and Progressive Reform* (New York: Oxford University Press, 1990); Allen F. Davis, *Spearheads of Reform: The Social Settlements and the Progressive Movement, 1890–1914* (New York: Oxford University Press, 1967); Kathleen D. McCarthy, *Noblesse Oblige: Charity and Cultural Philanthropy in Chicago, 1849–1929* (Chicago: University of Chicago Press, 1982); Linda Gordon, ed., *Women, the State, and Welfare* (Madison: University of Wisconsin Press, 1990); and Theda Skocpol, *Protecting Soldiers and Mothers: The Political Origins of Social Policy in the United States* (Cambridge, MA: Harvard University Press, 1992). Muncy offers a more nuanced interpretation of the tensions between expertise and the democratic aspirations of female reformers in *Creating a Female Dominion in American Reform, 1890–1935.*

45. Weinstein, *Corporate Idea in the Liberal State;* Lustig, *Corporate Liberalism;* Thomas Bender, *Intellect and Public Life: Essays on the Social History of Academic Intellectuals in the United States* (Baltimore: Johns Hopkins University Press, 1992). Allen, *Democracy, Inc.;* Morton Horwitz has argued in a similar vein that transformations in U.S. law over the course of the nineteenth century sought to develop nonpolitical criteria for legal principles. See Morton Horwitz, *Transformation of American Law* (Cambridge, MA: Harvard University Press, 1977), especially, 262–63; Ross, *Origin of American Social Science.* Jürgen Habermas has argued that such a trajectory in public life, in which knowledge to run society cannot be comprehended by the public, robs citizens of "the meaning

Democracy and the Progressive Era

While interpretations of Progressive Era reform emphasizing the rise of expertise have been valuable in outlining its possibilities for and its impact (usually assessed as negative) on American democracy and the growth of the national state, this emphasis has largely obscured important efforts at democratic reform, particularly at the local level.[46] This book contributes to a newly emerging historiography of democracy in the Progressive Era. It joins a number of works that focus on the city as an arena for democratic struggle but offers a new lens of democratic social knowledge through which to view it. In this section I outline several democratic themes emerging from recent historiography on the Progressive Era to indicate both how my work is connected to this scholarship and where it diverges from it.

An understanding of the reorientation of knowledge has underpinned many of the studies of democratic reform on the local level. Historians such as Robert Westbrook and James Kloppenberg chart how the decades surrounding the turn of the century occasioned a shift in intellectual life away from the use of abstract logic, deductive reasoning, and a British utilitarian empiricism that had little use for the study of history and culture.[47] Instead, intellectuals such as Dewey, William James, and Albion Small turned their attention to historical circumstances and cultural context as a basis for the social sciences. Pragmatic philosophers and social thinkers increasingly argued that knowledge did not grow exclusively out of abstract principles or formal logic but was both intertwined with culture, language, and experience and also socially constructed. This "radical theory of knowledge," as James Kloppenberg has called it, emphasized that knowledge and ethics resulted from empirical observation and inquiry, as well as the processes of human interaction and interpretation that gave meaning to personal and collective experience.[48]

The pragmatists' call for empirical study through the use of the scientific method helped lend authority to the social science disciplines. However, their insistence that knowledge was grounded in experience and was social in nature had great democratic potential; it offered a philosophical rationale for more inclusive ways to investigate urban problems and mediate social experience.

---

of their own actions," impoverishing the public sphere and ultimately democratic society. Jürgen Habermas, *Theory of Communicative Action*, vol. 1, *Reason and Rationalization of Society*, trans. Thomas McCarthy (Boston: Beacon Press, 1984), 302.

46. For an excellent overview of current efforts to rehabilitate Progressive Era democracy, see Robert D. Johnston, "Re-democratizing the Progressive Era: The Politics of Progressive Era Political Historiography," *Journal of the Gilded Age and Progressive Era* 1, no.1 (2002): 68–92.

47. Morton White, *Social Thought in America: The Revolt against Formalism* (Boston: Beacon Hill, 1959), 14; Kloppenberg, *Uncertain Victory*; Westbrook, *John Dewey and American Democracy*.

48. Kloppenberg, *Uncertain Victory*, 64–114.

Emphasizing that values, experience, and experimental action were integral parts of knowledge, pragmatism offered Chicago reformers and social scientists a framework for synthesizing their scientific methods with more interactive, participatory means to create social knowledge. This vision belied the equation of expertise with distanced observation and instead illustrated a tension between localized, interactive social science and the consolidation of intellectual life in the modern university.[49]

Though not an intellectual history, this book uses the crisis of knowledge to explore the tangled connections among social knowledge, reform, and politics. I argue that urban reform was not only an arena for the application of new social science expertise but also the site of intersecting, competing, and indeed colliding frameworks of knowledge. Democratic social knowledge offers an analytical lens that allows us to examine the ways in which democracy is tied to open-ended and inclusive processes of explaining social reality and shaping social institutions and how it fosters collective political action.

Situated within a historiography seeking to recover the democratic potential of Progressive Era reform, this book expands upon it by drawing our attention to the intersection of politics, knowledge, and everyday practices. It encourages us to understand democracy as praxis and a method for social action. Several works have helped lay the groundwork for this interpretation. Attentive to the potential of new urban arenas to foster democratic politics, a number of scholars have explored another important democratic theme: efforts to encourage participatory, deliberative politics.

Historical works, such as those of Robin Bachin, Kevin Mattson, and Philip Ethington, that tend to see this trend remind us that the Progressive Era was a moment of opportunities to redistribute power and reshape the state. Such historians have emphasized the expansion of the public sphere through a variety

---

49. Julie Rueben emphasizes that the intellectual transformation of this era has overstated the conflict between "advocacy and objectivity," arguing instead that late nineteenth-century intellectuals produced a complex discussion of the nature of scientific inquiry, one that might have allowed more room to reconcile a variety of ways of knowing. Rueben, *Making of the Modern University*; Westbrook, *John Dewey and American Democracy*; Kloppenberg, *Uncertain Victory*. As Robin Bachin has demonstrated, this tension was apparent at the University of Chicago. William Rainey Harper, president of the young university, encouraged its engagement in public life. He developed a large university extension program that offered college courses at locations throughout the city, as well as by correspondence. The university contributed its knowledge and research to the public sphere, thus making it available to people who did not have access to a traditional college classroom. But "the transmission of knowledge, according to this view, was centrifugal, emanating from the campus and moving out into various arenas of public life." This view stood in contrast to those of faculty and reformers influenced by pragmatism, who saw the extension classroom as "a chance for intellectual and civic exchange, in which workers, professionals, middle-class women, and academics could come together and better understand social conditions in the city and together learn a variety of approaches for bettering them." Robin F. Bachin, "Cultural Boundaries: Constructing Urban Space and Civic Culture on Chicago's South Side, 1890–1919" (PhD diss., University of Michigan, 1996).

of means, both by the expansion of voices and perspectives within civil society—as Ethington describes in his emphasis on journalism, political parties, and voluntary associations—and by the struggles over urban space and commercial culture—as Bachin argues in her discussion of Chicago's southside parks, baseball stadiums, and jazz and vice districts. Though Mattson also recovers a Progressive Era concern with deliberation as the foundation of participatory democracy, his work also implies that democracy must build on habits of mind. Thus he argues that, through deliberation, men and women educated themselves and each other into "an understanding of human beings' interconnectedness" and a "sense of fairness and inclusion, values utterly necessary for democracy."[50] Thus they came to a deeper understanding of the meaning of political equality.[51] Mattson suggests, as do some contemporary political scientists, that voting is not the only act that defines democratic behavior.[52]

A third theme emanating from the newer historiography is the Progressive Era as the transitional moment in U.S. history when new political subjectivities become possible, leading to the emergence of interest-group politics.[53] Historians concerned with democracy generally see such politics in a positive light, as opening up the political system to more players and providing the basis for collective action. Shut out of access to formal electoral politics, many of the social and political reformers appearing in historical studies built powerful networks that used methods of lobbying, mass meetings, and voter-education campaigns to gain access to political power. Bachin suggests that new civic identities served to "diffuse power and reshape municipal government through coalition building and the multiplication of actors on the political stage."[54]

What emerges from the historiography is a vision of expanding democratic politics marked by pluralistic interest groups. This was a significant shift from the autonomous (white male), individual political actor of classical liberalism, and it offered significant democratic potential for the redistribution of political

50. Kevin Mattson, *Creating a Democratic Public: The Struggle for Urban Participatory Democracy during the Progressive Era* (University Park, PA: Pennsylvania State University Press, 1998), 86, 58.

51. Ibid., 74.

52. Ronald Hayduk and Kevin Mattson, eds., *Democracy's Moment: Reforming the American Political System for the 21st Century* (New York: Rowman and Littlefield, 2002); Robert K. Fullinwider, *Civil Society, Democracy, and Civic Renewal* (Boulder, CO: Rowman and Littlefield, 1999), 355–74.

53. Livingston, *Pragmatism and the Political Economy of Cultural Revolution;* James Livingston, *Pragmatism, Feminism, and Democracy: Rethinking the Politics of American History* (New York: Routledge, 2001).

54. Bachin, *Building the South Side,* 8. See Zane Miller, *Boss Cox's Cincinnati: Urban Politics in the Progressive Era* (Columbus: Ohio State University Press, 1968), for discussion of how more traditional politics "drifted unsteadily away from its preoccupation with order and toward a concern with social justice and the preservation of an open society" (111). Miller's interpretation explores political parties and politics in a more traditional sense than this work.

power and social claims. The shift to interest-group politics made possible collective action against power structures woven into the state, the economy, and even private practices; over the course of the twentieth century, it has brought new laws, new rights, and new freedoms to previously marginalized groups.[55] Those participants introduced new forms of activism and also helped develop a new vocabulary of needs and rights that has contributed to twentieth-century contests over state responsibilities. In so doing, they contributed to a pluralist liberalism in which the state mediates among conflicting interests.[56]

While this shift to interest-group politics has been vitally important for the history of U.S. politics in the twentieth century, the historiography has not focused enough attention on the fact that interest-group politics that posits the state as mediator was an *unintended* consequence of the democratic aspirations of many reformers. I argue that, while we can understand the value of interest-group politics in opening up the public sphere, it was not at all the model of democracy or vision of the state that reformers proposed. Indeed, they sought to *transcend* and *unify* differences among groups. The ways in which they went about this work was at times problematic, as we see in the chapters that follow. But I also point to their successes as a way to think about the basis for collective, democratic politics. This interpretation of interest-group politics seems all the more important today as we see the way that the language of this type of politics has served to deflect claims by particular groups—"women" or "labor" or "environmentalist"—as those of a "special interest," not as claims that offer benefits to the broader society. As we see in chapter 6, the roots of this logic are visible in the Progressive Era.

In arguing for historical attention to a more complex view of collective politics in the Progressive Era, I join the work of other historians such as Glenda Gilmore and Robert Johnston.[57] Their works underscore the fluidity of racial and class boundaries in reform coalitions and suggest that we pay closer attention to how historical actors overcame social divisions to work together, as well as how groups, which were frequently politically marginalized, exercised more power and worked toward different visions of democracy than historians have generally recognized. Furthermore, a few works on Chicago have begun to sug-

55. Two important works that explore the transition to interest-group politics as an expansion of democratic power are M. Elizabeth Sanders, *Roots of Reform: Farmers, Workers, and the American State, 1877-1917* (Chicago: University of Chicago Press, 1999), and Elisabeth S. Clemens, *The People's Lobby: Organizational Innovation and the Rise of Interest Group Politics in the United States, 1890–1925* (Chicago: University of Chicago Press, 1997). These books are particularly helpful in understanding agrarian politics, a topic outside the scope of my book.

56. Clemens, *People's Lobby;* Ethington, *Public City;* Eldon J. Eisenach, *The Lost Promise of Progressivism* (Lawrence: University of Kansas Press, 1994).

57. Glenda Gilmore, *Gender and Jim Crow: Women and the Politics of White Supremacy in North Carolina, 1896–1920;* Johnston, *Radical Middle Class.*

gest that, despite strong attachments to racial, ethnic, or class groups, men and women worked across those boundaries.[58] In this book I point not only to the power of those men and women who forged common political visions but also to the possibility for collective politics to cut across categories of difference.

Building on these themes found in historiography—a reorientation of knowledge; attention to participatory, deliberative politics; the rise of new political subjectivities and its consequences for interest-group politics and the state—this book employs a framework of democratic social knowledge both to understand an important aspect of democratic thought in the Progressive Era (the focus on praxis) and to illustrate an epistemological and methodological dimension of democratic politics. Finally, in recognizing the role of sympathetic understanding as one aspect of democratic social knowledge, the book suggests a new direction for historiography: the role of affective ties in democratic politics. A lens of democratic social knowledge helps make visible emotional dimensions of reform while also helping us to see the limits and possibilities of sympathetic ties among political partners.

Democratic social knowledge as a practice that encourages and takes seriously all perspectives and ideas has potential dangers, too, a feature that Walter Lippman and particularly the elitist H. L. Mencken observed in the 1920s. Thus Johnston describes the rise of the Ku Klux Klan in Portland, Ethington suggests the way that marketing specialists and behavioral scientists used their expertise to manipulate voting behavior, and James Connolly argues that Boston's Irish and party politicians used Progressivism as a language to create a reactionary politics rooted in ethnic identity and circumscribing the power of other groups.[59] In this book, while we find potential for democratic social knowledge to bring more perspectives into political discourse, we also find that it could not always constrain prejudices that limit rather than expand the rights and freedoms of particular groups. The challenge of negotiating legitimacy and seemingly incompatible perspectives and claims proved to be the thinnest of tightropes for democratic social knowledge. The resilience of liberal republicanism, recast in the developmentalist logic of neoliberalism in the twentieth century, also dealt

---

58. For example, Robin Bachin (*Building the South Side*) emphasizes the importance of shifting alliances in contests over space in Chicago's south side. Richard Schneirov points out the significant role Chicago's working classes played in what he describes as the city's shift to new liberalism. Working with reformers and civic elites, workers were able to exercise a significant measure of political power. Maureen Flanagan argues that women, organized by gendered concerns, acted across boundaries of race, class, and ethnicity. Lizabeth Cohen describes the coalition building of Chicago's working classes that ultimately contributed to New Deal liberalism in *Making a New Deal: Industrial Workers in Chicago, 1919–1939* (New York: Cambridge University Press, 1990).

59. Johnston, *Radical Middle Class*, 234–47; Ethington, "Metropolis and Multicultural Ethics"; James J. Connolly, *The Triumph of Ethnic Progressivism: Urban Political Culture in Boston, 1900–1925* (Cambridge, MA: Harvard University Press, 1998).

serious blows to the framework of democratic social knowledge offered by Progressive Era reformers.

In the early 1890s, when this study begins, prevailing conceptions of liberal republicanism and its version of democracy were under tremendous pressure. Drawing upon their collective experiences as members of distinct groups, workers, women, and African Americans challenged the assumptions of classical political economy and atomistic individualism woven into Chicago's social fabric and shaping liberal republican ideas about public responsibility and the state. When the book ends in 1920, we see that social reformers had impacted the city, although not as dramatically as they would have liked. While the crisis in liberal republicanism and the intellectual reorientation that occasioned the development of democratic social knowledge was reframed during World War I and afterward, it gave rise to underlying questions about democracy that lingered.

Using an analytic lens of democratic social knowledge trained on Chicago reform in the Progressive Era, I find that it poses four overarching questions about democracy that were critical at that moment and are still unresolved today—albeit in different forms. Is it possible to develop epistemological and political models that help reconcile the tensions between democracy and expertise, personal subjectivity and distanced social science models that are limited in explaining and including human agency and experience? How can we (some might say *should* we) see multiple perspectives as resources and award social recognition and political legitimacy that incorporates both commonalities and seemingly irreconcilable differences? What constitutes justice in a liberal democracy? And finally, what are the dispositions necessary for a healthy and robust public life, and how can we foster them? Each of the chapters herein speak to different aspects of these issues, and they come together in the final chapter and epilogue, where I discuss in brief the charter campaign of 1906–7 to show a key example of how the struggles over democratic social knowledge illuminate these questions and to explore lessons we might find useful today. Indeed, even today, we continue to find examples of practices of democratic social knowledge in the social inquiry methods of participant observation and oral histories, some community organizing, and social activism—practices that cross boundaries of race and class and (frequently) gender to daily live out a democratic praxis.

But if we step back now to the 1880s and 1890s, before these struggles reached an impasse, we see a moment of crisis and possibility. Viewed in this light, Addams's rather dire description of a fatal drifting apart was not a pronouncement of an irrevocable future but was rather a call to action.

1

"He Who Merits Victory"

Liberal Republicanism and the Crisis of the 1890s

In the entire history of the world there is no clearer record of the fact that he who merits victory will win it than is found in the history of Chicago.[1]

In 1881, David Ward Wood published a salute to Chicago. Written in the grandiose style of booster literature, *Chicago and Its Distinguished Citizens* celebrated the city's vast economic growth and the entrepreneurial and civic leadership of its founders and early settlers. It narrated a story in which Chicago stood for all of nineteenth-century America. Within a generation, a western city grew where in 1818 only an abandoned fort and a few scattered trappers' huts had evidenced white settlement. After long efforts to fight off and then live together with white settlers, the Potowatamis who had lived on this marshy land sold it to the United States government at a bargain price and moved farther west. Speculation drove land prices up, and eastern investors began pouring money into the region. Settlers from Massachusetts, Virginia, New York, and Vermont, who had little money to invest but an adventurous spirit, moved to the growing city. A striking number made fortunes. It seemed no exaggeration for booster Elmer Barton to claim that "Chicago is more distinctively than any other city the embodiment of all that is most characteristic of the American people—a people who have within the limits of a single century risen from poverty and obscurity to a foremost place among the nations."[2]

The stories of Chicago's spectacular rise and the "old settlers" who built the city were legendary. They testified to American myths of the self-made man. Drawing from classical liberal political economy and republican free labor ideology, such narratives constituted the social knowledge of the American north

---

1. David Ward Wood, ed., *Chicago and Its Distinguished Citizens, or the Progress of Forty Years* (Chicago: Milton George, 1881), 185.
2. Elmer Epenetus Barton, *A Business Tour of Chicago* (Chicago: E. E. Barton, 1887), dedication.

29

in the antebellum decades, years that witnessed Chicago's rise. Highlighting autonomous independence and economic opportunities, these narratives set the parameters of a liberal republican social knowledge, knowledge that shaped elites' ideas about public responsibility, gave form to a conception of the universal (male) political actor, and set the boundaries of state action. But by the 1890s they were stretched thin. Newer residents—often workers and immigrants—experienced Chicago's economic and civic life, not as a land of opportunity, but as an unkept promise or as hostile terrain; they understood the city quite differently from those earlier arrivals who had made fortunes.

This chapter outlines the liberal republican social knowledge that shaped Chicago, first in the broader American intellectual context and then within the city itself as it informed practices of local government and public relief. I argue that as liberal republicanism shaped civic elites' understanding of their community and their place in it, and inscribed these lessons into public institutions, it functioned as a form of social knowledge, which, while not monolithic, set the boundaries of public debate and measured the legitimacy of political actors—and hence the democratic polity. The final section suggests that the depression of 1893 opened up an important moment when reformers sought new coalitions and new ways of understanding and solving their city's problems. This moment reflected the possibilities for creating democratic social knowledge, that redefined the practice of American democracy.

Liberal Republicanism and Chicago Civic Elites

Founded in 1832, Chicago grew up in a climate dominated by classical liberalism and free labor republicanism. The political economy that shaped the institutional and cultural life of the young city defined human nature as primarily self-interested. Derived from eighteenth-century moral philosophy, the field of political economy defined "man" as given to a truck and bartering nature; self-interest drove economic exchange as well as political choice and social relationships. Attributing self-interest to a universal human motivation helped make sense of cultural confusion and economic hardships surrounding the spread of an ideology that prioritized modern market relations. According to early political economists, the cash nexus, not personal relationships or feudal loyalties, bound individuals and societies together.[3] As business theorist Henry Wood wrote in his popular 1894 book, *The Political Economy of Natural Law*, "the predominant motive of social economy, on the present plane of human develop-

---

3. Albert Hirschman, *The Passions and the Interests: Political Arguments for Capitalism before Its Triumph* (Princeton, NJ: Princeton University Press, 1977).

ment, is self-interest."[4] For Wood this meant that "any inversion of this natural order will retard the coming ideal," whatever it may be.[5] This view endowed economics with properties of natural law and provided justification for laissez-faire policies; theorists argued that the economy would function best if governments defended private property and refrained from interfering with the complex system of business exchange and rational self-interest that held society together.[6]

In translating these abstract principles into a blueprint for their young nation, American theorists and politicians built upon ideas of self-interest and individualism. Pursuit of personal interest in economic life promised the quickest growth of the nation. Yet they expected to escape the problems wrought by excessive greed. Strong republican and evangelical Christian traditions upheld the importance of personal responsibility for the common good, expressed through public service and political participation.[7] This liberal republicanism was supported by a judiciary friendly to individual property rights. Closely related to a legal discourse couched in terms of natural law, economic principles themselves came to appear as inherent and immutable laws.[8]

Evolving alongside Calvinist traditions, this political economy complemented an American tendency to understand the course of the nation's development in millennialist terms. Seeing their country as God's chosen, Americans believed their history would unfold to produce the millennium. Enlightenment-inspired

4. Henry Wood, *The Political Economy of Natural Law* (Boston: Lee and Shepard, 1894), 13.

5. Ibid., 14.

6. Joseph Dorfman, *The Economic Mind in American Civilization*, vol. 2 (New York: Viking, 1949); Dorothy Ross, *The Origin of American Social Sciences* (New York: Cambridge University Press, 1991); Nancy Cohen, *The Reconstruction of American Liberalism, 1865–1914* (Chapel Hill: University of North Carolina Press, 2002); Jeffrey Sklansky, *The Soul's Economy: Market Society and Selfhood in American Thought, 1820–1920* (Chapel Hill: University of North Carolina Press, 2002); Daniel T. Rodgers, *Atlantic Crossings: Social Politics in a Progressive Age* (Cambridge, MA: Belknap Press of Harvard University Press, 1998), especially chapter 3, "Twilight of Laissez-Faire."

William Novak points out that the notion of laissez-faire was a fiction, for the state provided land, canals, and roads; passed laws that regulated exchange in the urban marketplace; required licenses; and so on. But my point here is a different one. While the reality belied the myth, most Americans *believed* in the notion of laissez-faire and the free market. Indeed, Novak shares my concern that the power of this narrative—what I frame here as liberal republican social knowledge—operated in the past (and continues in the present) to constrain ideas about the functions of the state. See William J. Novak, *The People's Welfare: Law and Regulation in Nineteenth-century America* (Chapel Hill: University of North Carolina Press, 1996), 1–18, 83–114.

7. James T. Kloppenberg, "The Virtues of Liberalism: Christianity, Republicanism, and Ethics in Early American Political Discourse," *Journal of American History* 71 (1987): 9–33; Drew R. McCoy, *The Elusive Republic* (Chapel Hill: University of North Carolina Press, 1980); Anne Norton, *Alternative Americas: A Reading of Antebellum Political Culture* (Chicago: University of Chicago Press, 1986); Mary O. Furner, "The Republican Tradition and the New Liberalism: Social Investigation, State Building, and Social Learning in the Gilded Age," in *The State and Social Investigation in Britain and the United States*, ed. Michael J. Lacey and Mary O. Furner, 174 (Washington, DC: Woodrow Wilson Center Press / Cambridge, England: Cambridge University Press, 1993).

8. Rodgers, *Atlantic Crossings*, chapter 3.

faith in rational progress and America's own history seemed to reveal the inevitable advance of democracy in the new nation. As the professional social sciences developed in the Gilded Age of the 1870s and 1880s, political and economic theorists incorporated belief in America's progress into their writings. These ideas all led to the conclusion that in a nation that enjoyed God's blessing, little economic tinkering was necessary.[9]

Both building on and contributing to these foundations of American political economy, Chicago civic elites cast their city as the finest example of the American exceptionalism underpinning liberal republicanism. Like a Horatio Alger plot, the story of the city's spectacular growth featured a combination of sound character, hard work, and good fortune—at least according to the boosters who wrote it.[10] Chicago was a frontier town in the midst of vast forests and agricultural land situated on the Great Lakes with their access to waterways in the east.[11] Its privileged position near to natural resources and rapid commercial and population growth seemed to bear out boosters' claims that the city, like the United States itself, was divinely chosen. With population surging, from 350 in 1833 to 300,000 by the Great Fire in 1871, the city boasted over a million residents by the time of the World's Fair.[12] Much of this growth came from immigration; by 1893, three-quarters of Chicago residents were foreign-born or the children of immigrants. Development of transportation infrastructure, first a canal and then railroads, made Chicago's growth as a market center possible. Exploiting its proximity to forests, the city became the largest lumber market center in the world by the 1850s. In that decade, Chicago also built the Board of Trade to regulate speculation and money use. By the Civil War, its financial strength attracted industrial ventures, particularly its famed meat-packing industry. These simultaneous developments of the spatial landscape, an industrial, time-ordered economy, and the Board of Trade which regulated market transactions, ensuring the value of money and commodities over long distances and periods of time, marked Chicago as an

9. Dorothy Ross, "Historical Consciousness in Nineteenth-century America," *American Historical Review* 89 (October 1984): 909–28; James Moorhead, "Between Progress and Apocalypse: A Reassessment of Millennialism in American Religious Thought," *Journal of American History* 71 (December 1984): 524–40.

10. Horatio Alger wrote more than 130 dime novels after the Civil War. His stories emphasized that the American dream could be attained by anyone who exercised strong determination and hard work.

11. This discussion of Chicago's economic growth is drawn from William Cronon, *Nature's Metropolis: Chicago and the Great West* (New York: Norton, 1991), 97–262. Cronon chronicles Chicago's economic rise in terms of its relationship to rural lands and resources as far west as Denver and its commercial and cultural mediation between the East and West.

12. Population figures are from Bessie Louise Pierce, *History of Chicago: The Rise of a Modern City*, vol. 3 (New York: Knopf, 1957), 515–16.

industrial, capitalist urban center.[13]

Chicago stood symbolically between the inhabited, civilized east and the wilderness of the west, and residents claimed the best of both worlds. As they encouraged the growth of the city, they looked to the west as an outlet for excess population and protection from the vices of urban luxury and indolence. Migrants from the hinterlands would reinvigorate the populace, as "physical development, power of endurance, indomitable courage, together with intellectual vigor, business instinct and inventive genius, gather into the great center from country homes." As one booster explained, "poor indeed would be the mental and physical status of the urban population were it not for the constant influx of the agriculturalist class."[14] Chicagoans thus drew upon a Jeffersonian vision of an abundance of uncultivated land offering an escape from the crowding, decadence, and class conflict of overgrown eastern and European societies.[15]

Chicago's civic elites made their fortunes from the opportunities the city offered. The earliest settlers laid the infrastructure that attracted a second generation of entrepreneurs in the 1850s. Most of these men were born into relatively modest circumstances in the Northeast, but made their fortunes in Chicago's booming economy. The city produced over two hundred millionaires in the late nineteenth century.[16] Marshall Field was the wealthiest of them all. Born on a farm in Massachusetts, he came to Chicago in search of economic opportunity. Working as a clerk, his employer noticed that he had a merchant's instinct and a rigid frugality. Field practiced his own philosophy: "The five, ten, or fifteen cents a day that is squandered, while a mere trifle apparently, if saved, would in a few years amount to thousands of dollars and go far toward establishing the foundation of a future career."[17] By 1866, only ten years after arriving in the city, he owned his own store which transacted over $9,000,000 worth of business. Field died one of the wealthiest men in the United States.

Field was only one among many of Chicago's newly wealthy who proudly told of their rise from poverty through hard work. In 1875, Philip Armour, a ditch-digger, arrived in the city. He rose to astounding fame and wealth by revolutionizing the meat-packing industry.[18] Armour enjoyed telling stories of his

13. David Harvey, *Consciousness and the Urban Experience: Studies in the History and Theory of Capitalist Urbanization* (Baltimore: Johns Hopkins University Press, 1985).

14. *The Biographical Dictionary and Portrait Gallery of Representative Men of Chicago and the World's Columbian Exposition* (New York: American Biographical, 1892), 522.

15. McCoy, *The Elusive Republic.*

16. Richard Schneirov, *Labor and Urban Politics: Class Conflict and the Origins of Modern Liberalism in Chicago, 1864–1897* (Urbana: University of Illinois Press, 1998), 299.

17. Quoted in Kathleen McCarthy, *Noblesse Oblige: Charity and Cultural Philanthropy in Chicago, 1849–1929* (Chicago: University of Chicago Press), 67.

18. Quoted in Donald Miller, *City of the Century: The Epic of Chicago and the Making of America*

difficult youth. The son of a family farmer, he left home at age nineteen to make his fortune in the California gold rush. Managing to save $8,000 through panning and digging sluices, Armour gambled on the meat-packing industry, and made his first million at the close of the Civil War. He invested in Chicago's future as a meat-packing center, making millions of dollars from the company that bore his name. Believing in practical education, he established the Armour Mission and Institute to teach needy boys useful trades. When the Institute opened in 1893, it was celebrated as "a place for developing character."[19] Armour frequently dispensed advice to students: "Let liquor alone, pay your bills, marry a good wife and pound away at whatever you want—and sooner or later you'll make good."[20] His success story, similar to those of Field's partner, Potter Palmer, railroad car magnate George Pullman, and T. W. Harvey, head of Chicago's most successful lumber firm, served as proof of the liberal republican myth that grew up around Chicago. Alluding to the mantra that came to define the new nation and its western frontier, Wood proclaimed, "Chicago is a self-made city, and those who have created it are self-made men."[21]

For Chicago's elites there were important moral and economic lessons in these success stories, lessons that enforced a social narrative privileging hard work, as a means to unify the city's diverse residents and to develop personal character. When asked about his success, Marshall Field explained simply, "I was determined not to remain poor."[22] He credited his individual drive as the source of his success. As historian Donald Miller observed about Field, "he had complete faith in the openness of the Chicago economy. In this city of boundless opportunity 'merit did not have to wait for dead men's shoes.' If he, the son of a struggling hill farmer, could make it in Chicago, anyone could."[23] Reflecting this sentiment, a booster asserted that "the history of human success has shown that only in exceptional instances has natural ability, legitimately applied, failed of a legitimate measure of achievement."[24] Such belief underlined the place of individualism and market ideology in elites' explanation of success. Chicago's many millionaires and the city's phenomenal economic growth testified that anyone who worked hard and exhibited personal initiative and ability was guaranteed success. Conversely, elites found it easy to blame the poor for their poverty.

(New York: Simon & Schuster, 1996), 220–22.

19. Clifford L. Snowden, "The Armour Institute of Technology," *New England Magazine* 16 (May 1897): 371.

20. Ernest Poole, *Giants Gone: Men Who Made Chicago* (New York: McGraw-Hill, 1943), 156.

21. Quoted in John J. Pauly, "The City Builders: Chicago Businessmen and Their Changing Ethos" (PhD diss., University of Illinois at Urbana-Champaign, 1979), 138.

22. Theodore Dreiser, "Life Stories," no. 12, "Success 1" (December 8, 1898), 7–8. Quoted in Miller, *City of the Century*, 257.

23. Miller, 258.

24. Wood, *Chicago and Its Distinguished Citizens*, 185.

A classical republican conception of labor and city-building also promised to mitigate the challenges presented by the city's pluralism. Chicago stood as a universal home welcoming anyone of a liberal economic persuasion. The shared task of building the city promised unity of purpose that would tie its residents, even the city's many ethnic groups, together: one businessman argued that "the enterprising man, no matter where he may be born, is naturally a citizen of Chicago."[25] This vision emphasized the importance of labor "as a work of responsible, patriotic citizenship."[26] Such a vision shaped the optimistic responses to the Great Fire of 1871. As one historian put it, "in destroying the city physically, the Chicago Fire renewed it symbolically, for the experience of building the city that had united the early settlers was now to bind the next generation as well."[27] Recreating the city had the moral effect of encouraging hard work and good character. "No longer was it necessary . . . to send America's children off to new settlements in order to preserve the pioneer ideals. All the virtues of pioneer life that had seemed on the wane before the fire would be required again if Chicago were to rebuild."[28] As the city quickly recovered, ministers and businessmen cast the experience in exceptionalist terms, offering it as proof of divine favor. At the dedication of the new Chicago Board of Trade, a local minister offered prayers of thanksgiving: "We went through fire and water, but Thou broughtest us out into a wealthy place."[29] Glossing over deep ethnic and class divisions in the wake of the fire, such memories entrenched a narrative justifying the unifying tendencies of Chicago's liberal republican social knowledge.[30]

For businessmen, Chicago's virtues were epitomized in the World's Fair of 1893, which showcased Chicago's physical growth, economic success, and cultural attainments.[31] Tellingly for the way organizers conceived of success, the Manufactures Building was the site of President Grover Cleveland's opening speech. It was the largest man-made structure on earth and was lit with over

25. Speech before the Chicago Historical Society, 1882, quoted in Pauly, "The City Builders," 138.

26. Wood, *Chicago and Its Distinguished Citizens*, 360–61. This was a theme heard often among American workers over the course of the century, though with a slightly different accent. See, for example, Sean Wilentz, *Chants Democratic: New York City and the Rise of the American Working Class* (New York: Oxford University Press, 1984).

27. Pauly, "The City Builders," 100.

28. Ibid.

29. *Dedication of the New Board of Trade Building . . . Dedicatory and Banquet Addresses* (1885), 7, quoted in Cronon, *Nature's Metropolis*, 348.

30. For discussion of division in the wake of the fire, see Karen Sawislak, *Smoldering City: Chicagoans and the Great Fire, 1871–1874* (Chicago: University of Chicago Press), and Carl Smith, *Urban Disorder and the Shape of Belief: The Great Chicago Fire, the Haymarket Bomb, and the Model Town of Pullman* (Chicago: University of Chicago, 1995).

31. Robert Rydell, *All the World's a Fair: Visions of Empire at American International Expositions, 1876–1916* (Chicago: University of Chicago Press, 1984); David F. Burg, *Chicago's White City of 1893* (Lexington: University of Kentucky Press, 1976).

127,000 lights, testament to American technological and economic success. The Fair's Court of Honor and Midway Plaisance attracted over 12,000,000 visitors—with approximately 1 out of 4 Americans making the trip to the White City. Cleveland hailed the Fair, Chicago, and the nation as one of the "'stupendous results of American enterprise . . . proud national destiny . . . and exalted mission."[32] The Fair celebrated the belief that abundant resources, free labor, liberty, assertiveness, and technological innovation came together to ensure unity and progress.[33]

Thus through their experience of building the city, civic elites identified the common good with economic growth. The success stories of Chicago's businessmen lent themselves to a social knowledge that emphasized economic rationality and hard work as its residents' defining characteristics. This social knowledge wove together classical liberal and republican strands of thought in which the autonomous individual succeeded through honest effort, and personal success would directly benefit the community as a whole. The ties that held residents together operated through the market and through city building, arenas that were implicitly masculine and white.[34] The lessons learned by Chicago's economic growth functioned as a form of social knowledge—though elites did not use the term. Their social knowledge—the narrative they used to explain Chicago's and their own successes—was visible in the city they built, structuring patterns of interaction, institutions, and politics. It was especially evident in their approach to public relief and private aid, and in their understanding of the proper role of the state.

32. Ray Ginger, *Altgeld's America: The Lincoln Ideal versus Changing Realities* (New York: Funk and Wagnalls, 1958), 19.

33. Alan Trachtenberg discusses how the business elite captured free labor ideology, convincing the middle class that competitive business led to fulfillment. This ideology had significant implications for many laborers who frequently experienced bouts of unemployment. Trachtenberg, *The Incorporation of America: Culture and Society in the Gilded Age* (New York: Hill and Wang, 1982), 87.

34. Rogers Smith, *Civic Ideals: Conflicting Visions of Citizenship in U.S. History* (New Haven, CT: Yale University Press, 1997), 30–39. On the connections between work and American civic identity, see Judith N. Shklar, *American Citizenship: The Quest for Inclusion* (Cambridge, MA: Harvard University Press, 1991); Carol Horton, "Liberal Equality and the Civic Subject: Identity and Citizenship in Reconstruction America," in *The Liberal Tradition in American Politics: Reassessing the Legacy of American Liberalism*, ed. David F. Ericson and Louisa Bertch Green, 115–36 (New York: Routledge, 1999); Evelyn Nakano Glenn, *Unequal Freedom: How Race and Gender Shaped American Citizenship and Labor* (Cambridge, MA: Harvard University Press, 2002); Nancy Cohen, *The Reconstruction of American Liberalism, 1865–1914* (Chapel Hill: University of North Carolina Press, 2002). For a description of liberalism and its theoretical connections to the market, see Dorothy Ross, "Liberalism," in *A Companion to American Thought*, ed. Richard Wightman Fox and James T. Kloppenberg, 397–400 (Cambridge, MA: Blackwell, 1995). On Chicago in particular, see Pauly, "The City Builders."

The Market, Moral Economy, and the State

By the 1890s, Chicago's market was the largest in the world and was imbued with extensive social meaning—and conflict. Belief in equal opportunity and promises of success to the virtuous hard worker were critical to the new city's and the new nation's economic and social narratives. They stood virtually as natural laws in mid-nineteenth century America, shaping ideas about the role of government in the economy and public responsibility for the poor and unemployed. Though Chicago's businessmen had benefited immensely from federal and state land grants, they did not recognize this as intervention. A laissez-faire framework shaped their worldview and structured their political policies. As one historian has explained, "unfettered capitalism was, [Chicago's business leaders] were absolutely certain, the underpinning of their city's, their country's, and their own well-being."[35] And elites' political ideas and local government practices emphasized individualism and laissez-faire. While the earliest settlers to Chicago depended on government aid and expected that city politicos would encourage development, by 1847 many Chicagoans no longer believed that municipal government should promote the city's growth. They "rejected both the redistribution of wealth through [public] improvements spending and the use of interest-group politics to make public works decisions."[36] Instead, through a program of special assessments which Robin Einhorn calls a "segmented system," Chicagoans ensured that only property owners affected by special taxes participated in the decision to levy them for improvements, thus limiting the municipal government's ability to create public works programs. This system prioritized the language of liberal property ownership, rejected an activist role for the state, and prevented discussion of the meaning of the public good. Indeed, Chicagoans privatized as many services as possible, such as police and fire protection, in the 1840s and 50s to remove "potentially divisive issues from the city council's agenda." Their program had a further advantage, they believed, because it "allowed Chicago's city government to provide services to property owners without redistributing their wealth."[37] Chicago's politicians built a system that upheld the primacy of private property, the autonomy of the individual political actor, and a limited role of the state.

The liberal republicanism that emphasized abundant opportunity and individual effort treated poverty and unemployment as temporary imbalances that the market would soon correct or as the result of laziness, mental dullness,

35. Miller, 121.

36. Robin Einhorn, *Property Rules: Political Economy in Chicago, 1833–1872* (Chicago: University of Chicago Press, 1991), 76.

37. Ibid., 144–45.

intemperance, even ethnicity or race.[38] Indeed, inspired by their predominantly New England Calvinist roots stressing individual salvation and viewing failure as a sign of weakness or sin, civic elites took a harsh view of the poor. Marshall Field captured this sentiment: "the man who is characterized by want of forethought, idleness, carelessness, or general shiftlessness cannot expect to succeed."[39] In such an economic and moral system, public social relationships entailed no further responsibility than those legally required in the liberal system of capitalism—fulfillment of economic contracts.[40] Dominated by the upper and middle classes, private charity undercut serious attacks on systemic poverty, unbalanced income distribution, or exploitative working conditions. Public codes emphasized the responsibility of the individual for his own welfare and made beneficence a matter of personal conscience and private choice, not a matter of public intervention. William Graham Sumner articulated this view in the 1880s in his popular sociological book, *What the Social Classes Owe Each Other*, which maintained that "in a state based on contract sentiment is out of place in any public or common affairs. It is relegated to the sphere of private and personal relations, where it depends, not at all on class types, but on personal acquaintance and personal estimates."[41] Sumner's code provided little room for state intervention in matters of charity and relief.[42] Private religious sentiment and duty had provided the rationale and framework to ameliorate the needs of the poor. But philanthropists' willingness to aid the poor was tempered by belief in the abundancy of economic success for all hard workers.[43] Charity too freely

38. Herbert Gutman, "The Failure of the Movement by the Unemployed for Public Works in 1873," *Political Science Quarterly* 80, no. 2 (1965): 254–76.

39. McCarthy, *Noblesse Oblige*, 67.

40. Amy Dru Stanley shows how, in the years following the Civil War, social relations followed definitions of freedom as contractual rights. See "Conjugal Bonds and Wage Labor: Rights of Contract in the Age of Emancipation," *Journal of American History* 75 (September 1988): 471–500, and "Beggars Can't Be Choosers: Compulsion and Contract in Postbellum America," *Journal of American History* 78 (March 1992): 1265–93. Also Eric Foner, *Reconstruction: America's Unfinished Revolution, 1863–1877* (New York: Harper and Row, 1988), and Morton Horowitz, *The Transformation of American Law, 1870–1960: The Crisis of Legal Orthodoxy* (New York: Oxford University Press), 187–213.

41. William Graham Sumner, *What the Social Classes Owe Each Other* (Caldwell, ID: Caxton, 1966), 24–25.

42. David J. Rothman, *The Discovery of the Asylum: Social Order and Disorder in the New Republic*, rev. ed. (Boston: Little, Brown, 1991); Bruce Dorsey, *Reforming Men and Women: Gender in the Antebellum City* (Ithaca, NY: Cornell University Press, 2002). In antebellum America, local and state governments supported public education, asylums for the mentally ill, or aid to orphans, widows, and abandoned women and children. Nonetheless, these institutions still focused on saving and reforming the individual; there was little belief that structural problems, as opposed to personal character flaws, were responsible for poverty.

43. McCarthy discusses this history of social reform in *Noblesse Oblige*. Also John Albert Mayer, "Private Charity in Chicago from 1871–1915" (PhD diss., University of Minnesota, 1978); and Paul Boyer, *Urban Masses and Moral Order in America, 1820–1920* (Cambridge, MA: Harvard University Press, 1978).

given was seen to undermine the lessons of the liberal market, casting paupers outside the imagined political community since their poverty rendered them "unable to know and act for the common good."[44]

In this environment, Chicago's local government and charities were very reluctant to provide relief to residents out of fear it would render them dependent. As Kathleen McCarthy observed in her study of Chicago philanthropy, "public resources for the care of the poor were limited and grudgingly rendered."[45] In the aftermath of the great fire, the privately run Relief and Aid Society (RAS), the largest institution devoted to charitable distributions, tried to prevent disbursements of the millions of dollars intended for fire victims to the "undeserving" poor. The RAS, with its board of prominent businessmen, feared that indiscriminate giving would foster laziness among Chicago's ethnic working classes.[46] Civic elites' efforts to limit relief helped entrench their liberal republican vision of limited public responsibility for the poor and unemployed. Moreover, elites' attempt to enact and enforce stricter fire codes to prevent future conflagrations further emphasized the limited role of the state solely as the protector of private property.

Similar views appeared in response to the depression of 1873. As working people sought public works programs, urban middle and upper classes responded with little sympathy. Instead they clung to a belief in opportunity and assumed that the market had separated out those who lacked character and drive. In Chicago, the superintendent of the Relief and Aid Society proclaimed that "most able-bodied men were 'loafing around the streets' and could find work 'if they were not too lazy to look for it.' He insisted: 'If the manifest destiny of a man is the poor house, we must let him go there. To aid some men will do them no good."[47] While Chicago socialists and unionists claimed a right to work, demanding government-sponsored public works, the *Chicago Daily Tribune* rejected them. It explained that Marx "foolishly rejected the classical economists" and denied that the "principles of current economic science" were "immutable," "necessary," and had "their roots in human nature." Socialists were dangerous because "they refuse to accept our political economy any more than a Mohammedan accepts Christianity."[48] Historian Herbert Gutman observes that although urban residents across the nation were themselves affected by the severity of the 1873 depression, they were "blinded by abstract ideologies and a

44. Glenn, *Unequal Freedom*, 24.

45. McCarthy, *Noblesse Oblige*, 54.

46. Sawislak, *Smoldering City*, 69–106; Smith, *Urban Disorder and the Shape of Belief*, part 1.

47. Herbert Gutman, "The Failure of the Movement by the Unemployed for Public Works in 1873," *Political Science Quarterly* 80, no. 2 (June 1965): 256. Quote is from the *Chicago Tribune*, December 23, 1873, and the *Chicago Times*, December 23, 1873–January 1, 1874.

48. Gutman, "Failure of the Movement," 272; *Chicago Tribune*, December 23, 25, 26, 1873.

devotion to 'natural' economic laws" and thus unwilling to adopt workers' calls for public works. Civic elites argued that the RAS was "able to take care of, to feed, to clothe . . . the wives and children of men who cannot work," ignoring that it rejected nineteen out of twenty applicants.[49]

Reflecting a belief in the widespread availability and transformative power of labor in the liberal market, the Illinois legislature passed a vagrancy law making it illegal to beg or loiter on the streets. This act lead to thousands of arrests in Chicago, and those who could not pay the fine were sent into compulsory labor for several months. Such laws made it illegal to eke out a living outside the market.[50] Charity reformers, and the civic elites who sponsored their work, invoked natural laws of political economy, expecting that punitive vagrancy laws and tough relief policies would compel the unemployed to sell their labor in the open market.[51]

Class conflict brought on by the Fire, the Panic of 1873, and the Great Uprising of 1877, in which the workers for the nation's four largest railroads staged a strike that ended violently, belied the universal acceptance of liberal republicanism and civic harmony that elites claimed. In the face of these growing attacks, prominent businessmen founded men's clubs to debate pressing urban problems. Representing the opinions and interests of a single class, elite clubs like the Citizens' Association and the Commercial Club served to solidify their members' explanations of social problems. Club members discussed topics such as "The Right of the State to interfere with vested and private rights" and "Unemployed laborers: What obligations rest upon the city or citizens for their support?"[52] As these discussions suggest, members were preoccupied with the role of the state as the defender of private property. Created in the wake of the general strike in 1877 to enforce this vision, the Commercial Club searched for ways to assert a stronger military presence in the city to prevent workers' attacks on capital. During 1877–78, the Citizen's Association spent $27,000 (nearly $500,000 today) on military expenses, financing the "equipment of Militia by purchase of arms, cavalry equipment, a battery, Gatling gun and ammunitions—supplying the police with arms and ammunition. The moral effect of this cannot be overestimated," the Association wrote.[53] The Commercial Club debated the matter and in 1879

49. Gutman, "Failure of the Movement," 274–75.

50. Stanley, "Beggars Can't Be Choosers," 1267.

51. Ibid., 1277. Stanley argues that politicians and economic theorists viewed vagrancy laws, with their compulsion to work, as an important aspect of maintaining the discipline and natural laws of the liberal market. See pp. 1282–83.

52. Commercial Club of Chicago, *Yearbook, 1908* (Chicago: Executive Committee of the Commercial Club of Chicago, 1908). This publication lists the topics of meetings up to the year of publication.

53. *Manual of the Citizen's Association, 1882–83*, 24. This pamphlet includes work of previous years.

invited a speaker on "The Military, as protectors of property, local and National."[54] Shortly thereafter, it took steps to bring an army installation to Chicago. The opportunity to bring a permanent federal presence to the city came in the wake of the 1886 Haymarket Affair, when fears of disintegrating public order left many upper-class citizens demanding police protection. Fort Sheridan opened in 1887, and Chicago's elites were relieved that the federal troops would "prevent a lot of riots occurring in Chicago because the soldiers could get there quickly."[55]

The discussion of public relief and the limited role of local government illustrates that Chicago's political economy rested on an assumption of naturalized liberal economic codes and relationships, especially laissez-faire and freedom of contract. As such, it cast the liberal republican narrative as commonsense and rendered it immutable. As a form of social knowledge, it shaped the terms of debate, the boundaries of legitimacy, and was inscribed in political and social institutions. It was the social knowledge against which alternative economic, social, and political ideas were framed. Any significant social reform would entail changing the content of that narrative, as well as finding justification for challenging the "natural law" it embodied.

Of course, the liberal republican narrative was far from monolithic. In 1866, the state legislature enacted a voluntary eight-hour law. Workers welcomed state intervention to limit their workday. As one worker suggested, "the eight hour system will have a tendency to keep society more upon an equality. It will give the laboring classes more time for study and thinking, and thereby they will become more independent of professional men."[56] They pointed out the corrosive effects of excessive labor that undermined the workers' independence and ability to contribute to democratic government. In the Panic of 1873, when local government refused to provide public relief, claiming its coffers were empty, workers demanded that a committee of ethnically diverse Chicagoans oversee the disbursement of RAS relief funds. Rather than leaving such efforts in private middle- and upper-class hands, as custom and classical liberalism dictated, workers argued that they had a vital role to play on such a committee.[57]

54. Ibid., 38.

55. John V. Farwell, quoted in *Haymarket Scrapbook: A Centennial Anthology*, ed. David Roediger, 130 (Chicago: Kerr, 1986). On the founding of Fort Sheridan, see William J. Adelman, "The Road to Fort Sheridan," in ibid., and Nina B. Smith, " 'This Bleak Situation': The Founding of Fort Sheridan, Illinois," *Journal of the Illinois State Historical Society* 80, no. 1 (Spring 1987): 13–22.

56. Quoted in Schneirov, *Labor and Urban Politics*, 34. Also William Andrew Mirola, "Fighting in the Pews and Fighting in the Streets: Protestantism, Consciousness, and the Eight-hour Movement in Chicago, 1867–1912" (PhD diss., Indiana University, 1995).

57. For the history of Chicago's charity and relief efforts see McCarthy, *Noblesse Oblige;* John Albert Mayer, "Private Charity in Chicago from 1871 to 1915" (PhD diss., University of Minnesota, 1978); Sawislak, *Smoldering City.* Amy Stanley ("Beggars Can't Be Choosers") illuminates the impact of free labor ideology on charity practices in the postbellum United States.

Contributing their labor to Chicago's development, they staked their claim as important members of the polity.

Rejecting immutable natural economic law, workers sought government intervention to curb what they saw as economic injustice. Doing so would not encourage laziness, as elites feared or make workers weak and dependent, but rather recognized what they claimed as their right to work and the power of the community to reorganize its social and economic arrangements accordingly. Similarly, in the wake of the Great Fire, women's organizations rejected the criteria and suspicion that greeted the needy when they sought help from the RAS. Women responded to the Fire by arguing that *all* were entitled to immediate help, not just those deemed "worthy" by the RAS. Their position recast public responsibility for relief as matters of debate, not questions answered by natural law.[58]

As the 1890s approached, unionists and clubwomen sought alternative ways to explain and respond to Chicago's problems. Their efforts suggest that Chicago's liberal republicanism couched in terms of natural law was giving way to a different form of discourse. Indeed, historian Mary Furner describes that in the latter nineteenth century, economic and social theory were increasingly conceived of as provisional and "defined rights, law, and state forms as cultural creations, shaped by the conditions and needs of particular historical context and subject to experimentation, growth, and change."[59] This historicism provided the intellectual backdrop for Chicagoans seeking new ways of explaining and shaping their society outside of the inherited assumptions of classical political economy.

"A Decade of Economic Discussion"

In May 1893, the stock market collapsed, triggering what was then the worst depression in American history. In Chicago, the depression, at first held at bay by the Columbian Exposition, set in quickly once the Fair closed at the end of October. As the immensity of social problems multiplied beyond the resources of private charity, the older conception of political economy seemed inadequate.[60]

58. Maureen A. Flanagan, *Seeing with Their Hearts: Chicago Women and the Vision of the Good City, 1871–1933* (Princeton, NJ: Princeton University Press, 2002), 27–29.

59. Mary Furner, "The Republican Tradition and the New Liberalism: Social Investigation, State Building, and Social Learning in the Gilded Age," in *The State and Social Investigation in Britain and the United States*, ed. Michael J. Lacey and Mary O. Furner, 174 (Washington, DC: Woodrow Wilson Center Press / Cambridge, England: Cambridge University Press, 1993).

60. Thomas L. Haskell, *The Emergence of Professional Social Science: The American Social Science Association and the Nineteenth-century Crisis of Authority* (Urbana: University of Illinois Press, 1977), particularly chapter 2, "Interdependence and the Rise of Professional Social Science."

Chicago, like the nation, faced an economic and cultural crisis that plunged the city into what Jane Addams described as "a decade of economic discussion."

While Chicagoans had been wrestling with social problems attendant to industrial capitalism and urbanization long before 1893, this moment was critical in ongoing debates about the future of American democracy. The depression threw into relief the claims workers had been making for decades: industrial capitalism brought wage dependency, which in turn undermined democracy rooted in classical liberal autonomy. American democracy was predicated on this autonomy, and without it, workers argued, the national experiment was imperiled. Historians have interpreted this moment differently. For example, Jeffrey Sklansky, noting the ascendancy of the social self by the 1890s, laments the death of a vision of democracy predicated on proprietary capitalism, since it undermined an important basis of workers' demands for economic justice.[61] In contrast, James Livingston welcomed the rise of the social self and its economic trope, corporate capitalism, arguing that it opened up the possibilities for creating multiple gender, racial, and class identities and forming a diversity of collective relationships and political actions.[62] These interpretations are important for our purposes here as they suggest the limits of what I have described as liberal republicanism and reinforce that moment as an opportunity to create a different social knowledge, one that was more inclusive than its predecessor. In forcing Americans to come to terms with the changing economy, it encouraged them to rethink the foundations of democracy, as well.

A public meeting on November 12, 1893 highlighted the possibilities of that moment. A spirited audience filled all 1500 seats of Central Music Hall and spilled into the downtown streets. Men and women, native-born and immigrants, workers, and civic elites packed the auditorium to hear English journalist and reformer William Stead, along with local reformers and union leaders, address what the *Chicago Tribune* parsimoniously labeled "Labor Topics." Local reformer Graham Taylor recalled the audience was "such a grouping of people from the extremes of life as no one could have imagined to be possible." He noted that "side by side sat leading businessmen and labor leaders, representatives of the city government and of its exclusive clubs, preachers and saloonkeepers, gamblers and theological professors, matrons of distinguished families and notorious 'madams' from houses of ill fame, judges of the courts and one of the men convicted in the Haymarket Riot trial who had recently been pardoned from the state prison by Governor Altgeld."[63]

---

61. Sklansky, *Soul's Economy.*
62. James Livingston, *Pragmatism, Feminism, and Democracy: Rethinking the Politics of American History* (New York: Routledge, 2001).
63. Graham Taylor, *Pioneering on Social Frontiers* (Chicago: University of Chicago Press, 1930), 29.

As the meeting reveals, the severity of the depression as well as the optimism inspired by the World's Fair, made possible new coalitions for forging alternative social knowledge. Stead had purposefully invited a broad cross-section of residents with the intention of opening dialogue among the many different groups of city residents. By bringing this cross-section of residents together, Stead elicited the perspectives of saloonkeepers and anarchists. He urged elites to listen to them before they passed judgments or made social improvements, admonishing that "before any one [sic] can speak with any right to be heard as to the condition of human beings he must do as Christ did and put himself in their place. You cannot live in velvet drawing-rooms and elegant boudoirs and philosophize about the subject."[64] Taylor, who would soon open a settlement house in the city, cautioned that urban problems could "not be solved until men and women come down from the suburbs into the center of the cities and live there for Christ's sake."[65]

Such arguments privileged a different epistemology than the naturalized assumptions of liberal republican social knowledge, one that posited knowledge as the product of collective experiences, mediated through social interaction and communal inquiry. As Taylor pointed out, the reconfiguration of the urban landscape along more socially and economically integrated lines demanded participatory inquiry rooted in shared experience. Indeed, John Dewey, who within the year would become the chair of both the departments of Philosophy and Pedagogy at the University of Chicago, explained, "social divisions as interfere with free and full intercourse react to make the intelligence and knowing of members of the separated classes one-sided." This was problematic since "barriers to intercourse prevent the experience of one from being enriched and supplemented by that of others who are differently situated." He argued instead that "since democracy stands in principle for free interchange, for social continuity, it must develop a theory of knowledge which sees in knowledge the method by which one experience is made available in giving direction and meaning to another."[66] Dewey's vision of democratic social knowledge encouraged the interaction Taylor described and included the experience (here he meant the experience of any group regardless of social position or education) as an important ingredient. The undercurrent of the meeting that day, then, suggested that different groups in the city offered a variety of perspectives on the city's problems. It laid out what was an emerging vision of democratic social knowledge.

Though by several measures the meeting was remarkably inclusive for a city that experienced deep division—women, workers, anarchists, social scientists, Native Americans, businessmen all rose to speak to each other—there was a brief

64. *Chicago Tribune*, November 13, 1893.
65. Ibid.
66. John Dewey, *Democracy and Education* (New York: Free Press, 1916), 344.

but striking interaction that foreshadowed limits to the inclusiveness of democratic social knowledge. As the meeting drew to a close, an African American man gained the attention of the audience. He began his remarks begging "the gracious indulgence of the audience," noting that "it has been asserted at this meeting that it is the first duty of a government to protect itself without regard to any poor and degraded class. As one of a down-trodden race . . ." He got no further as Stead interrupted him: " 'Sit down, sir,' said the Chairman. 'No one here has said anything like what you say and nobody here looks down upon your race. You have no right to introduce that subject.' "[67] Stead's dismissive response may have reflected his outsider's ignorance of the deepening problems of racial division in the city. Or it may indicate that he had been warned against permitting race to enter the public discussion. In either case, his reprimand was unwarranted in light of racial developments in the city throughout the early 1890s, when the possibility of social equality was increasingly decried in the city's newspapers, when Southern African American strikebreakers antagonized union members, and when the growing migration of blacks into the city began to form faint outlines of what became the south-side ghetto. By refusing to allow the African American man to speak that day, when women, immigrants, and workers were all vocal participants, Stead highlighted the depth of resistance African Americans confronted in gaining access to and legitimacy for *their* experience.

As Chicago reformers confronted the crisis of the 1890s then, they found that liberal republican social knowledge was inadequate for explaining the acute problems the city faced or defining democratic meaning, practices, and polity in an increasingly pluralistic, corporate industrial society. Throughout a decade of economic discussion, city reformers struggled to enact a new conception of democracy, one that would unify city residents, not through the competitive market, but through cooperation and social solidarity. The key to preventing a fatal drifting apart, many would argue, would come, not from pursuit of self-interested, contractual relations, but from building a more interactive, participatory, and sympathetic community life. At the end of the meeting, Stead offered a resolution—that those interested in redressing the city's problems create "a civic confederation" of various representatives to begin the tasks of social and political reform. The audience unanimously passed his resolution, and the Civic Federation of Chicago was launched. It offered a new arena in which to create democratic social knowledge.

67. *Chicago Tribune*, November 13, 1893.

2

"To Serve as a Medium of Acquaintance and Sympathy"

The Civic Federation and Conflicting Visions of Democratic Social Knowledge

To serve as a medium of acquaintance and sympathy between persons who reside in the different parts of the city, who pursue different vocations, who are by birth of different nationalities, who profess different creeds or no creed, who for any of these reasons are unknown to each other but who nevertheless, have similar interests in the well being of Chicago, and who agree in the desire to promote every kind of municipal welfare.[1]

In the days following the mass meeting of November 12, 1893, in which a wide range of Chicago's residents discussed the city's economic and social problems, settlement house founder Jane Addams, University of Chicago sociologist Albion Small, and journalist Ralph Easley joined with other reform-minded residents to organize the Civic Federation of Chicago (CFC).[2] The organization sought to bring different segments of the population together to investigate social problems, experiment with solutions, and promote political activism. According to its constitution, the CFC was to "serve as a medium of acquaintance and sympathy" for Chicago residents from different backgrounds. As a voluntary association with a diverse membership, the organization was in a position to act as a mediator of democratic social knowledge; through social science investigation, public education, and political mobilization, it sought to bring divergent groups into greater mutual understanding and offer an arena for them to bring their perspectives into a deliberative process.

1. The epigraph to this chapter is drawn from Civic Federation of Metropolitan Chicago Papers, Incorporation Papers, 1894, Chicago Historical Society, Box 1, Folder 1.

2. Ralph Easley was a journalist from Kansas who joined the staff of the *Chicago Inter-Ocean* in 1891. He left journalism in 1894 to become the secretary of the Civic Federation. In 1900 Easley founded the National Civic Federation in New York. Biographical information on Easley is available in the National Civic Federation Papers at the New York Public Library.

This chapter examines the efforts of the CFC to pursue social knowledge emphasizing interaction and cooperative activism and the epistemological tensions that ultimately undermined its goal of serving as "a medium of acquaintance and sympathy." Since labor leaders, club women, social scientists, business elites, and clergy all played a prominent role in its founding, the CFC offered an unusual opportunity to experiment with the processes of democratic social knowledge. In some respects, the organization indicated the elites' recognition of fundamental differences among social groups and a concession of their own inability to totally control the direction of Chicago's politics.

As a window onto the intersection between social knowledge and democracy, the CFC sheds light on the potential for interactive, cooperative strands of democratic social knowledge to inspire united political activism among very different social groups; through a reinvigoration of democratic political participation, the CFC hoped to avert a "fatal drifting apart." But the federation also illustrates how older conceptions of liberal republicanism, compatible with a growing elitist version of positivist social science, undermined goals of unity and collective activism. As two paradigms of social knowledge emerged in the organization, they foreshadowed later fissures in the CFC along class and gender lines. Ultimately, the CFC would fail to achieve its broadest goals of reconciling divergent social groups, but its possibilities and its failures are instructive as we consider the relationship between social knowledge and the practices of democracy.

Social Groups, Cooperation, and the Founding of the CFC

The Civic Federation of Chicago emerged during a transitional moment in Chicago's history when a reorientation of knowledge and social science met up with wider urban reform. This section illustrates the broad-based reform coalition that, for a brief period in the CFC's history, made the organization a creative model for forging democratic social knowledge. In drawing attention to the early diversity of the organization, the section highlights Chicagoans' recognition of divergent social groups. It is tempting to cast the CFC as an elite organization concerned with bringing orderliness and efficiency to public life and cleaning up Chicago politics. Indeed, most historical characterizations of the CFC describe it as simply a businessmen's reform group seeking to replace the political corruption associated with machine politics with honest government and municipal efficiency.[3] Through bureaucratization and rationalization of

3. The CFC is still awaiting a thorough study. For general discussions, see Andrew Feffer, *Chicago Pragmatism and American Progressivism* (Ithaca, NY: Cornell University Press, 1993); Maureen Flanagan, *Charter Reform in Chicago* (Carbondale: Southern Illinois University Press, 1987); Daniel Levine, *Varieties of Reform Thought* (Madison: State Historical Society of Wisconsin, 1964); David

business and government, such organizations entrenched middle-class interests and fostered an antidemocratic emphasis on efficiency and expertise. Another interpretation of businessmen's reform organizations maintains that functional problems explain the impetus for municipal reform: Socioeconomic pressures, such as population growth and industrialization, rendered inadequate older structures of city government and required new methods of administration that nonetheless maintained prevailing patterns of power relations.[4]

My discussion of the CFC's role in civic reform does not discount these interpretations; indeed, the federation disproportionately represented businessmen and professionals and within ten years of its birth had adopted an agenda aimed primarily at structural and fiscal government reform. By the 1910s it was a self-styled citizens' watchdog organization that was committed to promoting efficiency and economy in the spending of tax revenues.

However, most literature on the federation ignores working-class and women's membership in its early years. Several prominent unionists joined the CFC, and white women who held key roles in prominent female reform associations were active in the federation. Women in particular spoke regularly at the meetings and helped shape the CFC's methods and agenda. So while the characterization of the CFC as an elite male organization devoted to structural reform and business expertise has merit, it overlooks the different models of creating social knowledge brought by the organization's membership.

The Civic Federation's goal to form "an influential, non-political, non-sectarian association, embracing all the forces that are now laboring to advance the municipal, philanthropic, industrial and moral interests of Chicago" was broad and vague enough to capture just about any reform-minded group. And the six committees, created in its first year—municipal, industrial, philanthropic,

---

Marks, "Polishing the Gem of the Prairie: The Evolution of Civic Reform Consciousness in Chicago, 1874–1900" (PhD diss., University of Wisconsin, 1975); Thomas Pegram, *Partisans and Progressives: Private Interest and Public Policy in Illinois, 1870–1922* (Urbana: University of Illinois Press, 1992); Marguerite Green, "The National Civic Federation and the American Labor Movement, 1900–1925" (PhD diss., Catholic University of America, 1956, 1–14); Christopher J. Cyphers, *The National Civic Federation and the Making of a New Liberalism, 1900–1915* (Westport, CT: Praeger, 2002), 19–21. These works generally locate the CFC within the broader "organizational synthesis" of the late nineteenth century described by Robert Wiebe in *The Search for Order, 1877–1920* (New York: Hill and Wang, 1967), and Samuel Hays in "The Politics of Reform in Municipal Government in the Progressive Era," *Pacific Northwest Quarterly* 55 (1964): 157–69. For a different interpretation of the federation, one similar to that in this chapter, see Richard Schneirov, *Labor and Urban Politics: Class Conflict and the Origins of Modern Liberalism in Chicago, 1864–1897* (Urbana: University of Illinois Press, 1998).

4. Melvin Holli, *Reform in Detroit* (New York: Oxford University Press, 1969); Michael McCarthy, "Businessmen and Professionals in Municipal Reform: The Chicago Experience, 1887–1920," in *The Age of Urban Reform: New Perspectives on the Progressive Era*, ed. Michael H. Ebner and Eugene M. Tobin, 43–54 (Port Washington, NY: Kennikat, 1977).

moral, educational, political—offered opportunities for people with vastly different agendas to actively participate. The acceptance of differences among contending groups and the federation's efforts to both recognize and reconcile them through an agenda of democratic political and social reform marked a significant transformation in Chicago's political culture—one that challenged an ideal of a universal public good not infrequently equated with the liberal republican worldview of civic elites.

While businessmen, women, social scientists, ministers, and labor unions each had different reasons for joining the CFC, their alliance indicated a retreat from the republican belief that a political community should share a unitary conception of the public good. Their association also reflected growing optimism in social cooperation that had crystallized among reform-minded Chicagoans during the 1893 World's Fair. Models for a cooperative effort to pursue such social knowledge were readily available in the sociological work of CFC member Albion Small and to CFC founders, who helped organize the World's Auxiliary Congress. Divided into twenty departments, each covering topics such as religion, labor, music, literature, philosophy, and women, the congresses invited speakers from all over the world. These congresses offered a model for the integration and dissemination of social knowledge on an unprecedented scale. The CFC's organizing committee remarked in its first letter to would-be members that "such a movement should begin while our people are yet filled with the new ideas, new ambitions and inspirations drawn from the great Exposition and its valuable adjunct, the World's Congress."[5] The CFC also drew many of its earliest members from the fair's organizers and participants. Lyman Gage, the first president of the Columbian Exposition Board of Managers, accepted the presidency of the federation, and Bertha Honore Palmer, president of the Board of Lady Managers at the fair, was appointed vice president. Jane Addams helped organize the Social Settlement and Labor Congresses.

Following Stead's mass meeting, a committee of five was appointed to begin organizational work. The audience self-consciously chose individuals representing a variety of different groups in the city: "The first nomination was that of L. T. O'Brien to represent labor. Prof. [Edward] Bemis of the Chicago University was selected to represent education. T. W. Harvey to represent commerce, the Rev. Dr. [H. W.] Thomas, religion, and Miss Jane Addams of Hull House women [sic]."[6] Ralph Easley, a journalist turned reformer, provided the group

5. Letter dated November 23, 1893; Chicago Civic Federation Papers, Chicago Historical Society, Box 1, Folder 1A. The world's congresses would later provide a model for the CFC's educational work in sponsoring national conferences where men and women representing a variety of viewpoints gathered for discussion of labor arbitration (1894), primary election reforms (1897), foreign policy (1898), and trusts (1899).

6. *Chicago Tribune*, November 13, 1893.

with the organizational energy and full-time commitment necessary to get the CFC established. As secretary of the CFC through 1899, Easley exemplified a new style of progressive reformer. Part of the new middle class, he was dedicated to organizing and coordinating the variety of interests in the city and to bringing greater efficacy to reform efforts. He believed that multipartisan efforts to address problems in the city would ultimately prevent the divisions that threatened a permanent drifting apart. The CFC—and he himself as secretary—would serve to foster dialogue while remaining nonpartisan.[7]

The CFC was proud of its commitment to representing a diverse Chicago population. Though the membership did not proportionally represent Chicago workers or women, consciously seek a large number of ethnic representatives, or include any African Americans, it nonetheless was a significant departure from previous reform groups, which were almost universally divided along gender and/or class lines. Although many of its elite members—Franklin MacVeagh and Lyman Gage, for example—had belonged to the Citizen's Association (which had opposed working-class concerns in the past), the CFC embraced a wide range of issues such as arbitration, public health, and sanitation, long part of union and workers' agendas. Albion Small worked behind the scenes to ensure that businessmen held prominent positions in the new organization to avoid "the impression that the Civic Federation is a piece of scholastic idealism."[8] It thus encouraged cooperation similar to that of women's reform groups like the Illinois Woman's Alliance.

At the end of the first year the outgoing president, Lyman Gage, congratulated the CFC on its diversity:

> Almost every shade of political, religious and social opinion is represented. Almost one-sixth of the original members were persons identified with the labor organizations of the city, while professional men, educators, philanthropists, and persons interested in social reforms made up the remainder. The first officers of the association were selected to carefully represent the different elements of society. The president was a man of affairs and business, the first vice-president a woman, the second vice president a labor man. The association of all these people together, their consultation and work together has been one of the most useful features of the Federation.[9]

7. On Easley's role in founding the CFC, see Green, "National Civic Federation," 1–14; Cyphers, *National Civic Federation*. Easley's rise into the middle class as a journalist and his subsequent career in paid positions in voluntary organizations (the CFC and the National Civic Federation) places him among the new breed of professional reformers rather than the mugwump reformers seeking to secure their waning status, as Richard Hofstadter argues in *The Age of Reform: From Bryan to F. D. R.* (New York: Knopf, 1955).

8. Albion Small to Jane Addams, December 26, 1893, in Civic Federation Papers, Box 1, Folder 1.

9. Civic Federation of Chicago, *First Annual Report* (Chicago, 1895), 9. The officers he refers to

Gage's description is striking in its recognition of the officers as representatives of groups with implicitly distinct political identities and agendas. More than twenty years of activism on the part of women and workers perhaps made this point obvious to male civic elites, but its political and epistemological implications were significant. The organization "embodied a new definition of society as composed of interest and reform groups and classes rather than a moral hierarchy of individuals topped by the best men."[10] It threatened the unity assumed to underlie Chicago's liberal republicanism, while it sought to facilitate democratic social knowledge in which groups with different social locations contributed to an understanding of urban problems and their solutions.

The CFC's inclusiveness was both a recognition of new sociological theory regarding social groups and a valuable political strategy suggesting the reorientation of Chicago politics. Political events in the years after the Great Fire of 1871 had illustrated that businessmen were no longer able to shape Chicago's politics without courting working-class and women's organizations.[11] After the Great Fire and a later fire in 1873, for example, the newly formed Citizen's Association (CA) exerted its influence in politics. Under pressure from insurance companies, the CA worked to pass restrictive fire codes that would require businesses and homes to be built of brick. Workers, however, resisted since such measures would raise the price of homes out of their reach. Mobilizing their vote, workers forced the CA to compromise and limit the fire codes to a smaller business district. The Citizen's Association pursued other political work as well. Concerned with the growth of political machines, it began to keep track of the votes of aldermen and state legislators and made these available to interested voters. In 1882 the association also began a campaign for a civil service law, and over the course of the next decade it joined with other businessmen's organizations to form the Civil Service Reform League. In 1885, 1887, and again in 1893, however, its bills died in the state legislature.[12]

Their failures surely frustrated these civic elites, for in the past they had enjoyed significant political influence. But the compromises reached with unions suggested that alliances with the working class might lead to greater success, especially after 1889, when the labor vote became a decisive force in local elections.[13]

---

were Lyman Gage, president of First National Bank; Bertha Honore Palmer, wife of Potter Palmer; and L. T. O'Brien, labor leader.

10. Schneirov, *Labor and Urban Politics*, 334. Also Philip J. Ethington, *The Public City: The Political Construction of Urban Life in San Francisco, 1850–1900* (New York: Cambridge University Press, 1994), for discussion of the demise of republican belief in a unitary conception of the public good.

11. For a more detailed discussion of the widening of the public sphere to include more diverse interests, see Ethington, *Public City*.

12. Karen Sawislak, *Smoldering City: Chicagoans and the Great Fire, 1871–1874* (Chicago: University of Chicago Press, 1995).

13. Schneirov, *Labor and Urban Politics*.

That year elites joined with the Knights of Labor and the Trade and Labor Association in calling for independent candidates for a Sanitary District election. With the combined forces of business and labor, the independent candidates won all of the seats. The Citizens' Association and the Commercial Club had previously failed to recognize the importance of wooing labor's cooperation. Nor had their organizational strategy reached down into the wards and neighborhoods where these people lived and met and worked; even their attempt to encourage thoughtful voting by keeping electoral records in their offices was limited since it required voters to go downtown during working hours and to read English.

Though the alliance in the Sanitary District election marked the beginning of further cooperation between labor and civic elites, Chicago's workers were still perhaps the most unlikely group to join the CFC. Chicago had a violent labor history, making cooperation among the city's workers, businessmen, and government officials difficult at best. Lingering hostilities surrounding the Haymarket Affair had resurfaced shortly before the CFC's founding in 1893, when Governor Altgeld pardoned the convicted Haymarket radicals and the city erected a monument in honor of the policemen killed during the violence. However, despite this antagonistic history or perhaps because of it, working-class leaders had significant reasons for joining with the CFC. The Haymarket Affair and the repression in its wake seriously set back the cause of labor organization.[14] It also divided labor in the city, with the Trade and Labor Assembly (TLA) and moderate socialists distancing themselves from the Central Labor Union (CLU) and radical socialists and anarchists.[15] For James Linehan and William Pomeroy, moderate leaders of the TLA (later the Chicago Federation of Labor), the federation offered a way to rehabilitate the unions' public legitimacy.[16]

14. See Schneirov, *Labor and Urban Politics*, 183–259. See also Bruce Nelson, *Beyond the Martyrs* (New Brunswick, NJ: Rutgers University Press, 1988).

15. This split was apparent at the November 12 meeting. While M. H. Madden, James Linehan, and William Pomeroy played prominent roles at the gathering, pardoned Haymarket radical Sam Fielden left early to join twenty thousand comrades parading through the cold rain to Waldheim Cemetery in honor of the men executed in the aftermath of the bombing. See the *Chicago Tribune*, November 13, 1893, and the *Chicago Record-Herald*, November 13, 1893. Tommy Morgan, who had helped found the Central Labor Union but also remained active in the Trade and Labor Assembly, spoke at the meeting on November 12 but never appeared again in connection with the CFC. The divisions among Chicago's workers that day illustrated the decisive split in labor's strategy and tactics, with the TLA articulating a more conciliatory stance and seeking to establish itself as the official voice of laborers in the city. The TLA was open to alliances with business partly because of internal struggles that had brought William Pomeroy to leadership. A waiter by trade, he became a representative to the TLA in 1886 and rose to power as financial secretary almost immediately. By the early 1890s, he dominated the TLA and the Illinois State Federation of Labor, of which his friend, M. H. Madden, became president. Pomeroy claimed to have taken Stead on one of his tours of Chicago, and, in the formation of the CFC, the TLA emerged as the representative of labor. Jack Bizjack, "The Trade and Labor Assembly of Chicago" (master's thesis, University of Chicago, 1969).

16. As Pomeroy and his friends sought to bring labor into a friendlier relationship with businessmen and city officials, they drove a wedge further into the Chicago labor movement. Though he

The CFC's industrial committee took up several causes popular among union members, which the women at Hull House also pursued. In December 1895 the committee began an investigation of child labor in department stores. The state legislature was considering child labor regulations, and the information gathered was sent to the legislative committee.[17] The committee promoted arbitration, appointing its own negotiation committee and successfully sponsoring legislation for a statewide arbitration board. The following February and March, it attempted to mediate an impending garment workers' strike and called upon the mayor to intervene by notifying the State Board of Conciliation and Arbitration.[18] And the next month the committee campaigned for the Sulzer Bill, a measure before the U.S. Congress that proposed to ban sweatshop labor, and in October 1895 the CFC's industrial committee investigated discriminatory hiring practices in Chicago's restaurants.[19]

The changing relationship between business and labor was only one reason Chicago's elites and union leaders were willing to join an organization like the CFC. While their efforts to pass fire codes and civil service laws met with only limited success, businessmen watched as women attained significant reforms. In the summer of 1893 women's organizations and members of labor unions had successfully lobbied for an anti–sweatshop law that imposed maximum work hours for women and outlawed child labor. Together unions, social settlement workers, and powerful reformers with political connections formed a cross-class alliance to use educational methods and political agitation in sponsoring ward discussions and mass meetings that mobilized public opinion and lobbied the state legislature.[20] That same year, the Chicago Woman's Club also won demands for public kindergartens. The group organized and funded experimental programs for several years.[21] The popularity of the kindergartens convinced the state legislature to pass a law in spring 1893 that offered public funding.[22] Women's successes suggested the political value of new strategies,

---

was able to gain much legitimacy for Chicago's beleaguered labor movement, Pomeroy was also at the root of several internal scandals and was finally forced out of office. Eventually the TLA merged with other unions to form the Chicago Federation of Labor. Eugene Staley, "The History of the Illinois State Federation of Labor" (PhD dissertation, University of Chicago, 1928), 87–93; Schneirov, *Labor and Urban Politics*, 320–21.

17. CFC Minutes, December 25, 1895, Box 1, Civic Federation of Chicago Papers.

18. Ibid., February 20, 1896; March 19, 1896, Box 1.

19. Ibid., March 19, 1896; October 17, 1895, Box 1.

20. Meredith Tax, *The Rising of the Women: Feminist Solidarity and Class Conflict, 1880–1917* (New York: Monthly Review Press, 1980); Kathryn Kish Sklar, *Florence Kelley and the Nation's Work: The Rise of Women's Political Culture, 1830–1900* (New Haven, CT: Yale University Press, 1995).

21. Henrietta Greenebaum Frank and Amalie Hofer Jerome, *Annals of the Chicago Woman's Club for the First Forty Years of Its Organization, 1876–1916* (Chicago: Chicago Woman's Club, 1916); Jane Addams, *Twenty Years at Hull-House* (New York: Macmillan, 1910), 84.

22. Addams, *Twenty Years at Hull-House*, 84.

such as educational campaigns and lobbying, that their clubs and organizations pioneered.[23]

As they had much to give, women also had much to gain from the organization. While their successes illustrated the ways in which their reform organizations built networks that allowed them to exercise political influence without entering into the traditional male political culture, their prominent presence in the early work of the CFC illustrates a new phase in their strategy.[24] Seeking influence from within not only their separate female organizations but the citywide male power structures as well, they cultivated "the manly virtues: courage, frankness, and perseverance," as they put it, that they believed so important to their success.[25] "Learning to speak more like a man"—that is, publicly and authoritatively—helped them to pursue alliances with businessmen.[26] The CFC offered an opportunity to integrate their agendas into a city organization that sought to influence the traditionally male political power structure.[27]

The federation helped to legitimate women's efforts when they faced hostility from city leaders. In December 1894 a Mrs. Bradley, chair of the education committee of the Twenty-fourth Ward, read a report on the poor condition of the school building in that district. The executive council encouraged her to report the situation to the school board. A month later she returned to inform the council that the board rejected her report as incorrect. She requested the council to form a separate committee to investigate the school. In February 1895 a committee of male CFC members corroborated her account and sent a copy to the school board, which then acted on the complaints.[28] As in this case, women found the men of the CFC useful allies when they faced challenges to their public authority. Hoping to further publicize their work among different groups and gain greater political support, they eagerly joined the CFC.

The CFC especially offered a means of advancing a gendered version of social knowledge. Depicted most vividly in the contrasts between men's and

23. Elisabeth S. Clemens, *The People's Lobby: Organizational Innovation and the Rise of Interest Group Politics in the United States, 1890–1925* (Chicago: University of Chicago Press, 1997), especially 184–234; Kathryn Kish Sklar, "Hull-House in the 1890s: A Community of Women Reformers," *Signs: Journal of Women in Culture and Society* 10, no. 4 (1985): 658–77.

24. Ruth Bordin, *Women and Temperance: The Quest for Power and Liberty, 1873–1900* (Philadelphia: Temple University Press, 1981); Maureen Flanagan, *Seeing with Their Hearts: Chicago Women and the Vision of the Good Society* (Princeton, NJ: Princeton University Press, 2002); Anne Firor Scott, *Natural Allies: Women's Associations in American History* (Urbana: University of Illinois Press, 1991).

25. Frank and Jerome, *Annals of the Chicago Woman's Club,* 11; Sarah Deutsch, "Learning to Talk More like a Man: Boston Women's Class-bridging Organizations, 1870–1940," *American Historical Review* 97 (1992): 379–404.

26. Deutsch, "Learning to Talk More like a Man."

27. Among other things, the Chicago Woman's Club worked for school reform, revised criminal codes, and sought relief for poor people. See Frank and Jerome, *Annals of the Chicago Woman's Club.*

28. CFC Minutes, December 20, 1894; January 17, 1895; February 21, 1895.

women's agendas for the municipal committee, women's work within the CFC served to dissolve the boundaries between public and private spheres in a way that set them apart from many men in the organization. While the committee focused primarily on the physical needs of the city, often overlapping with the political committee, women investigated the sanitary conditions of bakeries and the purity of Chicago's milk supply, arguing that these issues touched families and the public health of the city.

Furthermore, they used their affiliation with the CFC to secure their own economic rights. For example, the education committee lobbied against a bill that would require the dismissal of married teachers, declaring it "manifestly unjust" and "distinctly class legislation."[29] The women rejected the state's attempt to add legal substance to separate spheres of ideology and thus essentialize gender. The law would have prevented middle-class married women from seeking employment in one of the only white-collar careers available to them. Further, it would have driven many wives of working-class men out of the schools and perhaps into lower-paying, more exploitative factory work. The women thus not only saw their work as an integral part of encouraging a more cooperative attitude toward civic life but also articulated an awareness that the gender and class implications of their reform efforts challenged the status quo.

The CFC thus recognized that social groups with competing interests, agendas, and viewpoints made up the urban landscape. This sociological shift was not merely pouring new wine into old bottles of political factions that James Madison had described in the Federalist Papers; rather it encompassed a new understanding of an epistemological gap posed by groups with disparate experiences and worldviews. The challenge for Chicago's social reformers was to find a way for the political trend toward interest groups—what was potentially a fatal drifting apart—to reconcile epistemological fragmentation through political and social reform. Given its members' aspirations to reinvigorate political culture and their previous reform experiences, the Civic Federation was an organization with the potential to foster democratic social knowledge.

Democratic Social Knowledge: The CFC as a Model for Interaction

This section emphasizes the potential of the CFC as a forum for interactive means of forging democratic social knowledge. It illustrates the ways the CFC drew from the expertise of its female members in creating interactive methods at the grassroots level and explores the epistemological implications of a social

---

29. *First Annual Report*, 83. The Chicago Women's Club also worked to prevent this legislation. Flanagan, *Seeing with Their Hearts*, 60–63.

scientific framework that embraced the divergent worldviews of various social groups.

Both the middle-class and elite women and the male social scientists who helped found the CFC brought with them important successes in using an interactive and activist model of social science for political ends. The women's knowledge and experience provided the CFC with successful models for addressing urban problems, while their organization and methods helped shape CFC methods. To encourage the participation of a cross-section of the population, the CFC helped neighborhood residents create ward councils with a liaison reporting to its executive committee. Such organization encouraged a communal process of investigation, discussion, and experimentation at the grassroots level. On the one hand these ward councils appear to have been an extension of men's political culture, as they worked feverishly to clean up government.[30] However, they also conducted the kind of firsthand investigations that female members had popularized in women's clubs, social settlements, and unions. In the Seventeenth Ward, CFC members employed a tenement inspector to gather data on living conditions there. The educational committee of the Twenty-fourth Ward council went into schools to assess the physical structure of the buildings. In ward councils throughout the city, residents compiled information about the state of garbage inspection and presented it to aldermen.[31]

Such ward councils were likely modeled after the Nineteenth Ward Improvement Club, an endeavor growing out of a series of meetings at Hull House social settlement in October 1892. The Improvement Club, like the ward councils that followed later, used local investigation and political organization to achieve its goals. The councils reflected the view that reform organizations had to rely upon neighborhood residents "not just to implement its goals, but to determine just what those goals should be."[32] Indeed the purpose of the CFC councils was to help each ward "make a thorough study of its own needs and conditions, and at the same time . . . endeavor to foster an intelligent and active interest in its local affairs."[33] Such investigations ensured that local knowledge shaped the agenda

30. *Chicago Tribune*, February 17, 1895; Minutes of the Seventeenth Ward Council of the Civic Federation of Chicago, 1894–96, in Graham Taylor Papers, folder titled "Civic Federation of Chicago," Newberry Library, Chicago.

31. Minutes of the Civic Federation, December 20, 1894; December 27, 1895; February 20, 1896; January 21, 1897; also Minutes of the Seventeenth Ward Council of the Civic Federation for other examples.

32. Quoted in Carol Nackenoff, "Gendered Citizenship: Alternative Narratives of Political Incorporation in the United States, 1875–1925," in *The Liberal Tradition in American Politics: Reassessing the Legacy of American Liberalism*, ed. David F. Ericson and Louisa Bertch Green, 156 (New York: Routledge, 1999).

33. Civic Federation of Chicago, "Suggestions as to the Work of the Ward Committees" (Leaflet No. 1), in Graham Taylor Papers, folder titled "Civic Federation of Chicago. Material Concerning

the CFC took up: garbage disposal, education, arbitration of labor disputes, investigation of political fraud and municipal ownership.[34] Initially concerned with issues of public health, the Improvement Club also challenged the logic of special assessments under Chicago's "segmented system" of collecting revenue. Under this arrangement, property owners seeking public improvements had to initiate and pay for projects even when they were not responsible for damages. But Improvement Club members "were able to prove that street paving had thus been reduced to a cedar pulp by the heavily loaded wagons of an adjacent factory, [and] that the expense of repaving should be borne from a general fund and not by the poor property owners."[35] New streets enhanced property values and enticed more prosperous ward residents to join their efforts. This endeavor brought the residents together in common cause to exercise their political power. "The alderman himself was obliged to come into such a popular movement," Addams recalled.[36] Like the Hull House Women's Club, which investigated sanitary problems and pressured local government for effective public health measures, the Nineteenth Ward Improvement Club helped redefine the city's responsibility to its residents.

Council representatives from other wards appeared regularly in the minutes of the early years of CFC. The ward councils' relationship to the executive committee suggests that the organization employed a proximate epistemology privileging firsthand experience and activism. The ward councils regularly brought concerns specific to their neighborhoods to the attention of the executive committee. Several wards complained of continuing sanitation problems. The Twenty-fourth Ward committee organized a separate educational subcommittee, and several wards reported concerns with political organization that later appeared in the CFC's agenda and shaped the objectives of the Municipal Voters League, an offshoot of the CFC.[37] The structure of the CFC and the council members' ability to shape the organization's agenda suggests the important emphasis placed on an interactive social knowledge.

1893–1897," Newberry Library, Chicago. On labor issues in particular, see CFC Minutes, December 25, 1895; February 20, 1896; March 19, 1896.

34. Several wards complained of continuing sanitation problems. The Twenty-fourth Ward committee organized a separate educational subcommittee, and several wards reported concerns about political organization. The ward councils also investigated local schools. See, for example, *First Annual Report*; Civic Federation of Chicago, "Suggestions as to the Work of the Ward Committees" (Leaflet No. 1), in Graham Taylor Papers, folder titled "Civic Federation of Chicago. Material Concerning. 1893–1897," Newberry Library, Chicago; *Chicago Tribune*, February 17, 1895; CFC Minutes, September 19, 1895; December 20, 1894; December 19, 1895; December 27, 1895.

35. Addams, *Twenty Years at Hull-House*, 186.

36. Ibid.

37. CFC Minutes, September 19, 1895; December 20, 1894; December 19, 1895; December 27, 1895. Papers of the Municipal Voters League can be found among the Citizens Association Papers and the Civic Federation of Chicago Papers, both at the Chicago Historical Society.

At the same time, the CFC also used more formal social science methods. Several social scientists worked with CFC committees to investigate sanitation, municipal government, and milk and water purity; results were disseminated in newspaper articles, printed reports, discussions, and speeches aimed at the general population.[38] Using investigation and expertise even at the ward level reflected the commitments of the social scientists who joined or supported the CFC. From the beginning, professors from the University of Chicago played an integral role in the organization; sociologists Edward Bemis, C. R. Henderson, and Albion Small were founding members. At the turn of the century Charles Merriam, a political scientist at the University of Chicago, helped write the new city charter proposed by the organization. They belonged to the generation of scholars that experienced the first tensions of professionalization. Many social scientists had entered their fields as an avenue to social reform, and they struggled to find acceptable outlets for their social values, as their professions increasingly clamped down on public activism. The CFC offered a home to professors who believed that "the scholar's duty is to aid in forming a judicial public opinion, as distinguished from the public opinion of a class and its special pleaders," and that local government was the "one field of practice in which a social scholar as a citizen must enter."[39] The CFC's willingness to experiment with social science investigation made it a hospitable organization for activists like Small and Henderson, who were seeking to put their social science theories into practice. Such investigations illustrated the growing authority of social science expertise in municipal reform during the Progressive Era.[40]

However, the CFC's interactive, communal model of producing social knowledge was unusual. The structure of the CFC and the ward council members' ability to shape the goals of the organization suggest that expertise needed not be associated with formal training and distanced neutrality alone. As it drew from the experiences of a variety of groups in the city, the CFC offered the potential to bridge an epistemological gap between academic knowledge and expertise

38. Chicago Civic Federation, *First Annual Report*, 54; Minutes, August 15, 1895; Civic Federation of Chicago, *Congress on Industrial Conciliation and Arbitration* (Chicago, 1895); Memorandum from Ralph Easley, December 12, 1896, "Accomplishments of the Past Year," in National Civic Federation Papers, Box 47, folder titled "Misc Papers," New York Public Library Rare Books and Manuscripts Division; Civic Federation of Chicago, *Biennial Report* (Chicago, 1905).

39. C. R. Henderson, "Business Men and Social Theorists," *American Journal of Sociology* 1 (January 1896): 385–97.

40. Thomas Haskell, *The Emergence of Professional Social Science: The American Social Science Association and the Nineteenth-century Crisis of Authority* (Urbana: University of Illinois Press, 1977); Muncy, *Creating a Female Dominion in American Reform*; Mary Former, *Advocacy and Objectivity: A Crisis in the Professionalization of American Social Science, 1865–1905* (Lexington: University Press of Kentucky, 1975); Camilla Stivers, *Bureau Men, Settlement Women: Constructing Public Administration in the Progressive Era* (Lawrence: University of Kansas Press, 2000). For the development of expertise more generally, see Robert Wiebe, *Search for Order*.

on the one hand and grassroots local knowledge on the other. Recognizing that groups' different social locations contributed to a richer social knowledge, the organization built on the democratic potential of intellectual trends beginning to appear in pragmatist philosophy.

In his utopian fantasy "No Mean City," Henry Demarest Lloyd offered a model of democratic social knowledge that blended expertise with community experience. The story begins with efforts to rebuild the White City as a permanent place outside of Chicago.[41] Exemplifying Lloyd's romance with British Fabianism, the project depended on experts for inquiry into the best examples of city management from around the world and for the planning and implementation of their findings.[42] Nevertheless, the significant role played by experts did not overshadow the contributions of others; cooperative labor, "with which professors, business men, ministers, workingmen, artists, men and women, had got into the habit of working in the World's Fair enabled this task of remaking the city to be carried on with marvelous efficiency and rapidity."[43] Indeed, Lloyd offered the story as a model for democratic social knowledge: "It is the essence of democracy that out of the conflict and comparison of the opinions and efforts of all will emerge as a resultant a better truth, a better decision, than can be had out of any narrower constituency."[44]

In a similar but more academic vein, Albion Small explained the communitarian nature of social knowledge. "Social knowledge," he wrote in his 1894 sociology textbook, was "something other than the mere addition of the impressions of individuals; . . . the standards of conduct of a given community are peculiar combinations of personal codes, which may vary widely from the former." Meetings like those of the CFC provided a forum to negotiate social knowledge. Each member held

a definite plan of action which he thinks should be carried out. A full discussion takes place. Each person expresses an opinion. Questions are asked and answered; objections are raised; suggestions are offered; statements of fact are made. At last a unanimous—a *one-minded*—decision is reached. It differs, in a greater or less degree, from the original idea of each member of the body; it is an organized unified product, not a mere addition of individual convictions.[45]

41. Henry Demarest Lloyd, "No Mean City," in *Mazzini and Other Essays,* ed. Jane Addams and Anne Withington (New York and London: G. P. Putnam's Sons, 1910), 201–32.
42. For discussion of Lloyd's interest in British Fabianism, see John L. Thomas, *Alternative America: Henry George, Edward Bellamy, Henry Demarest Lloyd, and the Adversary Tradition* (Cambridge, MA: Belknap, 1983).
43. Lloyd, "No Mean City," 209.
44. Ibid., 216.
45. Albion Small and George E. Vincent, *An Introduction to the Study of Society* (New York:

The product was social knowledge, as Small defined it. Significant in his description are both the process and the building blocks from which social knowledge is constructed. Those involved in the process hold an array of ideas and opinions that reflect different personal experiences. On their own they do not add up to a body of knowledge. Instead, they must be submitted to a process of discussion and questioning, reflection and mediation, whereby they are debated and molded into, as he perhaps too optimistically put it, one "unified product." Such discussions lead to transformations of the ideas and opinions of participants. Small suggested that this process of creating knowledge worked to incorporate different ideas while preventing the dangerous excesses of subjectivity.

The involvement of different groups was especially important, as Charles Henderson illustrated in an article defending the contributions of expert social theorists in constructing business ethics. Against businessmen's attitudes that "the class motives of employers and the laws of nature are the sufficient guaranty [sic] of social welfare" and that "economic forces are automatic, [and] natural," Henderson noted that human intelligence, will, and aspirations—in other words, components of social experience and political identities—must be taken into account.[46] He thus directly challenged the assumptions on which the older liberal republican social knowledge had rested. "It is the duty of the ethical theorist to show that the self-interest of the manufacturer and landlord do not secure the public welfare in any city of this country," he argued.

Figuring prominently in this project was the empirical knowledge embodied in the social scientists' "table of statistics, interpreted and illustrated by literary skill."[47] Henderson alluded here to two important cultural roles these statistics could play: popularized forms of social investigation provided empirical facts that could help establish a sense of order and causality in an increasingly complex world, and they acted to prod the moral imaginations of the capitalist community.[48] So while the CFC tried to promote a process of interaction whereby the social bases of knowledge were widened to include a range of social experience, it also recognized the important mediating function of social scientific knowledge.

In light of the trend toward expertise and professionalization in this period, the CFC's model of interaction between social science experts and community members appears as a more democratic social knowledge, as both social scientists

American Book, 1894), 306–8.

46. Charles R. Henderson, "Business Men and Social Theorists," *American Journal of Sociology* 1 (January 1896): 385–97, 392, 393.

47. Ibid., 389–90.

48. See Thomas W. Laqueur, "The Humanitarian Narrative," in *The New Cultural History*, ed. Lynn Hunt, 176–205 (Berkeley: University of California Press, 1989).

and community members shaped agendas and engaged in local investigations. Women, too, played a particularly important role in lending a framework for this type of social knowledge. Nonetheless, I do not want to essentialize their epistemological framework.[49] It was gendered, to be sure, but this was because women were best positioned to develop an interactive, proximate epistemology. Positioned outside of the academy and socially ascribed the role of nurturers and caretakers, they drew from a domestic discourse, as well as a growing discourse on social democracy. Such a framework was also used by non-elite groups—working classes and African Americans in particular—that were also feminized in the dominant culture.

Because the organization self-consciously included different segments of the population, it reflected the assumption that only through the contributions of different groups could society come to a fuller understanding of a complex and constantly changing social reality. The CFC combated social division through its efforts to create a more extensive social knowledge, believing, as member Jane Addams suggested, that "most of the misunderstandings of life are due to partial intelligence, because our experiences have been so unlike that we cannot comprehend each other."[50] CFC member Albion Small suggested that the organization grew out of the recognition that social knowledge was ultimately unitary but fragmented in the human experience. Forging a new social knowledge thus entailed coming to terms with the way experience shaped one's understanding of social problems. It laid open the possibility for reformers to see social values and practices as socially constructed, not as the result of natural laws.

The Social Organism, Civic Consciousness, and Democratic Cooperation

The CFC built on a growing conception of interrelatedness and desire for civic cooperation that framed middle-class political reform in the 1890s. This section examines the intellectual backdrop for the interactive, organic strand of democratic social knowledge. It helps us locate the CFC's project within a broader cultural effort to reconcile social fragmentation with democratic cooperation. The new civic consciousness was different from Gilded Age social divisions. In the 1880s a drifting apart along class and ethnic lines had made it difficult for urban groups to cooperate. The magnitude of the 1893 depression, however, forced

49. In a telling commentary, the Chicago Woman's Club, to which most of the female CFC members belonged, noted that their position in society was socially, not naturally, constructed: "These two departments of governments concerning the children and the poor and sick are quite in keeping with the place assigned to woman in the *social economy* and in direct line of development with *her position in society in the past*" (emphasis mine). See Frank and Jerome, *Annals of the Chicago Woman's Club*, 14.

50. Jane Addams, *Democracy and Social Ethics* (New York: Macmillan, 1902), 93, 175.

creativity, and growing conceptions of interdependence throughout American society fueled new ways of explaining the connectedness of urban groups.[51]

Henry Demarest Lloyd outlined reformers' hopes in "No Mean City" in describing the effects of an interactive form of democratic social knowledge on city residents. The greatest result it advocated was "something of the spirit of a religious revival." Residents constructed not only a perfected physical city, complete with paved streets, municipally owned electric streetcars and utilities, and practical and artistic education for all children but a new civic consciousness as well. Their efforts proved "that the city like the nation, or the church, or any other society could be successful only as far as it was a brotherhood."[52] His story illustrated how the process of structural reform offered opportunities for cooperative civic transformation. Through coordinated public participation, individuals developed a sense of organic civic consciousness with vaguely Christian undertones that linked them, through practice, to others sharing in the physical and moral project of city building.

The CFC's hopes for civic cooperation were fueled by sociological conceptions of organicism. The "organic concept" that Herbert Spencer popularized and sociologists such as Albion Small embraced described the "intimate interrelation and inter-dependence among the individuals and the groups which constitute society."[53] Thus, the organism is not homogeneous but has distinguishable parts that cooperate with one another.[54] In the late 1890s Americans increasingly used such social science theories of interdependence to reimagine the city as a group of interrelated yet differentiated parts.[55] Addams noted, for example, that settlement workers "regarded the entire city as organic" and sought to unify it.[56] Small further argued that the degree of cooperation directly influenced the "complete life of the whole," and "conversely, the life of the whole is diminished in so far as cooperation of the parts is incomplete."[57]

Against a growing discourse of economic interdependence and sociological theories of organicism, the CFC built its agenda. Members understood the "parts" of the city in terms of both space and identity. To serve as a medium of acquaintance and sympathy, the federation needed to reach into wards and

51. Samuel P. Hays, *The Response to Industrialism, 1885–1914*, 2d ed. (Chicago: University of Chicago Press, 1995), especially chapter 5, "The Reform Impulse"; Zane L. Miller, *Boss Cox's Cincinnati: Urban Politics in the Progressive Era* (Columbus: Ohio State University Press, 1968), 113–60; David P. Thelen, *The New Citizenship: Origins of Progressivism in Wisconsin, 1885–1900* (Columbia: University of Missouri Press, 1972), 33–85.

52. Lloyd, "No Mean City," 209.

53. Small, "The Organic Concept of Society," *Annals of the American Academy* 5 (1894): 89.

54. Ibid.

55. Patricia Mooney Melvin, *The Organic City: Urban Definition and Community Organization* (Lexington: University Press of Kentucky, 1987), especially 11–26.

56. Jane Addams, "Subjective Necessity of Social Settlements"; quoted in Melvin, *Organic City*, 20.

57. Small, "Organic Concept of Society," 88.

neighborhoods individually yet connect them within one overarching organization and coordinate groups with distinct interests and socioeconomic characteristics. The view of social knowledge that grew from such images stressed the
functional, systemic health of the urban organism, even as it recognized distinct
roles and functions of groups within the city. The metaphor of organicism, with
its analogy to biology and the body, was particularly apt in matters of public
health. References to the health of the entire city gripped the imaginations of
Chicagoans and helped them to realize that the health of individual neighborhoods affected the well-being of all. In turn, these public health concerns overlapped into political and economic reform.

Lloyd's story and Small's description of organic social knowledge nicely captured the challenges the CFC's model of interactive social knowledge and reform
presented to the older liberal republicanism. As we have seen, this social knowledge was closely tied to the segmented model of municipal government in which
public works decisions and the costs of building the city's infrastructure were
passed on only to those residents whose property was directly involved.[58] This
model of segmented government had fit nicely with antebellum liberal economic values that heralded the primacy of private property and small government.
While it avoided the political infighting of interest-group politics, it promoted a
privatism that limited residents' sense of responsibility for the well-being of the
entire city. Under such arrangements "it seems never to have occurred to anyone,
that the city might have a 'public interest' in the attractiveness, the convenience,
or even the health of neighborhoods that could not purchase these benefits
on their own."[59] Women, both inside and outside of the CFC, and the ward
councils countered this type of thinking. So too, Chicago's workers had encouraged a wider sense of urban connectedness and responsibility during the 1893
depression. Whereas liberal republicanism emphasized abstract classical economic principles as the basis for social knowledge and (segmented) government,
organicism offered a new framework of mutual responsibility and interdependence in which to think about them. Small recognized that "the sociologists'
theory of the organic structure of society had probably never been heard of by
the majority of the [CFC] committee, and they would have had little patience
with such abstractions, if they had been mentioned." Nonetheless, he reported,
the organization helped stir "the consciences of the members . . . in accordance
with the principles contained in that philosophical conception of society."[60] The

58. Robin L. Einhorn, *Property Rules* (Chicago: University of Chicago Press, 1991), 61–103,
discusses the segmented system.

59. Ibid.

60. Albion Small, "The Civic Federation of Chicago," *American Journal of Sociology* 1, no. 1
(1895): 79–103.

shared space of the city became a common denominator for all residents.[61]

An organic civic consciousness acknowledged different and even competing explanations of social experience and reality, thus opening up discussion about the nature of social knowledge. The CFC acknowledged that groups in the city did not know one another, rendering the possibility of sympathetic understanding extraordinarily difficult. Only through the contributions of different groups could society come to fuller understanding of a social reality that was complex, organic, and constantly changing. The interaction that the CFC fostered would ideally bridge this epistemological gap by drawing from the resources and experiences of a variety of groups in the city and incorporating them with an objective yet activist social science. Public discussion and mutual education served as mediators for this social knowledge.

Though several historians have demonstrated the growing sense of civic consciousness during the 1890s, which gave rise to new reform efforts, I want to emphasize the epistemological implications of the intersection of organicism and the new civic consciousness that took shape in the Civic Federation. The CFC's interactive, communal model of producing social knowledge and encouraging reform was innovative. It brought together social science methods and actual face-to-face interaction among a variety of groups. In creating a public arena for mutual recognition, it utilized an approach that appealed to a variety of members, from women seeking a wider milieu for their own reform work and unions hoping to rehabilitate their reputation and further their political ends, to social Christians seeking to foster God's kingdom on earth. The CFC's organic approach to social knowledge thus incorporated elements of an older republican tradition in that it suggested a singular common good that transcended self-interest. Yet it was significantly different in other ways, illustrating how social science had influenced political and reform organizations: This newer organicism acknowledged the particular experiences of different groups and encouraged their contributions to social inquiry and reform.

Social Knowledge and Politics

The social knowledge fostered by the CFC supported a new style of political activism by blending social science research and its popularization to inspire civic consciousness and using "investigation, publication, agitation and organiza-

---

61. See Robin Bachin, *Building the South Side: Urban Space and Civic Culture in Chicago, 1890–1919* (Chicago: University of Chicago Press, 2004), for discussion of how contests over urban space were connected with civic identity.

tion . . . to carry into effect the purposes of the Federation."[62] Balancing social science expertise with local experience and lobbying with democratic mobilization, the CFC adopted the activist social science and political methods of women's groups. To encourage public dialogue, the organization called mass meetings to talk about civic issues. This was a trend in other cities like Milwaukee and Cincinnati, as new organizations attempted to bring groups into discussion with one another to create "new patterns of political discussion."[63] Such methods reflected a new approach to democratic politics, emphasizing nonpartisanship, public debate, and citizen education.[64]

Historians of Chicago politics have suggested that a nonpartisan reform coalition, drawing from middle- and working-class residents, played an important role in reshaping Chicago politics in the mid-1890s.[65] From its beginning, the CFC portrayed itself as nonpartisan and dedicated to "the separation of municipal affairs from party politics." This was a familiar cry among reformers and businessmen concerned with creating more moral and efficient government at all levels, from federal to local administrations.[66] The rhetoric of "nonpartisanship" resonated soundly in Chicago's boisterous political atmosphere for several reasons. With voters swinging between Democratic and Republican candidates or an occasional third party, partisanship was not fixed.[67] Nor were the parties themselves formally organized on a citywide basis; power struggles among the different Democratic and Republican factions had yet prevented the rise of a unified machine that could consistently demand voters' loyalties.[68] Though

62. Charter and incorporation papers, Chicago Civic Federation Papers, Chicago Historical Society, Box 1.

63. Thelen, *New Citizenship*, 71.

64. On the emergence of new forums and ideas about the democratic public, see Kevin Mattson, *Creating a Democratic Public: The Struggle for Urban Participatory Democracy during the Progressive Era* (University Park: Pennsylvania State University Press, 1998).

65. Schneirov argues, for example, that the success of nonpartisan reform coalitions centering in the CFC and the MVL detracted from populist success in 1896. See *Labor and Urban Politics*, 346. Flanagan suggests that Chicago's success in ousting corrupt city councilmen contributed to a general sense of satisfaction with the structure of Chicago's ward system, though she cautions against taking "nonpartisan" rhetoric too seriously. See Flanagan, *Charter Reform in Chicago*.

66. Stivers, *Bureau Men, Settlement Women*; Patricia Wallace Ingraham, *The Foundation of Merit: Public Service in American Democracy* (Baltimore: Johns Hopkins University Press, 1995), 15–54; Frederick C. Mosher, *Democracy and the Public Service* (New York: Oxford University Press, 1982).

67. In this respect, Chicago was quite different from New York, where nonpartisanship frequently was a strategy to undercut the power of Tammany Hall. See Richard Skolnik, "1895: A Test for Municipal Nonpartisanship in New York City," in *Essays in the History of New York City: A Memorial to Sidney Pomerantz*, ed. Irwin Yellowitz, 132–44 (Port Washington, NY: Kennikat, 1978).

68. See Joel A. Tarr, *A Study in Boss Politics: William Lorimer of Chicago* (Urbana: University of Illinois Press, 1971), and Maureen Flanagan, *Charter Reform in Chicago*, for discussion of the tenuous nature of political machines in 1890s' Chicago. Nationwide civil service reform measures reflected a similar nonpartisan nature. See Carl Fish, *The Civil Service and Patronage* (New York: Longmans, Green, 1905).

Democrats increasingly attracted workers, significant interest in reform politics among both the middle class and workers permitted nonpartisan coalitions around public issues like sanitary reform or municipal ownership.

The CFC mobilized public support for civil service reform and against corruption in traction ordinances. These were classic concerns for urban reformers, and Chicago was no exception. Dating from the assassination of President Garfield in 1881 and the Pendleton National Civil Service Law (1883), Chicago's businessmen had unsuccessfully pursued legislation to combat patronage.[69] When in 1893 a disappointed office seeker assassinated the city's popular mayor, Carter Harrison Sr., sentiment for civil service reform increased.[70] The murder graphically illustrated the dangers of the spoils system and fanned long-smoldering sentiment in favor of civil service reform. A series of unusually violent elections further helped convince residents that political changes were necessary.[71]

Political machines and patronage raised the ire of Chicago's middle and working classes for several reasons. In the years after the Civil War and the Great Fire, Chicago government had undergone a transition to machine politics. While this centralized more power in the city council and thus overcame some of the problems of segmentation, it also led to widespread corruption.[72] The most notorious examples involved the traction magnate, Charles Yerkes, who had arrived in Chicago sometime around 1882 after serving a prison sentence for embezzlement.[73] By 1886 he had acquired majority interest in the North Chicago City Railway Company. Within two years Yerkes created other street railway companies and thus built his infamous monopoly over local transportation. While other companies continued to provide services, there was no coordination between them; the city council divided franchise rights along the routes into small parcels and contracted them out to private companies. As a result, customers often had to transfer several times, paying a new fare on each line, to get across the town. Yerkes offered councilmen cash or stock options to ensure their support.

69. For historical discussion of the civil service movement, see Cindy Sonic Aaron, *Ladies and Gentlemen of the Civil Service* (New York: Oxford University Press, 1987); Fish, *Civil Service and Patronage;* Ingraham, *Foundation of Merit,* 15–54; Mosher, *Democracy and the Public Service.*

70. Harrison was murdered by a disappointed office seeker, Patrick Eugene Prendergast. Immediately turning himself in, Prendergast announced, "I worked hard for Carter Harrison in his campaign. He promised he would make me corporation council. He failed to do this and I have shot him." Prendergast quoted in Marks, "Polishing the Gem of the Prairie," 166.

71. Sidney I. Roberts, "Businessmen in Revolt: Chicago, 1874–1900" (PhD diss., Northwestern University, 1960).

72. Einhorn, *Property Rules;* Sawislak, *Smoldering City;* Richard McCormick, "The Discovery That Business Corrupts Politics: A Reappraisal of the Origins of Progressivism," *American Historical Review* 86, no. 2 (1981): 247–74.

73. Sidney I. Roberts, "Portrait of a Robber Baron," *Business History Review* 35, no. 3 (Autumn 1961): 344–71.

Though Yerkes was the most notorious businessman manipulating the council, he was not the only one. Even on a smaller scale, companies could practically purchase franchise rights or buy city contracts by bribing councilmen. Indeed, aldermen came to expect such bribes, even postponing votes on pressing matters to drive up the prices for favorable votes.[74] Furthermore, as Graham Taylor described, partisan appointments were wasteful.[75] Contractors who neglected their duties were seldom fired, as partisan politicians sought to protect their friends. On many occasions the city hired unqualified men who did the work inefficiently or not at all, exasperating professionals who valued efficiency and order, as well as residents who wanted their streets and services maintained well.[76] Unions had additional reasons for wanting to displace machine politics. During the 1889 election of independent Sanitary Board commissioners, unions demanded that the money appropriated for the work go directly to labor, not to line the pockets of corrupt politicians. Female reformers were similarly concerned about corrupt politicians and believed civil service to be crucial to successful reforms.[77]

The CFC joined with the Citizen's Association and the Civil Service Reform League, which had been working for years on civil service legislation.[78] Using both its access to state politicians and its ability to mobilize voters through ward councils, the CFC pressured the state legislature to pass a civil service law in time for the spring 1895 municipal elections. Along with copies of the bill, the CFC sent out thousands of letters to Chicago voters, asking them to write three legislators and to ask two friends to each send letters as well. State politicians received more than seventeen thousand letters and entertained prestigious Chicago delegates, including CFC president Lyman Gage. The legislature passed the bill, but Chicagoans had to approve the law. To secure its passage, the federation circulated leaflets, hung posters, and arranged speakers, all in numerous languages. Men and women addressed factory workers during lunch hours, explaining the bill and answering questions. Ministers of middle-class Protestant churches joined with the Catholic clergy of working-class and ethnic neighborhoods in offering support for the bill in their Sunday sermons. The night before the election, the

74. Carter Harrison, *Stormy Years: The Autobiography of Carter H. Harrison, Five Times Mayor of Chicago* (New York: Bobbs-Merrill, 1935); Daniel T. Rodgers, *Atlantic Crossings: Social Politics in a Progressive Age* (Cambridge, MA: Belknap Press of Harvard University Press, 1998), 145–57.

75. Graham Taylor, *Pioneering on Social Frontiers* (Chicago: University of Chicago Press, 1930).

76. Martin V. Melosi, *The Sanitary City: Urban Infrastructure in America from Colonial Times to the Present* (Baltimore: Johns Hopkins University Press, 2000).

77. CFC Minutes, October 28, 1897. The example of the CFC resonates with scholarly literature on the civil service reform. See, for example, Ingraham, *The Foundation of Merit*, and Mosher, *Democracy and the Public Service*. On differences between male and female reformers on civil service issues, see Helene Silverberg, "'A Government of Men': Gender, the City, and the New Science of Politics," in *Gender and American Social Science: The Formative Years*, ed. Helene Silverberg, 156–84 (Princeton: Princeton University Press, 1998).

78. Marks, "Polishing the Gem of the Prairie"; CFC, *First Annual Report*.

CFC and other organizations sponsored forty meetings throughout the city. The campaign helped secure passage of the bill by a popular majority of forty-six thousand, an astounding 65 percent of the vote.[79]

While some Progressive Era historians suggest that political reforms, like civil service laws, were the province of civic elites and their new middle-class allies, the experience in Chicago suggests a much broader reform consensus. The nonpartisanship required to pass the bill illustrated the potential of a cross-class, interethnic political movement and the CFC to lead it.[80] Indeed, pressure to pass the bill had been so great that even the Democratic and Republican machines supported it. Although their endorsement was likely half hearted, the fact that they felt it necessary to give official support to the bill is testament to the reformers' ability to shape public opinion. Although the bill was more hotly contested in working-class neighborhoods, with police and firemen offering the greatest resistance, labor unions joined with the CFC in endorsing the bill.[81] Moreover, it still received majority support in several of these wards, and in no ward was it overwhelmingly defeated.[82]

The CFC was able to build on this reform consensus to unite public sentiment against Charles Yerkes and his supporters in the city council and state legislature. Like other cities across the nation, Chicago needed massive transportation restructuring.[83] When Yerkes entered Chicago's street railway business, he made a number of improvements, including electrifying and unifying the system.[84] Nonetheless, he remained extremely unpopular among Chicago residents, largely due to the poor quality of his services and his callousness toward consumers. Homeowners resented the aggressive way in which he gained frontage consents, and residents in all areas of the city were dismayed at his unsafe

---

79. Small, "Civic Federation of Chicago," 82; Ray Stannard Baker, "The Civic Federation of Chicago," *Outlook* 27 (July 1895); pamphlets titled "Workingmen" and "Vote 'Yes' for the Civil Service Law," in Jane Addams Papers, Reel 52; Marks, "Polishing the Gem of the Prairie," 168–69.

80. Addams, *Twenty Years at Hull-House.* Chicagoans were not alone in their use of nonpartisanship to invigorate participatory politics. Across the nation, farmers, women, and workers used strategies of nonpartisanship to shape local and state politics. See Elizabeth Sanders, *Roots of Reform: Farmers, Workers, and the American State, 1877–1917* (Chicago: University of Chicago Press, 1999); Clemens, *People's Lobby;* Kenneth D. Rose, *American Women and the Repeal of Prohibition* (New York: New York University Press, 1996), 24–25.

81. See flyer "Workingmen!" in Jane Addams Papers, Reel 52.

82. For election results see the *Chicago Tribune,* April 3, 1895. The support for political reform encouraged the formation of the Municipal Voters League, an offshoot of the CFC. The new organization would be able to give greater attention to political issues and reform politics, thus freeing the CFC to pursue other projects. For a discussion of the Municipal Voters League, see Roberts, "Businessmen in Revolt"; Sidney I. Roberts, "The Municipal Voters League and Chicago's Boodlers," *Journal of the Illinois State Historical Society* 53, no. 2 (June 1960): 117–48. Marks, "Polishing the Gem of the Prairie."

83. Holli, *Reform in Detroit.*

84. See Tarr, *Study in Boss Politics,* 80.

practices. Each year bystanders or children playing near tracks were injured or killed. In 1895 *Engineering News* reported that, in the previous year, 46 people were killed and 343 were injured in Chicago due to faulty overhead wiring. In response to "the appalling list of fatalities resultant from collision with electric and cable cars" and the "reckless disregard of human life shown by the street car companies," the Trade and Labor Assembly circulated a letter to "public spirited bodies," informing them of its resolution demanding "that the proper authorities compel the street car companies to properly safeguard with fenders the front of all electric and cable cars."[85] Workers, having a long history of animosity with railway companies because of brutally long hours of work, were further angered at the high fares Yerkes charged. Chicago residents were thus hostile to Yerkes, and when the state legislature passed a measure that extended traction franchises in the state for ninety-nine years, Chicagoans retaliated by voting its supporters out of office. Altgeld vetoed the law, but in 1897 Chicagoans had to confront Yerkes's political influence directly. The Allen Bill, which authorized the city council to grant streetcar franchises for up to fifty years, was enacted into law and sent to the Chicago city council for approval. Chicago residents, led by the CFC, the Municipal Voters League, and the Chicago Federation of Labor joined together to defeat the bill.

Hoping that a reinvigorated public life could save democracy from corruption and apathy, CFC members must have been pleased. The success of the civil service law and the defeat of the Allen Bill suggest that the CFC's cross-class alliances and coordinated educational and publicity tactics could successfully mobilize voters for democratic action. Furthermore, the nonpartisan tactics that the CFC employed embodied its expectation that political participation and moral education went hand in hand. This was not an unusual vision among Progressive Era reformers. Proponents of the social center movement argued that it educated citizens for political deliberation and decision making, and through the give-and-take of public debate, participants and their ideas would not be "annihilated" but transformed.[86]

The CFC's nonpartisan rhetoric calls for a critical look, however, for historians have long warned that appeals to nonpartisanship mask elite ideological strategies to entrench their own power. Certainly this is true. Republicans tended to support the civil service law more enthusiastically, particularly since they expected their mayoral candidate to win the 1895 election and thus be in a position to make changes before the law went into effect.[87] But during these early years the federation did not necessarily serve only Republican interests.

85. CFC Minutes, June 25, 1896.

86. See Mattson, *Creating a Democratic Public*, 67, and especially 91–102. Mattson's discussion of Mary Parker Follett is helpful on this point.

87. Flanagan, *Charter Reform in Chicago;* Harrison, *Stormy Years,* 128–29.

It worked to oust both Democrat and Republican state legislators who had supported the Yerkes traction bills. And when it set up its own commission to investigate and recommend political candidates, it included an equal number of Republicans, Democrats, and Populists who supported Democratic, Republican, and independent candidates.[88] When the Municipal Voters League grew out of the political work of the Civic Federation, it continued to endorse candidates of both parties who agreed to maintain the interests of the city against unfair franchises, supported civil service, promised to ensure the physical and sanitary needs of wards, and rejected gerrymandering.[89]

When we consider the tension between recognition of social fragmentation and the goal of civic harmony in an organization like the CFC, which acknowledged the wide differences in the social groups it hoped to coordinate, we see the cultural importance of its nonpartisan rhetoric. In terms of a classical liberal republican paradigm, the nonpartisan political actor was able to break free of ties to social groups and act in the best interests of the public good. This rational political actor was not tied to any particular party or social group and was able to temper selfish interest. Nonpartisanship facilitated an organic conception of the city, allowing citizens to define a wider public interest than that of the segmented system of government. The political battles over civil service and traction rights were concrete expressions of Small's organic conception of society as residents began to realize that matters affecting the quality of life in the city were interdependent on the quality of life in its various neighborhoods. Nonpartisanship furthered an imagined political actor able to cross boundaries of party, class, and ethnic loyalties and form alliances with others committed to a transcendent vision of the public good. The call for nonpartisan democratic activism thus might potentially temper the dangers of a civic life fragmented by the drifting apart of disparate social groups. However, as two different paradigms of social knowledge emerged—democratic and liberal republican—so did tension between the desire for social harmony and its potential to become coercive social control.[90]

Competing Paradigms of Social Knowledge

While the CFC's successes illustrate the possibilities of democratic social knowledge as a mediator of political interests, two different paradigms of social

88. CFC, *First Annual Report.* See also "Extract from the Regular Final Report of the Municipal Voters League for 1905," Citizen's Association of Chicago Papers, Box 5, Folder 3, Chicago Historical Society.

89. "Text of the Pledge," Citizens' Association of Chicago Papers, Box 19, folder titled "Municipal Voters League Committee and Board Minutes, Receipts, & Disbursements, February 1896–April 1899."

90. Mattson, *Creating a Democratic Public,* 49.

knowledge emerged in other reform efforts. One envisioned democratic social knowledge as emergent from the interaction among various social groups and comfortable with political activism and experimentation in an uncertain world. The other, reflecting a growing cultural climate less comfortable with uncertainty, privileged narrowly defined social science expertise seeking to make society more knowable and its future more predictable. These paradigms foreshadowed cleavages along gender and class lines and illustrated the potential of social science to foster a reform agenda whose end facilitated social control rather than democratic social knowledge.

Many middle-class and elite men in the CFC could not shake their investment in a liberal republicanism that privileged a liberal market rationality and labor exchange to mediate social relations. Their logic assumed that social life was built around market mechanisms resting on natural laws, and they used expert investigations that derived from distanced and neutral research to legitimize their epistemological framework. We can see this framework operating in several reform efforts led by men in the organization as the CFC struggled to balance the interaction of democratic social knowledge contributed by the women in the organization with positivistic expertise and liberal republicanism. The CFC's promotion of school reform, poor relief, and antigambling campaigns suggested disparities in members' ideas about the nature and process of achieving social knowledge. These disparities ultimately raised questions at the intersection of democracy and epistemology: Whose epistemological framework, experiences, and voices are included in efforts to shape society?

While no reports from the social scientists, engineers, and doctors remain, we can still infer much from the work of men in the organization whose appeals to efficiency and expertise and affiliations with other reform efforts increasingly privileged expert investigations that left little room for input from residents at the grassroots level. For example, the chairman of the CFC's education committee, William Rainey Harper, also chaired a citywide commission on education that turned to outside educational experts, school administrators from around the country, and professional organizations to outline a plan that would reduce the number of school board members and undermine teacher autonomy by giving the superintendent extensive power to decide all instructional issues.[91] Under Harper's leadership, the commission included other members of the CFC but not teachers or women active in educational reform, thus virtually denying their and their female supporters' experience and local, practical knowledge.

91. "Report to the Central Council of the Civic Federation," December 1897, University of Chicago Special Collections, Presidents' Papers, William Rainey Harper, Box 27, Folder 18; *Report of the Educational Commission of the City of Chicago* (Chicago, 1899). See also Julia Wrigley, *Class Politics and Public Schools: Chicago, 1900–1950* (New Brunswick, NJ: Rutgers University Press, 1982); David Hogan, *Class and Reform: School and Society in Chicago, 1880–1930* (Philadelphia: University of Pennsylvania Press, 1985).

The Harper Report touched off a controversy that served to solidify the CFC as an organization promoting a narrow vision of expertise as identified with professional training and aligned with Chicago's business interests. Over the next three decades, issues such as businessmen's domination of the board, the imposition of a hierarchical and centralized school administration, and conditions of teacher employment would divide the reform community, pitting the businessmen of the CFC against the predominantly female Chicago Teachers' Federation (CTF) and their allies. Fault lines appeared shortly after the CFC proposed an educational bill to the state legislature. Based on the Harper Report, the recommendations included expansion of the superintendent's power over hiring and curriculum decisions and a requirement that all new teachers hold a college degree. Since college graduation was rare—especially for women—the bill discriminated against female teachers from working-class backgrounds. The CTF and the Chicago Federation of Labor successfully mobilized against the bill, but the CFC continued to push for school restructuring that would give more power to educational experts—administrators rather than teachers. After the failure of the Harper bill, the CFC appointed a Committee of One Hundred to promote its educational goals, among them to secure the appointment of school board members "representative of the business and property interests, as well as of the intelligence and genuine unselfishness of the city."[92] In 1903 it again supported legislation to increase the superintendent's power, control teacher personnel issues, determine curriculum, and reduce the size of the school board.[93]

Teachers and their allies among the female members of the CFC offered a different version of educational expertise, one rooted in experience and couched in terms of democratic participation in school governance. They opposed decreasing the Board of Education since "this will bring about a membership of the palace-hunting class and may prevent complete and fair representation of the different sections of our large city."[94] Furthermore, they objected to the centralization of the superintendent's powers, arguing instead that the "idea of democracy should be encouraged. It is necessary, in a city like Chicago, for the people to be in close touch with the work of the school, made up, as it is of a mixed population" of numerous ethnic groups.[95] Margaret Haley, president of

92. Andrew Draper, "Common School Problems of Chicago," address delivered at a citizens' meeting under the auspices of the Commission of One Hundred of the Civic Federation of Chicago, December 1, 1900, 30.

93. Hogan, *Class and Reform*, 201.

94. *The Chicago Teacher and School Board Journal* 1, no. 3 (March 1899): 140.

95. Ibid., 141. The teachers were careful to recognize every ethnic group in the city: "American born, 488,000; German, 490,000; Irish, 248,000; Swedes, 111,000; Polish, 96,000; Bohemian, 89,000; Norwegian, 45,000; English, 44,000; Canadian, 34,000; Russian, 38,000; Italian, 23,000; Scotch, 22,000; French, 21,000; Afro-American, 25,000; Welsh, 3,000; Chinese, 2,000."

the CTF, spoke out against the CFC's 1903 bill, explaining that "it creates an administrative officer and confers on him all the duties and powers naturally and necessarily inherent in the whole teaching force, and the people, through their representatives, thereby setting aside the principles of democracy in the internal administration of schools."[96] Rather than create more administrative positions wielding expansive powers, the CTF maintained that the board should "build more elementary schools before anything else" since overcrowding meant that seventeen thousand children in the city's poorest areas were attending school for only a half day.[97] Finally, the teachers objected to the CFC's plan for outside experts to rate teacher efficiency since it "provides for a system of inquisitorial inspection, by people not necessarily qualified to know anything about the subject matter of teaching."[98] Putting more stock in practical knowledge, they rejected the idea of supervision by administrators—experts who may lack extensive classroom experience.

Two versions of expertise thus emerged from the CFC's role in the school controversies, one deriving from day-to-day experience in classrooms with children, another from training and experience in administration, a professional occupation that was located farther away from the classroom and its occupants. As Margaret Haley expressed it, "two ideals are struggling for supremacy . . . one the industrial ideal, dominating through the supremacy of commercialism, which subordinates the worker to the product and the machine . . . the other, the ideal of democracy, the ideal of educators, which places humanity above all machines." She objected to the CFC's and administrators' reforms, which would make the "teacher an automaton, a mere factory hand, whose duty is to carry out mechanically and unquestionably the ideas and orders of those clothed with the authority of the position, and who may or may not know the needs of the children or how to minister to them."[99] It is perhaps a testament to women's continuing influence in the CFC that, when Harper's report met strong opposition, the organization worked with the Woman's Club and the CTF to sponsor an open debate on the document.[100]

Tensions within the CFC over competing ideas of social knowledge—one that connected the logic of commercial society with expertise and another that cast expertise in experiential terms and called for the representation of numerous perspectives—were foreshadowed even at the founding of the organization in early 1894, when the CFC's Central Relief Association virtually ignored the

96. Margaret Haley, "Comments on the New Education Bill," *CTF Bulletin,* January 23, 1903, 1.
97. *Chicago Teacher and School Board Journal,* 140.
98. Ibid.
99. *CTF Bulletin,* March 6, 1903; Margaret Haley, "Why Teachers Should Organize," National Education Organization, *Addresses and Proceedings* (1904): 145–52; "Organization among Teachers," *Chicago Teachers Federation Bulletin* 1 (June 27, 1902).
100. Flanagan, *Seeing with Their Hearts,* 68.

input of working-class members. Born in the midst of economic depression, the CFC's first project provided unemployment relief. To guide its task the CFC had different models of relief from which to fashion its program. The Relief and Aid Society (RAS), the most prominent private charity organization in the city, offered one model. It had a long history of carefully screening—and usually rejecting—applicants. During the 1880s, the RAS gave aid to approximately one-fifth of its applicants and rejected outright more than 50 percent. In 1893 and 1894 the number of applicants rose, and the percentage of those rejected jumped to two-thirds.

In large part this was due to the RAS's suspicious outlook: its fear of encouraging dependence and its unwillingness to admit to the problems of structural economic downturns, even though they were, by this time, well recognized by economists. Most of its recipients were women, often with children, who were widowed or abandoned. The RAS did not customarily give help to unemployed men since it operated with the assumption that enough jobs were available to those who sought them. For the remainder of the decade, the RAS continued to reject between two-thirds and three-fourths of its applicants.[101] The Cook County Board of Charities also provided relief, but it routinely aided only one-third of those who sought help.[102]

Chicago workers offered a different model. During the depression the city's labor unions used public gatherings, speeches, and parades to pressure local government for public relief. Based on their contributions of physical labor to building the city, they challenged the roles of both government, which was usually passive on social welfare matters, and commercial elites, who had relied on their private success to translate into social benefits for the entire city. Responding to workers' pressure, the city created jobs for the unemployed. Arguing that their experiences had provided them with special knowledge of their condition and needs, they ultimately succeeded in pressuring Mayor Harrison to create the Committee of Relief and Public Safety.

Given the visible role of labor in the new organization, the CFC's Central Relief Association might have considered workers' approaches to relief when it began its project. Instead it constructed a program that lay somewhere between workers' demands and the model of the Relief and Aid Society. The first task of the Central Relief Association was "to ascertain, in the most expeditious, practicable way, the nature and extent of the want and distress" in the city, and to

---

101. Figures drawn from John Albert Mayer, "Private Charity in Chicago from 1871–1915" (PhD dissertation, University of Minnesota, 1978), 102–3.

102. Ibid., 464. For additional information on the RAS, see Sawislak, *Smoldering City*; Kathleen D. McCarthy, *Noblesse Oblige: Charity and Cultural Philanthropy in Chicago, 1849–1929* (Chicago: University of Chicago Press, 1982).

raise money for its relief.[103] This was an important process since disputes over the extent of unemployment affected the city residents' understanding of the economic depression. For example, the *Chicago Tribune*, in claiming that the number of unemployed was overestimated, implied that individuals were still largely to blame for their economic woes.[104] Agreeing that investigation was necessary, workers, government officials, and wealthier segments of the population turned to social scientific methods to guide their practice.

At its first meeting on December 9, 1893, the committee resolved to "make a thorough canvass of every block in the city and record everyone out of employment who may seem to be a proper subject for aid, or likely to be so."[105] Such social survey results found thousands of men out of work or nearing destitution. Once this information was officially obtained, the CRA was able to recognize that structural economic problems rooted in the depression, not individual workers' laziness and vice, caused rampant unemployment in the city. Here social science measurements helped ease some CFC members into an unfamiliar way of thinking about Chicago's economy. Still, in the guidelines they adopted, the CFC committee revealed lingering concerns about dispensing relief.

Even with the recognition of thousands of "deserving" poor in the city, the committee worried about providing aid to the "undeserving." As if to ease the minds of contributors, the CRA report noted tersely that, after the survey, "came the labor test."[106] The committee required a minimum of three hours of work each day in exchange for meals and a place to sleep. Men who worked more than three hours received tickets valued at ten cents per hour to exchange for clothes, shoes, or, in the case of married men, groceries.[107] Throughout the three months that the CRA operated its programs, an average of 2,275 men per day worked for approximately three and a half hours each.[108] Thus workers earned on average 34 cents per day or $2.04 a week for six days of work. Although it is impossible to determine how many were single men who worked just long enough to earn their meals and lodging and how many were married workers who lived at home with families and worked longer hours, by any calculation the 10–15 cents an hour the CRA paid was well below the average wages of 20 cents an hour or $8.75 a week in nonunionized, lower-skilled jobs.[109]

Furthermore, the CRA was unwilling to pay wages; rather, it distributed meals, clothing, lodging, and food staples to workers. To some extent this approach

103. CFC, *First Annual Report*, 31.
104. See, for example, *Chicago Tribune*, August 26, 1893.
105. CFC, *First Annual Report*, 32.
106. Ibid.
107. Ibid., 33.
108. Ibid., 36.
109. U.S. Bureau of the Census, *The Statistical History of the United States from Colonial Times to the Present* (Stamford, CT: Fairfield, 1965), 91.

reflected the nature of private relief efforts. Donations to the CRA often took the form of supplies rather than cash. But the CRA's decision to structure relief in such a manner also ignored the demands workers made on city government to provide paid public jobs that allowed them to maintain control over their wages. Refusing to trust workers, the CRA instead sought to maintain patriarchal control; its program undermined workers' own strategies of consumption, which often stretched their wages, particularly in lean times.[110] Nor did it help workers meet rent or house payments. In light of the kind of measures labor leaders had demanded, the actions of the CRA were conservative and even defensive.

Furthermore, the CRA, in contrast to the mayor's Committee on Relief and Public Safety, contained only one labor representative on the central committee. Although there are no records to indicate whether the committee recruited workers to survey neighborhoods and work with relief recipients, given the model from which the CRA drew, it is unlikely that the working classes were well represented. Workers' representatives had pressed Harrison to provide thousands of jobs building a drainage canal that bypassed private construction firms and were paid directly out of the city's budget. Although the city eventually sought contracts with private companies, the workers' plan extended the role of the city government as an employer to an unprecedented degree and enforced workers' claims of their right to a job.

However, the CRA retreated from such measures that would have expanded the responsibilities of city government and working-class representation. Private money financed the jobs it offered, and the CRA went to great lengths to use surveys and scientific charity to regulate and justify who received aid. The program the CRA adopted discouraged dependence by reinforcing labor not as a right but as a way to build character and responsibility. The advice that "competent, reliable men can get to the front" was printed on the back of a card given to each worker who applied for jobs. The CRA admonished workers to "please remember that your daily conduct and willingness to give a fair equivalent for what you receive is a test of character." Echoing Chicago's liberal republican civic myths, the card cautioned: "Good character and earnest endeavor will win the battle of life, especially in this free country, where there is generally work for all, if we find the right man for the right place."[111] Relying upon a definition of harmony as a trait of the free market, the CRA assured workers, "Our interests are mutual; let us be mutually helpful."[112] The association also registered working-

---

110. For discussion of these strategies, see Jeanne Boydston, "To Earn Her Daily Bread: Housework and Antebellum Working-class Subsistence," in *Unequal Sisters: A Multicultural Reader in U.S. Women's History*, 2d ed., ed. Vicki L. Ruíz and Ellen Carol DuBois (New York: Routledge, 1994), 44–56.

111. CFC, *First Annual Report*, 35.

112. Ibid.

men for relief and permanent positions since, as it asserted, a job provided the working man "a better chance" to be "a useful and helpful citizen."[113] Although labor unions shared this position, their rationale was different. Workers claimed a right to a job and wages that offered security for their families, even when the free market system failed. Viewing the matter through a lens that naturalized laissez-faire political economy, the CRA emphasized the moral lessons that labor offered. Struggle and failure in the market place served a didactic function that transformed the character of participants while encouraging them to accept the market as a means of dispensing fairness and justice.

In the face of workers' pressures, the CRA used its relief program to enforce the morality of the liberal political economy and an older liberal republican version of social knowledge. The magnitude of the depression had convinced many more well-off Chicagoans that economic problems, rather than individuals, were to blame for the city's unemployment and homelessness, but they still feared entering into relationships with the city's workers outside the mediation of the market. The possibilities for deception and abuse were high in the urban environment, where residents did not personally know each other. As though offering proof of this fact, the *Chicago Tribune* reported that the managers of one food distribution center turned away Bohemian women and gave alms only to Bohemian men when they suspected that several families were abusing the charity.[114] To CRA members, filtering aid through the process of labor exchange not only avoided contributing to working-class dependency but also served as a way to categorize and "know" the city's lower classes; "citizens" and "worthy" individuals were those willing to work. The CRA's program thus buttressed a stringent code of ethics that depended on the market, labor exchange, and scientific charity to mediate social relations. The CRA largely rejected workers' ideas and limited their role in formulating relief policies, thereby undermining the CFC's ability to construct a democratic social knowledge based on multiple classes.

After the Central Relief Association ended its program in spring 1894, the morals committee began an attack on gambling establishments, which further illustrated cultural anxieties surrounding classical economic social knowledge fostered by market exchange. In 1894 O. P. Gifford, an outspoken Baptist minister who led a citywide antigambling campaign, joined the committee. Shortly thereafter, it began its condemnation of gambling enterprises throughout the city. Although rendered illegal by both state and municipal laws, an estimated two hundred public gambling "hells" served fifteen hundred to two thousand "professional gamblers" and had fleeced countless innocent residents and

113. Ibid.
114. *Chicago Tribune*, September 6, 1893.

unwary World's Fair visitors. The police and mayor's office under Carter Harrison were implicated in accepting bribes and providing protection for these operations.[115]

Several months before the CFC was organized, Gifford had appeared at a Sunset Club meeting to discuss gambling, and there he explained how the vice undermined the rationality and ethics of market exchange.[116] Since a capitalist economy was ordered around the project of turning passion for gain into mutual interest in accumulating capital or goods, it required rational planning and personal habits of frugality, hard work, and the ability to keep promises. But gambling, Gifford proclaimed, "unfits a man for self-control" since the mental excitement it offers undermines "that calm and philosophic thought which is the condition of successful business."[117] Furthermore, "it gives gain without regard to merit."[118] And not only did it offer rewards based on luck rather than hard work, but it also exploited men since gain was won at the expense of another. Such practices inverted the morality of market exchange, Gifford explained, because "the very foundation of legitimate business is that man shall give something for something."[119]

Instead, gambling encouraged irrational waste of money, excessive and dangerous adventure, and dishonest intentions as gamblers used deception to achieve profit. John Philip Quinn, a former gambler, spoke at a Sunset Club meeting and described how dishonest gamblers plied their trade. He exhibited a number of gambling devices, explaining how "thieves and scoundrels" used them to win bets dishonestly while presenting themselves as honest, albeit very lucky, men.[120] His concern that unscrupulous people took advantage of the unwary reflected anxieties similar to those of the CRA, and he drew an even closer connection to gambling and commerce. Echoing century-long fears that in a money economy

115. CFC, *First Annual Report*. See also Bachin (*Building the South Side*, 256) on Harrison's role in moving the vice district to Chicago's south side, a transformation that further served to racialize vice in the city.

116. The Sunset Club fostered public debate and discussion on a wide range of social and political topics. Its speakers included national and local leaders, men and women, though its membership appears to have been male. Its yearbooks and publications are available at the Chicago Historical Society.

117. Sunset Club, *Sunset Club Yearbook* (Chicago, 1892–93), 194.

118. Ibid.

119. Ibid., 195.

120. A reformed gambler, Quinn took up a personal crusade to educate the public about gamblers' tricks. See Ann Vincent Fabian, *Card Sharps, Dream Books, and Bucket Shops* (Ithaca, NY: Cornell University Press, 1990). T. J. Jackson Lears insightfully discusses the tension between the manliness and self-control of calculated risk taking and the cultural stigma of gambling as irrational. Lears, "What if History Were Gambler?" in *Moral Problems in American Life: New Perspectives on Cultural History*, ed. Karen Halttunen and Lewis Perry, 331–40 (Ithaca, NY: Cornell University Press, 1998). Also Lears's discussion of gambling in *Something for Nothing: Luck in America* (New York: Penguin, 2003), especially 187–228.

clerks and employees might succumb to greed and steal from employers, Quinn emphasized rampant embezzlement cited in *Chicago Tribune* articles—ninety-eight million dollars since 1878. Speaking from his own observations, he ominously told the audience, "gambling beggars men, ruins their business, destroys the happiness of home, breaks the wifely heart, steals the bread from the baby's mouth, sends mothers and fathers to sorrowing graves, and at last drags the sin stained soul before the bar of God's dishonored justice."[121]

However, the danger of gambling extended far beyond individuals and their families because, as the Reverend William Burch asserted, "it is an anti-social form of pleasure" that threatened to unravel the nation itself. The gambler "cannot distinguish between his own dollar and the other fellow's dollar" and thus "cannot see the meaning of property aright."[122] Burch argued that this subverted the liberal foundations of the social order and shook the political order as well, for "there is nothing that so undermines republican institutions, nothing that so darkens the lustre [*sic*] of our old flag, as wrong ideas as to property."[123] Still, although Burch believed that victims of the gambling vice should be treated as insane and the keepers of gambling hells prosecuted, he professed little faith in laws. Rather, he argued for the power of moral suasion.

Critics in this discussion pointed out that it was hypocritical to condemn gamblers without also exposing business speculation as an enterprise that similarly sought profit without work or exchange of goods. In terms reminiscent of single taxers and agrarian populists, one opponent asked, "What distinction can be made between middle men of all kinds, whether they be gamblers, speculators, commission merchants, bankers, or what not?"[124] Pushing the indictment further, a Mr. F. A. Herring responded, "When a man buys that for which he never expects to pay; or agrees to buy that which the seller has not and never expects to get, and to pay for it with a check on a bank where the drawer has no deposits, he encourages something which saps the very foundations of morality, and which in my judgment, is the greatest danger towards which we, as a speculative nation are tending."[125] Attacks on speculation, part of an agrarian protest against the finance capitalism that emerged in the last quarter of the nineteenth century, thus shared a logic with antigambling campaigns.[126] One answer to the problem was to remind listeners that honesty, demonstrated by the availability of money to pay debts, ensured the legitimacy of speculation. Herring

121. Sunset Club, *Sunset Club Yearbook*, 202.
122 . Ibid., 205.
123. Ibid.
124. Ibid., 197.
125. Ibid., 203.
126. Lawrence Goodwyn, *Democratic Promise: The Populist Moment in America* (New York: Oxford University Press, 1976); Richard Hofstadter, *Age of Reform;* Nell Irvin Painter, *Standing at Armageddon* (New York: Norton, 1987); Thomas, *Alternative America.*

carefully discriminated between legitimate speculators, who can pay their debts, and frauds, who cannot: "So long as any man engaged in legitimate speculation buys only that for which he can pay, no matter how the market goes, there is no ruined home, there is no widow, there are no orphaned children."[127]

Chicago, as a leading site for national and international commodities trade, stood at the center of that "speculative nation," and several of its most prominent residents had a stake in legitimizing speculation. In the wake of several incidents of panic when investors were able to corner the commodities market, the Chicago Board of Trade sponsored campaigns to convince critics that its operations were honest and its function crucial to the economy. Against claims that speculators produced nothing and thus were parasites, the board argued that it created markets and prices, essential components of a market economy.[128] Against arguments that business itself was based on chance, the Reverend Gifford queried:

> Why, don't you know that the whole tendency of modern business is towards the elimination of speculation as much as possible? Every combine, trust and corner is the death of speculation. They do not bet on chance. They get money enough and brains enough together to control the modern grain market, as Joseph the Hebrew controlled the grain market of Egypt. . . . The whole tendency in this world is to do away with chance. The more we know of nature, the more we learn of the heart of things, the more we learn that there is no such thing as chance in the universe. It is unscientific to gamble. It is simply turning the tide of human affairs back to paganism and barbarism.[129]

Gifford thus juxtaposed the randomness and irrationality of gambling to appeals to scientific control of market society. A new intellectual universe in which "the emergence of probabilistic, statistical thinking suggested a new way of taming chance" was taking shape, one that stood in contrast to both a "culture of chance" marked by gambling behavior and to evangelical rationality, which posited a natural harmony of "providence and progress" unfolding in human history.[130] Thus, the CFC's line of attack on gambling, along with an effort to criminalize bucket shops, which engaged in speculation, legitimized the Board of Trade and financial capitalism in the face of those who held fast to the culture of chance or rejected speculation on the basis of evangelical rationality. The board received additional help when William Baker, its president in the 1890s, became president of the CFC in 1895.

127. *Sunset Club Yearbook*, 203.
128. Fabian, *Card Sharps, Dream Books, and Bucket Shops.*
129. Sunset Club, *Sunset Club Yearbook*, 209.
130. Lears, *Something for Nothing*, 200.

The Morals committee was unequivocal in its commitment to using state power to crack down on gaming houses. Gifford had laid some groundwork for the committee when he visited Mayor Hopkins on January 5. Following the meeting, Hopkins ordered police chief Brennan to close the gambling houses, but a month later they were again open for business. When the CFC entered the campaign against gambling, therefore, members felt it necessary to be more assertive in suppressing the vice. With the help of private detectives, the CFC drew up a list of gambling establishments and their owners, staged raids using crowbars and sledgehammers when necessary to gain admittance to "gaming hells," destroyed gambling paraphernalia, and brought owners and patrons alike into court.[131] In 1896 the CFC further aided the Board of Trade in its attack on gambling when the two organizations worked to indict and prosecute bucket shop owners throughout the city.[132]

Indeed, the Chicago Board of Trade's strategy of attacking bucket shops was part of its campaign to legitimize its own function. It effectively defined participation in the economy of finance capitalism as "rational" and "moral," while at the same time it criminalized behaviors that lay outside the logic of such an economic system.[133] The CFC's role in this campaign, when placed alongside its relief efforts in the winter of 1893–94, suggests how deeply some of the men in the organization tied civic consciousness to the liberal market economy. They sought not just to encourage municipal efficiency, as several historians have suggested, but also to entrench the ethics of classical liberal political economy in the regulation of personal behavior.

Gifford further connected antigambling rhetoric to a justification for civil service laws. Just as gambling enticed its victims with hopes of receiving something for nothing, so "professional politicians" used their positions for private gain by taking bribes or using public money in questionable business deals: "Gambling is wrong because it gives gain without regard to merit. The principle of civil service reform is making its slow and halting way into national, state and municipal politics. It is simply the recognition in political affairs of an eternal principle of righteousness that in the long run gain belongs to merit."[134] The notion that labor, enterprise, and virtue ensured economic success was the cornerstone of Chicago elites' social knowledge. It grew out of a classical political economy, the epistemology of which rested on the belief in natural economic laws above human alteration or legislative tampering.[135] In tying civic identity

131. CFC, *First Annual Report,* 92.
132. *Chicago Tribune,* March 1, 1896.
133. Fabian, *Card Sharps, Dream Books, and Bucket Shops.*
134. Sunset Club, *Sunset Club Yearbook,* 194.
135. For an excellent discussion of the social knowledge underlying classical liberal political economy as it was interpreted in postbellum America, see Nancy Cohen, *The Reconstruction of American Liberalism, 1865–1914* (Chapel Hill: University of North Carolina Press, 2002), particularly 23–60.

to the classical market economy, the CFC entrenched the belief that the market was the best mediator of justice. This worldview was at odds with the democratic social knowledge promoted by women and workers, who used experiential, first-hand knowledge to raise fundamental questions about power and the assumptions and justice of a classical political economy.

Even civil service reform reflected this epistemological conflict. Many men who supported civil service argued that it would bring about neutrality in government administration that would ensure fairness, justice, and especially efficiency. It would accomplish this by divorcing administration from politics. In doing so, its supporters ignored the challenges economic power posed to democracy, assuming instead that meritocracy would reward the fittest, best men just as the neutral market rewarded the most deserving. Nonpartisanship, rationality, and efficiency were thus linked with a positivist search for order and connected to the belief that the economy functioned according to laws best left alone.[136]

As the CFC developed, it promoted a new style of politics that linked interactive social knowledge, social science expertise, and social action. As ward councils investigated neighborhood conditions, social scientists informed discussions about sanitation, utilities, education, and politics, and women brought their experiences with using social science to advance moral claims, the CFC fostered faith in social scientific knowledge. Investigations, statistics, and experts could tell members about the way the city worked and help formulate the organization's agenda. These investigations, reports, and exposés, whether written in the lurid style of muckraking journalism or the dry prose of social science, awakened the sympathies of other residents and implicitly invited them to imagine themselves living in such conditions. Thus when members of the CFC conceived the organization as a "medium of acquaintance and sympathy" with a central body to bring together various groups and ward representatives, they looked to social knowledge as the mediator of concerted public action.

However, the CFC's different versions of social knowledge illustrated its deeply embedded epistemological and political tensions—tensions that were at

---

136. This position on nonpartisanship, while articulated by male reformers, was not strongly emphasized by women. Instead, as Helene Silverberg has argued, female reformers were "more concerned with achieving their social welfare goals than with reforming election procedures or ending the 'spoils system.'" Silverberg, "A Government of Men," 163. Robyn Muncy also points out the creative ways female social work professionals used national and state civil service regulations to create a network of like-minded women within the Children's Bureau. See Robyn Muncy, *Creating a Female Dominion in American Reform, 1890–1935* (New York: Oxford University Press, 1991), 31–33, 49–52.

the heart of the intersection between social knowledge and democracy. The CFC originated as an organization that sought coordination and ultimately cooperation among groups with distinct interests and identities. When these interests clashed over different models of relief or varying ideas about the role of the state in enforcing antigambling behaviors, for example, many CFC members used existing liberal republican principles—the basis of their social knowledge—as a blueprint for programs.

While workers also incorporated rhetoric upholding the value of labor, they espoused a different social knowledge. Though the CFC had set out to pursue a framework for civic unity that drew from both activist social science models and a democratic social knowledge, its Central Relief Agency used social science to reinforce fears of working-class fraud and dependency and to justify methods of social control that reinforced class divisions. By shaping its relief measures in such a way, it implicitly disregarded the experience and knowledge workers brought to the organization. Furthermore, both the terms of relief and the antigambling campaign revealed the distinctly masculine undertone of the CFC's ideas about civic identity. Its relief programs were specifically aimed at men, especially family men; it relied on other institutions in the city to address women's needs.[137] The debate over gambling linked masculine morality with participation in the liberal economy and, ultimately, political order; women appeared in the discussion only as dependents on men and passive victims of men's vices.[138] Yet the women who joined the CFC had sought to challenge such assumptions, which implicitly cast the economy, politics, and the public realm of the city as distinctly masculine domains. As we shall see in the next chapter, they took an important stance toward the state that challenged the laissez-faire implications of Chicago elites' liberal republicanism. Concerned with securing the best conditions in which to live and work, women pushed for an activist state.

In a similar vein, at the height of the depression, workers had demanded that the municipal government provide jobs programs. Their vision of an activist state undermined laissez-faire principles associated with classical political economy. In contrast, businessmen in the CFC held fast to the fears and principles that buttressed laissez-faire practices. Yet their policies toward gambling and vice suggested a more modern version of conservatism that sought to use the state to regulate private behavior.

---

137. Report of the Central Relief Agency in the Civic Federation of Chicago, *First Annual Report*, 38–41.

138. In light of the fact that the Women's Christian Temperance Union (WCTU) characterized wives of alcoholics in similar terms, it is interesting that women in the CFC did not appear to participate in the antigambling campaign. Given the ability of Chicago women to organize around moral issues, it might be that gambling was not a major domestic problem. Such a possibility further suggests the cultural anxieties about market behavior and morality. See Bordin, *Women and Temperance*, on the WCTU.

The reforms promoted by the federation thus illustrated the tensions over social knowledge and democracy. For some members, the CFC's organicism fostered a potentially democratic approach to social knowledge that would both recognize social difference and transcend it in the name of public good. But in several campaigns, its organic civic identity looked more like a hierarchical organicism of earlier political thought.[139] While groups in the city appeared as an interrelated and functioning whole, the "best men" and their conservation of classical political economy and its moral behaviors were called upon to define and promote public virtue. This construction of civic unity, with its appeal to natural economic laws, undermined a proximate epistemology with its emphasis on the social foundations of knowledge. The relationality and interaction encouraged in venues such as the city's social settlements as a means to foster a democratic social knowledge were at odds with the positivist and conservative direction the CFC headed. These tensions foreshadowed women's and labor leaders' eventual abandonment of the CFC. Although their influence lasted only a brief time, their presence in this organization can help us understand how competing visions of social knowledge were tied to questions of democracy: What epistemological frameworks legitimize the experience and knowledge of particular individuals and groups? What processes of creating social knowledge might include and mediate these different experiences and forms of knowledge? Who in a democracy can be knowers and contribute to public debate? As we see in subsequent chapters, there were alternatives to the liberal republican model that eventually prevailed in the CFC.

Conclusion

When we look at the CFC, what emerges is a social knowledge that constituted privilege and excluded workers and, to a lesser extent, women. Invested in market relations as the primary mediator of social relationships, most CFC men failed to take seriously competing visions of social knowledge by rejecting workers' and teachers' experiential knowledge during the depression and in Harper's educational report. Their epistemology was largely at odds with women and labor leaders in the organization, who used claims to firsthand knowledge and a model of interaction and participation to raise fundamental questions about power and the justice of a classical liberal political economy. Tensions between competing views of social knowledge reached their limits around the

139. Robert A. Burnham, "The Boss Becomes a Manager: Executive Authority and City Charter Reform, 1880–1929," in *Making Sense of the City: Local Government, Civic Culture, and Community Life in Urban America*, ed. Robert B. Fairbanks and Patricia Mooney-Melvin, 75–94 (Columbus: Ohio State University Press, 2001).

beginning of the twentieth century, when women and labor leaders found that men's commitments were increasingly irreconcilable with their own. They had largely abandoned the CFC by the time it spearheaded the charter campaign in 1906–7, to which I turn in chapter 6, when these different reform groups once again collided.

Jane Addams came to realize the differences most bitterly when a man from her neighborhood applied for aid from the Central Relief Association. Although he was a shipping clerk who, as Addams explained, was unaccustomed to working outdoors, the regulations demanded he take a job digging ditches to earn his food. Though Addams intervened on his behalf, the CRA stood firm. After laboring outdoors for two days, the man contracted pneumonia and died a week later. She concluded that "life cannot be administered by definite rules and regulations," as the CRA expected; rather, she learned from this incident "that wisdom to deal with a man's difficulties comes only through some knowledge of his life and habits as a whole."[140] Drawing from this experience, she remained critical of the rigid application of social scientific standards of efficiency and the use of positivist social knowledge alone to solve social problems. At the same time organizations like the CFC and individuals like Jane Addams sought to bring groups into greater identification with one another, clashes such as these would widen the gap in public discussions over the source of social knowledge. As we see in the next chapter, Jane Addams, through her work at Hull House, offered a different vision of democratic social knowledge.

---

140. Addams, *Twenty Years at Hull-House,* 97.

3

"To Add the Social Function to Democracy"

Jane Addams, Hull House, and Democratic Social Knowledge

I am not so sure that we succeeded in our endeavors to "make social intercourse express the growing sense of the economic unity of society and to add the social function to democracy. But Hull-House was soberly opened on the theory that the dependence of classes on each other is reciprocal.[1]

In her autobiography, Jane Addams recalled her neighbor's death during the 1893 depression with deep regret. She intimated it was the Civic Federation's standardized rules about unemployment relief and its unwillingness to learn "some knowledge of his life and habits as a whole" that led directly to his demise.[2] The lessons she learned from incidents such as this helped frame her approach to democratic social knowledge. Throughout her long reform career in Chicago as the founder of Hull House settlement in Chicago's Nineteenth Ward on the near west side, she forged an alternative to Chicago elites' liberal republicanism, offering a new vision of social knowledge growing out of "social intercourse" among city residents that would "add the social function to democracy."

This chapter places Hull House within a larger framework of Chicago reformers' attempts to reorient social knowledge. Addams and Hull House residents encouraged a variety of ways of knowing, and their forums for building social knowledge contributed to a new conception of democracy. In the course of their efforts they rejected a framework of liberal republican social knowledge, with its primary focus on atomistic individualism, in favor of a democratic

---

1. The epigraph to this chapter is drawn from Jane Addams, *Twenty Years at Hull-House* (New York: New American Library, 1981), 76.

2. Ibid., 97.

social knowledge that highlighted interconnections and relationality.[3] Addams in particular articulated a historicist understanding of social knowledge, ethics, and politics and, in so doing, rejected the assumptions of natural and divine law underpinning industrial capitalism, patriarchy, and even liberal politics, with its emphasis on the individual voter. Instead, she and her fellow residents posited the contours of a new democratic praxis that engaged directly with social needs and recognized the value of the experiences of divergent groups.

Using the analytical lens of democratic social knowledge, this chapter emphasizes a conception of democracy defined outside of formal politics. For Addams and many Hull House residents, democracy was enacted in daily prac-tices and social relationships, and this kind of praxis was a template for collective action. Shared experiences, joint projects, aesthetic expression, and delibera-tive forums in which all were free to speak were the grounds on which human commonalities, as well as cultural differences, became apparent and through which mutual bonds of social solidarity and equality were forged. Of course, the investigations, relationships, and projects emanating from Hull House inspired political activism as well, but it was an activism rooted in commitment to rela-tionships across class, gender, and ethnic lines, a concept of democratic praxis rather than political individualism exercised in the vote.[4] Democratic social knowledge was tied to such a vision since Hull House stood for the idea that one can know problems and offer solutions to them only by involving the people who were the most affected by them.

This chapter offers a few key examples of the many rich activities eman-ating from Hull House that together challenged liberal republicanism. They

---

3. Addams did not reject the value of liberalism entirely. Indeed, she played an important role in extending one of its most important tenets—the right of the individual to self-determination—to women, but she also argued that rights and even the self were socially constituted. James Livingston, *Pragmatism, Feminism, and Democracy: Rethinking the Politics of American History* (New York: Rout-ledge, 2001), 57–84. On the social self more generally, see Jeff Sklansky, *The Soul's Economy: Market Society and Selfhood in American Thought, 1820–1920* (Chapel Hill: University of North Carolina Press, 2002). Sklansky is far more critical of the emergence of the social self and its role in adjusting social thought to the emergence of corporate capital than is Livingston, who sees it as opening up possibilities for new subjectivities, especially for women, and for new forms of cultural politics. See Livingston, *Pragmatism, Feminism, and Democracy*, 5–6.

4. By noting class, gender, and ethnic identities, I do not mean to imply that these categories were fixed. Indeed, they were continually being reconstituted, especially during this period. Nor do I mean to suggest that there was not a range of diversity and conflict within categories such as women, immigrants, workers, or even businessmen. See, for example, Mae Ngai, "The Architecture of Race in American Immigration Law: A Reexamination of the Immigration Act of 1924," *Journal of American History* 86, no. 1 (June 1999): 67–93; Nan Enstad, *Ladies of Labor, Girls of Adventure: Working Women, Popular Culture, and Labor Politics at the Turn of the Twentieth Century* (New York: Columbia University Press, 1999); and Howell John Harris, "The Making of a 'Business Commu-nity,' 1880–1930: Definitions and Ingredients of a Collective Identity," in *Federalism, Citizenship, and Collective Identities in U.S. History*, ed. Cornelius A. van Minnen and Sylvia L. Hilton, 123–40 (Amsterdam: Vu University Press, 2000).

demonstrate the range of ways that social knowledge and democracy intersected within Chicago reform. The chapter has two parts. Part 1 selectively highlights aspects of Addams's intellectual biography to indicate the development of her reform ideas and their relationship to her gender and class setting. Addams is useful in understanding the emergent democratic social knowledge, both because she embodied many of the experiences, ideas, and motivations of other men and women of her social class and because her democratic ideas were still unusual for her time. Part 2 then widens the analytical lens to explore five different aspects of Addams's and Hull House's democratic social knowledge: mutuality; aesthetics and sympathetic understanding; deliberation and interaction; activism; and narrative translation.

These five aspects of democratic social knowledge overlapped one another, yet separating them, even in an artificial way, offers a clearer picture of the facets of that knowledge. They offer a frame of reference for later chapters, and we will return to them as we move through the remainder of the book. In this chapter, the highlighted, roughly chronological examples of democratic social knowledge reflect both the evolution of Hull House residents' praxis and the changing reform context in which they and their neighbors operated. Each of these examples illustrates frameworks through which middle-class and elite Hull House community members experimented with moving across the class and ethnic boundaries that threatened a "drifting apart," causing psychic and political alienation, and prevented democratic solidarity. As we saw in the previous chapter, these examples also foreshadow the difficulties confronting democratic social knowledge.

Part 1. Early Ideas

Addams's biographers have provided a rich portrait of the formative influences and experiences that shaped her mature ideas. While a full recounting of her biography is not the purpose here, selected examples afford us a window onto the cultural milieu in which her democratic social knowledge emerged. They illustrate the importance of religion, family history, domesticity, and Romanticism for Addams's early ideas.[5]

5. Biographies of Addams are numerous, and I borrow extensively from them. See, in particular, Victoria Bissell Brown, *The Education of Jane Addams* (Philadelphia: University of Pennsylvania Press, 2004); Louise W. Knight, *Citizen: Jane Addams and the Struggle for Democracy* (Chicago: University of Chicago Press, 2005); Allan Davis, *American Heroine* (New York: Oxford University Press, 1973); James Farrell, *Beloved Lady: A History of Jane Addams' Ideas on Reform and Peace* (Baltimore: Johns Hopkins University Press, 1967); Daniel Levine, *Jane Addams and the Liberal Tradition* (Madison: State Historical Society of Wisconsin, 1971); Jean Bethke Elshtain, *Jane Addams and the Dream of American Democracy* (New York: Basic Books, 2002). Dorothy Ross, "Gendered Social Knowledge:

Born in 1860, Addams was steeped in traditions of domesticity, social Christianity, and Romanticism and was well acquainted with new sociological studies, all of which encouraged her to identify connected ways of knowing and emotional bonds as constitutive of both self and community. Her political upbringing emphasized a republican commitment to the common good, and that, along with her youthful inclination toward stewardship, was reflected in her sense of duty to serve the social welfare of the community. Indeed, it must have been a powerful sense of love and duty that brought this well-to-do woman into Chicago's Nineteenth Ward. Home to fifty thousand poor and working-class immigrants representing eighteen nations, the neighborhood had all of the problems associated with economically deprived areas: "[T]he streets [were] inexpressibly dirty, the number of schools inadequate, sanitary legislation unenforced, the street lighting bad, the paving miserable and altogether lacking in the alleys and smaller streets, and the stables foul beyond description."[6] The ward was one of Chicago's poorest and most neglected.

Seeking to serve the needs of the district, Addams opened Hull House as a project of fellowship and cultural uplift that betrayed her youthful arrogance and paternalistic tendency toward moral priggishness. But Hull House soon became much more. By 1893 it was a day care and community center, a meeting place for immigrants and labor organizations, a site of local and state political activity, and the nerve center of an increasingly powerful network of women's reform activities. In 1894 the settlement had fifteen permanent residents and, after 1900, more than fifty people lived at Hull House.[7] The residents' widespread participation in ward, city, and state politics, their involvement in relief efforts, and their sponsorship of cultural and intellectual activities made Hull House a civic space fostering interaction among Chicagoans. Like the settlement's activities, Addams's reform sensibility expanded as well during her first years in the settlement, transforming her conception of democracy and framing the local epistemology that soon placed Hull House and its most famous resident at the center of a reform community wrestling with social knowledge and democracy.

Domestic Discourse, Jane Addams, and the Possibilities of Social Science," in *Gender and American Social Science: The Formative Years*, ed. Helene Silverberg, 235–64 (Princeton, NJ: Princeton University Press, 1998), also offers a very useful discussion of intellectual influences on Addams.

6. Addams, *Twenty Years*, 81. The Nineteenth Ward was composed primarily of German, Irish, Italian, Bohemian, Polish, Russian, and Jewish immigrants. *Hull-House Maps and Papers* (New York: Macmillan, 1895).

7. Though women were a majority, men composed one quarter of the residents at the turn of the century, and most of the residents, regardless of sex, were primarily middle-class college graduates. All of the new residents went through a probationary period, in which they created their own program or sought a niche in the settlement. Those already living there voted on whether to extend permanent residency to the new person in question. Robyn Muncy, *Creating a Female Dominion in American Reform* (New York: Oxford University Press, 1991), 13–14.

The settlement offered ways for various groups to interact and forge common experiences. Addams's personal journey, from her ambitious, arrogant youth caught up in heroic dreams of individual triumph, "to a warm and sympathetic woman who 'folded ambition for herself into ambition for democracy,'" suggested that in the best situations commitment to democratic social knowledge was mutually transforming, making the reformers the "reformed."[8] Hull House's art programs, its women's clubs and gendered uses of social science, and its forums for economic and political discussion all encouraged social interaction. In so doing they offered a model of democratic social knowledge that highlighted relational, interpretative, and sympathetic ways of knowing and wedded them with social science methods.

While building on recent work on Addams and Hull House, my interpretation departs from well-known characterizations of this famous woman and the settlement movement. Much of the literature on Jane Addams and Hull House describes Addams as a benevolent crusader, a chauvinistic meddler, or a forebear of professional social work.[9] More recently, scholars have focused on the significance of Addams and Hull House within women's political culture.[10] Such works have identified the settlement as a significant locus in generating a gendered social science that women used to shape the emerging welfare state. To varying degrees these descriptions capture Addams's place in American social reform. She devoted her life to helping working people and immigrants; in the process she redefined many ideas about the urban environment and the role of the state. She was a significant leader of Progressive Era women who linked their experience within a female network of social reform to the suffrage movement and a gendered conception of citizenship. However, she was also deeply influenced by her upper-middle-class background, and at times her interactions with her poor and ethnic neighbors reflected the problems of power and hierarchy in social reform. Ultimately, she moved toward a conception of social knowledge that was

8. Brown, *Education of Jane Addams*, 6.

9. Shannon Jackson, *Lines of Activity: Performance, Historiography, Hull-House Domesticity* (Ann Arbor: University of Michigan Press, 2000); Davis, *American Heroine;* Farrell, *Beloved Lady;* Levine, *Jane Addams and the Liberal Tradition;* Kathryn Kish Sklar, "Hull House in the 1890s: A Community of Women Reformers," *Signs* 10, no. 4 (1985): 658–77. Muncy, *Creating a Female Dominion,* and Allan Davis, *Spearheads of Reform* (New York: Oxford University Press, 1967), focus on Addams's contributions to American social work and the formation of the welfare state. For a more critical view of Addams, see Rivka Shpak Lissak, *Pluralism and Progressives* (Chicago: University of Chicago Press, 1989).

10. Jackson, *Lines of Activity;* Kathryn Kish Sklar, *Florence Kelley and the Nation's Work* (New Haven: Yale University Press, 1995); Muncy, *Creating a Female Dominion;* Regene Henriette Spero Silver, "Jane Addams: Peace, Justice, Gender, 1860–1918" (PhD diss., University of Pennsylvania, 1990); Rebecca Sherrick, "Private Visions, Public Lives: The Hull-House Women in the Progressive Era" (PhD diss., Northwestern University, 1980); Helen Lefkowitz Horowitz, "Hull-House as Women's Space," *Chicago History* 12, no. 4 (December 1983): 40–55.

more democratic and relational, driving her and the residents at Hull House to work *with* the poor, not *for* the poor.[11]

Several recent studies have placed Addams and Hull House within a burgeoning literature on gendered social knowledge. Building on feminist theory, this literature argues that women activists and social thinkers offered ways of knowing that emphasized the contingent, the situational, and the relational.[12] Its subject of study most often focused on women and children or the domestic sphere. Sharing much with pragmatism, women social scientists and reform activists emphasized the primacy of experience and proximity, sought to create communal processes for experimentation and reflection, and wed inquiry and social action. Such methods were the hallmark of Hull House and Addams's mature thinking, as Dorothy Ross, Charlene Haddock Seigfried, Shannon Jackson, Katherine Kish Sklar, Victoria Brown, Louise Knight, and others have shown. This chapter owes much to these works on Addams, and many of the incidents and interpretations here will be familiar to historians knowledgeable about literature on Addams and Hull House. These previous works allow me to situate them as a part of the broader reorientation of social knowledge underway in Chicago social reform. Let me now highlight some significant features of her biography that laid the foundation for democratic social knowledge.

Jane Addams must have felt at home in the world of Chicago's philanthropists and club women when she moved to the city in 1889. Born in 1860 in Cedarville, Illinois, she shared the small-town background of many of Chicago's leading citizens and had been educated as a privileged daughter of the northern Illinois commercial and political elite.[13] She attended Rockford Female Seminary, where

11. Brown emphasizes this point in *The Education of Jane Addams*. Closely analyzing Addams's letters, her upbringing, and the influences upon her youth, Brown explores Addams's transformation toward participatory democracy. In *Citizen*, Knight presents a slightly different but intriguing account of Addams's journey toward democracy. She explores intellectual influences such as Christianity, idealism, and humanitarianism, as well as Addams's friendships and experiences as formative in her more gradual evolution toward her democratic theory.

12. Charlene Haddock Seigfried, *Pragmatism and Feminism: Reweaving the Social Fabric* (Chicago: University of Chicago Press, 1996); Jackson, *Lines of Activity*; Ross, "Gendered Social Knowledge"; Sklar, "*Hull-House Maps and Papers*: Social Science as Women's Work in the 1890s," in *Gender and American Social Science*, ed. Silverberg, 127–55; Elshtain, *Jane Addams and the Dream of American Democracy*.

13. Kathleen McCarthy, *Noblesse Oblige: Charity and Cultural Philanthropy in Chicago, 1849–1929* (Chicago: University of Chicago Press, 1982), and James Gilbert, *Perfect Cities: Chicago's Utopias of 1893* (Chicago: University of Chicago Press, 1991), both examine the small-town heritage of many of Chicago's leading citizens in the 1890s. John Huy Addams was perhaps the most influential figure of Jane's formative years. He belonged to no church and contributed financially to all four denominations in Cedarville, and he instilled in his daughter the importance of personal integrity

her father had served as a trustee. The seminary emphasized social duty and service, and Addams wrestled with her conscience over matters of religious faith, a
task no doubt made more difficult by pressure from faculty members and classmates to have a conversion experience and take up missionary work.[14] Plagued
by doubts, Addams rejected such religious commitments, however. When she
graduated in 1881, she had no clear path for her future.

However, following her graduation, Addams was caught up in the "family
claim," struggling, as did many women of her class, to carve out a life for herself
that offered freedom and intellectual stimulation and still conformed to society's
gendered expectations. Her father died shortly after her graduation, and Addams
split her time attending to her stepmother and helping her married siblings. The
years she spent with her stepmother, Anna Haldeman Addams, were difficult,
though they prepared the young woman for Chicago society life; they also positioned her as a peacekeeper in the family.[15] Her widowed father had remarried

in spiritual matters. His strong belief in stewardship impressed young Jane, as did his belief that
education and religion could transform society. His political career, both as a founding member of
the Republican party and a state legislator, helps explain his daughter's political savvy. Since Jane's
mother died when Jane was barely three, her father exercised the most pervasive moral and intellectual influence over her during her childhood and adolescence, encouraging her to read the entire
contents of his library, including works such as Thomas Carlyle's *Heroes and Hero Worship* and
Plutarch's *Lives,* as well as numerous Emerson essays and treatises. Farrell, *Beloved Lady,* 36; Brown,
Education of Jane Addams; Addams, *Twenty Years* (1981), 27, 41, 48–49.

For discussion of issues of historical accuracy and intriguing narrative threads in Addams's
construction of her memoir, see Victoria Bissell Brown, "Introduction," in Jane Addams, *Twenty
Years at Hull-House,* ed. Victoria Bissell Brown, 11-30 (Boston: Bedford/St. Martin's, 1999). See also
Brown, *Education of Jane Addams,* for discussion of this issue. For interpretation of Addams's rela-
tionship with her father that emphasizes his patriarchal authority in making decisions, particularly
educational ones, for his daughter, see Louise W. Knight, "Biography's Window on Social Change:
Benevolence and Justice in Jane Addams's "A Modern Lear," *Journal of Women's History* 9 no. 1
(Spring 1997): 111–38.

14. Like Mount Holyoke, Rockford's religious affiliations were Congregational and Presbyterian.
On Addams's school days see Brown, *Education of Jane Addams,* and Farrell, *Beloved Lady,* 27–39.
Also see Addams, *Twenty Years* (1981), 46–59; Crunden, *Ministers of Reform;* and Brown, *The Education of Jane Addams,* 58–59, as well as the following chapters for discussions of Addams's religious
struggles.

15. Victoria Brown explains that, during this time, Addams's family became ever more complicated, putting her in the position of mediator. Her brother Weber struggled throughout his life with
mental and physical illness, leaving his wife and daughter in need of family help. Her sister Alice
married her stepbrother Harry Haldeman, creating complex fissures in the family. Her overly sensitive stepbrother George never married and spent much of his adult life battling mental illness, while
his mother grew ever more bitter at her circumstances—and her stepchildren. Addams coped with
her family throughout this period—and throughout her life—with equanimity, attending to family
needs when possible but refusing to be drawn into their battles. By emphasizing this context, Brown
helps us understand the origins of Addams's personal style and her political commitments after
she moved into public life at Hull House. Her refusal to take sides and her unflagging belief that all
conflicts could be resolved grew out of the disposition she fashioned as the family mediator. Addams
escaped to Europe in 1886 with a group of friends, including Ellen Starr. It was on this trip abroad
that she visited Toynbee Hall and decided to open a settlement house herself. Addams's decision to

when Jane was eight, and by all accounts, Anna Addams was an accomplished Victorian lady who ascribed to the ideals of domesticity. She encouraged Jane to take on the roles of wife and mother and pressured her to choose a genteel lifestyle. Perhaps to fulfill her own social aspirations, as well as influence her stepdaughter, Anna moved the family to Baltimore and into eastern social circles following John's death. Socializing, parties, and European travel completed Jane's education for a woman's upper-middle class Victorian life.[16] In the midst of these social functions, Addams found herself suffering from "nervous depression and [a] sense of maladjustment."[17] Anna's aspirations for Jane underscored the difficulties the young woman faced. Her father's moral influence, her college education, and her extensive reading in social criticism and literary classics had taught her the value of service.[18]

Looking back on these years, Addams saw her struggles in light of the classed gender transformation women of her cohort experienced. She posited that the first generation of college women "had departed too suddenly from the active, emotional life led by their grandmothers and great-grandmothers[,] that the contemporary education of young women had developed too exclusively the power of acquiring knowledge and of merely receiving impressions." Women had struggled to obtain higher education but found few career opportunities. Furthermore, Addams decried the fact that "somewhere in the process of 'being educated' they had lost that simple and almost automatic response to the human appeal, that old healthful reaction resulting in activity from the mere presence of suffering or of helplessness."[19] Suggesting that women had legitimate work as caretakers, a mature Addams took a critical view of service that was stripped of humanitarian connection. But hers was not an essentialist view of women's emotional nature. Rather, it reflected a pragmatist understanding of the role of emotion in human thought and action. For pragmatists, emotions pervaded experience. When the emotional experience is one of perplexity or social sympathy, it serves as the basis for inquiry and a motivation for action.[20] An education that encouraged young women to observe and analyze life but frowned on their

open a social settlement was a complex one, though her visit to Toynbee Hall was formative in her thinking about the kind of place she wanted to create.

16. For accounts of Anna Haldeman Addams and her relationship with her step-daughter, see Brown, *Education of Jane Addams*, chapters 7–10.

17. Addams, *Twenty Years* (1981), 67.

18. Ibid., 57.

19. Ibid., 64.

20. Charlene Haddock Seigfried, in her introduction to Jane Addams, *Democracy and Social Ethics* (Urbana: University of Illinois Press, 2002), xxiii–xxv. Seigfried offers an especially helpful discussion of Addams's ideas about social morality and sympathy in comparison to John Dewey and William James. For discussion of a pragmatist's reconciliation of emotion and objectivity, see Seigfried, *Pragmatism and Feminism*, 164–69. Dewey suggested that "Emotion is an indication of intimate participation" (ibid., 164).

active participation in the public realm encouraged a sense of uselessness and passivity.[21]

The sense of maladjustment and restlessness Addams experienced had a religious, as well as gendered, root. During her college years, she searched for a spiritual foundation that would reconcile her weak loyalties to any particular Christian church and her strong desire for a code of ethics that demanded committed humanitarian action. Addams believed it crucial that she resolve such dilemmas, and she ultimately forged her own brand of ethical action.[22] Imagining the deity in feminine terms helped her in her quest. She wrote of trying to dig to the bottom of all systems of religion, "back to a great Primal cause—not nature, exactly but a fostering Mother, a necessity, brooding and watching over all things, above every human passion."[23] As historian Victoria Brown suggests, contrary to early nineteenth-century Christian masculine images of God as patriarchal father or stern judge, Addams's vision of God was motherly, nurturing, and concerned about her earthly creation. Even so, Addams reclaims for her feminized version of God the masculine traits of a God who is "quiet, calm, dignified, self-reliant, even brooding, even cold."[24] Addams's vision of God thus maintained a masculine strength that avoided the excesses of female sentimentality. In such musings, Brown points out, Addams flirted with the idea of gender as a cultural construct, but more important, she valorized the feminine. By characterizing the deity in such terms, she seemed to be seeking a way to claim both masculine and feminine traits for women.

Addams valued women's unique social experience and the intuition and insight it encouraged. In a speech at the Rockford Seminary junior class convocation, she linked her religious vision with an ethical code, again conveyed in gendered terms.[25] Drawing upon "the old ideal of womanhood—the Saxon lady

21. Ellen Fitzgerald, *Endless Crusade: Women Social Scientists and Progressive Reform* (New York, 1990); Barbara Solomon, *In the Company of Educated Women: A History of Women and Higher Education in America* (New Haven: Yale University Press, 1985).

22. Her personal need for religion prompted her to "go ahead building my religion where I can find it, from the Bible and observation, from books and people, and in no small degree from Carlyle." More important to Addams than evangelical notions of faith and salvation, then, was her belief in finding a path to ethical action, as it was revealed through religion, experience, and history. Jane Addams to Ellen Gates Starr, November 22, 1879; Jane Addams Microfilm, Swarthmore College Peace Collection (hereafter cited as JAP), Reel 1.

23. Jane Addams to Ellen Gates Starr, August 11, 1879; JAP, Reel 1. See Brown, *Education of Jane Addams*. Ellen Gates Starr (1859–1940) was a classmate of Addams for a year at Rockford Female Seminary. She left after only one year, but she and Addams remained close friends, corresponding, traveling, and eventually living together. See *Notable American Women, 1607–1950; A Biographical Dictionary*, ed. Edward T. James, vol. 3 (Cambridge, MA: Belknap Press of Harvard University Press, 1971), 351–53.

24. Brown, *Education of Jane Addams*, 88–89. As Brown points out, such a literary and intellectual move helped her rationalize the "masculine" ambition and public role she envisioned for herself.

25. For more on the following interpretations of "The Breadgivers" and "Cassandra," see ibid.,

whose mission it was to give bread unto her household," Addams likened the call of her generation to that ancient female role. "We have planned," she announced, "to be 'Bread-givers' throughout our lives, believing that in labor alone is happiness, and that the only true and honorable life is one filled with good works and honest toil, we have planned to idealize our labor, and thus happily fulfil [sic] woman's noblest mission."[26] Echoing traditional liberal republican notions of labor and separate spheres, her language cast labor as character forming, even redemptive, and seemingly located women's work in the private realm of the home. However, in Addams's essay, the educated woman's "noblest mission" was not to minister to her family alone but to the wider family of humanity; Addams implied as much in her recognition that perhaps a "turn of fortune" would confine some classmates "to the literal meaning of our words," leaving them enclosed in the private, domestic world. While she acknowledged that such work offered spiritual fulfillment, Addams herself was seeking a means to make women's work—her own work—public rather than entirely private.

She followed "The Breadgivers" with a valedictory address that likened the intuition woman gained from her social experience with a feminized construction of knowledge. This time she drew upon the Greek tragedy of Cassandra, a Trojan woman gifted with prophecy who foretold the destruction of her city. Emphasizing that Cassandra "had no logic to convince the defeated warriors, and no facts to gain their confidence," Addams illustrated the paradoxical situation in which nineteenth-century women found themselves.[27] Their "feminine trait of mind" provided them with "a mighty intuitive perception of Truth which yet counts for nothing in the force of the world." To overcome the subjective and suspect qualities of intuition in an intellectual environment that increasingly privileged social science, Addams counseled women to study science, so that they might gain "*aeuthoritas,* the right of a speaker to make herself heard." She recognized that scientific knowledge offered women public authority. Women could "prove to the world that an intuition is a force in the universe, and a part of nature; that an intuitive perception committed to a woman's charge is not a prejudice or a fancy, but one of the holy means given to mankind in their search for truth." By merging this perception with scientific methods, women might "bring this force [of intuition] to bear throughout morals and justice."[28] Considering her female audience, it is not surprising that Addams's discussion of intuition is feminized. But more significant is her marriage of intuition and empiricism as a starting point for inquiry. This vision of epistemology was at odds with the growing scientism that privileged a positivist empiricism alone.

92-99 and Ross, "Social Knowledge."

26. Addams, "The Breadgivers," quoted in the *Rockford Register,* April 21, 1880.

27. Addams, "Cassandra," JAP, Reel 27.

28. Ibid.

These two college essays provide insight into the foundation of Addams's maturing worldview, which later shaped her activities at Hull House. In the "Breadgivers" Addams idealizes labor, particularly that which ministers to biological needs and is historically women's work; the labor of providing food, literally and figuratively, assumed a spiritual significance that gave meaning to life, particularly as it became public work. Addams implied that all people were bound together by their dependence upon the fulfillment of the essential physical demands of food, shelter, and clothing. These biological necessities, particularly the instinct to feed and care for the young, subsumed all else. By expanding the purview of women's domestic responsibilities into a context wider than the family, Addams extended this feminine ideal into a basis for a broadly humanistic ethic that challenged the individualism and self-interested aspects of liberal republicanism. Such an understanding, however, was still embryonic during her college years.

In "Cassandra" she more directly explained women's contributions to social knowledge. Furthermore, she envisioned social science as the result of a pragmatic effort; it would take "the active busy world as a test for the genuineness of [woman's] intuition."[29] Long before she read William James or met John Dewey, Addams had proposed a pragmatic test for the validity of social knowledge. By the end of her college years, she had thus articulated the core values that served as the foundation for her life's work: a spiritualized and cooperative labor modeled on social Christian principles; a gendered social knowledge based not on an essentialist understanding of womanhood but on women's social experience, a knowledge that might broaden public responsibility along more humanitarian lines; and a pragmatic basis for knowledge and social truth that justified a prominent place for women in social science and reform.

Absent from her ideas at this time were the democratic implications of working alongside society's marginalized. She still clung to a vision of heroic stewardship, though it would soon be transformed. Addams spent her college years and the eight years following in coming to terms with the fact that traditional forms of private domestic life and heroic stewardship did not offer her a viable way to pursue these ends. In January 1889, then, after years of searching for a way to act upon the ethics she articulated when she left Rockford Seminary, Addams settled upon work in Chicago.

The Scheme: Gender, Class, and Networks of Reform

When Jane Addams moved to Chicago in 1889 to open Hull House, she joined an active reform community that was rich with women's clubs, philanthropic associations, and cultural institutions. These networks were shaped by gender

29. Ibid.

and class in ways that were important for the settlement and its founders. This section outlines this broader community in order to locate Hull House in Chicago's reform landscape.

On Friday, February 14, 1889, Mrs. T. W. Harvey visited Addams. The venerable Mrs. Harvey, wife of the city's wealthy lumber and railroad car magnate, frankly told Addams she had come to investigate her. Addams knew Julia Harvey only by her reputation as "a great power in the Woman's [sic] Club in which she [had] held various offices."[30] Mrs. Harvey had heard of Addams from friends in the Chicago Woman's Club who had learned of the plan to open a social settlement house. Modeled after Toynbee Hall in east London, the young women's settlement would stress the importance of neighborly relationships between middle- and upper-class residents and working people of the city.[31] Like Toynbee Hall, cultural uplift initially shaped its reform and educational goals. However, Toynbee Hall was a male project, connected to Oxford University, and headed by a local minister. Addams and her friend Ellen Starr proposed something different; they would run the secular settlement themselves.

The superintendent of the Armour Mission and Dr. Hollister, a member of its board, were their first enthusiastic converts and invited Addams to speak before the entire board on February 9.[32] On the appointed day, Addams, with Dr. Hollister beside her on the platform, told her audience of the plan to open a house, complete with upper-middle-class comforts and refinement—but in the midst of one of Chicago's poor, immigrant sections—where she and Ellen Starr would live as neighbors to the local residents. "The effect was mixed," she wrote to her sister. "Mr. McCord the old minister who presided evidently thought I was . . . talking sheer nonsense."[33] The idea of two single women choosing to live unprotected in the poverty and danger of the city was certainly what one audience member described as "the strangest thing he had met in his experience."[34] But

30. Jane Addams to Mary Addams Linn, February 19, 1889; JAP, Reel 2. For discussion of the female reform network in which the club operated, see Maureen Flanagan, *Seeing with Their Hearts: Chicago Women and the Vision of the Good City, 1871–1933* (Princeton, NJ: Princeton University Press, 2002).

31. Mina Carson, *Settlement Folk: Social Thought and the American Settlement Movement, 1885–1930* (Chicago: University of Chicago Press, 1990); Standish Meacham, *Toynbee Hall and Social Reform, 1880–1914: The Search for Community* (New Haven, CT: Yale University Press, 1987); Addams, "The Outgrowths of Toynbee Hall," JAP, Reel 47.

32. The Armour Mission on Thirty-first and Clybourne Avenue was opened through the efforts of Plymouth Congregational Church and funding by Philip D. Armour. Despite its original church affiliations, it professed to be nonsectarian and offered self-improvement programs such as manual training classes for boys, domestic courses for girls, and a library. See Kathleen McCarthy, *Noblesse Oblige*, 93–94.

33. Addams to Mary Addams Linn, February 12, 1889; JAP, Reel 2.

34. Addams, *Twenty Years* (1981), 88. As Joanne Meyerowitz has described, middle-class gender expectations discouraged women from living alone. See Joanne J. Meyerowitz *Women Adrift: Independent Wage Earners in Chicago, 1880–1930* (Chicago: University of Chicago Press, 1988).

the younger listeners were enthusiastic and offered their support if the women began work in the neighborhood of the mission. Alan Pond, a rising architect who later served on the Hull House board of trustees, "assured me that I had *voiced* something hundreds of young people in the city were trying to express, & that he could send us three young ladies at once who possessed both money and a knowledge of Herbert Spencer's 'Sociology' but who were dying from inaction and restlessness."[35] It was this earnest young woman with such odd ideas that Mrs. Harvey came to investigate.

Upon hearing of the scheme, Mrs. Sears, a member of the Woman's Club and a volunteer at the Armour Mission, told Addams and Starr she did not want them to become "the adjunct of any mission" and undoubtedly spurred Harvey and the Woman's Club to action.[36] Mrs. Harvey arranged for Addams and Starr to present their plan to the Woman's Club philanthropy committee. Upon hearing of the idea, the shocked older ladies on the committee cried that "surprises never cease," and a lively discussion ensued. By the end of the meeting, Addams must have sighed with relief, for the "effect was very good," and the two friends added the club members to their growing list of supporters.[37]

Even with the support of the Woman's Club, the idea of two young ladies living alone in a poor neighborhood greatly challenged the mores of Chicago's society set and the city's patterns of philanthropy. The two decades of urban growth and reconfiguration following the Great Fire had transformed Chicago's philanthropic activities and the elites' conception of their civic stewardship.[38] The growing middle class, seeking to emphasize its own status, increasingly frowned upon contact with the poor; working-class areas of the city were deemed unpleasant and even dangerous, and women abandoned their former patterns of benevolent work that had brought them into the homes of their poorer neighbors. Instead they organized clubs that discussed social issues, sponsored projects to discover and advance humanitarian principles, and threw charity balls, dispensing the money to institutions that other people, increasingly (male) professionals, ran.[39] Friendly visiting of the sort their mothers and grandmothers engaged in gave way to impersonal financial management on behalf of charities such as the Relief and Aid Society.

As we saw in chapter 2, the RAS employed the techniques of scientific charity such as registration of needy recipients, friendly visiting, and work tests,

---

35. Jane Addams to Mary Addams Linn, February 12, 1889; JAP, Reel 2.
36. Ibid. For discussion of the gendered differences in the way the project was received in Protestant circles, see Brown, 214–16.
37. Jane Addams to Mary Addams Linn, February 19, 1889; JAP, Reel 2. As Brown notes, Addams undoubtedly exaggerated her meetings with Harvey and the Women's Club philanthropy committee to win family approval for her scheme. Brown, 372, *Education of Jane Addams*, n. 36.
38. McCarthy, *Noblesse Oblige*, 27.
39. "Resolution" in Chicago Woman's Club Minutes, December 12, 1883.

with the express purpose of preventing fraud and dependence believed to be encouraged by indiscriminate giving. The RAS served as a bulwark against direct contact between the rich and the poor: "[I]ts work is to offer to all persons in Chicago who are disposed to help the suffering and worthy poor, but have not the time nor inclination to do it themselves with the caution which the subject demands."[40] Founded in 1883, the Charity Organization Society (COS) competed with the RAS. While the RAS accepted the permanence of poverty, the COS instead sought the elimination of pauperism through social science methods and neighborliness.[41] In 1888 the two organizations merged, but the more powerful RAS took over and transformed the COS. When Addams presented her plan to Chicago's elite, the dominant attitude among the wealthy philanthropists reflected the attitude of the RAS and continued to discourage them from seeking personal contact with the poor.

The entrenchment of the RAS as Chicago's primary philanthropic body also brought new patterns of gender relations within such organizations. Whereas women had almost exclusive leadership of antebellum charity and relief institutions, their leadership dwindled following the Civil War and the Great Fire, when the predominately male RAS emerged as the leading institution among Chicago's charities. Yet women still challenged assumptions about power and the public good. Women's response to the fire, their argument that all were entitled to immediate help, not just the "worthy," put them at odds with civic elites and recast matters of relief as public questions.[42] In light of these differences along gender lines, it is suggestive that Mrs. Sears, a volunteer for the male-dominated Armour Mission, steered Addams and Starr away from the mission. Perhaps she feared their work and their independence would have been lost within the institution and its powerful male sponsors. Indeed, activist-minded women were busy building their own networks and alliances to promote municipal reform and women's suffrage outside of male-dominated organizations.[43]

Women's organizations took root in Gilded Age Chicago and by the 1890s were actively promoting cross-class and cross-ethnic endeavors. The Chicago Woman's Club was organized in 1876 with the intention of fostering discussion about social problems; early topics included free trade, sociology, and women's relation to church and state.[44] Study and internal debate soon turned into

40. Chicago Relief and Aid Society, *Annual Report,* 1880, 8.

41. Charity Organization Society, *Annual Report of the Directors of the Charity Organization Society of Chicago,* 1886; W. Alexander Johnson, "Methods and Machinery of the Organization of Charity," from the *Annual Report of the Charity Organization of Chicago,* 1887; John Albert Mayer, "Private Charity in Chicago from 1971 to 1915" (PhD diss., University of Minnesota, 1978); McCarthy, *Noblesse Oblige.*

42. Flanagan, *Seeing with Their Heart,* 27–29.

43. See Flanagan, *Seeing with Their Hearts,* 31–55.

44. Henrietta Greenebaum Frank and Amale Hofer Jerome, *Annals of the Chicago Woman's Club*

action as the club sponsored the first kindergarten in the city, obtained appoint-ments of women to the Board of Education, and joined forces in 1885 with the Women's Christian Temperance Union, the Cook County Woman's Suffrage Club, the Moral Education Association, and other organizations to establish the Protective Agency for Women and Children, which worked within the legal system to secure safety and justice for victims of domestic abuse; it was the only organization of its kind in the nation.[45] Care of children and the poor, tradi-tionally defined as the province of women, sparked coordinated reform efforts among African Americans, immigrants, native-born residents, middle-class club women, and working women. The Illinois Woman's Alliance, for example, was created in 1888 by representatives of various women's organizations, including the Chicago Woman's Club, Ladies Federal Labor Union, Cook County Suffrage Association, and the Chicago Trade and Labor Assembly.[46]

As government began to intervene in matters believed to be women's prov-ince (largely because women pressured it to do so), female activists argued that their social experiences must be brought to bear in public discussion. Women used this domestic discourse to position themselves as experts with practical experience and knowledge about education, child rearing, the home, and the ways that political and economic practices touched their lives, homes, and neighborhoods.[47] This logic of municipal housekeeping invoked arguments of

---

for the First Forty Years of Its Organization, 1876–1916 (Chicago: Chicago Woman's Club, 1916), 30.

45. Ibid., 53; Meredith Tax, *The Rising of the Women* (New York: Monthly Review Press, 1980), 74–75; Elizabeth Pleck, *Domestic Tyranny: The Making of Social Policy against Family Violence from Colonial Times to the Present* (New York: Oxford University Press, 1987), especially 88–107.

46. Sparked by outrage over sweatshop labor, the Illinois Woman's Alliance developed a solidar-ity around three fundamental principles: "1) the actual status of the poorest and most unfortunate woman in society determines the possible status of every woman; 2) the civilization of the future depends upon the present condition of the children; 3) public money and public officials must serve public ends." Tax, *Rising of the Women*, 71. These principles, reflecting activism based upon gender identity, challenged the boundaries of traditional liberal republicanism. The first principle indicated a recognition of the precarious position of women, particularly in a male-oriented political economy. As women faced limited property and legal rights, they understood that, regardless of class or ethnic background, their status was largely dependent on men and subject to circumstances often beyond their control. All women might be treated as the "poorest and most unfortunate woman in society." They implicitly emphasized the relational nature of society and the need for group organi-zation. Individualism simply would not help women achieve power and rights. The second principle furthered this position by building on a maternalist ethic to care for the marginalized. It politicized women's efforts on behalf of themselves and their children by suggesting an argument for an ethic of care and public responsibility. And in the third principle they articulated the logical conclusion—an activist government whose public ends were not narrowly defined as business interests. See Evelyn NaKano Glenn, *Unequal Freedom: How Race and Gender Shaped American Citizenship and Labor* (Cambridge, MA: Harvard University Press, 2002), 46; Pleck, *Domestic Tyranny*.

47. For further discussion of women's use of expertise, see Camilla Stivers, *Bureau Men, Settle-ment Women: Constructing Public Administration in the Progressive Era* (Lawrence: University Press of Kansas, 2000), and Robin Bachin, *Building the South Side: Urban Space and Civic Culture in*

women's social experiences to explain their entrance into politics: "[T]hese two departments of government concerning the children and the poor and sick are quite in keeping with the place assigned to woman in the social economy and in direct line of development with her position in society in the past."[48] On the one hand, such appeals along gendered spheres of influence suggest the pervasive hold of sex roles and the elaborate rationalizations needed to justify the expansion of the "woman's sphere." On the other hand, women carefully avoided reference to an essentialist special nature in their description of the role "assigned to women in the social economy."[49] This shared identity encompassing women's social experience served to bridge class, ethnic, and racial lines, just as abolitionists two generations earlier had hoped the commonalities of womanhood would draw white and African American women together.[50]

Men also spearheaded another form of charity that emerged among elites in the 1880s and 1890s—that of cultural philanthropy. Illustrating ideas popularized in Andrew Carnegie's "Gospel of Wealth," Chicago's numerous self-made men envisioned a society held together by cultural institutions bestowed by the rich and patronized by the "fit."[51] Fearing that materialism and the declining intrinsic value of labor would lead to individual and collective moral degeneration, they turned to the arts to promote civic life. Business elites built a myriad of cultural institutions aiming to foster order, stability, and civic pride among citizens. Drawing on the ideas of John Ruskin and Matthew Arnold, cultural philanthropists believed that art could express the fixed, natural ideal of human existence, and they relied on its didactic power to counter the materialism and dehumanization of industrial Chicago.[52] The Newberry Library, Field Museum, Art Institute, Chicago Public Library, and Crerar Library were opened with the hope that they would help Chicago's citizens appreciate "higher" culture. By locating these institutions in the downtown

---

Chicago, 1890–1919 (Chicago: University of Chicago Press, 2004). On domestic discourse see Nancy Cott, *Bonds of Womanhood;* Ross, "Gendered Social Knowledge."

48. Frank and Jerome, *Annals of the Chicago Woman's Club,* 14.

49. In *Seeing with Their Hearts,* Maureen Flanagan implicitly essentializes the differences between men's and women's civic visions. Though clearly some women were committed to a maternalist agenda because they believed in their essential differences from men, others, as the earlier quote from the Chicago Woman's Club illustrates, were aware of the effects of social and cultural narratives of gender. The gendered strategy worked since those cultural definitions of "woman" were in a state of flux in the 1890s, with older associations between womanhood and the domestic sphere holding a tight grip on the popular imagination.

50. Jean Fagan Yellin and John C. Van Horne, eds., *The Abolitionist Sisterhood: Women's Political Culture in Antebellum America* (Ithaca, NY: Cornell University Press, 1994).

51. McCarthy, *Noblesse Oblige,* especially 51–72. See also *Handbook of Chicago Charities,* available Chicago Historical Society.

52. Helen Lefkowitz Horowitz, *Culture and the City* (Chicago: University of Chicago Pres, 1976); Raymond Williams, *Culture and Society* (New York: Columbia University Press, 1983).

area, the businessmen sought to draw residents into the city, thus reintegrating them into civic life.[53]

Addams thus publicized and sought support for her ideas among a reform-minded elite that espoused a range of beliefs about social responsibility and the nature of philanthropy. To each of these groups her plan offered exciting possibilities. To older society men and women, Addams harked back to pre-fire memories of women's neighborly duty. To educated young men and women, Hull House provided a practical means to use the social science principles they learned in college and read about in popular sociology. Since Addams modeled her scheme on Toynbee Hall, a project dedicated to reform through education and uplift, it struck several responsive chords in Chicago's cultural philanthropic circles. And Addams appealed to the Woman's Club at a transitional point in its history, when it was increasingly politicized and sought to redefine its activities with a gendered notion of social responsibility. In spite of their differences, however, everyone could agree that Addams's desire to live and work directly among the poor transgressed the social boundaries of safe and ladylike activity.

What Addams and Starr proposed doubly challenged class and gender expectations since young, single women living alone were already morally suspect, and members of the upper class living intimately with workers, paupers, and vice peddlers was ignoble—even for those who sought to reform them. In her youth, Addams had fashioned a "heroic stewardship" that emphasized the important role an individual could play in ameliorating human distress.[54] But by the time she and Starr began mingling with Chicago philanthropists, she had adopted a different paradigm of social change, one in which sharing the daily experiences of and living in neighborly relation to the poor and working classes were essential. The seeds of her transformation were planted in her youth, though they did not mature until after her move to the Nineteenth Ward.

Part 2. Adding the Social Function to Democracy: Mutuality in Democratic Social Knowledge

Opening a settlement house wrought a transformation in Addams's naïve ideas about social reform and led her toward a life of adding the social function to democracy. She struggled to break free of conventional feminine roles while still finding ways to bring the valuable insights of female social experience to bear on public life and to challenge the conventional class expectations of a

53. Horowitz, *Culture and the City*, 117.
54. Brown, *Education of Jane Addams*.

reformer, which would have distanced her from the immigrants and poor people with whom she worked. Settlement work offered Addams a template for more direct interaction with these populations, and the version of settlement work she and Starr espoused valorized the feminine. The early years that unfolded at Hull House took its residents toward a relational and proximate democratic social knowledge born of shared experience, toward a respect for the insight and experience that neighbors were able to offer to reform, and toward a version of democracy defined in terms of social relations and everyday practice.

In perhaps an autobiographical account of this time in her life, Addams captures the sense of alienation permeating urban life that settlement living might overcome:

> You may remember the forlorn feeling which occasionally seizes you when you arrive early in the morning a stranger in a great city: the stream of laboring people goes past you as you gaze through the plate-glass window of your hotel; you see hard workingmen lifting great burdens; you hear the driving and jostling of huge carts and your heart sinks with a sudden sense of futility. The door opens behind you and you turn to the man who brings you in your breakfast with a quick sense of human fellowship. You find yourself praying that you may never lose your hold on it all. A more poetic prayer would be that the great breasts of our common humanity, with its labor and suffering and homely comforts, may never be withheld from you. You turn helplessly to the waiter and feel that it would be almost grotesque to claim from him the sympathy you crave because civilization has placed you apart, but you resent your position with a sudden sense of snobbery.[55]

Describing the figure as a "stranger in a great city," Addams evokes a sense of isolation and of the fatal drifting apart fostered by the urban landscape. The division appeared along class and gender lines, particularly in the appropriation of space. Because it is physically insulated from work and the public street, the "solitary figure" seems feminine and resonates with the dissatisfaction Addams felt as an educated woman discouraged from active participation in those realms. She also returns here to the valorization of labor and a feminine image of a mother-god figure. But in this description the reference to a feminine deity is much less distant than in her letter to Starr a decade earlier, conjuring up images of physical interaction with her children through the uniquely female role of nursing. The universal experience of original helplessness and need of a mother for sustenance and comfort suggest a commonality that binds all people. Yet Addams goes on to illustrate how modern society has interfered with basic

55. Addams, *Twenty Years* (1981), 92–93.

human connections. As the entrance of the waiter suggests, the class nature of modern industrial society precluded interaction; indeed, the middle-class woman and the working man are unable to speak to each other in any meaningful way even when brought face to face.

The image of the plate-glass window suggests that the isolation of urban life is spatial, highlighting that in the modern city one spectates but does not participate. Addams's description richly illustrates the ideas of social theorists who have argued that transformations in social behavior wrought by the nineteenth-century city made public behavior a matter of observation, passive participation, and a kind of voyeurism. The "invisible wall of silence" that separated city dwellers "meant that knowledge in public was a matter of observation—of scenes, of other men and women, of locales. Knowledge was no longer to be produced by social intercourse."[56]

The social settlement sought to overcome these problems of isolation and distanced observation. Its encouragement of social interaction grew out of a belief in sympathetic human nature then current in social science theory. Evolutionary sociology and social psychology posited sympathetic and cooperative foundations of social life as they articulated a new social self. Such theories developed in reaction to Herbert Spencer's and William Graham Sumner's laissez-faire sociology. Lester Frank Ward's *Dynamic Sociology* (1883) led such attacks. Ward agreed with social Darwinists that human society was evolutionary, but he explained progress not in terms of survival of the fittest but as the result of human effort; cultural gains accrued through cooperative endeavors to further intelligence and improve the human environment.[57] Such ideas appeared throughout the young social science disciplines, particularly in the American Economic Association, founded by notable social scientists such as Richard Ely and Henry Carter Adams, who became acquaintances and supporters of Addams.[58] Developmental psychology and philosophy further explained social life and language as cooperative endeavors; the individual's realization of its self and development of reason occurred only in relation to the community and was mediated through symbolic action.

Such social science theories only confirmed what Hull House residents learned inductively in the Nineteenth Ward. The patterns of relationship among settlement neighbors emphasized the sociability and interdependence of life in urban communities. The poor depended upon extended family, neighbors, churches, and ethnic societies for help in times of unemployment and illness.

56. Richard Sennett, *The Fall of Public Man* (New York: Cambridge University Press, 1977), 27.

57. Ross, *The Origins of American Social Science* (Cambridge, New York: Cambridge University Press, 1991), 91–94; Ellsworth R. Fuhrman, *The Sociology of Knowledge in America, 1883–1915* (Charlottesville: University Press of Virginia, 1980), 75–99.

58. Ross, *Origins of American Social Sciences*; Sklansky, *Soul's Economy*.

In times of trouble, families often relied upon a neighbor to share a meal or take them in when eviction left them homeless.[59] Addams noted that "the fact that the economic condition of all alike is on a most precarious level makes the ready outflow of sympathy and material assistance the most natural thing in the world."[60] Such practices countered suspicion and the concern for social control that lay beneath rigid standards of middle-class scientific charity. While her comments here illustrate Addams's tendency to romanticize and universalize her neighbors' generosity, it also captures an important survival strategy. Mutuality, whether in the form of ethnic societies, labor unions, or religious ties, shaped the lives of immigrants and the working classes. These forms of mutuality, particularly that of labor unions, show how their social experience stood at odds with a liberal republican social knowledge that valued independence over mutuality and the didactic lessons of self-interested market behaviors over sympathetic understanding.

Addams challenged middle- and upper-class men and women like herself to learn from the immigrants and working poor of the Nineteenth Ward. Perhaps writing about her own education and personal transformation at Hull House, Addams observed that the reformer or charity worker who actually lives among poor people "is chagrined to discover that in the actual task of reducing her social scruples to action, her humble beneficiaries are far in advance of her, not in charity or singleness of purpose, but in self-sacrificing action. She reaches the old-time virtue of humility by a social process. . . . She has socialized her virtues not only through a social aim but by a social process."[61] Such humility was critical, for "we learn how to apply the new [moral knowledge] only by having attempted to apply the old and having found it to fail."[62] Humility came from the willingness to recognize multiple perspectives and confront the problems of power inherent in charity and social reform.

Addams suggested that, in order to explore dogmatic beliefs and speculative assumptions, the reformer had a moral and political responsibility to embrace diverse experiences and know firsthand the lives of others. Without sympathetic understanding, derived from "tentative and observant practice," democratic reform was impossible. In characterizing settlement work as tentative and observant practice, Addams pointed to the pragmatic nature of its social inquiry. The settlement worker wove together concrete experience and action, observation, and fact gathering. Illustrating the importance of domestic discourse on her thinking, Addams presented this inquiry as dialogic. New knowledge and

59. John Albert Mayer, "Private Charity in Chicago from 1871 to 1915" (PhD diss., University of Minnesota, 1978, 408–412).
60. Addams, *Democracy and Social Ethics* (New York: Macmillan, 1902), 19–20.
61. Ibid., 68–69.
62. Ibid., 74.

personal transformation, which were inseparable in her mind, resulted from interaction and human relationship. The proximate, relational ways of knowing inherent in domesticity served as a model for larger social inquiry.

Hull House residents found that one of the earliest means of forming connections with their neighbors was to offer the kinds of material assistance common among the women in the ward—such as caring for children and nursing the ill. Thus their assistance was not in the form of traditional philanthropy but was rather a neighborly exchange of watching a baby or borrowing catsup. Such "utilitarian sociability," as scholar Shannon Jackson describes it, provided the foundation for relationships within material exchange and was reminiscent of the ways that economic necessity drove sociability in the lives of the poor.[63] Such lessons put settlement residents into a reciprocal relationship with their neighbors in a wider sense. The upper classes shared their privileged lifestyles, their "training and cultivation," and more important, their abundance of time, access to meeting space, and centers of political power, while their neighbors offered important lessons of mutuality and sympathy. Invitations to attend immigrants' "weddings, their funerals, and christenings as welcomed guests" helped Addams to break down her own class prejudice and morality that distanced her from her neighbors.[64] Moreover, Hull House residents' willingness "to wash the newborn babies, and to prepare the dead for burial, to nurse the sick, and to 'mind the children'" provided a way for their neighbors to accept their help.

Desire to overcome alienation is a theme that appeared frequently in Addams's writings and was the key to both her social ethics and democratic vision. "Nothing so deadens the sympathies and shrivels the powers of enjoyment as the persistent keeping away from great opportunities for helpfulness, and the ignoring of the starvation struggle, which makes up the life of at least half of the race," Addams argued.[65] Building on her college essay, "Breadgivers," she spiritualized the unity in the labors associated with securing the necessities of life. Sharing life rituals and daily labor helped to minister to "the deep-seated craving for social intercourse that all men feel" and establish such a relationship.[66] Addams thus interpreted different cultural manifestations of life rituals as part of a universal attempt to provide human meaning to the life process itself. Such neighborly helpfulness and participation in life rituals reflected her belief in a common human nature. Addams suggested that "the things which make men alike are finer and better than the things that keep them apart," for "these basic likenesses, if they are properly accentuated, easily transcend the less essential differences of race, language, creed, and tradition."[67]

63. Jackson, *Lines of Activity,* 60.
64. Addams, "Outgrowths of Toynbee Hall," 13.
65. Ibid., 3–4.
66. Addams, *Twenty Years* (1981), 88.
67. Ibid., 89.

In her experiences with her neighbors, we see Addams struggling for a basis on which to overcome the social differences born of economic disparities and ethnic diversity. We also see her shaping an alternative to the narrative of Economic Man, with its logic of self-interested rationality. Her struggle to both recognize diverse experience and find commonalities that were explained not by self-interested greed but by shared emotional experience and life practices served as the foundation for her social knowledge and democratic ideas. Within a few months of moving to Hull House, Addams began to understand the value of proximate knowledge and to deepen her belief in human sympathy and mutuality as a way to overcome a fatal drifting apart. Furthermore, she had begun to wrestle more deeply with the class implications of a democratic social knowledge. Lessons in mutuality turned on its head the traditional reform relationship, with its hierarchy, its patronizing tone of the rich working *for* the poor rather than *with* the poor.

As the transformative nature of working with poor people became clearer to her, Addams began to describe democracy in social terms as interactive, relational, and mutually dependent, both for material purposes and spiritual lessons.[68] Indeed, in contrast to the individualism and self-sufficiency of liberal republicanism, Addams argued that "to attempt to attain a social morality without a basis of democratic experience results in the loss of the only possible corrective and guide. . . . A man who takes the betterment of humanity for his aim and end must also take the daily experiences of humanity for the constant correction of his process."[69] By appealing to the intimate daily routines, typically the traditional domain of women, Addams suggested that women's social experience provided a foundation on which to recognize commonalities. Additionally, in emphasizing the importance of classes joining together "in the starvation struggle," Addams illustrated how the daily struggles of her neighbors to meet their basic needs offered a realm of shared experience for overcoming the social and economic alienation she so feared.

Living in the Nineteenth Ward, Addams learned firsthand the inadequacy of a liberal republicanism that denied the value of the social experience of her neighbors. As a founder of the pragmatic tradition, Addams sought new ways to facilitate social knowledge. She remarked that settlement workers were motivated by "a desire to use synthetically and directly whatever knowledge they, as a group, may possess, to test its validity and to discover the conditions under

68. Knight argues in *Citizen* that Addams had not yet completed her democratic transformation until the late 1890s, while Brown dates it to an earlier point, suggesting that her essay on the Pullman Strike, "A Modern Lear," indicates her democratic disposition. I find important shifts in Addams's thinking in these early years of the 1890s as the pressure of her experiences in the ward pushed her toward a more complex democratic theory.

69. Addams, *Democracy and Social Ethics,* 176.

which their knowledge may be employed."[70] Conceiving of knowledge as the result of inquiry and reflection on the diversity of everyday experiences, Addams sought venues to encourage such processes to unfold. Drama afforded one area in which to build the social relations necessary to a democratic social knowledge, as did the study clubs, public discussions, and political activities associated with the settlement.

"A Sense of Compassion of the Experiences of Others": Aesthetic Knowing and Sympathetic Understanding

Addams believed that aesthetic expression, particularly drama, was useful in promoting sympathetic understanding. The Hull House arts program, in both its formal agenda and its creative process, was built on the relational and proximate knowledge and the democratic interactions with their neighbors that residents strove for on a daily basis.[71] The political power of performance, as both an analytical category and an aesthetic form, lies in its potential to evoke common emotions and connect individuals. This was the idea behind Hull House theater productions, which involved children, teens, and young adults in the neighborhood.

Addams had been attracted to the humanitarian and didactic potential of art since the days of her youthful education. Her familiarity with Romanticism encouraged an understanding of art as an expression of human individuality that also sought unification. Indeed, she believed it to be part of human nature. Her visits to galleries, ancient catacombs, and pyramids confirmed her belief as she observed aesthetic creation in all cultures throughout history.[72] Addams traced this creative instinct back to the critical moment of a child's self-realization. She suggested that "the most precious moment in human development is the young creature's assertion that he is unlike any other human being, and has an individual contribution to make to the world."[73] However, children also experienced in this realization "a sense of solitude, of being unsheltered in a wide world of relentless and elemental forces, which is the basis of childhood's timidity" and is never quite outgrown.[74] This moment brought terror, as well

70. Addams, "A Function of the Social Settlement," in *Jane Addams on Education*, ed. Ellen Condliffe Lagemann, 77 (New York: Teachers College Press, 1985).

71. Jackson, *Lines of Activity*, 203–47.

72. Merle Curti, "Jane Addams and Human Nature," *Journal of the History of Ideas* 22 (April–June 1961): 240–53. Addams was also clearly influenced by the aesthetic theories of Matthew Arnold and John Ruskin, with whose works she was familiar. See Matthew Arnold, *Culture and Anarchy: An Essay in Political and Social Criticism*, ed. J. Dover Wilson (Cambridge: Cambridge University Press, 1960), and John Ruskin, *Art and Life: A Ruskin Anthology* (New York: Alden, 1900).

73. Addams, *Spirit of Youth and the City Streets* (New York: Macmillan, 1909), 8.

74. Addams, *Twenty Years* (1981), 30.

as creativity. Art was both an outlet and an opportunity to merge one's self with a wider human endeavor and therefore decrease loneliness. Human desire for solidarity thus undergirded art, and to suppress this instinct meant "the hungry individual soul . . . without art will have passed unsolaced and unfed."[75] Viewed in its widest sense, artistic expression was a tool to provide common ground by evoking universal human tendencies that transcended immediate differences.

Addams believed drama to be a unifying aspect of human expression, and the theater indeed provides a useful metaphor for understanding her version of sympathetic social knowledge.[76] Drama draws the audience in and invites the spectator to step into the shoes of the characters and emotionally experience the story. She argued that drama "[warms] us with a sense of compassion of the experiences of others" and that the arts offered "a sense of the genuine relationship which may exist between men who share large hopes and like desires, even though they differ in nationality, language, and creed."[77] Because it was shared by all people and all civilizations, Addams envisioned artistic expression as a way to foster sympathetic understanding and to unify individuals through a universal search for meaning that had no national or class boundaries.

Several plays produced by Hull House clubs lent themselves to both didactic and spiritual lessons for their working- and middle-class audiences by depicting the problems of ward residents and transcending the immediate ethnic and class-based nature of those problems.[78] *The Son of the Immigrant* portrayed the difficulties not only of settlement in a new country but also of a generation gap as native-born sons insolently broke from their immigrant parents. But instead of isolating the Italian immigrant characters and audience members, it helped them recognize a common experience of intergenerational conflict that transcended ethnic origins. Witnessing the effect of the play, Addams rhetorically asked, "Did the tears of each express relief in finding that others had had the same experience as himself, and did the knowledge free each one from a sense of isolation and an injured belief that his children were the worst of all?"[79] The *Three Gifts* told the story of a striking bricklayer and the effects of unemployment and immigration, themes familiar to Nineteenth-Ward actors and audiences. Residents noted the introspective portrayals the actors gave and the

75. Ibid., 258.
76. For discussion of theater and the arts through the analytical lens of performance studies, see Jackson, *Lines of Activity*.
77. Addams, *Twenty Years* (1981), 268, 32.
78. Laura Dainty Pelham, Hull House theater director after 1900, recalled that the settlement sought opportunities to produce original plays dealing with local conditions. The following discussion draws from Jackson, *Lines of Activity*, 204–69.
79. Quoted in ibid., 227.

sympathy with which the play was received. In 1911 Hilda Satt Polacheck dramatized Leroy Scott's novel *The Walking Delegate*.[80] The fictional story was inspired by a New York labor scandal, in which union organizer Samuel Parks was convicted of extortion. Scott's book explored the issue of dishonesty in labor unions, juxtaposing an honest hero, Tom Keating, with Buck Foley, a character based upon Parks. In the climax of the story, Keating exposes Foley, saving his own slandered reputation and that of the union. The lesson in the *Walking Delegate* was clear: Personal responsibility and honesty could redeem the labor movement. But while Scott depicted the conflict between honesty and dishonesty in trades unions, he also illustrated the same conflict in the ranks of employers. Scott exposed businessmen as complicit in corruption and portrayed the honest union man as the moral superior. The play depicted a more complex view of the labor movement and the working classes, serving a didactic function not only for its working-class audience but for its middle-class viewers as well.[81]

Plays such as these used aesthetics to foster interactive, sympathetic social knowledge. Addams viewed the purpose of art as she did civic reform: as a sympathetic exercise that enables the spectator to explore and experience another's point of view and even merge with intangible spiritual truths. Such ideas about art harked back to her "Cassandra" essay on intuition and truth. Reflecting Romanticism's belief that aesthetic pursuits could access transcendent truth, drama offered a means for individuals and social groups to understand each other's experiences and at the same time search for truth beyond the particular circumstances of those experiences. Significantly, she suggested that "a play can tell certain things more potently and persuasively than can all the sociological pamphlets that ever fell from the groaning presses."[82] Simon Patten, a political economist, an active member of the settlement movement, and lecturer at the New York School of Social Work, agreed: "[T]he renewed imagining of hate, love, terror, curiosity, danger, daring, and fury—all the elemental stuff—concentrates the thoughts and momentarily rouses mental forces to a keener effectiveness than any scheme of night schools has yet discovered."[83] Viewed in this manner, art provided an emotional means to facilitate democratic social knowledge by encouraging sympathetic and intuitive insights into common human experiences.

80. The idea for this project apparently originated with Addams. Polacheck describes the writing and production of the play in her autobiography, *I Came a Stranger: The Story of a Hull-House Girl* (Urbana: University of Illinois Press, 1991), 118–26. See also chapter notes on pp. 222–27 for references and reviews.

81. Hull House theater drew middle-class as well as neighborhood audiences. See Polacheck, *I Came a Stranger.*

82 "Hull-House Bulletin" (1905–6), 17. See Stuart Joel Hecht, "Hull-House Theatre: An Analytical and Evaluative History" (PhD diss., Northwestern University, 1984).

83. Quoted in Carson, *Settlement Folk,* 127.

The actors themselves found the experience transforming. Children and young adults from different nationalities and religious backgrounds participated in the drama groups. The son of a Russian Jewish immigrant remembered that "the remarkable thing about it as I look back was the diversity of the background from which the kids came. . . . Various nationalities that came from different levels, there were some from working class families, most I would say came from working class families at different levels of culture."[84] Another participant recalled, "it was really an education[;] it was really wonderful for all of us, for instance, we were given a Chinese play, and we had to learn gestures."[85] Hull House drama director Edith de Nancrede took the whole class down to Chinatown and "had us meet some of the people and talk to them, you know how do we do this and how do we do that so that it wasn't just the play, we were getting other things, you know, like being together." They were, as she explained, "experiencing different cultures, different ways of life."[86] This was true for the audiences as well, which were composed both of neighborhood residents—Italians, Russian Jews, and others from across the city, some of whom came from the wealthy North Shore. When they came to Hull House, they experienced an array of cultures and interacted with people from different parts of the city and diverse parts of the world.[87]

The drama club had important political implications. Hull House used art and drama to forge humanistic bonds reflecting Addams's effort to bridge an epistemological gap among people with widely divergent experiences and worldviews. For reformers like Addams, who were concerned with a "drifting apart" and its effects on civic unity, aesthetics offered a way to transcend those differences and create a common vision of the public good.[88] Her democratic vision then was shaped by a recognition of fundamental human commonalities and cast differences as culturally created. In this respect, Addams was ahead of many of her contemporaries who saw ethnic, class, and gender differences as biologically determined, though her commitment to the resolution of differences still strikes modern readers as naïve, particularly as it foreclosed recognition of potentially unbridgeable differences in worldviews. Yet it was consistent

84. Interview with Alex Epson, October 12, 1980, Stuart Hecht Collection, Folder 1, University of Illinois–Chicago, Special Collections.

85. Interview with Nicolette Malone, March 10, 1980, in ibid.

86. Ibid.

87. Interview with Elizabeth Elson Cohen, November 7, 1980, 14; interview with Mrs. Nat (Goldie) Kalyn, October 21, 1980, both in ibid.

88. Aesthetics and cultural expressions were of course matters of extensive debate during this era. Addams's vision was only one of many ways people of her class envisioned the political function of art and cultural institutions. For alternative ideas that emphasized the role of culture in creating, rather than overcoming, class barriers, see Lawrence Levine, *High Brow/Low Brow: The Emergence of Cultural Hierarchy in America* (Cambridge, MA: Harvard University Press, 1988); Lefkowitz, *Culture and the City.*

with Addams's ideas that democratic politics must grow out of daily practice that built a democratic personality capable of exercising humility, dignity, and sympathetic understanding.[89]

The Working People's Social Science Club: Interaction and Deliberation

Thus far we have seen how democratic social knowledge was emergent in relational and proximate social life and in connection with aesthetic knowing and sympathetic understanding. Each of these ways of knowing emphasized interaction across class and ethnic lines. Hull House's Working People's Social Science Club expanded upon this conception of interaction as a process for forging democratic social knowledge. At weekly meetings, the club encouraged debate among the intellectuals, politicians, public officials, women, and working people who attended, with the hope of increasing civic consciousness on the part of the participants. It provided an interactive and deliberative public forum in which to blend social science investigation, political policy, and participant experience.[90]

The club was modeled on a number of citywide economic conferences organized after the Haymarket Affair. Lyman Gage had initiated these cross-class meetings with the purpose of amelioration. Recalling his motive, he explained that "it was evident that the social fabric was being torn by mutual misunderstandings, which might be healed or at least mitigated by a better comprehension of the ideas and motives which actuate men in their relations to each other in the social." With faith in a liberal model of discourse to solve social problems, Gage organized the Economic Club. Twenty-four members, representing varying shades of opinions, including anarchist and socialist, met monthly at his home. Out of this group grew the idea for "economic conferences"—public meetings "for orderly discussion of the ideas and 'isms' which were splitting up into hostile groups, many well disposed, if misguided people."[91]

Gage's description of the conferences suggests both a recognition of subjectivity (men brought different "ideas and motives" to their relations with one

---

89. Victoria Brown explains that Addams's refusal to acknowledge that some differences are irreconcilable was rooted in her particular democratic vision. See Victoria Bissell Brown, "Advocate for Democracy: Jane Addams and the Pullman Strike," in *The Pullman Strike and the Crisis of the 1890s: Essays on Labor and Politics*, ed. Richard Schneirov, Shelton Stromquist, and Nick Salvatore, 130–58 (Urbana: University of Illinois Press, 1999).

90. The club nurtured the type of deliberative public that Kevin Mattson describes as the cornerstone of participatory democracy and was a forerunner of the school center movement he discusses in *Creating a Democratic Public: The Struggle for Urban Participatory Democracy during the Progressive Era* (University Park: Pennsylvania State University Press, 1998).

91. Lyman J. Gage, *Memoirs of Lyman J. Gage* (New York: House of Field, 1937).

another) and the dangers it posed to common civic consciousness ("hostile groups" developed). It also reveals a commitment to deliberative democracy and the belief that public discussion and debate could bridge social barriers and misunderstandings. The meetings grew into public conferences where "every possible shade of opinion was freely expressed," including those of a man "who had been involved with the group of convicted anarchists, and who doubtless would have been arrested and tried, but for the accident of his having been in Milwaukee when the explosion occurred."[92] Interest was high as a hall seating five hundred consistently filled for the conferences.

The Working People's Social Science Club arose from a similar belief that public discussions could ease class and ethnic animosity. Its organizers "expected that a full and calm discussion of the various labor questions, will enable all who attend to gain a better and clearer idea of the problems that are demanding solution, and the various remedies that are proposed."[93] The club embodied an effort to widen participation in the deliberation of social problems. It focused on topics popular with both social scientists and the lay public. Economic and labor matters received the greatest attention, although municipal government, social-ism, and immigration issues also frequently appeared on the agenda. As the city faced legislation on labor issues, police matters, municipal control of utilities, and civil service reform, the club tried to represent a wider range of ethnic, occupational, and political views. During the campaign for an Illinois Factory Act, the club hosted lectures and discussions on the topic.[94] One CFC member, Franklin MacVeagh, spoke on "Civil Service Reform in Municipal Affairs" dur-ing the Civil Service Law campaign. That same year, Judge C. G. Dixon and labor leader George Schilling debated "Arbitration in Labor Troubles" versus "The Futility of Legal Enactment."[95]

The club thus encouraged dynamics that brought together social investigation and experience in debates over the meaning of class, economic, and gender rela-tions. For example, one evening in 1893, a visitor to the club recalled a lecture by a Baptist minister and sociologist from the University of Chicago, probably C. R. Henderson. "Trying to prove that it is wrong to make individuals responsible for changes caused by the advance of trade," since these were unintended results, "he asks of the laborer patience, steady effort, and the economy so seldom practiced in America, just as he asks of the rich, in order somewhat to equalize matters,

---

92. Jane Addams, *Twenty Years* (1981), 134.

93. Alfred D. Hicks to "Dear Sir," April 7, 1890; JAP, Reel 51. When the Chicago Commons opened in 1894, it adopted a similar model for its weekly Free Floor meetings. See Louise C. Wade, *Graham Taylor: Pioneer for Social Justice, 1851–1938* (Chicago: University of Chicago Press, 1964), 127.

94. Working People's Social Science Club, schedule, 1892; JAP, Reel 51.

95. Ibid., program, 1893; JAP, Reel 3.

generous sacrifices which can only be voluntary."[96] Henderson's emphasis on the voluntary nature of the elite's sacrifices indicated a liberal republican position that rejected the state's regulation of the economy. The audience, however, pointed out that he failed to understand the effects of industrial capitalism on laborers. One Bohemian shoemaker illustrated the problems created by industrial division of labor. "Suppose I offer now to make a shoe, myself alone, when there are machines for nailing and sewing all the separate parts! The man who has learned a trade and can no longer support himself by it, is dismissed without any compensation."[97] "Savings indeed!" another scoffed. "One would think a man had nothing to do but to go to the bank and deposit his little hoard. Christ did not save; he had no home."[98] After several such reprimands, the minister relented; "perhaps I spoke too severely of vagabonds, who do nothing worse than to secure food and lodging; they too are my brothers."

Henderson's comments illustrate the transformative potential of an interactive and communal process of social inquiry. Initially the professor assumed that labor unions attempted to undermine natural economic laws. He counseled workers against trying to subvert those laws; they should remain patient and acquiesce to the unfolding process of industrialization. Implicitly Henderson assumed that workers who protested against economic laws were irrational and immoral, as were the unions that represented them. His interactions at the Social Science Club, however, challenged those assumptions. Workers' experiences, when brought up against the professor's theories, helped him to recognize as legitimate their demands for basic social needs of food and shelter. Significantly, though, the workers won his recognition using his own terms and positioning themselves as Christ-like. And indeed, Henderson recognized their claims in Christian terms; it is not clear to what extent he recognized them in material terms.

As this exchange illustrates, meetings were lively and fraught with serious discussion that often challenged the dominant cultural values of individualism and competition. In this respect, the club functioned as an alternative to local saloons.[99] Like the saloon, the Social Science Club offered a location for neighborhood residents to gather and discuss political and intellectual matters significant to the working classes. Unlike the saloon, however, which was often segregated along ethnic, gender, or class lines, the club aimed specifically to draw together a wide variety of people. The conservative speaker, "very

96. Madame Theresa Blanc, *The Condition of Woman in the United States*, trans. Abby Langdon Alger (1895; repr., Freeport, NY: Books for Libraries Press, 1972), 78–79.

97. Ibid., 79.

98. Ibid., 83.

99. Roy Rosenzweig, *Eight Hours for What We Will* (New York: Cambridge University Press, 1985); Perry Duis, "Whose City?: Public and Private Places in Nineteenth-century Chicago," *Chicago History* 12 (March 1983): 2–23.

correct in his white collar and long frock coat," offering "A Defense of the Right to Acquire Property" or "A Defense of the Chicago Board of Trade," faced members of a "club where social science gladly uses the language of anarchy."[100] A wide range of people—Germans and Bohemians, Catholic Irishmen, and Russian Jews—regularly attended the meetings. But the inclusion of white women and college professors was perhaps even more unusual than interethnic participation. Initially women stayed away, but after 1893, when Alzina Stevens and Florence Kelly addressed the club, the meetings attracted more women. By spring of 1895, female speakers outnumbered male presenters seven to six, and the fall's program featured a special six-week series by Charlotte Perkins Gilman.[101]

For the college professors and social scientists, the Social Science club offered a location to build a social knowledge based not only on expertise or natural laws but also on the experiences and perspectives of the people in question.[102] Their presentations before the club indicated a willingness to place their theories under the scrutiny of members of the working class. In these interactions, workers' experiences accorded them the status of experts, much as women claimed their domestic experiences as a basis for special knowledge regarding municipal housekeeping.[103]

Groups such as the Working People's Social Science Club led John Dewey to reflect that "there is a socialism regarding which there can be no such dispute—socialism of the intelligence and of the spirit. To extend the range and the fullness of sharing in the intellectual and spiritual resources of the community is the very meaning of the community."[104] Such ideas about social knowledge reflected Addams's own pragmatic interests. In suggesting that "social perspective and sanity of judgment come only from contact with social experience; that such contact is the surest corrective of opinions concerning the social order, and concerning efforts, however humble, for its improvement," Addams counterbalanced trends to isolate academics and experts within the academy and away from the wider social life they studied.[105]

The Working People's Social Science Club privileged personal and group experiences as an important ingredient in the formation of democratic social

100. Blanc, *Condition of Woman*, 74.

101. See programs and schedules for the Working People's Social Science Club; JAP, Reel 51.

102. For discussion of the role of University of Chicago faculty members in the city's settlement houses, see Bachin, *Building the South Side*, 104–9.

103. The inverted relationship between workers and professors made a few of the latter uncomfortable; indeed, at the close of seven years, the secretary reported that only twice had a speaker lost his temper, and in each instance it was a college professor "'who wasn't accustomed to being talked back to.'" Addams, *Twenty Years* (1981), 140.

104. John Dewey, "The School as Social Center," in *100 Years at Hull-House*, ed. Mary Lynn McCree Bryan and Allen F. Davis, 103–7 (Bloomington: Indiana University Press, 1990).

105. Addams, *Democracy and Social Ethics*, 7.

knowledge. It legitimated workers' special insights and upset hierarchies in its promotion of communal processes of mediating social knowledge. The format provided workers, policy makers, and intellectuals personal access to each other, and in this respect the club served as an arena of mutuality and relationship that, while not daily and intimate, still helped bridge the epistemological gaps among social groups.

However, the club also illustrated some differences. Primarily based on rational discourse and argumentation, its format was reminiscent of male political traditions. Its method of public debate stood in contrast to women's practical knowledge and organization, with its emphasis on doing rather than theorizing. Still, the club provided a location for a pivotal point in the process of social inquiry. Participants reflected on their own experiences and learned of multiple perspectives. By 1895, then, the outlines of Hull House's democratic social knowledge, with its emphasis on relation and proximity, aesthetics and sympathetic understanding, and interactive, socially mediated knowledge, came into focus. This democratic social knowledge, with its gendered implications, was more fully developed in Hull House's social science inquiry and political activities.

"Only When Accomplished by the Whole Human Consciousness": Experience and Activist Social Science

Daily interactions with their neighbors helped Hull House residents articulate a desire for a democratic praxis predicated on relationship and communal processes of democratic social knowledge. It also deepened their understanding of the economic and social problems raised by the laissez-faire nature of liberal republicanism and the problems it posed for democratic social relationships. Addams noted that "there was always present the harrowing consciousness of the difference in economic condition between ourselves and our neighbors."[106] With the arrival of Florence Kelley in 1892, Addams and the women at Hull House learned the tools of social science to confront the economic problems that separated them.[107] In contrast to the developing social science disciplines in universities and professional societies, their social science was born of experience with the problems they studied. They were not distanced or neutral observers but active participants in the lives of the people and the communities they studied. Even more important, like the Working People's Social Science Club, residents sought to enlist their neighbors in their inquiries, making theirs an activist social science based on experience.

---

106. Addams, *Twenty Years* (1981), 80.
107. For biographical information on Kelley, see Sklar, *Florence Kelley and the Nation's Work*.

Florence Kelley had fled her abusive husband and come to Illinois seeking a divorce under the state's lenient laws. Having completed a bachelor's degree at Cornell University, she pursued graduate study at the University of Zurich, where she espoused socialism and translated into English Friedrich Engel's *Condition of the Working Class in England*. An expert social investigator, Kelley prodded Hull House residents to employ more scientific investigation. In her valedictory address, "Cassandra," Addams had argued that women's search for authority required them to merge their female experience and intuitive insight with scientific study. Kelley had argued a similar point in an article published in 1882, just after her college graduation. Titled "Need Our Working Women Despair?" Kelley argued that a new social science was emerging that had "humane interest, and can never be complete without help from women."[108] The new science required not only statistical work but also interpretation. And interpretation "can be complete only when accomplished by the whole human consciousness, i.e., by that two-fold nature, masculine and feminine, which expresses itself as a whole in human relations."[109] Both women recognized the potential of social science to provide a more inclusive and fuller social knowledge, but unlike Addams, Kelley had developed the social scientific skills to realize it. After her arrival in 1892, Addams helped her secure an appointment as sweatshop investigator for the Illinois Bureau of Labor Statistics. That same year, Carroll Wright, the federal commissioner of labor, asked her to survey the city's slums. These two jobs launched Hull House's earliest and best-known forays into social science inquiry.

To investigate the neighborhood, Kelley and the men and women she worked with used social survey methods. Their work first provided the material for reports to the Illinois Bureau of Labor Statistics and to Carroll Wright; then it became the basis for *Hull-House Maps and Papers*. With attention to emerging social science standards, Agnes Holbrook, a graduate of Wellesley's science program and Hull House resident, wrote the introduction to the maps. She reported that "the facts set forward [in *Hull-House Maps and Papers*] are as trustworthy as personal inquiry and intelligent effort could make them." Each house, tenement, and room was visited, and "in many cases the reports obtained from one person were corroborated by many others and statements from different workers at the same trades and occupations, as to wages and unemployed seasons, served as mutual confirmation."[110] Living in the midst of the neighborhood, Hull House residents relied on the mutual relationships they had with neighbors to render more reliable information.

---

108. Florence Kelley, "Need Our Working Women Despair?" (November 1882), 512. Sklar discusses this essay in the context of Kelley's early developing social science and reform critique in *Florence Kelley and the Nation's Work*, 69–82.

109. Sklar, *Florence Kelley and the Nation's Work*, 69–70.

110. Ibid., 126.

The studies provided a solid foundation for political action. As we have seen, unions and women's organizations had joined forces as early as 1889 to demand legislation ending sweatshop labor, but they had been unsuccessful until their political connections had grown and, significantly, until Kelley had carefully prepared her statistics to lend weight to their claims. Fellow settlement residents were optimistic about her contributions to the campaign: "She is so amazingly clever ... and she's got such a load of good black and white statistics."[111] Kelley's statistics were significant in an age avidly devoted to social investigation. Indeed, the seemingly dispassionate use of statistics and tables facilitated imagination in creating a "humanitarian narrative" sufficient to mobilize readers to action.[112] Such narratives, taking the form of the realistic novel, the autopsy, the clinical report, or the social inquiry, spoke "in extraordinarily detailed fashion about the pains and deaths of ordinary people in such a way as to make apparent the causal chains that might connect the actions of its readers with the suffering of its subjects" and thus mobilize readers to action.[113] Her numbers told the story of domestic life destroyed by the sweating system, as fathers, mothers, and children of all ages worked from morning until late in the evening. It told the story of people "noticeably undersized and unhealthy" who looked "dwarfed and ill-fed," whose "narrow chests and cramped hands are unmistakable evidence of their calling."[114] In this way, social science was an important medium for prompting emotional response and moral indignation. The attention to the visible effects of industrial labor on the human frame posited the body as a location of social knowledge. The bodies of wage laborers emphasized a concrete experience of industrialization that was overlooked in economic theory. Embodied knowledge of this sort potentially served as a corrective to abstract economic principles and pervasive business practices.[115]

Hull House residents' admiration for Kelley and her statistics was not misplaced; in 1893 the state legislature passed the Illinois Factory Act. Settlement work wedded with social science and public action turned women into producers and theorizers of knowledge, not merely consumers; it gave women the authority Addams sought for her sex.[116] The example of *Hull-House Maps and Papers* encouraged further studies linking Hull House residents' proximity and

111. Quoted in Jackson, *Lines of Activity,* 272.

112. On the use of social science in framing the "humanitarian narrative," see Thomas W. Laquer, "Bodies, Details, and the Humanitarian Narrative," in *The New Cultural History,* ed. Lynn Hunt, 176–204 (Berkeley: University of California Press, 1989).

113. Ibid., 177.

114. Alice Holbrook, introduction to *Hull-House Maps and Papers.* See also Jackson, *Lines of Activity,* 280.

115. Daniel E. Bender, *Sweated Work, Weak Bodies: Anti-Sweatshop Campaigns and Languages of Labor* (New Brunswick, NJ: Rutgers University Press, 2004); Laura Hapke, *Sweatshop: The History of an American Ideal* (New Brunswick, NJ: Rutgers University Press, 2004).

116. Ross, "Gendered Social Knowledge."

activism with social science methods. Studies of housing, truancy, child labor, and immigrant experiences furthered the Hull House women's roles in creating social knowledge.

Hull House women's social and political authority was deepened with the publication of *Hull-House Maps and Papers* in 1895. The book illustrated how women's contributions to social knowledge helped render the problems of Chicago's workers and ethnic groups knowable in new ways. Carefully drawing together the information on wage and ethnic groups, Hull House women converted these statistics into maps that visually illustrated where ethnic groups lived and how much money they made. The interpretative essays that accompanied the maps further explained the class and gendered nature of the problems with which ward residents struggled. Despite a liberal republicanism that posited men as wage earners and women as caretakers of the home, the maps and essays revealed that men did not earn a wage capable of supporting their wives and children. Rather, the volume demonstrated the persistence of a family economy. In discussing the wage map, Agnes Holbrook added textured description to the story its colored blocks told:

In this neighborhood generally a wife and children are sources of income as well as avenues of expenses; and the women wash, do 'home finishing' on ready-made clothing, or pick and sell 'rags' the boys run errands and 'shine'; the girls work in factories, get places as cashgirls, or sell papers on the streets; and the very babies sew buttons on knee-pants and shirt waists, each bringing in a trifle to fill out the scanty income. [117]

Pointing out the way that women and children contributed to the household, Holbrook lashed out against the atomism of liberal republicanism: "The theory that 'every man supports his own family' is as idle in a district like this as the fiction that 'every one can get work if he wants it.'"[118]

Furthermore, the labor that took place within the tenement apartment violated domestic norms as work permeated every area of the house. The Sweatshop Law prohibited non–family members from working in the kitchen or any room in the apartment that required them to pass through sleeping and eating areas. Poignantly illustrating the difficulties of enforcing this law, however, Kelley reported that one nighttime investigation revealed a garment worker who, with "his family, a wife and four indescribably filthy children," occupied a kitchen and two bedrooms:

117. Holbrook, introduction to *Hull-House Maps and Papers*, 21. See also Jackson, *Lines of Activity*, 273.

118. Holbrook, introduction to *Hull-House Maps and Papers*, 21.

The farther bedrooms could be entered only by passing through the other rooms. This farther bedroom, where the man was found at work, was 7 x 7 x 8 feet, and contained a bed, a machine, one chair, a reeking lamp, and two men. The bed seemed not to have been made up in weeks; and in the bed, in a heap, there lay two overcoats, two hats, a mass of bed-covers, and nine fine tan-color capes trimmed with ecru lace, a tenth cape being in the machine in process of stitching. The whole dwelling was found to be crawling with vermin, and the capes were not free from it."[119]

This promiscuous mix of living and work space—of men, women, and children sweating side by side—ridiculed middle-class pretensions of a peaceful domestic sphere sheltering working men from the rough world of business and lending its unspoiled moral influence to their political behavior.

Conditions like those in the Nineteenth Ward inspired Chicago's female reformers who attacked the laissez-faire implications of liberal republicanism. *Hull-House Maps and Papers* revealed the ways in which industrialization violated gender and family norms and rendered unrealizable the boundaries between public and private domains. Drawing upon a logic of municipal housekeeping, women turned their domestic concerns for health and cleanliness, protection of the home, and child nurture toward addressing public issues such as sanitation and education. With the boundaries increasingly blurred between public and private responsibilities, growing numbers of women carved out active political identities for themselves that argued for the value of their social experience and the knowledge it accorded them. As *Hull-House Maps and Papers* suggested, much of the basis for an emerging feminized civic consciousness lay in gendered forms of social knowledge and social science methodology. Its gendered nature was apparent first in the subjects of study: the intimate, daily lives of men, women, and children, as well as the emphasis on the deleterious effects of laissez-faire business practices on the family, particularly on the bodies of women and children. Mixing public and private concerns, gendered social knowledge was thus marked by its intimacy as a basis for inquiry and action and its practical commitment to wedding facts with a moral vision for social change.

The methodology of producing this social knowledge was further gendered, as Shannon Jackson has argued, in its attention to relationship and locality and to a proximate epistemology that privileged authority and knowledge in shared experience and personal interaction. Thus Kelley observed that "you must suffer from the dirty streets, the universal ugliness, the lack of oxygen in the air you daily breathe, the endless struggle with soot and dust and insufficient water

---

119. Kelley, "The Sweating System," in *Hull-House Maps and Papers*, 30. Also cited in Jackson, *Lines of Activity*, 278–79.

supply, the hanging from a strap of the overcrowded street car at the end of your day's work . . . if you are to speak as one having authority."[120] The use of social science helped position middle-class women in the working-class areas of the city; it provided a rationale beyond neighborliness and benevolence for their work in ethnic and working-class communities, many of which already had their own mutual-aid networks. Such social science was attentive to the needs of women and children and served to legitimize women's role in political action. Indeed, the Illinois Factory Act Law, the publication of *Hull-House Maps and Papers*, and the numerous surveys and investigations conducted under the auspices of the settlement lent the weight of the social sciences to women's claims to moral authority.[121] And this point became clearer as Hull House's early forays into social inquiry became a tool, not just for middle-class women but also for cross-class means of pursuing knowledge and seeking a shared gender consciousness.

The campaign for the Sweatshop Law illustrates the ways that pursuit of a more inclusive, relational, and experiential social knowledge facilitated political activism and brought women into the political arenas in important ways. During the Sweatshop Law campaign and later when the Illinois Manufacturers Association challenged the law, working women held meetings at Hull House to discuss the law's impact on their lives and map out a strategy to defend it.[122] By encouraging women to meet and plan how they might become part of the public discussion about labor legislation, Hull House helped crystallize the political consciousness of both middle-class and working women, encouraging them to envision citizenship and the public role of government in activist terms.

Neighborhood residents of the Hull House Women's Club were able to use lessons about investigation and agitation learned during the Sweatshop Law campaign to procure more efficient garbage removal. After discussing research on the high death rate in urban areas, the club decided to conduct its own investigation into sanitary conditions to better understand why the ward had the highest infant death rate in the city. Armed with municipal sanitary codes, neighborhood women began a careful investigation of alleyways. Throughout August and September 1895, they reported 1,037 violations of health codes. Their efforts to secure more efficient garbage removal resulted in the appointment of Addams as neighborhood garbage inspector. The club then mobilized

120. Kelley, "Hull-House," *New England Magazine* (July 1898), 550. Also see Jackson, *Lines of Activity*, 272.

121. Sklar, *Florence Kelley and the Nation's Work*; Fitzgerald, *Endless Crusade*; Ross, "Jane Addams and Gendered Social Knowledge."

122. On businessmen's attacks on the law, see Sklar, *Florence Kelley and the Nation's Work*, 254–60. Papers related to the Illinois Manufacturers Association's attack on the law can be found in the Illinois Manufacturers Association (IMA) Papers, Box 1, Folder 1, Chicago Historical Society.

the community to begin a cleaning brigade that sorted garbage, burning what it could, badgering the city to remove the numerous rotting dead animals, and hauling away the rest. Eventually they unearthed a paved alleyway eighteen inches below the surface. This alley became a source of pride in the neighborhood, and residents fought to get the city to repave it.[123] Through the women's persistence, three city inspectors in a row were transferred from the ward for failing to perform their duties, and their efforts helped focus citywide attention on the magnitude of the sanitary problems and political corruption.

By influencing public opinion on such matters, Hull House and its neighbors helped crystallize civic consciousness and citywide reform such as that taken up by the Civic Federation of Chicago. Their successful campaigns led them to enlist the city to study garbage renewal and agree to municipal ownership of garbage removal in the interests of public health.[124] Their efforts became the model for other female organizations, such as the Women's City Club and the Juvenile Protective League, which drew together firsthand experience, investigation, and activism and, as we saw in chapter 2, influenced the Civic Federation's early approaches to social investigations.[125]

The women's research and agitation further combined personal knowledge of their neighborhood with systematic social science methods in a manner that helped educate them about their political potential. By directly involving neighborhood women in the formulation of problems, research, and solutions, the women's club built on the activist social science offered in *Hull-House Maps and Papers*. In both projects, the interaction of middle-class women's social science and working-class women's experiences fostered a broadened sense of female political authority and shaped an activist agenda that pressured government to protect public health. This approach to democratic social knowledge and democracy more generally opened up questions about the proper role of the state and the nature of justice. The demand for local and state government to

123. Jane Addams, *Twenty Years* (1981), 202–4.
124. See Flanagan, *Seeing with Their Hearts*, 96–98, 102–3. See also *Women's City Club Bulletin* 6, no. 1 (May 1917) in Women's City Club Papers, Box 1, Folder 9, in the University of Illinois–Chicago Special Collections; "Ten Years of Civic Work," *Women's City Club Bulletin* 9, no. 1 (May 1920) in Women's City Club Papers, Box 2, Folder 12, in the University of Illinois–Chicago Special Collections.
125. For discussion of the Women's City Club, see Maureen Flanagan, "The City Profitable, the City Livable: Environmental Policy, Gender, and Power in Chicago in the 1910s," *Journal of Urban History* 22, no. 2 (January 1996):163–90. *The Women's City Club Bulletin*, available in the Women's City Club Papers in the University of Illinois–Chicago Special Collections, is an excellent record of women's investigations and activism in the 1910s. Anne Meis Knupfer discusses the Juvenile Protective Agency in *Reform and Resistance: Gender, Delinquency, and America's First Juvenile Court* (New York: Routledge, 2001). Also available in the University of Illinois–Chicago Special Collections are the Jane Addams Papers, which, along with the Hull House Papers there, provide a fascinating record not only of the types of women's reform work but also their activist social science methods.

address ward problems challenged the laissez-faire nature of liberal republicanism. The use of imagination and sympathetic understanding as a guide in social ethics illustrated the transactive nature of democratic social knowledge that recognized the daily struggles and suffering of the poor as social experiences and the foundation for public action rather than a just and didactic feature of the industrial market. Justice instead emerged as social action to alleviate the struggles and suffering; democratic justice included the voices of the entire community in meeting social needs. This vision of civic bonds as relational, communal, and gendered challenged the atomistic and masculinized liberal republicanism.

"Perplexity and Clashing of Different Standards": Narrative Translation and Democratic Social Knowledge

Jane Addams was an accomplished author who reached a nationwide audience through her essays and books. Her use of parable-like descriptions of people in her neighborhood, the middle-class and elite men and women she encountered in her public work, and her own autobiographical experiences provided vivid images and lessons to her readers. Her stories helped make legible her neighbors, who were frequently invisible, demonized, or caricatured in public culture. She likewise sought to help her readers understand their own deeply rooted motives and the effects of their actions on her neighbors. As author, she thus became a translator, and her narrative provided an imaginative entree into the lives of people who rarely came into meaningful contact with one another. Her descriptive translations thus fostered another form of democratic social knowledge and served to break down barriers by helping people to recognize their commonalities.

Addams's narrative translations are exemplified in her first book, *Democracy and Social Ethics* (1902), which offers an example of her interpretive, relational sociology.[126] In the book, knowledge "was shown to emerge from the interpersonal experience and sympathetic relation between the sociological interpreter and her subjects."[127] Her gendered social knowledge brought together domestic discourse that privileged the home as a moral space and women's social experience in a bustling urban neighborhood; it also emphasized the educative value of experience, especially the sympathetic, interpersonal experience of the parent-child relationship. The references to Goethe and Emerson that appear throughout her writing also indicate that Romanticism—with its valorization

126. Ross, "Gendered Social Knowledge."
127. Ibid., 237. Shannon Jackson also argues that Addams offered an alternative interpretative method of sociological inquiry to that developing within the male-dominated academic discipline. See *Lines of Activity*, 249–303.

of feeling, subjectivity, intuition, and individuality—figured in her formulation of social knowledge. As we have seen, these traditions, along with the later influence of pragmatism and experiences at Hull House, laid the foundation for a social knowledge that was proximate, situational, and relational.

Addams's social ethics in the book contributed to pragmatic philosophy. As philosopher Charlotte Haddock Seigfried illustrates, Addams emphasized the "importance of attending to the diverse sexual, class, ethnic, and other cultural relations that constitute persons and to the disparities of power operative in the resolution of moral dilemmas."[128] In *Democracy and Social Ethics*, she accomplishes these through her attention to perplexity as the pivot around which social problems are understood. Her commentaries share an emphasis on her deeply human, personal approach to social inquiry. In contrast to positivist methods of attaining social knowledge that collected discrete facts and categorized people, Addams's essays illustrate how concrete experience, told in narrative form, serves as a form of social knowledge. Indeed, after the publication of *Hull-House Maps and Papers*, Addams turned away from social scientific writing, preferring to mix autobiography, imaginative prose, and sociological observation in a modernist literary style that Katherine Joslin has called "moral experimentalism."[129]

With its emphasis on human intention, crisis, and resolution, her essays served to foster an imaginative, interactive experience similar to that of drama or living in a diverse neighborhood. Remarking upon a conversation with an Irish woman whose years of living near several Italian families led her to change long-held stereotypes, Jane Addams invoked a notion of "extended experience" that encompassed one's interaction with texts. She suggested that this woman's experience "is exactly the thing . . . we hope for when we read books about all kinds of people—to get over the differences raised by barriers and traditions, that really we may be fair-minded and may know people as they really are."[130] Addams's understanding of literary practices as a form of experience illustrates the cultural changes wrought by modern economic growth. At a time when individuals were becoming more aware of their dependence on people across town whom they did not know, across the nation, and even across the world, journalism, arts and literature, and other forms of print culture increasingly served as a

---

128. Charlene Haddock Seigfried, introduction to Addams, *Democracy and Social Ethics*, xxx.

129. Katherine Joslin, *Jane Addams: A Writer's Life* (Urbana: University of Illinois Press, 2004). Joslin's fascinating discussion of Addams's literary style explores the reformer's place among the most important American authors of her generation—Theodore Dreiser, William Dean Howells, Frank Norris, Hamlin Garland, Vachel Lindsey—as well as authors like Emerson, Whitman, Tolstoy, and Zola, who influenced her unique brand of writing.

130. Jane Addams, "The Hull-House Women's Club," *Club Worker* 3 (November 1901): 1, quoted in Anne Ruggles Gere, *Intimate Practices: Literacy and Cultural Work in U.S. Women's Clubs, 1880–1920* (Urbana: University of Illinois Press, 1997). Addams was well aware of the limitation of literature, however, dwelling upon it in *Twenty Years* (1981).

means to connect individuals and communities.[131] She was not alone in valuing literature as social critique and a way of knowing. As a Columbia humanities professor has summarized, "literature provides us with noble pleasure, but it finds its chief function as criticism and interpretation of life. . . . The object of language is to convey thought and feeling from one mind to another without loss of moving power."[132] While she did not see them as substitutes for actual experience, Adams's essays reached thousands of readers unable to participate in settlement work directly.

Democracy and Social Ethics articulates two themes: the passing of an older code of ethics—atomistic individualism—and its replacement in the form of democracy "extended to all social affairs," where identity, social knowledge, and public ethics were constructed through civic interaction. The book introduces several modern relationships that cause personal and social division: the college-educated young woman and her family; the middle-class housewife and her domestic servant; the industrial employer and the factory worker; the ward boss and his immigrant constituent. She clearly sets up the perplexity of relationships and seeks a way out of them by translating apparent differences into moral dilemmas both groups could understand, discuss, and solve. Addams emphasized that social relationships always bring intersecting points of view that occasion the necessity for deeper understanding.[133] As author, Addams served as the translator for these points of view, and she uses a dialogic style to evoke the relational nature of experience in the ward. Her essays use the multiplicity of voices of common people to turn upside down the "authoritative discourse" of the typical social tract. In her writing, their stories become the powerful, richly textured lessons of urban life, "making social science more like imaginative fiction."[134] She uses them creatively, not just to explain social problems but also to explore deeply rooted, almost mystical, questions about the human condition.

In each of her examples, Addams carefully explains the intentions of both parties and poignantly articulates the problem that they pose. Her narrative style uses familiar discourses of domesticity, classical political economy, and Christian philanthropy to both engage the middle-class reader and reinterpret those same discourses. In laying bare the assumptions that shape social attitudes, interactions, and institutions, she tries to depict social reality, not through an omniscient

131. Thomas Haskell discusses economic interdependence in *The Emergence of Professional Social Science* (Urbana: University of Illinois Press, 1977), chapter 1. See also Benedict Anderson, *Imagined Communities: Reflections on the Origin and Spread of Nationalism* (London: Verso, 1991), for an interesting discussion of the ways that print culture can create a means to imagine unknown others as having similar experiences as oneself and thus contribute to a sense of community.

132. Quoted in Julie A. Reuben, *The Making of the Modern University: Intellectual Transformation and the Marginalization of Morality* (Chicago: University of Chicago Press, 1996), 220–21.

133. Ross, "Gendered Social Knowledge," 250.

134. Joslin, *Jane Addams*, 94.

eye but through the consciousness of the groups involved. Multiple perspectives and the perplexity they create thus become clearer and suggest the need for new social meanings worked out in social and political reform.[135] For example, she describes the confusion and misunderstanding between immigrants and charity workers over their different conceptions of aid. Pointing out the numerous examples of mutual aid that made survival in the lower ranks possible, Addams explained to her middle-class audience that the poor are "accustomed to help each other and to respond according to their kindliness."[136] In contrast, however, the delay and caution of the charity worker's scientific standards appear to the needy "as the cold and calculating action of a selfish man."[137] The relationship between charity visitors and poor people thus often resulted in the "perplexity and clashing of different standards, with the consequent misunderstandings."[138] Furthermore, recipients must play along with the charity workers, lauding temperance, saving, and cleanliness, even "though in their eyes a glass of beer is quite right and proper when taken as any self-respecting man should take it; though they know that cleanliness is an expensive virtue which can be required of few; though they realize that saving is well-nigh impossible when but a few cents can be laid by at a time."[139] Addams describes the moral framework immigrants maintain and in so doing challenges stereotypes. And she further exposes the power dynamics of the charitable relationship, with the immigrant forced to conform, at least superficially, to the standards of the charity worker.[140] The goal of such interpretive methods of knowledge production was to see things "from the point of view of the immigrant people themselves."[141] Such writing "celebrates the dialogic world of independent and equally valid voices," voices that contribute to a democratic social knowledge emergent from the blending of cultures in urban America.[142]

These interpretative features of Addams's narratives, along with the relational, proximate, and interactive epistemology Hull House fostered, thus contributed to a social knowledge in which a broader range of experiences is central to the process of inquiry. In another telling example of this methodology, Addams writes her own experience into the relationships under examination, ensuring

---

135. Seigfried, introduction to Jane Addams, *Democracy and Social Ethics,* xxv–xxx.

136. Addams, *Democracy and Social Ethics,* 25.

137. Ibid., 22–23.

138. Ibid., 27.

139. Ibid., 22–23.

140. For historical discussion of this point, see Alan M. Kraut, *The Huddled Masses: The Immigrant in American Society, 1880–1921* (Arlington Heights, IL: Harlan Davidson, 1982), 127–33. Also Lissak, *Pluralism and Progressives.*

141. Addams, "Social Settlements," *Proceedings of the National Conference of Charities and Corrections* (1897), 344–45.

142. Joslin, *Jane Addams,* 61, 62.

that the middle-class young woman's perspective is clearly explained. She illustrates the strained family relationships when "young women's impulse to act her part as a citizen of the world" clash with parental expectations.[143] Daughters' attempts to assert themselves are made more difficult, she claims, "due to the fact that for so many hundreds of years women have had no larger interests, no participation in the affairs lying quite outside personal and family claims." Parents conclude that "her attempt to break away must therefore be willful and self-indulgent."[144] But women's movement into the public realm signaled that "our democracy is making inroads upon the family, the oldest of human institutions, [with a claim] being advanced which in a certain sense is larger than the family claim."[145] By explaining both parents' and daughters' positions, she illustrates how new choices for women lead to uncertain family identities and challenges the patriarchy of the traditional family structure in which the daughter is a "family possession."[146]

In *The New Radicalism in America*, Christopher Lasch argues that what Addams described in her discussion of the relationship between parents and their daughters was a cultural crisis, that "middle-class parents found themselves unable any longer to explain to their children why their way of life was important or desirable," and that children were "equally unable to communicate a sense of why they could not pursue the goals their parents held up before them."[147] However, Lasch fails to acknowledge that Addams was describing a *daughter's* experience, an experience defined by the patriarchal Victorian culture in which she grew to adulthood. This patriarchy was the backdrop for the individualist ethics she critiqued in both her writings and her settlement work.[148] She was indeed describing a cultural crisis, but the class terms in which Lasch articulated it was only part of the story. As historian James Livingston argues, Addams strove to reconcile individualism with a new conception of the social self and social ethics that developed in tandem with corporate capitalism. Her new moral universe was predicated on social solidarity, with subjectivity and agency not an a priori fact in the political actor but constituted in relationships. Livingston argues that the feminist individualism that Addams helped forge rejected the notion that subjectivity was found in proprietary capitalism. Instead, feminist individualism opened up new models of subjectivity in which the social self or "the collective

143. Addams, *Democracy and Social Ethics*, 85.

144. Ibid., 74.

145. Ibid., 77.

146. Ibid., 82.

147. Christopher Lasch, *The New Radicalism in American Life, 1889–1963: The Intellectual as a Social Type* (New York: Knopf, 1963), 36.

148. Marilyn Fischer, "Jane Addams's Critique of Capitalism as Patriarchal," in *Feminist Interpretations of John Dewey*, ed. Charlene Haddock Seigfried, 278–96 (University Park: Pennsylvania State University Press, 2002).

identity forged by cooperation appears as the alternative to the morbid isolation of the lordly male proprietor."[149] The feminine and masculine, elite and lowly voices she blends in her work thus point to a new way to understand class and gender identities, and with them, democracy.

When viewed through the lens of class formation, Addams's role as a translator appears somewhat problematic. On the one hand, her efforts to take seriously and make legible the cultures, experiences, ideas, and aspirations of Chicago's immigrants, workers, and daughters was important cultural and epistemological work in an environment that frequently infantilized them.[150] Although as a woman—and a woman with an uncomfortable message—she often ran the danger of marginalization, her public reputation and elite status put her in a better position to gain a wider hearing among middle-class men and women than spokespeople from the populations she wrote about. Nonetheless, it is Addams's interpretation—her voice—that represents these people in public debate. Like other middle-class men and women seeking to secure their new roles in social work and public policy, she ran the danger of silencing, romanticizing, or misinterpreting her neighbors, even as she gained new class status for doing so. To do so would be to undermine the very democratic social knowledge she sought to create and the democracy she wished to build. That she remained aware of this danger, sought to break down the psychological barriers of the class divide, worked with her neighbors to define and carry out their own cultural and political projects, and publicly explained the dangers of a democracy that did not include the experiences and voices of people like those she came to know in her neighborhood, suggests her strong commitment to avoiding the pitfalls of her class position, though of course she could never entirely escape it.

As in her work at Hull House, we see in her writing the embodiment of the Progressive reformers whom William Allen White summarized in *American Magazine* in 1909: "And so with all our reforming conditions about us, by the millions and millions we are first of all reforming ourselves. We are promoting democracy by forgetting ourselves in the thought of others."[151] Jane Addams, Hull House, and the rich female network of Chicago reform suggest that we

149. James Livingston, *Pragmatism and the Political Economy of Cultural Revolution, 1850–1940* (Chapel Hill: University of North Carolina Press, 1994), 75. Livingston discusses the intersection of pragmatism, corporate capitalism, and feminism on pp. 70–78 and in *Pragmatism, Feminism, and Democracy*.

150. Laura Hapke, *Labor's Text: The Worker in American Fiction* (New Brunswick, NJ: Rutgers University Press, 2001).

151. Quoted in Joslin, *Jane Addams*, 111. Immigrants and workers also recognized the fact that settlement residents used their class position differently. As union organizer Abraham Bisno noted, "My acquaintance with the people at Hull House was an eye-opener to me. People who did not belong to our class took an interest in our lot in life." Abraham Bisno, *Abraham Bisno, Union Pioneer* (Madison: University of Wisconsin Press, 1967), 115–16.

might consider class not only in terms of occupation or income but also as an identity with fluid boundaries capable of creating new political alliances and subjectivities. Chicago's wealthy and middle-class women and Chicago's workers and immigrants forged such relationships, as we see in the following two chapters, making Progressive Era Chicago a politically vibrant arena indeed.

Conclusion

Throughout the 1890s, Hull House served as a kind of stage for civic interaction. Participants in its activities could act out new roles in ways that were both promising and problematic for democratic social life. In discussions at the Working People's Social Science Club, workers became experts. In women's cross-class investigations of municipal street cleaning, they participated in a common project that connected their own domestic lives to broader political aims. In addition, art offered a means for a transcendent sympathy. As Hull House encouraged mutual experience, discussion, and artistic pursuits as arenas for civic interaction, it emphasized the social foundations of knowledge and democracy as daily practice.

Nevertheless, the basis of mutual recognition at the root of its democratic social knowledge did not always address fundamental differences between participants. Addams was always clear that residents should *not* live like their neighbors; a settlement should instead be a reflection of the elite and middle-class tastes and style of its residents. This included furnishings, social manners, even the employment of servants. Addams herself admitted that economic and cultural differences haunted settlement work even as it attempted to transcend them.[152] Perhaps Hull House became so popular not only because it addressed the need for middle-class women to create meaningful public work for themselves and was at the center of a multifaceted approach to humanizing industrial capitalism's worst effects but also because it responded to a problem that was ultimately political: the survival of democracy in a fragmented city. Ultimately it positioned middle-class reformers, particularly women, as democracy's saviors. As mediators trying to explain differences, recognize multiple voices, and make divergent classes and ethnic groups legible to one another, these middle-class

---

152. This recognition of power differentials is significant. Any form of representation is fraught with inevitable differences between intermediaries and those whom they represent. Yet as sociologist Alberto Melucci has suggested, "a necessary condition of democratization is the refusal to deny this problem ideologically: only if and when it is acknowledged does it become possible to look for ways controlling and reducing the distance separating power from social demands" (253). See "Social Movements and the Democratization of Everyday Life," in *Civil Society and the State: New European Perspectives*, ed. John Keane, 245–60 (London: Verso 1988).

reformers helped diffuse class and ethnic tensions between diverse groups, enabling them to understand and work together politically. Thus the democratic social knowledge Hull House promoted served as the basis for democratic politics both in the everyday dynamics of power relations and in the formal arena of electoral politics.

In so doing, Hull House put a new twist on the middle-class domestic model of reform. The project turned the middle-class home into a public space available to neighbors and people from all over the city, who were welcome to socialize in its rooms, leave their children, and join its numerous clubs and discussions. It aimed at solidarity along humanistic lines. One British settlement worker captured the challenges Hull House posed: "In emphasizing the wide universal brotherliness and responsibility, Addams seemed to break down the nucleus of family obligations and eliminate meaningful social hierarchies" that middle-class domesticity taught.[153] By creating such an environment, Addams implicitly recast liberal republicanism and aligned social responsibility more closely with women's domestic duties carried into the public realm. Addams thus departed from prevailing notions of democracy and citizenship that shaped Chicago's political economy during its decades of spectacular growth. Where the political agent had been cast as male, buttressed by private responsibilities and privilege and closely aligned with the moral value of work, Addams defined it as an ethical responsibility to care for the community. Its roots, then, were gendered and Christian; she drew from the example of women's labor in the "Breadgivers" and widened the definition of the family to include social gospelism's concept of a brotherhood of humanity united through Christ.

The goal "to add the social function to democracy," then, meant to foster a process by which "identification with the common lot which is the essential idea of Democracy becomes the source and expression of social ethics."[154] Since "the Social Gulf is always an affair of the imagination," a combination of social science, shared experience, and Christian and domestic ideals of sympathy could bridge it.[155] She attacked "the selfish people of our acquaintance" who share "the conviction that they are different from other men and women, that they need peculiar consideration because they are more sensitive or more refined," and who "'refuse to be bound by any relation save the personally luxurious ones of love and admiration, or the identity of political opinion, or religious creed."[156] Addams's ideas about human nature led her to search for

153. Helen J. Gow, April 11, 1897, Helen J. Gow Diaries, vol. 3, Duke University, Durham, NC, quoted in Sklar, *Florence Kelley and the Nation's Work*, 204.

154. Addams, *Democracy and Social Ethics*, 11.

155. Addams, "Address of Miss Addams [on Settlement Work], University Settlement Society of New York, *Annual Report for 1902*, 55. Quoted in Ross, "Gendered Social Knowledge."

156. Addams, *Democracy and Social Ethics*, 10.

commonalities on which to ground a relational, sympathetic, interactive democratic social knowledge.

When Addams maintained that the social gulf is a problem of imagination, she argued against what she believed to be the psychological barriers to democracy and turned to a democratic social knowledge to overcome those divisions. Implicitly suggesting that equal social relations were as much an affair of the imagination as were economic boundaries, Addams worked to foster sympathetic understanding that recognized commonalities. Proximate knowledge made the Other more visible and understandable; mutuality, experience, and interactive social knowledge fostered democratic praxis rooted in relationships across class and ethnic differences. Though a democracy built on daily practices and social relationships did not appear immediately political in a culture that defined politics narrowly, it quickly became so in the activist environment of Progressive Era Chicago. It offered an alternative to—indeed ultimately challenged—liberal republicanism's emphasis on market relations and commitment to business prerogatives and upset class, ethnic, and family hierarchies. As Addams confronted the problem of power as it was manifested in daily interactions, as well as social, economic, and political institutions, she clung to a vision of democracy in which those unequal power relationships would be replaced by mutuality, in which proximate, interactive knowledge was connected to activism, and in which recognition of common humanity transcended without crushing differences of culture, class, and experiences, thus preventing a fatal drifting apart. This vision of democracy explains why, during World War I, Addams broke ranks with so many of her Progressive allies to remain pacificist.[157] She refused to accept that some problems might be irreconcilable; for her, violence was no substitute for sympathetic understanding, reason, and humility.

Addams's broadly based formulation of democratic social knowledge placed her apart from the Civic Federation. Though the social settlement and the CFC shared a commitment to interaction across class and gender lines to address urban problems, epistemological differences—and their impact on democratic social knowledge—soon became apparent. Whereas the CFC was increasingly attracted to expert social science, Hull House sought ways to foster an alternative model of democratic social knowledge based in local relationships, proximate experience, and activism. While each offered a different approach to social

157. On Addams's opposition to World War I, see *The Second Twenty Years* (New York: Macmillan, 1930); Kathryn Kish Sklar, "'Some of Us Who Deal with the Social Fabric': Jane Addams Blends Peace and Social Justice, 1907–1919," *Journal of the Gilded Age and the Progressive Era* 2, no.1 (January 2003): 80–96.

knowledge, both faced tensions around class, inclusion of the Other in the polity, and representations of collective experience and knowledge, as well as expertise, in political debate. The controversies taken up in the next chapter surrounding Pullman Town, its famous strike, and the debate over arbitration it fostered further point to the possibilities and limitations of democratic social knowledge.

4

"Such a Piece of Business Folly"

Labor Arbitration and Class Struggles over Democratic Social Knowledge

The demand [workers] made before quitting work was that the wages should be re-stored to the scale of last year. . . . It must be clear to every business man and to every thinking mechanic that no prudent employer could submit to arbitration the question whether he should commit such a piece of business folly.[1]

Despite the differences that divided Hull House and the Civic Federation, during the turbulent Pullman Strike both organizations agreed on one thing: Chicago's labor conflicts required an intermediary if the city was to avoid a "fatal drift-ing apart." Both settlement reformers, like Jane Addams, and the CFC's Board of Conciliation, created in early 1894, envisioned themselves in this role.[2] Their optimism about mediation was tested in June 1894, when thousands of workers at the Pullman Palace Car Works went on strike after months of wage cuts, shop abuses, and grievances about the way George Pullman managed the company town where one-third of his employees lived. While workers asked Pullman to sit down with them and negotiate an end to the strike, he maintained that he had nothing to arbitrate—indeed that arbitration itself was "such a piece of business folly." Through the lens of the Pullman Strike and the labor strife that followed, we see conflicts over liberal republican social knowledge and an alter-native democratic social knowledge imbedded in the debates over conciliation, arbitration, and collective bargaining.

1. The epigraph to this chapter is drawn from the testimony of George Pullman, in U.S. Strike Commission, *Report on the Chicago Strike of June–July, 1894* (Washington, DC: U.S. Strike Commission, 1895), 552 (hereafter cited as *Chicago Strike*).

2. The CFC organized an industrial committee soon after its founding in an attempt to prevent and mediate labor struggle. Social settlement leaders frequently played prominent roles in mediating strikes across the city. For example, Graham Taylor was called upon to serve as a third-party arbitra-tor in a number of strikes during the 1890s, as were Addams and McDowell.

This chapter examines arbitration debates as exemplifying broader struggles over democratic social knowledge. Just as the Civic Federation sought new ways to shape social knowledge through mutual discussion and political endeavors and Jane Addams and Hull House residents used civic interaction to bridge the gap of disparate social experiences, so middle-class reformers believed arbitration offered a method of democratic praxis, one that brought hostile parties together. Early arbitration theorists among reformers and social scientists suggested that it recognized a kind of worker knowledge and promoted mutuality and understanding between workers and employers, thus encouraging democratic social relations.[3]

Seen in this light, arbitration was an important aspect of democratic social knowledge emphasizing mutuality, respect, interaction, and discussion of shared problems. Reformers were particularly concerned that industrialization had increased social distance between owners and employers and had heightened class conflict. In the wake of serious conflicts like the Pullman Strike, new mechanisms were clearly needed to foster peaceful work relations. Arbitration, as a process that brought unionists and employers into greater proximity and knowledge of one another, promoted the kind of interactive, proximate social knowledge critical to harmonious cross-class relations. Its success in doing so required employers and unions to first recognize and then respect each other's particular knowledge and use it to achieve a greater collective knowledge of business practices and their impact on workers' lives. In an environment in which owners saw their business prerogatives as sanctioned by "natural" economic law, arbitration served to raise the epistemological status of workers by legitimizing their contributions to business practices. Arbitration was thus tied to efforts to create an interactive, inclusive, participatory social knowledge, one closely connected to democratic praxis that recognized the importance of workers' experiences and contributions to social debate and economic decisions.

Against the backdrop of shifting conceptions of democracy and anxiety over the transformation of the U.S. economy, reformers imagined arbitration in complex ways: as a set of relationships between different social actors and with the state; as a potential solution to the impersonal nature of industrial capitalism;

3. By equalizing the forces of labor and capital and bringing them into negotiation, it also offered an industrial democracy predicated upon the principles of political democracy. During the 1880s and continuing into the new century, arbitration attracted attention from workers, progressive businessmen, and reformers alike who sought to overcome the social strife that had exploded in strikes and riots over the previous two decades. William E. Akin, "Arbitration and Labor Conflict: The Middle-class Panacea, 1886–1900," *Historian* 29, no. 4 (August 1967): 565–83. In 1886, for example, New York produced a report drawn from arbitration advocates around the country and in England. State Board of Arbitration, *Views of Arbitration as Means of Settling Labor Disputes* (Rochester, NY: Union and Advertiser Company's Printers, 1886). For other works on arbitration from the period, see John P. Peters, ed., *Labor and Capital: A Discussion of the Relations of Employer and Employed* (New York: G. P. Putnam's Sons, 1902), 179–304. For the efforts of unions around the nation to secure arbitration, see David Montgomery, *The Fall of the House of Labor: The Workplace, the State, and American Labor Activism, 1865–1925* (New York: Cambridge University Press, 1987).

and as a way of promoting industrial peace. Arbitration exemplified the reformers' vision of a democratic social knowledge that sought new processes by which to understand and explain social reality. They believed it would foster owners' and employers' reasonableness and encourage open deliberation about economic questions. Some theorists even suggested that arbitration was part of a larger goal of industrial democracy, one that expanded political rights and equality into economic relations.[4] In contrast, many industrial capitalists' steadfast opposition to arbitration reveals an epistemological framework that privileged classical economy as a set of natural laws that, not coincidently, protected their business interests. In debates over arbitration, we thus find important epistemological positions at stake, conflicting ones that variously privileged workers' collective practical knowledge, the assumptions of classical liberal political economy, or social science. By focusing on arbitration in this way, the chapter shows how arbitration was part of a cultural dialogue—and battle—over democratic social knowledge.

The Pullman Town and strike have been well noted in labor and urban historiography; however, viewing it through the lens of struggles over social knowledge offers us a new window onto debates about arbitration and democratic social knowledge as well.[5] My interpretation of arbitration as part of a struggle over democratic social knowledge complicates the usual characterizations of arbitration. Recognizing that most union leaders from the Progressive Era were wary of compulsory arbitration and that even voluntary arbitration was frequently promoted by conservative unionists who sought to avoid radical transformation of economic relations, labor historians tend to view arbitration

4. Howell John Harris, "Industrial Democracy and Liberal Capitalism, 1890–1925," in *Industrial Democracy in America: The Ambiguous Promise*, ed. Nelson Lichtenstein and Howell John Harris, 43–66 (New York: Woodrow Wilson Center Press and Cambridge University Press, 1993).

5. Labor historians have focused on the strike's contribution to the evolution of railroad transportation and regulation, the American Railway Union and the career of Eugene Debs, and to President Cleveland's use of the injunction as a new weapon in labor disputes. See, for example, Richard Schneirov, Shelton Stromquist, and Nick Salvatore, eds., *The Pullman Strike and the Crisis of the 1890s: Essays on Labor and Politics* (Urbana: University of Illinois Press, 1999); Nick Salvatore, *Eugene V. Debs: Citizen and Socialist* (Urbana: University of Illinois Press, 1982); William E. Forbath, *Law and the Shaping of the American Labor Movement* (Cambridge, MA: Harvard University Press, 1991). Likewise, urban historians have drawn attention to Pullman Town itself since it was one of the first towns built using the theory of environmentalism to inform urban planning. Carl S. Smith, *Urban Disorder and the Shape of Belief: The Great Chicago Fire, the Haymarket Bomb, and the Model Town of Pullman* (Chicago: University of Chicago Press, 1995); Stanley Buder, *Pullman: An Experiment in Industrial Order and Community Planning, 1880–1930* (New York: Oxford University Press, 1967). The strike and its aftermath also served as a lightening rod for ongoing discussion among social scientists and businessmen about the transformations in the U.S. economy in the decades following the Civil War. Nancy Cohen, *The Reconstruction of American Liberalism, 1865–1914* (Chapel Hill: University of North Carolina Press, 2002), 192–202, and Mary O. Furner, "The Republican Tradition and the New Liberalism: Social Investigation, State Building, and Social Learning in the Gilded Age," in *The State and Social Investigation in Britain and the United States*, ed. Michael J. Lacey and Mary O. Furner, 171–242 (New York: Woodrow Wilson Center Press and Cambridge University Press, 1993).

suspiciously.[6] Historians who focus on the transformation of the liberal state see it as an important step toward new liberalism, which sought voluntary solutions to economic conflict and placed the state in the position of brokering between associated groups of businessmen and workers. Still, the outcomes of state intervention were disappointing, as alliances between corporations and government came to dominate economic policy and practices, including arbitration, by the end of the Progressive Era.[7] From the vantage point of the 1880s and 1890s, however, arbitration appeared as a hopeful, democratic solution—though not without its pitfalls—to the era's labor conflicts.

Pullman is an important place to begin not just because the strike intensified national discourse about arbitration but also because the car magnate and his town allow us a window into how class impacts ideas of social knowledge. As Pullman and other businessmen, reformers, union officials, economists, and workers themselves wrestled with the social and economic significance of arbitration, they raised questions about democracy and epistemological agency: Who in industrial capitalism can be knowers? Could arbitration and, later, collective bargaining serve democratic purposes? Might they not counteract the alienating effects of the modern, corporate world and encourage mutual and equitable relations between business and capital, transforming both sides in the process? Balancing against a free-market paradigm, could arbitration serve as a mechanism of redistributive justice?

This chapter begins with an exploration of the social knowledge Pullman espoused, which shared a belief in the justice of the market and classical economic principles with liberal republicanism. It then explores the views presented at the CFC's arbitration conference in late 1894. This event provides us with a snapshot of arguments for arbitration from the perspectives of various commentators—historicist economists, social reformers, and unionists. Finally it examines the course of arbitration in Chicago after the Pullman Strike. These examples illustrate the tenacity of a liberal republican rhetoric and logic among business elites and the ways that unionists used arbitration to make claims for their own legitimacy and for new standards of justice.

"We Treat Them as Individuals and as Men":
Liberal Republicanism and Resistance to Arbitration

By the time of the Pullman Strike, Chicago businessmen and unions had been struggling over union recognition and arbitration for two decades. Since the

---

6. Montgomery, *Fall of the House of Labor.*
7. James Weinstein, *The Corporate Ideal in the Liberal State, 1900–1918* (Boston: Beacon, 1968).

late 1870s, arbitration had been a part of the platform of the Chicago Trades Assembly and its younger incarnation, the Trades and Labor Assembly.[8] The Typographical Union had secured arbitration agreements in the 1870s, and M. J. Carroll, one of its leaders and a CFC member, reported that union recognition and arbitration went hand in hand in the printing trades and tended to prevent strikes.[9] In the 1880s a series of successful strikes in the building trades led to arbitration agreements and settlements generally favorable to unions.[10] In 1890 the United Carpenters' Council (UCC) won unions' biggest victory toward securing arbitration. After calling a strike to pressure Chicago contractors to recognize the union, it won recognition, a wage increase, and a provision for a joint arbitration committee to settle disputes and create stable agreements between the contractors and union workers. The World's Fair directors, led by president Lyman Gage, noted the power of the organization, as contractors agreed to an eight-hour day and compulsory arbitration of all disagreements.[11] In March 1891, when leading contractors signed a two-year agreement with the UCC stipulating arbitration, collective bargaining became a reality in Chicago's building trades.[12]

8. Jack Bizjack, "The Trade and Labor Assembly of Chicago" (master's thesis, University of Chicago, 1969); Truman Cicero Bingham, "The Chicago Federation of Labor" (master's thesis, University of Chicago, 1924).

9. Testimony of M. J. Carroll, *Chicago Strike*, 460.

10. Richard Schneirov and Thomas J. Suhrbur, *Union Brotherhood, Union Town: The History of the Carpenters' Union of Chicago, 1863–1987* (Carbondale: Southern Illinois University Press, 1988).

11. With 70–90 percent of the carpenters organized, the union joined with bricklayers to form the Building Trades Council (BTC). As Schneirov and Suhrbur demonstrate, the strength of the BTC was a turning point in the ability of separate unions to carry out successful strikes and command arbitration.

12. Schneirov and Suhrbur, *Union Brotherhood, Union Town*, 38–41. As Schneirov and Suhrbur make clear, because of fierce competition among contractors, most of them rejected arbitration and collective bargaining until the union was able to ensure that the majority of carpenters would not accept wages lower then the negotiated rate. Once the Building Trades Council was powerful enough to ensure this, contractors agreed to union recognition and arbitration. The BTC's successful bid for arbitration indicated the strength of Chicago's craft economy, a strength that was in part predicated on craftsmen's ability to negotiate trade agreements and arbitrate disputes with employers. As Andrew Wender Cohen has demonstrated, Chicago was the site of struggle between a petite bourgeois of craftworkers and small businessmen and larger industrial concerns. The ability of men in trades such as construction, trucking, and shop keeping to control the local economy belies the organizational and corporate liberal explanations of U.S. economic development in the Progressive Era. In these small-scale enterprises, unions were able to assert a collective identity and power in preventing national corporations from dominating whole sectors of Chicago's economy. They succeeded largely through their ability to enforce union rules and pressure employers to enforce trade and arbitration agreements. The lessons of Chicago's craft economy suggest the importance of collective action, union recognition, and, when necessary, arbitration of disputes. Andrew Wender Cohen, *The Racketeer's Progress: Chicago and the Struggle for the Modern American Economy, 1900–1940* (New York: Cambridge University Press, 2004), 1–57. Cohen argues that the struggle

Still, this struggle was bitter. Employers maintained a paradigm of individualism at odds with unionization. Though economic knowledge was shifting at this moment, with businessmen, public intellectuals, and unionists developing a nuanced understanding of the emerging corporate economy, the language of classical liberal individualism and a conception of liberal republican social knowledge still set the terms of popular debate; employers used it to cast unions and union claims outside the boundaries of legitimacy.[13] In response to the UCC's gains in the 1880s, contractors met in Chicago to found the National Association of Builders (NAB) in 1887. Invoking individualism implied in freedom of contract, the NAB asserted the "absolute personal independence of the individual to work or not to work, to employ or not to employ." The NAB rejected all arbitration "on this fundamental open-shop principle, which it considered the basis of 'our whole social fabric.'"[14] In 1893 the World's Fair directors managed to roll back union successes when the directorate refused to fire nonunion workers. Taking refuge behind the federal government, Lyman Gage explained that "We could not grant this demand [for the closed shop] if we were personally disposed to do so. The World's Columbian Exposition is an institution created and fathered by the U.S. Government. The United States have [sic] decided that we cannot accede to this demand."[15] As Graham Taylor, sociologist, minister, founder of Chicago Commons social settlement, and close observer of Chicago labor battles, remarked, "American business and industry still cling in the main to that individualism which resulted from boundless resources and unhampered enterprise which no longer exist. . . . Labor organization has not yet been accepted in principle by employers in general."[16] Against this backdrop, the status of unions and arbitration was uncertain when the Pullman Strike began a year later.

Owners' opposition to unions made securing arbitration all the more important. Because arbitration inherently depended upon a recognition of the union and all that it represented—workers' equal status with employers, their particular collective knowledge, their voice in economic decision making—it cut right

over the modern economy influenced labor law and provided the basis for industrial organization during the New Deal.

13. Nancy Cohen, *The Reconstruction of American Liberalism, 1865–1914* (Chapel Hill: University of North Carolina Press, 2002); James Livingston, *Pragmatism and the Political Economy of Cultural Revolution, 1850–1940* (Chapel Hill: University of North Carolina Press, 1994); Cohen, *Racketeer's Progress;* Alan Trachtenberg, *The Incorporation of America: Culture and Society in the Gilded Age* (New York: Hill and Wang, 1982).

14. Richard Schneirov, *Labor and Urban Politics: Class Conflict and the Origins of Modern Liberalism in Chicago, 1864–97* (Urbana: University of Illinois Press, 1998), 249.

15. Quoted in Schneirov and Suhrbur, *Union Brotherhood, Union Town,* 52–53.

16. Graham Taylor, "Draft of Report on the Church and Economic and Industrial Problems for the Universal Christian Conference on Life and Work," n.d., in Graham Taylor Papers, Box 48, Folder 2258, Newberry Library, Modern Manuscripts Collection.

to the core of conflicts over democratic participation in the industrial economy and over working-class legitimacy to shape social explanations of economic realities.[17] Rejecting the collectivist implications of unions, owners like Pullman relied upon the principles of individualism, as well as the laws of supply and demand and laissez-faire to determine their interactions with their workers, and they assumed that the liberal market promoted social harmony rather than class conflict. Pullman's explanations of the strike and his refusal to arbitrate illustrate these points.

On the surface the strike appeared to grow out of circumstances arising from the depression of 1893–1894, but much more was at stake in the way Pullman, workers, and reformers framed the terms of debate. Between August 1893 and April 1894, the company made several wage cuts, amounting on average to 25 percent of a typical paycheck, although some employees fared much worse. Pullman justified these cuts on business principles: Because the demand for its railcars had declined during the depression, the company had to either close the shop or underbid on contracts, forcing them to lower workers' wages accordingly. Choosing the latter measure, Pullman agreed to take several contracts that would amount to a $50,000 loss to the company. The terms of the contracts also meant a total loss of $62,000 of workers' wages. Drawing from the language of classical liberal economics, Pullman justified these cuts to the federal commission investigating strike. "The wage question is settled by the law of supply and demand," he explained. "We are obliged to reduce wages in order to . . . compete with other people in the same business that are doing the same thing."[18] To raise wages when the economy was depressed would amount to "a gift of money" to his employees—an act of generosity neither Pullman nor the liberal republicanism of Chicago's elites endorsed.

Furthermore, Pullman argued, in such pressing times "a mutual sacrifice must be made. . . . The men must work a little harder and the Pullman company must use its profits that it has made in its business."[19] In his eyes, economic wisdom and common sense clearly dictated this course of action.[20] He assumed that the invisible and benevolent hand of the market served as a mechanism to coordinate and harmonize a variety of interests held by laborers and employers, and he appealed to the laws of supply and demand to settle questions of wages, prices, and production. This language permeated popular, as well as academic,

17. For linkages between arbitration and union recognition, see William B. Weeden, *Arbitration and Its Relation to Strikes* (Boston: G. H. Ellis, 1887), 12; U.S. Commission on Industrial Relations, *Final Report and Testimony*, vol. 19 (Westport, CT: Greenwood, 1970), 805; originally printed 1900–1902 by U. S. Government Printing Office, Washington, DC.

18. Testimony of George Pullman, *Chicago Strike*, 557.

19. Ibid.

20. The strike commission pointed out the financial advantage the company gained in keeping its works operating rather than shutting them down. *Chicago Strike*, 565–66.

economic discussions. As settlement leader and frequent arbitrator Graham Taylor explained, "the typical American employer considers that wages are properly determined by the play of the labor market, in accord with what he calls immutable economic laws."[21] If left alone, the market would bring the most just distribution of wages and profits. Joseph Weeks, a leading student of arbitration, explained that the most popular theory for preventing and settling labor differences is laissez-faire—unrestricted competition: "It is asserted that not only will competition determine accurately and inevitably what is a 'fair day's wage' for a 'fair day's work,' but that it will redress all economical grievances."[22]

Pullman's comments assumed that the worker and employer shared an interest in expanding company profits since this would increase the wage fund; from his position, the liberal market brought social harmony rather than conflict.[23] Pullman had long held such positions. Indeed, his stance was reflected in a remarkable series of editorials in Pullman Town's newspaper, *Arcade Advertiser*. Published several days after workers staged a walkout in May 1886, the newspaper laid out the company's vision of economics in articles such as "A Dollar," "Peaceful Industry," "A View of Wealth," "How the Individual Works," "Civil Society," and "Manufacturing." The articles add up to a careful articulation of an economic worldview that emphasized social harmony through productive labor for the good of the company and the nation. After explaining that "the railroads, the steamship, and the telegraph have almost obliterated time and space, and have made the whole world a common market," the paper goes on to explain that "the great natural advantages of the United States make it possible for our country to become the manufacturing center of the world, and the largest prosperity of our people seems destined to come through a realization of our possibilities as manufacturers." The paper reinforces the company's position that "every man works directly for others and indirectly for himself." While this seems to suggest a collectivist vision akin to that espoused by unions, taken together the articles suggest a commitment ultimately to the success of business and the growth of profits. Thus it argues for the importance of steady labor costs, so that contracts can be fairly bid and won. It implies that strikers' demands for higher wages threatened the survival of the company and individual families. A "citizen

21. Taylor, "Draft of Report on the Church"; Julia A. Reuben, *The Making of the Modern University: Intellectual Transformation and the Marginalization of Morality* (Chicago: University of Chicago Press, 1996), 145–52.

22. Joseph D. Weeks, "Labor Differences and Their Settlement: A Plea for Arbitration and Conciliation," Economic Tracts No. XX (New York: Society for Political Education, 1886), 15.

23. Josephine Shaw Lowell, "The Arbitration of Labor Disputes," *Locomotive Firemen's Magazine* 23, no. 2 (August 1897): 114; Josiah Strong, "Are the Interests of Employer and Employed Mutual, and, if so, How Can This Mutuality of Interests Be Made Effective?" in *Labor and Capital: A Discussion of the Relations of Employer and Employed,* ed. John P. Peters, 13–21 (New York: G. P. Putnam's Sons, 1902).

of Pullman" noted that "men with families dependent upon them cannot afford to be idle. . . . I sincerely hope that work in all the shops will speedily be resumed, and I believe that every man with a home here holds the same view, for the creation of products is as much a necessity as is the consumption of products."[24]

Expounding economic laws that assumed an identity of interests between labor and capital, Pullman not only believed workers would accept a wage cut during the 1894 depression; he also expected them to act in accordance with principles of possessive individualism. Indeed, in ascribing self-interest as the primary human trait shaping economic interactions, possessive individualism stood as one of the cornerstones of the liberal market economy.[25] As Weeks described it, "this theory [of laissez-faire or competition] assumes that both employer and employe [sic] understand what is their highest interest in an economical sense, and will surely seek it . . . and as the result of this contest waged by each to get all he can, there will result perfect justice to all."[26]

Because they represented a collective association in which the individual subordinated his personal interest to the good of the whole, unions stood in opposition to this individualism, and for this reason employers like Pullman rejected unionism. Pullman Company vice president Thomas Wickes explained the company's decision not to arbitrate: "We treat them as individuals and as men."[27] Juxtaposed with the mutualism of unions, which frequently adopted the motto "an injury to one is the concern of all," Wickes's statement helps explain the significance of battles over arbitration at this particular moment in economic transformation since arbitration required the recognition of unions and workers' rights to equal representation in disputes with management. Pullman further explained that it was "impossible to submit to arbitration" the matter of wages because doing so would violate "the principle that a man should have the right to manage his own property."[28] Drawing on reasoning rooted in the individualism of liberal political economy, he observed that "it must be clear to every business man and to every thinking mechanic that no prudent employer could submit to arbitration the question whether he should commit such a piece of business folly."[29]

Everett St. John, general manager of the Chicago, Rock Island, and Pacific Railway Company and president of the General Managers' Association (an

24. *Arcade Advertiser*, May 8, 1886, Pullman Strike Scrapbooks, Reel 10.
25. Cohen, *Reconstruction of American Liberalism*, 38; Jeffrey Sklansky, *The Soul's Economy: Market Society and Selfhood in American Thought, 1820–1920* (Chapel Hill: University of North Carolina Press, 2002), 14.
26. Weeks, "Labor Differences and Their Settlement," 16.
27. Testimony of Thomas Wickes, *Chicago Strike*, 621.
28. Testimony of George Pullman, *Chicago Strike*, 556.
29. Ibid., 552.

employers' association of railroads operating through Chicago), shared Pullman's views. In his dual capacity, he appeared before the U.S. Strike Commission investigating the Pullman boycott. In his second day of testimony, St. John asserted that "to very many minds the law of supply and demand must still govern. It is a principle as old as government itself, and has proven in the years past effective as applied to both employer and employee."[30] Though St. John recognized that "in the minds of many" this principle of supply and demand "might prove ineffective in the future," he remained unclear about what might replace it as a means to determine wages."[31]

By refusing to arbitrate matters that he saw as natural economic law, Pullman rejected the workers' collective knowledge of the work process and industrialization's effects on their lives. This position reflected his paternalistic attitude: In reducing them to individuals, he suggested he had nothing to learn from individual workers and their singular experiences. On the contrary, he figured himself as a teacher, using the town and its resources to shape worker behavior. Even more striking than the 1886 editorials themselves is the handwritten scrawl left by a Pullman Company employee explaining that "following editorial articles embodying statements of laws of trade and principles of political economy were read in every household in Pullman Saturday and Sunday. Suggestive forms of statement were used in order to have readers make their own applications of truths."[32] Pullman's approach to the labor problems of the day illustrated a framework of knowledge about the environment and behavior that suggested that residents could be educated—or manipulated, depending on one's perspective—into becoming model workers. His paternalism delegitimized the epistemological status of his workers and residents.

Pullman granted social science experts the intellectual and moral authority to manipulate the environment, even as he maintained the inviolability of natural economic laws.[33] Seeking to improve the lives of his workers, Pullman

30. Testimony of Everett St. John, *Chicago Strike*, 253.

31. Ibid. Everett St. John quoted an opinion of Judge Thomas Cooley that suggested that arbitration might be an effective means of settling some matters but not issues such as sympathy strikes. He left open the possibility of a board of arbitration but equivocated on whether the state should involve itself in such matters: "The personal liberty of both the employer and the laborer is necessarily to be respected, and every man must be left to determine for himself whether he will observe and perform such moral or sentimental obligations or recognize such claims as the State has never deemed it wise to convert into legal duties or legal rights." Quoted in testimony of Everett St. John, *Chicago Strike*, 254.

32. *Arcade Advertiser*, May 8, 1886, Pullman Strike Scrapbooks, Reel 10.

33. George Pullman was born into modest circumstances in upstate New York and came west in 1859 to earn his fortune. Though he rose quickly to success in the city's booming economy, he was concerned about the social divisions between capital and labor. Pullman had joined a number of reform organizations in the city, but none inspired him as much as Charles Read's novel, *Put Yourself in His Place: A Novel* (1870). The novel takes its name from a stock phrase of one of the characters "who believes that the key to social harmony lies in one's ability to see the world through the eyes of

combined theories of environmentalism with the goal of business profits into a grand experiment.[34] Pullman Town was indeed extraordinary for the time. As we have seen, Chicago and its early environs had developed haphazardly under the segmented system encouraged by the free market, but social theorists and architects had begun to question the practice of building urban landscapes in this manner. Increasingly they believed that as urban planning solved the problems of sanitation and disease that plagued the city, it could also affect behavior.[35] In this context, Pullman Town was a sociological experiment in planned community, and in positivistic fashion the experiment offered a means to gather knowledge about the influence of environment on working-class behavior. Rather than permit the randomness and vice that usually accompanied city growth, Pullman's project offered visitors firsthand observations of moral order fostered by urban planning.

Delegates from state departments of labor, industrialists, and social scientists visited the town and most hopefully praised the use of social science principles to shape the built environment; such a unification seemed able to remake the character of the working class and also resolve problems of worker and employer relationships.[36] One delegation thought Pullman Town "one of the most attractive experiments of the age seeking to harmonize the interests of labor and capital." After visiting the town, measuring its sewer pipes, counting residents' books and pianos, and surveying the religious and ethnic backgrounds of the workers, the delegates concluded that the Pullman factory and town should "be held up to the manufacturers and employers of men throughout the country as worthy of their emulation."[37] The social scientific nature of these visitors' methods and their own distance from Pullman and his town lent weight to the supposed objectivity and neutrality of the knowledge their reports disseminated. Most investigators seemed to agree with Pullman's own proud observations of the town's success: "Evidently, [workers] were striving to make their homes correspond to their surroundings, and if able to do nothing more than beautify them, they at least kept them cleaner and planted flowers in their windows."[38]

others." It attacked employers' indifference toward dangerous working conditions, and the protagonist, like Pullman himself, sought to "combine a craftsman's skill, an inventor's imagination, and an entrepreneur's boldness to remake the world around him for the better." Quoted in Smith, *Urban Disorder and the Shape of Belief*, 202.

34. Ibid., 203.

35. Buder, *Pullman Town*, 60–76; Smith, *Urban Disorder and the Shape of Belief*, 180–88; Gwendolyn Wright, *Moralism and the Model Home: Domestic Architecture and Cultural Conflict in Chicago, 1873–1913* (Chicago: University of Chicago Press, 1980).

36. For discussions of reactions to Pullman Town, see Buder, *Pullman Town*, "Public Opinion and the Town," 92–104; Smith, *Urban Disorder and the Shape of Belief*, 184–208.

37. Quoted in Smith, *Urban Disorder and the Shape of Belief*, 192.

38. Ibid., 194–95.

Pullman Town reinforced several features prominent in liberal republican-ism. By offering a living environment free from saloons, gambling halls, and brothels and that further provided appealing and harmonious dwellings and public spaces, Pullman believed he could transform his workforce. The town would attract upstanding workers, especially family men, and the atmosphere would discourage vice. Such an environment helped instill middle-class values promulgated by capitalists: sobriety, thrift, stability—traits that the civic elites of the CFC also espoused. Indeed, as we saw in chapter 2, the CFC's Central Relief Association rhetoric echoed such assumptions of the harmony of interests between employers and employees. Pullman calculated that his town would also help workers to recognize the financial and moral interests they shared with the company, thus encouraging loyalty. Yet his town was built on the patriarchal paternalism beneath Chicago's liberal republicanism. Pullman and his workers shared a "conviction that men should work; that women, children, and other dependents should be cared for; and that the family was the critical center of the social order."[39] The specifics of who was responsible for providing for women and children was often debated, but commentators, workers, most of the wives, and Pullman alike seemed to share a framework of Victorian domesticity.

Of course, critics pointed to the town's hypocrisies: Pullman refused to sell property to workers; the city lacked independent newspapers, churches, and meeting halls; and the watchful eye of the company undermined independent voting.[40] The generally favorable response the town and Pullman's treatment of his workers received among social scientists and businessmen illustrated a ten-dency to prioritize urban order and cleanliness over political and human rights.[41] Several historians of the Progressive Era have remained skeptical about the era's democratic rhetoric for such reasons. Citing a tendency toward social control, they are quick to point out reformers' efforts to create administrative bureaucra-cies and local organizations aimed at controlling public and private behavior that conformed with middle-class gender norms and domestic arrangements, economic and fiscal practices and policies, and Americanization programs. New business practices, particularly those of corporate welfare, buttressed these efforts. As a forerunner of corporate welfare, in which companies attempted to head off union pressures and state intervention by meeting some of the social needs of their employees, Pullman Town offered an example of how the marriage of tech-

39. Janice L. Rieff, "A Modern Lear and His Daughters: Gender in the Model Town of Pullman," in *Pullman Strike and the Crisis of the 1890s,* ed. Schneirov, Stromquist, and Salvatore, 66–86, 68.

40. Richard T. Ely, "Pullman: A Social Study," *Harper's Monthly* 70 (1885): 452–66.

41. This was a point Ely made and on which Smith elaborates. See Smith, *Urban Disorder and the Shape of Belief,* 207. The book illuminates the way in which portrayals of Pullman Town, the strike, and their legacy have revealed tensions in Americans' imaginations of the city as a place of disorder and chaos on one hand and freedom and democratic potential on the other. Such mixed views, Smith argues, have significantly shaped urban policy making. See especially 266–79.

nology, corporate practices, and social science might be used to promote a certain social knowledge—one that emphasized domesticity and a virtuous, acquiescent workforce that believed in the harmony of interests between capital and labor.

The moral and economic discourse surrounding Pullman Town and the 1894 strike reflected Chicago's broader debates over social knowledge. At this moment of economic transformation, when class relations were in flux, Pullman's refusal to arbitrate indicated his suspicion of workers, his rejection of their knowledge and experience as valuable additions to economic and social dialogues, and his adherence to economic knowledge that naturalized a language of classical liberal thought and affirmed employers' prerogatives to shape business practices according to market-driven ideals of fairness and justice. However, Pullman's was not the only conception of economic and social reform. For those who espoused different visions, arbitration offered a means for democratic interaction that elevated the epistemological status of workers and provided a forum for advancing economic and business knowledge.

Arbitration, Democratic Process, and Social Knowledge

The Pullman Strike was a watershed in debates about arbitration and drew national attention to the issue.[42] While some observers believed that Pullman was in the right and that owners need not ever arbitrate matters of wages,[43] other high-profile, pro-business men such as Mark Hanna reacted to Pullman's position in no uncertain terms: "A man who won't meet his men half way is a God-damn fool."[44] In Chicago, despite some conservative opposition to unions and arbitration, a coalition of labor representatives, social settlement workers, and some progressive-leaning businessmen weary of Chicago's industrial conflict looked hopefully to arbitration, expecting much from the CFC's Board of Conciliation.[45] Even the conservative Illinois Manufacturers Association, many of whose members also belonged to the CFC, invited M. H. Madden, president of the State Federation of Labor, to meet with them and discuss the possibilities

42. William E. Akin, "Arbitration and Labor Conflict: The Middle-class Panacea, 1886–1900," *Historian* 29, no. 4 (August 1967): 565–83, 575–76.

43. *Wall Street News,* July 2, 1894, and Lyman Abbott's editorial in *Outlook,* July 7, 1894, both reprinted in *Proceedings of the General Managers' Association of Chicago, Chicago, June 25, 1894–July 14, 1894,* in appendix, "Extracts from the Press," 1–3 (Chicago: Knight, Leonard, 1894).

44. Thomas Beer, *Hanna* (New York: Knopf, 1929), 133, quoted in Akin, "Arbitration and Labor Conflict," 577.

45. Schneirov, *Labor and Urban Politics,* discusses alliances forged between workers and businessmen. He argues that such cooperation was part of a larger move toward association and new liberalism that encouraged political and reform alliances across Chicago's classes throughout the 1890s.

of arbitration in their industries.[46] The membership of the CFC and its Board of Conciliation, with its business and labor representatives, seemed to appeal to both sides in the strike. Lyman Gage, president of the federation and a good friend of George Pullman, had publicly refused to support the strikers. In addition, the board included several prominent businessmen and professionals likely to be friendly toward Pullman: E. B. Butler, president of Butler Brothers wholesale notions; A. C. Bartlett, vice president of a wholesale druggist firm; and attorney Arthur Reyerson. However, other members had been active with working-class causes: Prof. C. R. Henderson; M. J. Carroll, editor of the *Eight-hour Herald* and a thirty-year member of the typographic union, which had practiced arbitration for two decades; Henry Demarest Lloyd; and Jane Addams. The board, in fact, proved "eminently satisfactory" to M. H. Madden, president of the State Federation of Labor.[47] Noting that labor had "wanted arbitration and tried in vain to get it, except in a few isolated cases, for fifteen or twenty years," Madden hoped that the "Civic Federation's board will take the place of a state board." Under such circumstances, he thought, "the great mass of capitalists and employers will be glad to welcome arbitration now that it comes to them in a quasi-official guise."[48] The stakes surrounding their efforts were heightened when George Howard, vice president of the American Railway Union, suggested that, "if the Civic Federation, representing all the best elements in this community, cannot effect so desirable a result [as an agreement to arbitration], it cannot justify its existence."[49] When Pullman refused to meet with the board, hopes for arbitration were shaken, and the government, as well as reformers, sought to reshape public opinion about mediation.

In the strike's aftermath, the federal government appointed a commission, led by long-time arbitration advocate and U.S. Labor Bureau Commissioner, Carroll Wright. Under the leadership of Wright, long a partisan of arbitration, the commission released a report that denounced Pullman and his refusal to arbitrate and encouraged national laws that instituted the practice. At the federal level, legislators pushed for a national arbitration law for the railroad industry that would protect the rights of labor, capital, and the public. Though it took four years and several attempts, Congress passed the Erdman Law in 1898.[50]

46. Illinois Manufacturers Association Minutes, June 11, 1894, Box 1, Folder "Minutes" in Illinois Manufacturers Association Papers, Chicago Historical Society. Established in response to the 1893 Sweatshop Law, the IMA successfully challenged limitations on women's hours in the 1895 case Ritchie vs. the People.

47. Gage cited his friendship with George Pullman as a reason that he would not donate to relief funds for the strikers. *Chicago Times,* June 8, 1894. M. J. Carroll described his position regarding arbitration in his testimony in *Chicago Strike,* 460.

48. M. H. Madden, in *Chicago Mail,* June 1, 1894, Pullman Strike Scrapbooks, Reel 14.

49. George Howard in *Chicago Herald,* June 2, 1894, PSNL, Reel 14.

50. Later, in 1904, following Theodore Roosevelt's arbitration in the anthracite coal strike of

The federal government's interest increased after the turn of the century, when two different committees on industrial relations issued reports (1902 and 1915) encouraging union recognition, collective bargaining, arbitration, and the pursuit of industrial democracy.[51] Locally, the CFC called its own conference to build support for legislation to create a statewide arbitration commission. In the wake of the Pullman Strike, debates about arbitration thus appeared on a very visible local and national stage.

After the strike, the CFC conference brought together prominent figures such as Carroll Wright, labor leaders Samuel Gompers and M. M. Garland, reformers Josephine Shaw Lowell and Jane Addams, and economist Henry Carter Adams to discuss various aspects of the topic—from its European roots to its contemporary practices and implications. By assembling national representatives for discussion and debate, the CFC's conference was modeled on its local efforts to bring city residents with divergent opinions and ideas into conversation with one another.[52] The conference marked a turning point as well in the organization's commitment to understanding the new economy from the perspective of business and labor representatives and promoting reforms based on scientific knowledge.[53] Economists Henry Carter Adams, Jeremiah Jenks, John R. Commons, and Edward Dana Durand, all of whom were researching issues related to arbitration, helped organize the conference and made presentations. The national conference became the model for others the CFC sponsored—on primary election laws, foreign policy, and trusts—which sought to bring together participants with academic and practical expertise. It foreshadowed the influence that people with expertise would come to exercise in policy decisions. As we saw in the CFC's battle over educational reform, dedication to "neutral" social science and the narrowly defined expertise signaled the organization's increasingly positivist bent.[54]

1902, Congress proposed a bill to create a National Arbitration Tribunal, which would have the power to arbitrate in a number of different industries. Such interest in mediation and collective bargaining continued throughout the early twentieth century and culminated in the National War Labor Board and the Wagner Act's provisions for the National Labor Board during the Great Depression. See, for example, David McCabe, "Federal Intervention in Labor Disputes under the Erdman, Newlands and Adamson Acts," in *Proceedings of the Academy of Political Science*, vol. 8, *Labor Disputes and Public Service Corporations, January 1917*, No. 1, 94–107 (New York: Academy of Political Science, Columbia University, 1928–1991); Hearings before the Committee on Education and Labor, National Arbitration Tribunal, Fifty-eighth Congress, April 7, 1904.

51. Valerie Jean Conner, in *The National War Labor Board: Stability, Social Justice, and the Voluntary State in World War I* (Chapel Hill: University of North Carolina Press, 1983), argues that the Industrial Commission's reports and the National War Labor Board pointed to a growing interest at the federal level in industrial democracy.

52. M. M. Garland, *Congress on Industrial Conciliation and Arbitration*, 55.

53. Clarence E. Bonnett, *Employers' Associations in the United States: A Study of Typical Associations* (New York: Macmillan, 1922), 397; Christopher J. Cyphers, *The National Civic Federation and the Making of a New Liberalism, 1900–1915* (Westport, CT: Praeger, 2002), 22.

54. Cyphers, *National Civic Federation*, 21–24.

Most of the participants at the conference denounced Pullman's strict adherence to the principles of laissez-faire and supply and demand, though none went so far as Chicago judge Murray Tuley, who had arbitrated several disputes in the construction industry and argued for compulsory arbitration. They also rejected the paternalistic spirit behind the Pullman Town experiment. Envisioning arbitration as a process for building democratic relations in the emerging industrial order and for articulating such views, they offered an alternative social knowledge about economic relations. Thus, while the participants at the conference did not come to radical conclusions (indeed, those with radical views were not invited), the speakers did suggest a different lens through which to view arbitration. Not only did they consider mediation from the vantage point of contemporary debates over economic and political theory, but embedded in their presentations were also clues to the epistemological and political functions arbitration might play in economic transformation.[55]

During the two-day conference, several participants illustrated the ways that conciliation and arbitration were envisioned as promoting economic knowledge and self-transformation, overcoming social alienation, raising the social and political status of workers, and challenging the foundations of liberal republicanism. The conference is useful for our purposes, as it illustrates how at this particular moment, reformers imagined mediation as a process that promoted democratic social knowledge. In contrast to Pullman's language of classical liberal economics, some of the participants envisioned arbitration as a process that both promoted and increased workers' knowledge, thus enhancing their epistemological position in debates about economic practices. And in contrast to Pullman's paternalistic and coercive efforts to fabricate loyal and productive workers, the reformers envisioned intercession as a means to encourage personal attributes of reason and trust, which were valued in a democratic market economy. Other participants emphasized that arbitration promoted social harmony by serving as a transformative process that encouraged traits such as mutual respect, honesty, and fairness required for democratic character. Still others considered negotiations as part of a trend toward industrial democracy, shaped by historicist economics, which might replace a paradigm of classical liberal political economy, which functioned as natural law.

Arbitration and Historicist Economics

Reflecting on the Pullman Strike months later, Jane Addams wrote a measured

---

55. For discussion of the conference from a perspective of its contributions to economic theory, see Furner, "The Republican Tradition and the New Liberalism."

but critical essay on the walkout. Illustrating the contingent nature of knowledge, "A Modern Tragedy" posited that "the virtues of one generation are not sufficient for the next any more than the accumulations of knowledge possessed by one age are adequate to the needs of another."[56] Instead, Addams, like a growing contingent of historicist economists, exhorted that knowledge about the liberal market had failed to adapt to changes brought about by industrial capitalism and advocated instead that a new basis for industrial relations be sorted out.

Conflict over the labor question and a host of economic concerns about production and distribution, wage-fund theory, competition and consolidation, state regulation, and the development of marginalist economics pointed to a moment when liberal political economy was in the painful throes of transformation. Conflict between historicist and neoclassical economists who addressed the need for new economic knowledge dominated the profession in the last two decades of the nineteenth century.[57] These debates demonstrated a struggle over differing views of the nature of knowledge, particularly as they were manifested in disputes about arbitration.

Efforts to "know capitalism," as historian Mary Furner terms it, ran the gamut from social scientific research, to state-sponsored inquiries drawing on the testimony of workers and employers, to journalists' and reformers' exposés—and, as this chapter suggests, to the process of arbitration itself. Because reformers envisioned arbitration as a democratic dialogue that mediated various lived experiences, it was one aspect of a much larger discussion over democracy and the cultural authority to shape economic practices.

Arbitration, collective bargaining, and trade agreements between the consolidated forces of labor and capital caught the attention of historicist economists since they responded to the reality of economic consolidation by encouraging businessmen to recognize unions while promising greater efficiency and productivity and avoiding costly strikes.[58] Arbitration even suggested a means of identifying and solidifying new social rights expressed in the economic realm,

56. Addams, "A Modern Tragedy," JA Microfilm, Reel 47, 9. Victoria Bissell Brown, "Advocate for Democracy: Jane Addams and the Pullman Strike," in *Pullman Strike and the Crisis of the 1890s*, ed. Schneirov, Stromquist, and Salvatore, 130–58, argues that Addams staked out an important position as a neutral advocate. Brown describes Addams's neutrality as a courageous and vital part of her democratic commitment.

57. For discussion on these traditions within economic thought, see Furner, "Republican Tradition and the New Liberalism." Also Cohen, *Reconstruction of American Liberalism*.

58. Although these terms were often used interchangeably, they were distinct. The object of conciliation was for employers and workers to discuss questions of common interest, including wages, hours of work, and shop conditions, and to come to mutual agreement regarding them. In contrast, arbitration involved outsiders in settling a particular question over which the parties could not otherwise agree. See Address of Josephine Shaw Lowell in Industrial Committee of the Civic Federation, *Congress on Industrial Conciliation and Arbitration* (Chicago: W. C. Hollister & Bros., Printers, 1894), 41. See also John R. Commons, ed., *Trade Unionism and Labor Problems* (Boston: Ginn, 1905).

even as it avoided the wholesale transformation of the free market economy by maintaining the primacy of contractual relations. As John Bates Clark, the architect of marginalist economics, argued, arbitration shored up the justice of contracts but emphasized organized business and labor instead of individuals as the parties. Collective bargaining and arbitration thus offered a corporatist approach to labor relations that steered a middle course between legal individualism in which laborers had no rights to organize and the statist proposals of democratic collectivists who rejected the identification of any private interest with the public good and maintained that the state was the proper instrument to check selfish interest.[59] By the middle of the twentieth century, arbitration and collective bargaining were seen as a means to regulate the economy; economists noted that even "critical decisions concerning utilization of resources and distribution of the proceeds from production have come within the scope of the bargaining process."[60]

This vision of arbitration conflicted with the neoclassical economics coming into vogue during the 1880s and 1890s, which was heavily influenced by the "classical discourse of the law, with its characteristic references to legal knowledge as the product of a gradual, incremental process of discovering and perfecting natural laws embedded in human nature and reflected in the constitutional order." In such discourse, "rights were inherent and immutable," and thus this view of knowledge was "at odds with the developing discourse of the new economics, whose leading figures in this period understood theory as provisional, relative to the current economic and technological order, and defined rights, law and state forms as cultural creations, shaped by the conditions and needs of a particular historical context and subject to experimentation, growth, and change."[61] Two different conceptions of knowledge emerge from these debates: one formal, naturalistic, and unchanging; the other contingent and socially created.[62]

Joseph Weeks, an early student of arbitration, explained the differences between these two schools of thought in an early discussion of arbitration. Speaking of classical liberal economics, he noted that it "assumes the existence and efficacy of what are termed economical laws or forces, whose action is inevitable, and to which, without any interference, must be left the settlement of these vexed questions." In contrast, "the other theory, while it recognizes the existence, and within certain limits, the authority of economical laws, denies

59. Cohen, *Reconstruction of American Liberalism*, 195–197; Furner, "Knowing Capitalism," 245.

60. Arnold R. Weber, ed., *The Structure of Collective Bargaining: Problems and Perspectives. Proceedings of a seminar sponsored by the Graduate School of Business, University of Chicago, and the McKinsey Foundation* (New York: Free Press of Glencoe, 1961), vii.

61. Furner, "Republican Tradition and the New Liberalism," 174.

62. These conceptions of knowledge mirrored debates in philosophy between rationalism and pragmatism. See James, *Pragmatism*.

that they are fixed and unalterable."[63] He, like historicist economists, pragmatic philosophers, and their reform allies, argued that social practices and relationships, such as those embodied in the capitalist economy, were humanly created and thus subject to human intervention. In light of this latter conception, arbitration theoretically served a dialogic function to mediate different perspectives, economic principles, and justice. It was a process not just to settle differences; the very act of opening up economic ideas and practices to dialogue signaled a transformation in the locus of economic power away from the exclusive domain of businessmen and toward a vision of industrial democracy in which workers participate in decisions relevant to their work.[64]

Henry Carter Adams, economist at the University of Michigan and one of the founders of historicist economics, argued that arbitration was essential to creating a new form of liberty, one that accommodated the realities of economic transformation in the late nineteenth century. Adams depicted unions and arbitration not as irrational and dangerous but as essential to the process of determining new rights for labor.[65] "Do we recognize any undeveloped and unexpressed labor rights?" he asked. "If so, is it not wise to establish a machinery necessary to discover what those rights are?" Unlike Pullman, who held strict adherence to immutable natural laws, Adams encouraged arbitration as a mechanism to explore a new basis for the distribution of profit and the determination of rights: "[T]he question of arbitration is at the bottom a question of personal liberty, and implies the creation of new and unusual rights which, when realized by that great class who are now the possessors of no property, shall come to be for them a veritable property."[66]

Other participants at the conference described how the conflict between

63. Weeks, "Labor Differences and Their Settlement," 14.

64. Lichtenstein and Harris, eds., *Industrial Democracy in America;* Milton Derber, *The American Idea of Industrial Democracy, 1865–1965* (Urbana: University of Illinois Press, 1970).

65. Henry Carter Adams, address before the Congress on Industrial Conciliation and Arbitration, in *Congress on Industrial Conciliation and Arbitration,* 66.

66 Ibid., 68. Like other theorists of his time, Adams was wrestling with the problems of proprietorship, which historians James Livingston and Jeff Sklansky have recently explored. Adams's tentative solutions, building modern liberty on a new conception of independent property in the form of a voice in the industrial process, is an interesting addendum to both historians' discussion of corporate capitalism. Livingston argues that corporate capitalism made possible a wide variety of new relationships and identities, and indeed, Adams seems to make a similar point—arbitration would create a new set of rights that, when understood as a form of property, ensured workers' participation in the mechanics of the economy, much as the vote made them participants in government. Sklansky argues that the demise of proprietary capitalism and the emergence of consumerism ultimately undermined the foundation on which unions and reformers could offer significant cultural critique and radical politics seeking a redistribution of wealth. Adams's willingness to replace material property with a property of social rights and voice in the governance of the economic sector raises the same kinds of questions as does Sklansky a century later about the nature of power and freedom.

neoclassical and historicist economics played out on the ground. James Weeks explained that "the old schools of political economy say this question [of distribution of the product] must be settled by competition. The doctrine of laissez-faire is the only thing that has brought it right. It is eternal law; it has existed from all eternity and it will exist through eternity; and any attempt to interfere with the doctrine of unrestricted competition is perfectly useless."[67] Garland followed Weeks to the platform and reiterated that "the main controlling spirit of wage [sic] today . . . is the law of supply and demand."[68] Businessmen's "gospel of grab," as he called it, sanctified self-interest while failing to recognize laborers as legitimate voices in economic discourse. He stated that objections to arbitration grew "out of the assumption that the right to decide questions that arise between employer and employe [sic] rests with the employer alone"—an assumption that clearly denied the value of laborers' experiential knowledge. Workers, thus devalued, were subjected to the employer's power: "[W]hen the decision is given, labor's only choice is to accept or go elsewhere."[69]

Henry Demarest Lloyd, member of the CFC's Board of Conciliation and long-time friend of labor, painted the problem more vividly in an article titled "Arbitration": "The attitude of the employer amounts simply to this: Reason shall not arbitrate between us, because there is a Judge sitting on your case who always decides in my favour, if he has time enough—Judge Hunger."[70] The specter of Judge Hunger, waiting out labor disputes in alliance with employers, pointedly suggested the failure of the liberal market to distribute the necessities of life and emphasized what many unionists and reformers understood as the underlying inequity in employers' power over workers. As Weeks asserted, "the tendency of economical forces acting without direction or guidance is not to right economical wrongs, or establish justice, but to perpetuate and augment existing burdens and add others" onto the backs of workers.[71] Such debates over arbitration revealed a shift characteristic of historicist economic thought away from a formalist conception of immutable laws of the liberal market and toward a recognition of the economy as embodying socially created standards of justice; as such, it exemplified a struggle over cultural authority to define social reality and principles of justice.

67. Address of James D. Weeks, *Congress on Industrial Conciliation*, 50.
68. Address of M. M. Garland, *Congress on Industrial Conciliation*, 53.
69. Address of Weeks, *Congress on Industrial Conciliation and Arbitration*, 52.
70. *Hand Book of the National Association of Steam and Hot Water Fitters and Helpers* (1892). Despite his close support of the labor movement, Lloyd supported compulsory arbitration. Peter Coleman explains that Lloyd's socialism led him to support compulsory arbitration because he believed the collective interests of the community had to take precedence over the interests of any one group. See Peter J. Coleman, " 'Strikes Are War! War Is Hell!': American Responses to the Compulsory Arbitration of Labor Disputes, 1890–1920," *Wisconsin Magazine of History* (1987): 195.
71. Weeks, "Labor Differences and Their Settlement," 19.

Reformers' Moral Challenge

Social reformers envisioned arbitration as a moral challenge to the prerogatives of capitalists, seeing it as an alternative means to secure social harmony
by overcoming class alienation and promoting self-transformation and democratic equality. Rejecting Pullman's idea that a market governed by laissez-faire
or fabricated through the patriarchy of a company town brought social harmony—a belief also shared by many Chicago elites of his generation—they
looked for other means to ensure a democratic process for bringing industrial
peace. Pullman's vision of social harmony may have been possible in a society of
small proprietary capitalists in which apprenticeship figured prominently and
promoted personal interaction. But by the 1880s and 1890s, as anxiety about
industrial capitalism increased and social relations were in flux, commentators argued that industrial organization bred mistrust: "[T]he close personal
relationships which formerly existed was [sic] broken up with the advent of
machinery and the creation of large fortunes. The immense affairs are managed
by agents, whose interest it is to return the largest profits to a capitalist, or a
number of them, who know little of the army of employes [sic] which is daily
helping to pile these fortunes still higher."[72] Consequently, "there is good reason
to suppose that the favored classes know very little of the real condition of the
average workingman, and have no conception of the difficulties with which he
is surrounded and bound down in the place in which our industrial system has
fixed him."[73]

Commentators on the Pullman Strike noted Pullman's alienation from his
workers. One town resident and minister, William Carwardine, for example,
explained that Pullman "has not kept himself in touch with the laboring men
. . . and there never would have been a strike in Pullman if Mr. Pullman had been
in closer relations to his men."[74] In a similar vein, Jane Addams emphasized the
social distance between Pullman and his employees.[75] Pullman "cultivated the
great and noble impulses of the benefactor until the power of attaining a simple
human relationship to his employes, [sic] that of frank equality with them, was
gone from him."[76] Reflecting a local epistemology that privileged proximity and
intimacy as the basis for knowing others, Addams charged that the "modern
tragedy" Pullman embodied was the social and psychological distance between
employers and employees.

72. Charles F. Peck, in *Views of Arbitration*, 13.
73. Ibid., 14.
74. Testimony of Rev. William H. Carwardine, *Chicago Strike*, 446.
75. For discussion of this essay, see Smith, *Urban Disorder and the Shape of Belief*, and Victoria
Brown, "Advocate for Democracy: Jane Addams and the Pullman Strike," in *Pullman Strike and the
Crisis of the 1890s*, ed. Schneirov, Stromquist, and Salvatore, 130–49.
76. Addams, "A Modern Tragedy," JA Microfilm, Reel 47, 4.

Seeing arbitration as a promising way to bring workers and owners into conversation with each other to overcome their distance, reformers imagined mediation as an important component of democratic interaction that might recapture the personal nature of a small-scale, proprietary capitalist economy that corporations like the Pullman Company had eclipsed. As the head of the Massachusetts Bureau of Labor Statistics, Carroll Wright, had explained, arbitration promoted "mutual confidence and respect between these two classes."[77] Describing conditions in Nottingham, England, an arbitration proponent noted that "a most friendly feeling has taken the place of hostility and confidence and mutual respect exist where formerly all was suspicion and hatred."[78] Reformers expected that "the chief advantage in arbitration, in the United States, would be the personal contact which it would bring about between the two great classes of industrial society. . . . The great trouble is, men are getting so far apart that they do not understand one another, and consequently have no mutual sympathy and good-will."[79] Arbitration, then, might go far in preventing a fatal drifting apart of capital and labor. The *Outlook,* a national reform-oriented paper, suggested that as employers began embracing arbitration, "there seems less danger than before that the two classes of our citizens should drift hopelessly apart."[80]

By encouraging discussion and respect, supporters believed mediation promoted equitable social relations, and they drew from a language of democracy as embodying reason and rationality, trust, and honesty to describe its promise. Prominent reformer Josephine Shaw Lowell emphasized that arbitration required that "a man must be willing, and he must also be able, to see the other side; he must be ready to be convinced; he must have sufficient mind to be able to understand the arguments put forward to convince him."[81] Likewise, James Weeks, representative of capital and editor of *American Manufacturer and Iron World,* suggested that workers and employers must be able to practice proximate relations, to put suspicion aside, and to "sit down face to face, like honest men, and talk the matter over and say, 'Now, we are not scoundrels; we don't

77. Carroll Wright, in *Views of Arbitration,* 9. Also see Wright, *Industrial Conciliation and Arbitration* (Boston: Rand, Abery, 1881), for a detailed discussion of ideas about arbitration and early attempts to institute mechanisms of arbitration.

78. Joseph Weeks, *Views of Arbitration,* 23.

79. Ibid., 29–30.

80. *Outlook,* December 1, 1894, 896, quoted in Shelton Stromquist, "The Crisis of 1894 and the Legacies of Producerism," in *Pullman Strike and the Crisis of the 1890s,* ed. Schneirov, Stromquist, and Salvatore, 184.

81. Josephine Shaw Lowell (1843–1905) was one of the most influential women in charity movements following the Civil War. In 1882 she helped found the New York Charity Organization Society, in which she was a guiding force for twenty-five years. Her concern for labor problems and her attempts to publicize what she considered to be the most constructive elements of the labor movement led her to publish "Industrial Arbitration and Conciliation" (1893). See *Notable American Women,* ed. Edward T. James (Cambridge, MA: Harvard University Press, 1971), vol. 2, 437–39.

believe that you are scoundrels.'"[82] Lowell pointed out that arbitration encouraged the participant "to have faith in the honor of others and a strong sense of honor himself."[83] Arbitration encouraged a basic recognition of reasonableness, honesty, and legitimacy of claims between the parties—traits essential for both market relationships and democratic deliberation.

The influence of the social gospel was apparent in the reformers' description of arbitration. Lowell intoned Christianity in arguing that it prioritized justice over selfishness, as the basis for arbitration. Arbitration "requires an advanced moral and intellectual development," [84] she asserted and equated this development directly to Christianity: "A fair, a true, a noble, in one word, a Christian relation should be striven for, and 'conciliation' is the technical word which has been selected to describe this relation."[85] In a similar vein, Weeks denounced the "gospel of grab" encouraged by laissez-faire economics and suggested that "if you will examine into the fundamental principles of our Christian civilization you will find that it is a civilization of association. It is a civilization where men come together, giving up certain rights to others, and giving up certain things that they claim belong to them for the good of all, that out of it all may come the highest justice for all. It is a theory of association, and not a theory of unrestricted competition."[86]

Because arbitration required capitalists and union representatives to meet face to face, it afforded a proximate epistemology built on interaction and focusing on the practical effects of industrial capitalism rather than the formal laws of classical liberalism. Weeks decisively asserted, "Christian civilization is dependent upon getting together, respecting each other and talking face to face and settling your disputes like men and not like brutes and savages."[87] Christianity offered a model to further the imaginative process necessary to put oneself in another's place and thus to break down barriers. This process entailed a similar exchange of selves that Addams's notion of sympathetic knowledge and Dewey's description of experience and communication offered. These methods encouraged a more imaginative and personalized approach to the creation of social knowledge. If putting oneself into another's shoes promoted a deeper

82. Address of James D. Weeks, *Conference on Industrial Conciliation*, 51.

83. Address of Josephine Shaw Lowell, *Conference on Industrial Conciliation*, 45. Arbitration thus offered opportunity for a practical business and civic education. It required employers, union officials, and workers to keep their promises. Indeed, educational efforts of the nineteenth century emphasized the need to internalize these lessons since fulfilling contracts was an essential aspect of market behavior. Employers, however, had long criticized the unions for failing to ensure that their members complied with their contracts. Consequently, employers looked suspiciously on unions and often depicted their members as irrational and dangerous.

84. Address of Josephine Shaw Lowell, *Conference on Industrial Conciliation*, 45.

85. Ibid., 41.

86. Address of James D. Weeks, *Conference on Industrial Conciliation*, 50.

87. Ibid., 20.

understanding of others' experiences, it might then encourage a rethinking of the ways in which economic and social arrangements promoted ideals such as fairness, individual liberty, independence, and freedom. Consequently, social Christianity privileged arbitration as pedagogy that challenged the laws of liberal economics by focusing on social and personal dynamics rather than abstract logic.[88]

Reformers imagined arbitration as a democratic process fostering equality and mutual relationships. In this respect, the interaction required for arbitration went hand in hand with the experiential, relational epistemology of many Chicago reformers. They emphasized that parties in the midst of arbitration or conciliation must be able to see each other's point of view, and such an image harked back to the kind of civic interaction idealized by the CFC's hope to serve as a medium for various groups to come into greater understanding and recognition of one another.

It was also similar to the interactive social knowledge Addams was formulating in her writings on immigrant and working-class cultures and the role she had carved out for settlements as an interpreter between cultures and classes. In *Hull-House Maps and Papers,* Addams argued for the role the settlement house could play as a translator in her discussion of the union organization of cloak makers. Skilled men in this field, mostly Russian Jews, had lost substantial ground to untrained women working in sweatshops, and these men had hoped to meet with the women to organize their labor. However, the women, primarily Irish and American, refused to go to the saloon where the men usually met. They finally agreed to meet at Hull House, but immediately the cultural barriers were obvious. "They were separated by nationality, by religion, by mode of life, by every possible social distinction," including their gender.[89] An interpreter stood between the men on one side and the women on the other and "was baffled by the social aspect of the situation," not so much by the economic issues. The real challenge was to get the groups to understand each other's point of view.

In Addams's configuration, however, the parties themselves could not overcome the divide. Though the interpreter was puzzled by the situation, she was still present, bringing the two groups together. Thus it was with arbitrators, as well. The most popular mechanism for arbitration among middle-class reformers was a three-person board, with one member each chosen by capital and labor and a third agreed upon by the other two. This model had the benefit of bringing to the discussion an assumed neutral—and moral—umpire, who nonetheless had to meet with the approval of both sides.

88. Social gospelists were interested in arbitration. See Walter Rauschenbusch, *Christianity and the Social Crisis* (New York: Macmillan, 1907). Also Derber, *American Idea of Industrial Democracy,* 77–80, 151–58.

89. Jane Addams, *Hull-House Maps and Papers* (New York: Crowell, 1895), 190.

In the wake of the Pullman Strike, this third party was often described as representing the public.[90] Even though the Strike Commission's report was read as a pro-labor document, it argued strongly that arbitration should represent the interests of the public. The nature of the railroad industry—its central role in moving people and the necessities of life, both of which had been disrupted during the Pullman Strike—warranted state intervention into labor disputes. Carroll Wright observed that debate that had begun during the strike taught "the public the necessity of placing labor and capital on a strong business basis of reciprocal interests, but interests which recognize the public as their chief master."[91] Railroad workers thus became "quasi-public servants." As historian Nancy Cohen has explained, this depiction was an important one as it "up-ended historical conceptions of the citizenry as a body of producers" and argued for the federal government to act as a neutral arbiter in the public interest—a public that was increasingly defined as a body of consumers.[92]

The insertion of the neutral third party into the debate was an interesting ideological maneuver. It advanced the interests of a consuming public over those of any one group, be they employers or workers. Thus, workers and employers owed their livelihood to the public. It also positioned the growing ranks of middle-class government administrators in agencies such as the Bureau of Labor as neutral parties who could simultaneously mediate between conflicting parties and in the interests of the public. This vision of arbitration carved out a new role for the state as both protector of a consuming public and arbiter of conflicting class interests. While these ideas were not widely accepted by workers, employers, or the public, they would reemerge in the first decades of the twentieth century.

Although Carroll Wright's emphasis on the rights of the public spoke to an emerging debate over the role of that state and a new liberal conception of justice, it did not preclude the older reform vision that arbitration encouraged self-transformation. As journalist and reformer Ray Stannard Baker observed in 1920,

---

90. *American Federationist* 8, no. 6 (June 1901).

91. Carroll D. Wright, "Chicago Strike," quoted in Cohen, *Reconstruction of American Liberalism,* 199.

92. Cohen, *Reconstruction of American Liberalism,* 199. Cohen suggests that Wright redefined the public as a body of consumers, whose interest in the free flow of commodities would be protected by the federal government, operating through neutral boards of experts. She suggests that while Wright believed this role for the federal government was a democratic protection of workers' interests, it was fundamentally undemocratic in nature (199–202). For further contemporary discussion of the public's interest as superseding that of labor and capital, see Julius Henry Cohen, "A League to Enforce Industrial Peace," in *Proceedings of the Academy of Political Science* 17 (1917): 108–44, and Rabbi Joseph Krauskopf, "Necessity of Industrial Arbitration," in *Annals of the American Academy of Political and Social Science; Settlement of Labor Disputes* 36, no. 2 (September 1910): 57–66.

To see the labor managers on one side and the labor leaders on the other dealing day after day with these inflammable human elements in industry, trying to give to short sighted selfishness a little wider vision, trying to mitigate competitive ferocity with a touch of the spirit of cooperative understanding, trying to get into the dull brain of prejudice some little glimpses of the problem of the other man, is not only to appreciate the immense difficulty of the problems involved, but to be filled with admiration for the determined idealism, the patience, the faith of these leaders, and to wonder that they have got as far toward a new reign of law as they have.[93]

Using language similar to that of reformers twenty-five years earlier, these advocates continued to cite its psychosocial benefits: a way of encouraging democratic equality, respect, and mutual understanding between employers and employees.

Unions, Knowledge, and Rights

Before the Pullman Strike, unions had pushed for arbitration for several reasons. Like middle-class reformers, they described its potential to establish democratic equality between workers and employers. They discussed it in terms of the recognition and legitimacy it afforded them; indeed, arbitration presupposed both parties' recognition of each other as partners and as having valid ideas and visions. Furthermore, many unions sought to avoid costly strikes whenever possible. Nonetheless, in the 1880s arbitration was a delicate matter for most unions, which were nearly unanimous in their denunciation of compulsory arbitration.[94] An editorial in the *Locomotive Firemen's Magazine*, edited by Eugene Debs, suggested that "arbitration of a voluntary character is well

93. Ray Stannard Baker, "Shop Council Plan Real Aid to Public," in *The Hart, Schaffner, & Marx Labor Agreement: Industrial Law in the Clothing Industry,* comp. Earl Dean Howard (Chicago: n. pub., 1920), 92.

94. Coleman, "Strikes Are War! War Is Hell!" 187–210. The *Locomotive Firemen's Magazine* reported that compulsion would be good to the degree "that corporations could not assert with arrogance that there was 'nothing to arbitrate,'" but it rejected the idea that the law should set the rate of wages. *Locomotive Firemen's Magazine* (December 1894): 1156; Walter MacArthur, "The American Trade Unions and Compulsory Arbitration," *American Federationist* 8, no. 5 (May 1901): 107–114; *Locomotive Firemen's Magazine* (June 1894): 602–5. MacArthur, editor of the *International Seamen's Journal,* accepted the idea of voluntary arbitration, but like many union leaders of this time, likened compulsory arbitration to "involuntary servitude" (111); an editorial in the *American Federationist* (September 1894) argued the same position. For a historical perspective on compulsory arbitration, one that sees more support from unions in the nineteenth and early twentieth centuries, see Josiah Bartlett Lambert, *"If the Workers Took a Notion": The Right to Strike and American Political Development* (Ithaca, NY: Cornell University Press, 2005), 91–95.

enough, but the instant compulsory arbitration is suggested, manhood, citizenship, independence and self-respect revolt."[95] Workers feared the courts' hostility and scoffed at the idea that compulsory boards would be disinterested.[96] Furthermore, efforts to make arbitration compulsory and binding undermined the power of strikes, which were, for the American Federation of Labor and its affiliates, the workers' ultimate source of power. But despite their skepticism, the unionists still sought voluntary arbitration.

For the unionists, securing a living wage while avoiding costly strikes was one of the primary reasons for submitting to mediation.[97] L. S. Coffin, representing the Brotherhood of Railway Trainmen, explained that the living wage constituted "such wages as to enable a temperate, fairly economical and industrious man to support a family as an American laborer's family should live," and he encouraged negotiation before a "competent authority or arbitration or conciliation commission when necessary."[98]

Much of the recent literature on arbitration emphasizes its role in the emergence of collective bargaining between unions and employers after the turn of the century. Collective bargaining, these accounts argue, represented a decisive split within labor union ideology away from politics as a means of widespread economic reforms. Instead, collective bargaining emphasized the transition to business unionism, where workers focused on bread-and-butter issues within the workplace itself and they were more likely to be successful. These accounts tend to focus on the way unions and employers adjusted to the emerging corporate liberal economy, but because historians have seen this transition as one of loss (of the potential of radical unionism), they have overlooked arbitration as both an indicator of a significant shift in assumptions about economic knowledge and as a mechanism to create knowledge and redefine justice.[99]

95. *Locomotive Firemen's Magazine* (February 1894): 137. For the unions' rejection of compulsory arbitration, see W. C. Carter, "Objections of Labor to Compulsory Arbitration," *Proceedings of the Academy of Political Science*, vol. 7, *Labor Disputes and Public Service Corporations*, 36–43, and George E. Barnett et. al., "Discussion of Trade Unions and Compulsory Arbitration," in ibid., 81–93; John L. Lewis, "The Settlement of Disputes among the Mine Workers," *Annals of the American Academy of Political and Social Science* 36, no. 2 (September 1910): 79–85; Opinion of the Illinois State Board of Arbitration on Compulsory Arbitration, in *Reports of the Industrial Commission on Labor Organizations, Labor Disputes, and Arbitration, and on Railway Labor*, vol. 17, 701.

96. Experience proved that the federal government, businessmen, and legal arbiters were too frequently interested participants. *Locomotive Firemen's Magazine* (February 1894); "Favors Strike as a Remedy," *Chicago Tribune* (March 27, 1900); Salvatore, *Eugene V. Debs*, 131.

97. Furner, "Republican Tradition and the New Liberalism," 207. On the living wage, see Lawrence B. Glickman, *A Living Wage: American Workers and the Making of Consumer Society* (Ithaca, NY: Cornell University Press, 1997). For an alternative reading of the emergence of consumer society, see Cohen, *Reconstruction of American Liberalism*. Cohen credits social scientists, rather than workers, with securing the logic of consumer society.

98. Address of L. S. Coffin, *Conference on Industrial Conciliation*, 26.

99. Andrew Cohen has suggested that collective bargaining and arbitration functioned to

Yet this is not how the unions saw things. Their emphasis on wages and standard of living reflected a significant reorientation of economic knowledge and social justice, away from businessmen's appeals to liberal market principles of laissez-faire and supply and demand as the primary mechanism of justice and toward a belief in the socially created nature of economic laws and the search for a process that opened up questions of the meaning of justice and the importance of meeting human needs.[100]

This ideological move was apparent in the arbitration of a 1912 electric railway strike, for which unions and employers both carefully prepared, citing their calculations and arguments for and against the "American standard of living," as the living wage was often called.[101] As economist Henry Carter Adams alluded, unions had come to use arbitration as a mechanism for defining new rights and making new claims, in this case, the right to a living wage. One of the reasons unions supported arbitration, then, was its potential to legitimize new principles of justice. Indeed, twenty-five years after the Pullman strike, theorists, businessmen, and unionists alike still grappled with the economic principles implicit in labor arbitration. While most economists found that mediation could not offer a wage distribution theory that would withstand the scrutiny of their discipline's methods, they observed that arbitration pitted against each other two ideals of distributive justice—one social and exemplified in workers' demands for a living wage and the other individualistic, competitive, and articulated by owners' efforts to continue to treat their workers as individuals rather than as members of unions.[102]

Unionists in the 1880s and 1890s saw in conciliation and arbitration a means to assert the power of unions and collective knowledge of workers, thus bringing parity to workers' and employers' epistemological positions that were still in flux. Carroll Wright explained the psychological dynamics wrought by this inequality by pointing out that workers felt "regarded as holding a subservient position," and "manufacturers [felt] that theirs is a dominant one."[103] In times of wage reductions, workers "are not inclined to credit [employers' claims], and

exercise control over the local economy and stave off the advance of corporate, industrial capitalism. Still, he cautions that craftsmen generally rejected arbitration. See Cohen, *Racketeer's Progress*, 9, 122.

100. Kathleen G. Donohue, *Freedom from Want: American Liberalism and the Idea of the Consumer* (Baltimore: Johns Hopkins University Press, 2005); Lawrence Glickman, *Living Wage*.

101. For an extensive discussion of how employers and unions fought over the notion of "the American Standard of Living," both marshalling the methods of empirical social science and the language of justice and fairness, see John Harrison Kolb, "Arbitration in the Chicago Street Car Controversy of 1912" (PhD diss., University of Chicago, 1913). Kolb's work points out that arbitration was the arena in which both sides tried to determine an appropriate, "just" standard of living.

102. Wilson Compton, "Wage Theories in Arbitration," in *Trade Unionism and Labor Problems*, ed. John R. Commons, 2d ser., 694–713 (Boston: Ginn, 1921).

103. Carroll D. Wright, in *Views of Arbitration*, 10.

believe that affairs are not as represented."[104] For their part, he said, employers "seem to regard sitting at the same table and talking over the rate of wages, hours of labor, and other matters, as being beneath their dignity and as conceding too much."[105]

However, the labor representatives at the conference stressed that workers acquired a greater knowledge of their craft through regular discussions with management. M. M. Garland, president of the Amalgamated Association of Iron, Steel, and Tin Workers, explained that participation in arbitration prompted workers "to keep close watch on the values of their products and to take account of all cost entering into its production."[106] Indeed, he continued, "what may be called the commercial knowledge of the wage worker, especially as it concerns his own trade, has of late years been advancing at a rapid rate."[107] These ideas reflected an earlier position on cooperation between capital and labor in which arbitration "treats labor as a brain force as well as hand power."[108] In an earlier formulation of this position, Joseph Weeks had suggested that permanent boards of arbitration allowed workers "to obtain a correct and measurably complete knowledge of the condition of trade, prices, demand, etc."[109]

Weeks also explained that, through arbitration, "the employer obtains a closer insight into the surroundings and needs of the employee."[110] Conciliation and arbitration thus positioned workers, both as individuals and a collective body, as economic and social teachers; they schooled employers about the effects of company policies on the production process and on their private lives. In the heat of the Pullman conflict, the need for workers to play such a role resonated among the strikers. Although Frederick Taylor would not publish his complete statement on scientific management until 1903, the Pullman Company consulted with Taylor and adopted the principles of scientific management in the years preceding the 1894 strike.[111]

104. Ibid.
105. George Howell, in *Views of Arbitration*, 24.
106. M. M. Garland, *Congress on Industrial Conciliation and Arbitration*, 55.
107. Ibid.
108. *Views of Arbitration*, 17–18.
109. Weeks, "Labor Differences and Their Settlement," 45.
110. Ibid.
111. For discussion of scientific management policies in the Pullman Company, see Montgomery, *Fall of the House of Labor*, 126–31. In response, the workers increasingly sought to protect themselves from both the loss of autonomy wrought by these changes and the vagaries of economic cycles. They expressed a distinct culture, with work standards and a code of ethics that helped militate against losses of autonomy in the reorganization of workplace practices in the latter nineteenth century. Through workplace standards and, later, union rules, workers struggled to maintain control over output quotas that would stave off an overly rapid work pace or prevent wages from falling so low that slower workers could not earn a living. In the absence of other means of influencing wages, such techniques allowed workers to intervene with the mechanism of the market to help maintain both a sense of control over their labor and a living wage. Ibid., especially chapter 1, "The Manager's

The growth of piecework and corporate managers—moves toward scientific management—significantly impacted the daily lives of Pullman workers. Thomas Heathcote, a Pullman car builder and strike leader, explained that a new general manager had appointed "unexperienced men in almost every department, men who were his friends" but who were unfamiliar with the work. Such practices led to "a great deal lost by mismanagement, since in order to be manager of car works of such magnitude as the Pullman company has[,] the manager must be a practical car builder. Now Mr. [Harvey] Middleton," Heathcote complained, "does not understand car building." The general foreman "is not an expert mechanic or is not experienced in the business; and some of the other foremen are not experienced, and consequently there is a great deal of work gotten out and spoiled by the foreman, the management, etc.," losses that ultimately impacted workers' incomes.[112] For example, when management furnished low-quality lumber for the construction of a car, only to have the inspector reject the finished product, the workers were assessed the cost of new materials and were not paid for the time spent on the inferior and unusable products.[113] Heathcote's arguments turned on its head what was, at the time, an emerging logic of modernist division of labor that foreclosed the possibility that those who occupied the lower tiers of the production process have knowledge. Instead of accepting this logic, he positioned management as inferior; his manager's knowledge of the work process was inadequate, thus costing both the company and its employees valuable time and money.

Such complaints illustrated what Big Bill Haywood and Frank Bohn, leaders of the Industrial Workers of the World, articulated in their work, *Industrial Socialism*. Pointing out the importance of workers' knowledge, they quipped, "the manager's brains are under the workman's cap."[114] This was precisely the point that Heathcote and others made in their grievances against costly mismanagement at Pullman. Attempts to reorganize production, particularly through piecework rates and the implementation of scientific management principles, struck at the autonomy workers maintained by both nullifying their traditional knowledge gained through practical experience and chipping away at their ethical code of honor and mutualistic ethics. Frederick Taylor explained this process, noting that "managers assume . . . the burden of gathering together all of the

---

Brain under the Workman's Cap," 9–57. By replacing day wages with piecework rates, scientific management techniques not only undermined workers' authority in the production process but also compelled them to work harder to earn the same or even reduced wages.

112. Testimony of Thomas Heathcote, *Chicago Strike*, 423–24. Also testimony of Merritt Brown, *Chicago Strike*, 442–43.

113. Testimony of Merritt Brown, *Chicago Strike*, 442–43. Also *Chicago Herald*, May 28, 1894, Pullman Strike Scrapbooks, vol. 14, p. 71.

114. William D. Haywood and Frank Bohn, *Industrial Socialism* (Chicago: Kerr, 1911), 25, quoted in Montgomery, *Fall of the House of Labor*, 45.

traditional knowledge which in the past has been possessed by the workmen and then of classifying, tabulating, and reducing this knowledge to rules, laws, and formulae which are immensely helpful to the workmen in their daily work."[115] Workers' testimony to the Strike Commission and in numerous government and arbitration reports drew attention to the value they put on their experience; it was a form of knowledge crucial to efficient and economical business practices.[116]

Drawing from their experience, workers not only had a unique perspective on the economics of the workplace; they also had special insight into the social implications of industrial capitalist economic practices. As Jennie Curtis, a seamstress in the repair shops, reported, "We worked as hard as we possibly could and doing all we could, too. The most experienced of us could only make 80 cents per day, and a great many of the girls could only average 40 to 50 cents per day." These earnings reflected a dramatic wage cut resulting from piecework; before the strike, Pullman seamstresses earned on average $2.25 a day.[117] Pullman had defended piecework as an "educational tool in that it offered incentive to the worker to improve his [sic] skills."[118] Workers, however, emphasized a different lesson: Declining wages threatened moral order. They testified that their wives and daughters increasingly took jobs outside of their homes, thus undermining the gendered division of spheres and the patriarchal moral and political order Pullman Town was built to encourage.[119] Children stopped attending school because parents needed their wages or could not afford decent clothes and books. They illustrated that such economic practices led to a dangerous decline in their standard of living that pushed them toward the social unrest that Pullman Town was designed to thwart. In this case the workers' contributions to social knowledge came from their structural relationship to an industrial capitalist system. Their experience, embodied in their cultural practices and protests of strategies like piecework, and complaints about high rents in company-owned

115. Fredrick Winslow Taylor, *The Principles of Scientific Management* (New York: Harper, 1911), 36.

116. Industrial Commission Report. The persistent value of the workers' experiential knowledge is demonstrated by the notion of "work-to-rule actions," in which workers follow procedures exactly as laid out by management. Since their practical experience helps them develop more efficient ways of doing their jobs—ways that workers frequently do not share with bosses or that employers do not bother to learn—work-to-rule actions generally result in a slowdown. Such actions demonstrate that stipulated work procedures are usually not as productive or efficient as the techniques workers themselves figure out. I am grateful to Deborah Cohen for pointing this out. For a variation on this idea, see Mary R. Schmidt, "Grout: Alternative Kinds of Knowledge and Why They Are Ignored," in *Democracy, Bureaucracy, and the Study of Administration*, ed. Camilla Stivers, 110–122 (Boulder, CO: Westview, 2001). Also of interest is Ralph P. Hummel, "Stories Managers Tell: Why They Are as Valid as Science," in ibid., 87–109.

117. Testimony of Jennie Curtis, *Chicago Strike*, 434.

118. Quoted in Buder, *Pullman*, 141. Also Montgomery, *Fall of the House of Labor*, 129.

119. Rieff, "A Modern Lear and His Daughters."

towns and high prices in company stores reflected knowledge gained not only from experience in doing their jobs but also from their location in the class system. It provided them with ample evidence of an exploitative dimension within industrial capitalism.

Garland's argument that arbitration advanced workers' commercial knowledge was significant in light of Pullman's growing use of scientific management practices based on positivist techniques that analyzed, systematized, and controlled each step of the labor process. The purpose of scientific management "was systematic separation of the mental component of commodity production from the manual. The functions of thinking and deciding were what management sought to wrest from the worker, so that the manual efforts of wage earners might be directed in detail by a 'superior intelligence.'"[120] In contrast, arbitration encouraged workers to gain a more unified knowledge of the whole production and business process. As Carroll Wright, commissioner of the U.S. Bureau of Labor, argued, regular meetings of an arbitration board furnished an opportunity "for the workmen to obtain a knowledge of the needs of trade and the demands of the future both upon them and the manufacturers."[121] Arbitration encouraged workers to both defend and deepen their material knowledge of the production process.

Implicitly, mediation expanded democratic rights into the workplace and secured labor's position of equality and power. "One of the chief advantages," as M. M. Garland explained, "is the bringing together of employer and employe [sic] in conference and discussion."[122] The benefits of such a system lay in the fact that "actual business rules are here brought into play and the workman in possession of material knowledge which enables him to discuss intelligently all the intricacies of his trade, stands equal with the employer, a conversationalist in the conference room, and reason ruling." Garland pointed out that, "with increasing knowledge of the business end of their trade, workmen have found the means of better defending their rights." Indeed, he attributed the frequency of strikes in the 1880s and 1890s to the fact that workers "imbibe a spirit of independence, and do not hesitate to throw down their tools in defense of their position after the employer shows himself impenetrable to reason."[123]

Such an interaction had political and psychological effects that contributed to the formation of the workers' democratic character. Weeks suggested that "the employe [sic] on the one hand asserts both his industrial independence

---

120. Montgomery, *Fall of the House of Labor*, 252. In *The Principles of Scientific Management* (New York: Harper and Brothers, 1911), Taylor describes the process by which employers could capture and monopolize the functional knowledge of the worker.

121. Carroll D. Wright, quoted in *Views of Arbitration*, 10.

122. Address of M. M. Garland, *Conference on Industrial Conciliation*, 55.

123. Ibid.

and his equality with his employer, and demands his living as his right, not as a favor, and a voice and equal power in the decision of the questions that affect his interests in his relations to his employer, his work and his product."[124] In the face of economic transformations that threatened the foundations of the democratic character—ones usually attributed to the autonomy of proprietary ownership—the terms used to describe arbitration—independence, equality, rights—suggest a cultural search to find new ways to forge a democratic personality.

The unions' power lay in their ability to act as an agent for a collective body of workers. Together the workers pooled their knowledge and skills to defend themselves against both small-scale businessmen and industrial capitalists. Increasing proletarianization meant that workers lost sight of the whole process of production, but through unionization, the unions believed that workers gained access to a larger understanding of both production and broad economic principles. The U.S. Industrial Commission concluded that one of the benefits of unions for the individual worker was that

> his ignorance of market conditions will be partly remedied, both through the combination of the knowledge of all the members of the union, and, in some cases, by the broader outlook which the union officials, wholly or partly exempted from daily application to manual work, may be able to obtain. The whole matter of bargaining can be put into the hands of the most skillful; and the officers and leaders may develop a skill in bargaining, by constant practice, comparable to that of their opponents. . . . When he dealt as an individual with his employer, he had to accept regulations and rates of pay which he had little or no voice in determining. He was under an industrial authority which left him no freedom except the freedom to leave its jurisdiction. The union is a democratic government in which he has an equal voice with every other member. By its collective strength it is able to exert some direct influence upon the conditions of employment. As a part of it, the individual workman feels that he has a voice in fixing the terms on which he works. He exchanges the sense of subjection to the employer for a certain sense of free action.[125]

So, "to the mind of the union man the fixing of minimum wages by the union does not seem to involve any diminution of his liberty."[126] Joseph Weeks went

124. Address of James D. Weeks, *Conference on Industrial Conciliation,* 52. For unionists and historians who have suggested that arbitration signaled labor's retreat from an effort to reconstruct economic life, Weeks's point is informative.

125. *Final Report of the Industrial Commission,* originally printed in 1900–1902 by the U.S. Government Printing Office, Washington, DC, for the U.S. Industrial Commission (Westport, CT: Greenwood), 806.

126. Ibid., 807.

further, arguing that arbitration served to help both unions and employers alike to gain a broader understanding of business practices and their social effects. One of the benefits of boards of arbitration, he asserted, was that "there is brought in these boards or committees not the knowledge, perception, and judgment of one class only, which are apt to be imperfect, clouded, and biassed [sic], but the combined intelligence, information, and judgment of both employer and employed, standing at different sources of information and looking at these questions from different points of view."[127]

The epistemology suggested here is reminiscent of that taking shape at Hull House and the CFC. Like the Working People's Social Science Club and the Hull House Women's Club, it legitimized workers' firsthand experience and sought a mechanism through which to process and reflect on that experience. Like that pushed by the Civic Federation and other Hull House programs, it was interactive in laying down a means for groups to meet, collectively define problems, and work toward solutions. Like Hull House theater and the social settlement itself, it was relational in that it emphasized understanding between parties and an exchange of selves that sought to bring personal transformation of behavior and attitudes. By implication, if employers respected the knowledge workers brought to the process of determining the various aspects of trade, duties, conditions, and wages, they might also recognize their equality in the arbitration process.[128] In opening such matters up for discussion and compromise, arbitration offered a means outside of classical liberal market logic to regulate the economy. And, perhaps more important, it would serve as an interactive process to mediate cultural definitions of justice. As such, arbitration attempted to balance economic principles and interests with human needs.

While the unions represent a collective body of workers, workers as individuals rarely speak about arbitration in the historical record. When they do, it is primarily to position themselves as sympathetic figures worthy of public support. Scattered throughout the record of the Pullman Strike are voices of individual workers: Jennie Curtis, the Pullman seamstress who appears as a heroic female innocent, paying off her father's debts and supporting her family after his death; Thomas Heathcote, one of the Pullman workers who emerged as a leader during the strike by rallying individual workers to join the union and its fight. The testimonies of these workers did not appear in the CFC's arbitration conference, but these workers did provide testimony to the U.S. Strike Commission investigating the Pullman Strike. In this, the commission was modeled on congressional investigations into labor conflicts in the 1870s and 1880s that

127. Weeks, "Labor Differences and Their Settlement," 37–38.

128. For further discussion on the democratic implications of arbitration, see William H. Pfahler, "Co-operation of Labor and Capital," *Proceedings of the American Academy of Political and Social Science* 20, no. 1 (1902): 96–97.

reflected the republican tradition of gathering information from the people. It included the testimonies of small proprietors, workers, and union representatives, as well as businessmen and local reformers.[129] The commission looked to the experiences of all of the participants as important pieces of a larger picture of economic transformation. The federal government increasingly built on this foundation in its numerous investigations, particularly its massive reports from 1899 to 1901.

The Strike Commission deliberately sought the perspectives of a number of workers, suggesting a perspectival approach to social knowledge. This approach assumed no hierarchy between knowers but merely sought to illuminate different perspectives to gain a fuller social knowledge. However, letters to Chicago newspapers expressed some public suspicion of worker testimony by raising the issue of the epistemological position of workers at this moment of class formation. One letter to a Chicago paper attacked the commission for calling upon

> strikers who have pressed their way to the front, without invitation, to preach the fallacies, absurdities and falsehoods with which the public was regaled daily, while the strike was in progress, from the Debs literary bureau. The stuff going into the records of the commission is a rehash of the blatherskite orations daily heard at [a local union hall] and the blatherskite editorials in the newspaper organs of the strike.

This public response frames knowers and knowing in class terms, assuming that workers' testimony is deliberately falsified whereas businessmen's accounts are true. "In view of these facts," the writer went on, "it is difficult to see what public service, what purpose or usefulness, the commissioners are meeting by their deliberations."[130] By attempting to delegitimize workers' contributions to social explanations of the Pullman Strike, the letter writers similarly delegitimize workers' contributions to the development of democratic social knowledge. At this moment of democratic struggle, then, epistemological status intersected with class formation. Another paper suggested, without editorial comment, that the labor commission "had obtained much information relating to the labor troubles at Pullman, a few facts concerning the grievances of the railway employes [sic] who participated in the recent general strike and the opinions of the several witnesses who testified upon the best methods of avoiding strikes in the future. All this came from wage workers and was just what the commission desired."[131]

129. Furner, "Republican Tradition and the Liberal State," 199.

130. "Inquiries of the Strike Commission," from Elliot Anthony Pullman Scrapbooks, p. 2 (ca. 1894), Chicago Historical Society. Also Pullman Scrapbooks, Reel 10, p. 80, "Questions for the Strike Commission," and p. 112, "Not Investigating the Strike."

131. "Story of the Strike—Told by Those Who Took Part in It," in Elliot Anthony Scrapbooks,

As these observations suggest, the workers' fight for epistemological legitimacy went hand in hand with labor contests in the city and with the federal government positioning itself to recognize workers' testimony and broker between the testimony of the conflicting parties. Thus, the Strike Commission not only heard from businessmen and union representatives but also called upon individual workers, local reformers, and "experts" like University of Chicago professor Edward Bemis. In the end, its report offered several suggestions to avoid conflicts like the Pullman Strike in the future, including expanding the role of the federal state as a neutral arbiter of future labor conflicts. The commission was so certain of the wisdom of this step that it suggested that arbitration in the railroad industry become compulsory.[132] Though few unionists or businessmen endorsed compulsory arbitration, the Strike Commission's recommendations reflected a growing public desire for state mediation of labor conflict. Positioning the higher voice of the people along with the state as a disinterested and thus fair and moral voice in labor conflicts, increasing numbers of arbitration proponents pushed for governments—local, state, and federal—to establish arbitration boards.[133]

Still, acceptance of state arbitration would be a long time in the making. Many reformers, including CFC secretary Ralph Easley, hoped to find alternative voluntarist means to encourage arbitration. In 1900 Easley left the Civic Federation to found the National Civic Federation (NCF), an organization that brought together leaders from unions, businesses, and the public—who were usually social scientists—to both mediate labor conflicts and investigate and educate all of the parties about economic problems. The Chicago Civic Federation, with its effort to assemble social science experts and groups holding divergent viewpoints, thus provided a model for what became an important national voluntary agency in the first two decades of the twentieth century. The model of investigation and arbitration the NCF offered attempted to bridge class conflict without resorting to state intervention, though it did work with agencies at the state and local levels.[134] As yet another approach to mediation and arbitration, it was beyond some reformers' vision of a democratic collectivism aided by the state. In Chicago in the early years of the twentieth century, both a state board and voluntarist approaches existed side by side, though neither would prove entirely successful as the nation headed into World War I.

---

p. 2 (ca. 1894), Chicago Historical Society.

132. Report of the Commissioners, *Chicago Strike*, lii–liii.

133. In Chicago, for example, the Civic Federation lobbied for legislation to create a state arbitration board.

134. On the National Civic Federation, see Marguerite Green, "The National Civic Federation and the American Labor Movement, 1900–1925" (PhD diss., Catholic University of America, 1956); Cyphers, *National Civic Federation and the Making of a New Liberalism*.

"Property above the Man and the Delivery Wagon above the Citizen": Arbitration after Pullman

Despite the fact that economists, reformers, businessmen, and workers embraced the idea of voluntary arbitration, it is important to note the different frameworks of meaning each held. For businessmen and economists, social harmony was still restricted to the shared interest of capital and labor and indeed assumed that capital's profit subsumed labor's interest in wages. Negotiating the two was merely a means to avoid costly strikes, not a redefinition of the foundation for social harmony per se. Reformers, however, had a different vision of social harmony—one that assumed a shared interest in meeting human needs and was secured through democratic participation. Conciliation, collective bargaining, and arbitration were significant indicators of that collective life and thus a means to democratic progress. In the years after the Pullman Strike, arbitration remained a contested issue among the players in Chicago's economic struggles, all the more so because it was so closely tied to union recognition and difficult debates over distributive justice. Despite the creation of a state arbitration board and the emergence of joint arbitration agreements in several craft industries, employers resisted arbitration and began an assault on closed-shop practices.

In the two decades following the Pullman Strike, ideas about arbitration as an interactive, democratic, self-transformative process challenging liberal republicanism met strong resistance from the industrial, corporate business community. This opposition to arbitration embodied struggles over union legitimacy and power, the rights of property, and alternative visions of economic knowledge and justice.[135] Businessmen's continued reluctance to embrace arbitration was dramatically apparent after the Illinois legislature created a state-wide Board of Arbitration. The CFC sponsored an arbitration bill supported by reformers

---

135. Court mediation had been championed by Chicago's jurist Murray Tuley since his decision in building strikes in 1887. He was popular enough among the unionists to garner an invitation to speak before the 1890 National Convention of Carpenters and Joiners. See *Chicago Tribune*, August 5, 1890, and Jane Addams, *The Excellent Becomes the Permanent* (New York: Macmillan, 1932), 73–82. In testimony before the Strike Commission, Eugene Debs also suggested that a state court, complete with judge and jury, might prove a helpful solution. "Establish the court the same as our other courts of law are established and maintained for the purpose of meting out justice to litigants. It seems to me where there is trouble of a local character between an employer and employees in a factory or mill a State court established of that kind that would necessarily have the confidence of the people" (Eugene V. Debs, testimony before the Strike Commission, *Chicago Strike,* 164). Debs clarifies, however, that this approach would work only for local disputes; it would provide no remedy for large-scale, interstate industrial disputes such as the Pullman Strike since few employers and workers would find legitimate the authority of unfamiliar mediators. Court mediation was the least popular remedy because the legal system was too slow and potentially too biased to be of help. Andrew Wender Cohen shows, however, that the courts in Chicago had been favorable to unions in past (*Racketeer's Progress,* 71).

and unions, which the legislature passed in 1895.[136] The board was composed of three members appointed by the governor. Using the rhetoric of middle-class reformers, the board described itself as "a far-reaching educative influence, increasing the habitual regard of both employers and employes [sic] for their respective rights and obligations, and teaching men the wisdom of settling their differences by pacific means and avoiding the strike and the lockout."[137]

However, the board's optimism glossed over the fact that employers and to a lesser extent the employees rejected its assistance altogether.[138] Their hostility to state-sponsored arbitration was evident in their numerous refusals to arbitrate conflicts. Employers used the rhetoric of classical liberalism to refuse arbitration and enforce the claim that only they had the right to determine business practices. For example, in February 1896 several Chicago clothing manufacturers announced that previous agreements with the Garment Cutters and Trimmers Association would be void. Employees would have to agree to "submit to such terms of employment with them as the manufacturers might elect to fix."[139] When the workers rejected the employers' announcement, they found themselves locked out the following Monday. Despite the efforts of the Board of Arbitration, the employers refused to submit the matter to mediation; instead, echoing the Pullman Company's position and refusing to accept the collectivism of unions, "they insisted that they must be permitted to treat with the men as individuals, and not as members of a trades organization."[140] These arguments

136. For a description of the Board of Arbitration and its responsibilities, see the U. S. Department of Labor Bureau of Labor Statistics, *Mediation and Arbitration Laws of the United States* (Washington, DC: Government Printing Office, 1913), 17–19. Although one party to a conflict might petition the board to investigate and publicize a labor dispute with the goal of bringing public censure, both parties had to agree to arbitration before the board could make binding recommendations; if only one party agreed to the investigation, the board's decisions would be nonbinding. In this respect it was voluntary rather than compulsory and served as an instrument of conciliation. See also *Reports of the Industrial Commission on Labor Organizations, Labor Disputes, and Arbitration, and on Railway Labor,* vol. 17 (Washington, DC: Government Printing Office, 1901), 429.

137. *Fourth Annual Report of the State Board of Arbitration of Illinois* (Springfield, IL, 1899).

138. The board faced difficulties in securing state funds to cover travel expenses. The lack of funds kept members from quickly getting to the location of labor disputes. In order for the board to begin an investigation, a majority of employee signatures was needed, but where disputes involved several hundred or more employees, this became an organizational headache, delaying or in some cases precluding investigation. Moreover, once employees requested arbitration, employers had to agree, and most were reluctant to do so. The law offered no means of enforcement of the board's decisions. Governor Tanner, in an address before the Illinois legislature in January 1899, pointed out this problem and asked for amendments to the law. Later that spring, the House and Senate overwhelmingly agreed to changes that would allow the board to use the courts more vigorously to subpoena wage and employment records and witnesses and to impose penalties on those who did not comply. Likewise, the courts could establish fines for failure to comply with an arbitrated agreement.

139. *First Annual Report of the State Board of Arbitration of Illinois,* 18; *Hull-House Bulletin,* April 1896, 4, and May 1896, 5.

140. *First Annual Report of the State Board of Arbitration of Illinois,* 19.

on the part of the employers remained the largest obstacle to arbitration. Indeed, in the first year after the law took effect, workers attempted to initiate arbitration on eight separate occasions, while employers sought the help of the board only once.[141] This pattern continued for the first several years of the board's existence, with employers usually rejecting arbitration proposals.[142]

Despite resistance to the state board, two factors helped arbitration gain a stronger foothold in Chicago. One was that the mediation process was growing in the craft sector of the economy; the other was public support.[143] In Chicago's craft economy, where the social distance between employers and workers was quite small, joint arbitration agreements often worked well, and their relationships tended to be familiar and friendly. As John Mangan, president of the International Association of Steam-Fitters commented, after an 1892 agreement, "even though slight differences appeared on the surface at times, still to the credit of both sides be it said those outside the conference never heard of any disputes or differences and I feel that the harmonious feeling prevailing can be attributed largely to the fairness of our contractors."[144] Though Mangan perhaps exaggerated the harmony between the employers and their employees, his comment suggests that their relationships were not always at odds.[145] In the local economy, where social mobility was fluid and propriety capitalism remained a potent explanatory force, craftsmen and their employers enjoyed conditions more conducive to cooperative regulation of the market. Under such conditions,

141. See *First Annual Report of the State Board of Arbitration of Illinois.*

142. See, for example, the annual reports for the board's first five years (1896–1900); *Reports of the Industrial Commission on Labor Organizations, Labor Disputes, and Arbitration, and on Railway Labor,* vol. 17, 412. This pattern extended to public servants as the school board refused to arbitrate teachers' salaries with the Chicago Teachers' Federation. *Union Labor Advocate* 3, no. 6 (February 1903): 16. Despite the employers' reluctance, the unions continued to call on the board and welcomed a branch office when it opened in Chicago. *Union Labor Advocate* 3, no. 10 (June 1903). For a notable exception, see Schneirov and Suhrbur, *Union Brotherhood, Union Town,* 54–55. They argue that the Carpenter's Union opposed arbitration after 1893 because the arbiters had decided against them in a labor dispute over wages.

143. Though in 1900 Chicago was the site of a growing, modern, industrial economy whose business leaders were hostile to unions, it retained a vibrant craft economy in which joint arbitration boards were common means of settling disputes. This craft economy, unlike the industrial economy that was engaged in the large-scale production of heavy goods, consisted of smaller businesses in trades such as construction, trucking, and shop keeping. As unions within the craft economy gained recognition and entered into collective bargaining and trade agreements with employers, they often created joint arbitration boards, where employers and unions each appointed or elected members to resolve disputes.

144. John Mangan, *History of the Steam Fitters,* 24, 38, quoted in Cohen, *Racketeer's Progress,* 86.

145. Cohen, *Racketeer's Progress.* Robert D. Johnston also makes a strong case for the fluidity and alliances of the working class and petite bourgeoisie in *The Radical Middle Class: Populist Democracy and the Question of Capitalism in Progressive Era Portland, Oregon* (Princeton, NJ: Princeton University Press, 2003).

"collective bargaining became a tool for the joint control of competition, all the more powerful for harnessing the growing strength and legitimacy of labor unions in the city."[146] Thus the building trades and teamsters unions were able to advance the cause of arbitration.

Public support for arbitration also spread. In 1902 the *Typographical Journal* commented that, in the face of such public opinion, "the bosses are beginning to wonder whether they hadn't better stay off their high horses [and refuse to arbitrate] instead of mounting and afterward landing with a hard bump."[147] During an economic boom between 1902 and 1904, "employers did frequently accede to industrial conciliation, and thereby, at least informally, recognized unions as legitimate bargaining agents."[148] Ralph Easley, the former secretary of the CFC who left in 1900 to found the National Civic Federation, a group of industrial capitalists and unionists who promoted arbitration, reported that he was "much impressed with the arbitration machinery that had been perfected by the teamsters and their employers."[149]

As unions and employers' associations' allied themselves on boards of arbitration, collective bargaining became a way of regulating the market, and in so doing, it chipped away at the liberal republicanism of Chicago's industrial elites.[150] For example, Ralph Easley praised the Chicago Board of Arbitration (CBA), which teamsters and their employers formed to consolidate their power by assuming jurisdiction over local labor disputes. The board offered its mediation services to every industry, whether it was welcomed or not. Because most businesses relied on the teamsters to deliver their materials and products, the CBA was able to exert pressure on employers who refused to hire union labor or join employers' organizations. Using the CBA, the alliance was able to set wages and work rules, effectively exercising regulation over Chicago's local economy.[151]

Their successes, however, undermined the ability of corporations in the city to expand into new territories, thus sparking a corporate industrial attack on unions and small-scale employers' associations and a rejection of arbitration. Resistance began first in the building trades, where unions had been most successful and prior to the Pullman Strike had secured arbitration. In 1899 business elites initiated a lockout to undermine the ability of the union to set limits on productivity. Several attempts at arbitration failed. The lockout continued until

146. Cohen, *Racketeer's Progress*, 86, 104.

147. *Typographical Journal* 20 (June 15, 1902): 4.

148. Georg Leidenberg, "Working-class Progressivism and the Politics of Transportation in Chicago, 1895–1907" (PhD diss., University of North Carolina–Chapel Hill, 1995), 168.

149. *American*, January 26, 1903, quoted in Leidenberg, "Working-class Progressivism," 168.

150. Cohen, *Racketeer's Progress*, 104.

151. Ibid., 103.

the financial community forced Mayor Carter Harrison to provide police protection against assaults on nonunion scabs.[152]

In 1903 a strike at Kellogg Switchboard and Supply Company resulted in a court decision that undermined the unions' ability to demand the closed shop. Employers celebrated this decision. The Illinois Manufacturers Association distributed a pamphlet to its members that explained the verdict and praised the businessmen's campaign for the open shop: "It is only by uniting to uphold the laws that we can prevent any infringement upon the liberty to contract, which is so precious to every manufacturer."[153] Striking here is the employers' insistence that uniting in their own associations would ensure the individualism of liberty of contract; they refused to recognize the workers' similar logic.

Corporate leaders soon found an opportunity to push the limits of their victories in the open-shop campaign and attack another of the Chicago unions' powerful weapons—the sympathy strike. In November 1904 several thousand United Garment Workers walked off their jobs at Montgomery Ward to protest sweatshop conditions and the fact that the local Wholesale Clothiers Association, in alliance with the National Association of Manufacturers and the National Association of Clothiers, had reneged on their contracts with the unions by proclaiming an open shop.[154] Emboldened by the Kellogg decision, the representatives of Montgomery Ward and clothing manufacturers refused to meet with the garment workers to settle the dispute directly or turn the matter over to arbitration.

As the months dragged on with no resolution in sight, the union appealed to other labor organizations for help.[155] In solidarity with the garment workers, the teamsters agreed to a sympathy strike.[156] The months that followed witnessed escalating violence, as the clothing manufacturers used strikebreakers and police to battle the teamsters' efforts to control the streets. Determined to challenge the sympathy strike as it had the open shop, the employers stood firm and refused arbitration overtures from Mayor Edward Dunne, a private Citizens Committee, and veteran arbitrator Judge Murray Tuley.[157] In the end, the strike weakened the

152. For discussion of the lockout see *Report of the Industrial Commission of the Chicago Labor Disputes of 1900, with Especial Reference to the Disputes in the Building and Machinery Trades* (Washington, DC: Government Printing Office, 1901), vol. 8; Leidenberg, "Working-class Progressivism," 46–61; Cohen, *Racketeer's Progress*, 108–111.

153. *Annual Report of B. A. Eckhart, President, to the Members of the Illinois Manufacturers Assn.* (Chicago: M. A. Fountain, 1903), 10–11.

154. Elizabeth Anne Payne, *Reform, Labor, and Feminism: Margaret Dreier Robins and the Women's Trade Union League* (Urbana: University of Illinois Press, 1989), 89. See also Howell John Harris, *Bloodless Victories: The Rise and Fall of the Open Shop in the Philadelphia Metal Trades, 1890–1940* (New York: Cambridge University Press, 2000), for further discussion of attacks on the open shop.

155. *Chicago Tribune*, April 9, 1905.

156. Chicago Federation of Labor Minutes, April 9, 1905, Chicago Federation of Labor Papers, Chicago Historical Society.

157. Leidenberg, "Working-class Progressivism," 185.

teamsters' unions, leading to a split and a denunciation of the sympathy strike and labor militancy by one faction. It also turned public opinion against the union and encouraged employers' associations to seek prosecution of corrupt union leaders.[158]

Taken together, the employers' open-shop campaign represented a repudiation of the democratic processes that unions and reformers had been trying to integrate into Chicago labor relations since the 1880s. It was a powerful assertion of capital's prerogatives to govern industry according to its own property interests and to ignore a growing rejection of classical liberal economic principles. The Pullman Strike Commission's observations continued to hold true for Chicago's business elites a decade later: "We . . . have employers who obstruct progress by perverting and misapplying the law of supply and demand, and who, while insisting upon individualism for workmen, demand that they shall be let alone to combine as they please." Drawing from a historicist economics, the commission rebuked such a position by stating that modern industry "has seriously disturbed the laws of supply and demand."[159] Using a discourse of classical liberalism, the industrial and corporate capitalists were able to slow the unions' gains, but they were not able to stop them. Chicago's union membership continued to fluctuate, and the strikers continued to demand union recognition and arbitration procedures as part of the settlements. During the teamsters' strike, the strikers articulated a critique of the industrial capitalists' position that was shared by many unionists and reformers in Chicago. They rejected the employers' conception of justice and rights and chastised them for putting "property above the man and the delivery wagon above the citizen."[160]

On the one hand, the violence of Chicago's labor conflicts suggested that the reformers' vision of arbitration as a process of personal and social democratic transformation was insufficient. Commenting on this failure, the *Daily Labor Bulletin* wrote in the midst of the Teamsters' strike, "strange that human nature is such, that after bitter experience and loss to selves and others, that pride stands in the way of bridging the chasm that all desire to cross."[161] The employers' open-shop campaign and the teamsters' strike suggested that arbitration was a limited means of mediating between labor and capital, but perhaps because of these escalating conflicts, the reformers' rhetoric still held powerful sway well into the 1910s. After another bitter garment workers' strike in 1910, the workers succeeded in using arbitration to secure fuller recognition of their rights, thus pointing to a significant victory for the advocates of arbitration.[162]

158. Ibid., 186–96; Cohen, *Racketeer's Progress*.
159. *Chicago Strike*, xlvii.
160. *Daily Labor Bulletin*, May 25, 1905.
161. Ibid., May 26, 1905.
162. See Payne, *Reform, Labor, and Feminism*.

The Hart, Schaffner, and Marx Strike and the Possibilities of Arbitration

In 1910 forty thousand garment workers, one-tenth of Chicago's labor force, went on strike against Hart, Schaffner, and Marx and other clothing makers. Remembering her decision to lead the walkout, Annie Shapiro Glick explained that the issue was not only about wage reduction and poor treatment. "We had to be recognized as people," she explained.[163] Lasting more than four months, the strike brought "girl strikers" like Shapiro into the homes of Chicago's wealthy women to explain their stand and drew these same influential women and other members of women's clubs onto the picket lines in support of them. As the Chicago papers reported, the strikers were indeed gaining "social recognition."[164] The sympathetic support of Chicago's clubwomen and the media helped the strikers prevail.[165] In January 1911 the company signed an agreement that recognized the United Garment Workers' union, created a board of arbitration, and put into place procedures for handling grievances. These measures reflected a significant step forward for arbitration and collective bargaining in the city. As historian Elizabeth Anne Payne has observed, the "creation of arbitration procedures between management and workers laid the foundation for the introduction of the preferential shop in 1913 and the closed shop thereafter."[166]

The arbitration machinery was developed in the year after the strike. With the creation of a Trade Board and a Board of Arbitration thereafter, the company and workers instituted an appeals process and weekly meetings of representatives of management and labor. In the agreement, the workers articulated their "intention and expectation that they pass from the status of wage servants, with no claim on the employer save his economic need, to that of self-respecting parties to an agreement which they have had an equal part with him in making; that this status gives them an assurance of fair and just treatment."[167] This language echoed that of labor reformers in the 1880s and 1890s, who believed arbitration would put employers and workers on a more even playing field and thus foster a greater sense of democracy in economic practices.

163. Interview (1976) of Hannah Shapiro Glick by Rebecca Sive-Tomashefsky, Manuscript Collection, Preston Bradley Library, University of Illinois–Chicago, quoted in Payne, *Reform, Labor, and Feminism*, 88.

164. Payne, *Reform, Labor, and Feminism*, 90.

165. During the strike, the workers met frequently at Hull House with reformers, settlement workers, and sympathetic members of the public. As in the teamster strike five years earlier, several arbitration attempts failed. The city council appointed a board to try to mediate, but it failed. Later the Illinois Senate sent a committee of five members to broker a settlement, but they too were unsuccessful. J. E. Williams, Sidney Hillman, Earl Dean Howard, *The Hart, Schaffner, & Marx Labor Agreement, Being a Compilation and Codification of the Agreements of 1911, 1913, and 1916 and Decisions Rendered by the Board of Arbitration* (Chicago, 1916), 18–19.

166. Payne, *Reform, Labor, and Feminism*, 91–93.

167. Williams et. al., *Hart, Schaffner, & Marx Labor Agreement*, 2.

The agreement also reflected a vision of social harmony to counter the tendency toward a drifting apart in industrial life by stating that "the parties to this pact realize that the interests sought to be reconciled herein will tend to pull apart, but they enter it in the faith that by the exercise of the co-operative and constructive spirit it will be possible to bring and keep them together." The language here also recognized the divergent interests of labor and capital while still articulating the belief that arbitration's transformative potential would prevent those divisions:

> This will involve as an indispensable pre-requisite the total suppression of the militant spirit by both parties and the development of reason instead of force as the rule of action. It will require also mutual consideration and concession, a willingness on the part of each party to regard and serve the interests of the other, so far as it can be done without too great a sacrifice of principle or interest. With this attitude assured it is believed no difference can arise which the joint tribunal cannot mediate and resolve in the interest of co-operation and harmony.[168]

When the company agreed to arbitration in 1911, it did so reluctantly and spent the next year trying to provoke a strike and thus "discredit the arbitration procedures."[169] In a report to the federal government three years later, however, Hart, Schaffner, and Marx executives offered a new perspective born out of their experience. The Trade Board and Board of Arbitration "protect us against ourselves and make it impossible to violate or overlook the rights of the employees."[170] The company at times found this "vexatious," and "innumerable cases have arisen where we have been obliged to change plans and policies much against our will yet where the final results were better because of the change."[171]

In language strikingly different from that which Pullman used two decades earlier, the company explained that "patience and self control are essential in administering a business on this basis" but that "it ensures exhaustive discussion of every matter of importance, gives everybody an opportunity to express his opinions, frequently brings to light valuable suggestions, and makes possible a higher degree of team-work." Indeed, echoing the complaints of the Pullman employees in 1894, who envisioned arbitration as a remedy, the company observed that "inefficient methods of foremen, lack of watchful supervision, and inaccurate information as to prevailing conditions on the part of higher executives" are brought out through this process and "could not long survive when

---

168. Ibid.
169. Payne, *Reform, Labor, and Feminism*, 92.
170. Williams et. al., *Hart, Schaffner, & Marx Labor Agreement*, 24.
171. Ibid.

every complaint brought by a workman was thoroughly investigated."[172] Even the third arbiter on the board, J. E. Williams, was chosen because "he is a man peculiarly capable of aiding in creating sympathetic understanding on the part of all."[173] Reflecting the hope that mediation could recapture the harmonious relations of smaller enterprises, the company explained its process as "simply the natural and healthy relation which usually exists between the small employer and his half dozen workmen, artificially restored."[174]

Joseph Schaffner, secretary-treasurer of the company, explained that the new mechanisms helped him to know his employees better. He explained that, prior to the strike, he believed he understood his employees and told a friend he was proud of "the happy and contented condition of our employees," but he admitted he was out of touch and needed a way to develop better relations with them: "That was just two days before the strike. I thought they were just as happy as they are now. I did not know any different."[175] In testimony before the commission, one of the company's officers asserted that " 'not in a thousand years' would his corporation consider any proposal to revert to the old system of individual bargaining."[176]

Hart, Schaffner, and Marx's ringing endorsement of arbitration was perhaps due to increased efficiency following a reduction in labor stoppages and strikes, but it does not seem to be idle rhetoric. It reflects the company's more positive relationship with its workers following the institution of the Trade Board and the Arbitration Board. Between April 1912 and June 1914 the boards peacefully adjusted 1,401 complaints. Most of these were made by the union. While 84 percent were adjusted by representatives of each party, 14.7 percent were referred to the Trade Board, and 2.3 percent went to the Board of Arbitration. Most of the decisions went in favor of individual workers or the union.[177]

Unionists and workers shared the company's enthusiasm for arbitration. Sidney Hillman, president of the Amalgamated Clothing Workers of America, praised the company in the wake of a new trade agreement in 1916. Well acquainted with Hart, Schaffner, and Marx, where he spent considerable time working to mediate grievances in the wake of the 1910 strike, Hillman testified that the firm was "absolutely fair to organized labor. . . . I have no hesitancy in saying that there are very few concerns in this country where the conditions of labor are as good as in your establishment."[178]

172. Ibid., 27–28.
173. Ibid., 23.
174. Ibid., 28.
175. U.S. Commission on Industrial Relations, *Final Report and Testimony,* vol. 1, 575.
176. Charles H. Winslow, *Collective Agreements in the Men's Clothing Industry,* U.S. Department of Labor, Bureau of Labor Statistics (Washington, DC: Government Printing Office, 1916), 10.
177. Ibid., 13.
178. Sidney Hillman to Messrs Hart, Schaffner, and Marx, April 26, 1916, reprinted in *Hart,*

The employees testified to the "moral as distinguished from the material benefits."[179] In reporting to the Industrial Commission, an employee related that "the people actually feel like men and women now, while previous to the agreement there was no such feeling in the shops."[180] Another explained that "the fear of being wrongfully discharged has disappeared, because of the right to demand redress. Wages or prices can not be reduced; if attempted to, the price committee, a creation of the trade board, will be there and investigate the case."[181]

The board also reflected the unions' vision of arbitration and collective bargaining as an arena for making collective knowledge. It was composed of representatives of various departments of the industry, and the company believed that "by drafting its membership from the various departments the board is made to possess collectively a complete and intimate knowledge of the conditions and character of the work in all departments. This intimate and complete knowledge is absolutely essential as a condition of intelligent procedure."[182] The value of bringing together individuals who possessed a particular, albeit incomplete, knowledge raised the workers' epistemological status in the workplace by recognizing as important the experiences and insights that they held about each step in the production process. It was a means for their collective knowledge to be brought to bear on decisions affecting their working conditions and wages.[183]

Conclusion

Like the debate over arbitration surrounding the Pullman Strike twenty years earlier, the experiences of the workers and employers at Hart, Schaffner, and Marx illustrate the importance of understanding arbitration through the lens of democratic social knowledge. With the definition of industrial class relations in flux, union leaders and their middle-class allies tried mightily to ensure that

---

Schaffner, & Marx Labor Agreement, 42. Also see Winslow, Collective Agreements, 6, for successes in this area in general and at Hart, Schaffner, and Marx specifically. Benefits to the company are discussed on pp. 9 and 12.

179. Winslow, 12.

180. Quoted in ibid., 12.

181. Quoted in ibid., 11.

182. Winslow, 43.

183. Likewise, workers had demanded that employers open up their books to scrutiny during the collective bargaining process, providing workers with economic information bearing on wages and other terms of employment. For example, John Mitchell argued that union representatives must be informed "not only about wages in their own and other industries but also the cost of living, the cost of production, the charges for transportation, the state of the market, the price, cost, and quality of competing products, and the character of machinery and processes used" (Derber, American Idea of Industrial Democracy, 125). Providing this information suggested that the unionists would better understand the position of the employer and be more fully informed before making demands.

the industrial workplace became a site of democratic practice. Arbitration was a way to accord rationality and respect to workers and to recognize unions as a viable and valuable representative of workers' collective knowledge and agency. For reformers, this process was transformative for both parties, and where the conflicting sides could not accomplish this feat themselves, the reformers were happy to step in as moral arbiters. Democracy would be enacted through the equality afforded the parties in cases of mediation, arbitration, and collective bargaining. By configuring democratic praxis in such a way, arbitration laid open to question all sorts of deeply embedded social and economic assumptions that cast the unions as irrational and the workers as irresponsible children; that privileged individualism and businessmen's prerogatives; and that maintained hierarchal economic relations.

By destabilizing assumptions about a "naturalized" economic and social world view—in this case the liberal republican practices and language invoked by Pullman and other employers—arbitration also opened the door to understanding how social knowledge was contested and shaped at multiple levels. Likewise, it shows how class figured into and confounded democratic social knowledge. At the point of production, workers' shop-floor experience offered a critical piece of knowledge about the most efficient and effective ways to do the work. Their experiences also provided information about the social effects of business practices and industrial capitalism's abilities to meet human needs.

Economists and reformers wrestled with ways to include the workers' input in the mechanisms of distribution of profits and social rights in order to negotiate an acceptable standard of living. Arbitration seemed a hopeful way to make those processes more democratic by according recognition and status to working people through their union representatives. As the struggle over arbitration illustrates, epistemological status was bound to a degree of equality and respect and to political agency. To the extent that workers were able to avoid violence and mediate differences, the reformers were able to cut across class and make alliances with workers against intractable employers who refused arbitration altogether. Moreover, they were successful enough to convince the public, both in the city and ultimately nationwide, of the virtues of arbitration.[184] As the public joined with workers and employers to demand that *its* rights also be protected, the state increasingly became an agent of justice by protecting rights, particularly of weaker parties. It was the arena in which claims were negotiated.

By the time of World War I, the context for discussion over labor arbitration

---

184. When the struggles turned violent, however, reformers and the public became more ambivalent about organized labor. This was especially apparent in the 1905 Teamsters' strike, though it dated back much earlier to the Haymarket Riot and Pullman Strike. See Leidenberg, "Working-class Progressivism," 193–94. Cohen (*Racketeers' Progress*, 129, 136) also points out that reformers were particularly concerned that unions adhere to the rule of law and maintain industrial peace.

had changed dramatically, as the Hart, Schaffner, and Marx agreements suggested. Though corporate elites' attitudes toward arbitration varied by industry, mediation was more commonly practiced than it had ever been, even though there was still no consensus in every case or in each industry.[185] World War I further opened the door to the extension of state intervention in labor conflict.[186] Historians know labor's disappointments of the postwar years, when businessmen were able to quash unions in many industries or undermine them through corporate welfare practices and shop committees. However, from the vantage point of 1918, the moment when government-appointed arbitrators took their side was an optimistic one for many unions.[187] As head of the Chicago Federation of Labor, John Fitzpatrick received several requests for help from unions in the region hoping to bring disputes before the War Labor Board, and he worked closely with National War Labor Board (NWLB) chairman Frank Walsh to ensure that workers received a sympathetic hearing.[188] In a landmark settlement in Chicago's packinghouses that set the standards for future NWLB decisions, federal mediator Samuel Alschuler instituted an eight-hour day, overtime compensation, living wage increases, and arbitration and conciliation processes.[189] Putting aside the "ofttimes embarrassing and influential contention that . . . prices and income are so fixed by law or otherwise," Alschuler put justice above the laws of supply and demand.[190] Fitzpatrick and Walsh, who had

185. Support for arbitration remained uneven among both employers and unions. As one observer explained, "If you happen to be in control of the situation, or think you are in control, you are not for arbitration. If you happen to be weaker than the other party, or think you are, you are a sturdy advocate of the principle of arbitration." Julius Henry Cohen, "A League to Enforce Industrial Peace," in *Proceedings of the Academy of Political Science*, vol. 8, 113.

186. Montgomery, *Fall of the House of Labor,* chapter 8, "This Great Struggle for Democracy," 370–410.

187. For discussion of labor's losses following World War I, see ibid., 411–64. Also see Conner, *National War Labor Board.*

188. John Fitzgerald to William B. Wilson, Department of Labor Secretary, June 13, 1918, and an unidentified letter also requesting Judge Alschuler to handle the dispute, all in Chicago Federation of Labor Papers, John Fitzgerald Papers, Box 7, Folder 7, Chicago Historical Society. Also see "Outline of Grievance" to National War Labor Board from hotel and restaurant employees in Folder 50.

189. For the full text of the decision, see *In the Matter of the Arbitration of Six Questions concerning Wages, Hours, and Conditions of Labor in Certain Packing House Industries, by Agreement Submitted for Decision to a United States Administrator* (Washington, DC: Government Printing Office, 1918).

190. Ibid., 11. For examples of cases Chicago workers brought to the NWLB, see "Before the War Labor Board, Transcripts of Proceedings in Chicago Vicinity, 1918–1919," twelve volumes. Typescripts available from Northwestern University Library. Some specific cases include Chicago Typographical Union No. 16 vs. Chicago Local American Newspapers Publishers Association, Docket No. 404, November 11, 25–27, 29, 1918, vol. 3, pp. 1–379; International Association of Machinists vs. Burke and James, Inc., Docket No. 588, November 4, 1918, vol. 3, pp. 1–76; Employes [*sic*] vs. Eugene Ditzen Co., Docket No. 244, October 7, 14, 21, 1918, vol. 3, pp. 1–1086; and Amalgamated Association of Street and Electrical Railway Employees of America, Division 241 & 308 vs. Street and Elevated Railway Lines of Chicago, IL, & Evanston, IL, Docket No. 59, July 1918, vol. 7, pp. 60–189.

argued the workers' case and who, along with former president William Howard Taft chaired the NWLB shortly thereafter, delighted in the decision. As Walsh wrote to Fitzpatrick, if Alschuler were made labor administrator of the United States, "we could all go home, quit our foolishness, and go to work."[191] Unions welcomed the federal government's role as mediator as they used the moral force of the state to press their claims for living wages, the right to arbitration and collective bargaining, and improved safety and working conditions, all of which they had been fighting for since the 1870s.[192]

The NWLB thus offered unions a means to push their vision of economic justice and thereby create a precedent that posited the state as the mediator of last resort. Indeed, as numerous frameworks for arbitration emerged in the early twentieth century, the neutral third party was sometimes envisioned as a means to support workers' claims. This was not to suggest that the state necessarily took their side but rather that it served to equalize the power dynamics of an economic relationship that was unequal at its core. In the 1915 Industrial Commission report, labor commissioner and economist John R. Commons argued that the state should equalize the bargaining situation.[193] By 1916, when the United States was deeply enmeshed in World War I and on the brink of joining the Allied cause, the state was more readily recognized as protecting not just the public interest but workers as well. This commitment positioned the state as a moral arbiter and in so doing opened up twentieth-century debates about its role in determining, distributing, and protecting contested claims such as the American standard of living or, as Franklin Roosevelt would later cast it, "freedom from want."[194] Indeed, perhaps most important for the course of the

---

Issues in these cases range dramatically, though they all incorporate aspects of union agendas since the Civil War: working conditions, living wages, maximum hours, union recognition, and collective bargaining.

191. Frank P. Walsh to John Fitzgerald, June 13, 1918, Chicago Federation of Labor Papers, John Fitzpatrick Papers, Box 7, Folder 49, June 1–30, 1913, Chicago Historical Society. For a report of Walsh's testimony before Alshuler see *Chicago Herald,* February 12, 1918, "Clash at Hearing of 'Yards' Dispute," in Women's Trade Union League Scrapbook, Box 2, Folder 8, University of Illinois–Chicago, Daley Library Special Collections Department. For Walsh's position on arbitration and collective bargaining, see Women's Trade Union League Scrapbook, Box 2, Folder 8, University of Illinois–Chicago, Daley Library Special Collections Department.

192. Conner, in *National War Labor Board,* discusses the NWLB standards on a number of issues including the living wage, the eight-hour day, and the right to mediation and arbitration. For recent discussion of this era and its lost potential, see David Brody, *Labor Embattled: History, Power, Rights* (Champaign: University of Illinois Press, 2005); Joseph Anthony McCartin, *Labor's Great War: The Struggle for Industrial Democracy and the Origins of Modern American Labor Relations, 1912–1921* (Chapel Hill: University of North Carolina Press, 1997); Shelton Stomquist, *Reinventing the People: The Progressive Movement, the Class Problem, and the Origins of Modern Liberalism* (Champaign: University of Illinois Press, 2005).

193. Derber, *American Idea of Industrial Democracy,* 121.

194. See Donohue, *Freedom from Want,* for discussion of the shift in economic thought and the state's role in establishing the notion of freedom from want.

twentieth century, at that moment arbitration served as an arena for loosening the grip of liberal republicanism's vision of justice mediated through the market; it made it possible to envision a redistributive justice mediated through state intervention.

That workers were able to gain a hearing and in most cases prevail in their claims to the NWLB suggests the long road traveled since the Pullman Strike, when many employers refused to recognize unions and to seek any mediation of differences with their employees. As the Hart, Schaffner, and Marx case illustrates, arbitration could indeed serve the goal of democratic social knowledge by fostering democratic interaction and the creation of a fuller knowledge in the workplace. In their most optimistic formulations, these new relations would not just transform the individuals involved but also provide a solution to the problems of democracy in an industrial economy. Of course, most employers did not see it that way and during the early twentieth century worked to ally themselves with the federal government. Though we must not lose sight of the democratic hopes that mediation, arbitration, and collective bargaining embodied in the early twentieth century, the growing relationship between businessmen, the federal government, and the reformers and social scientists interested in these issues ultimately helped secure a particular type of liberal democracy—one that privileged the political and policy-making power of social scientists and businessmen. It harnessed the growing bureaucratic apparatus of the state to support a logic that privileged capitalist growth and consumption. This brand of liberal democracy failed to incorporate an activist social science or the participatory deliberation encouraged by and necessary to democratic social knowledge. Thus the potential for democratic social knowledge to redress significant matters of class and democracy was undermined. As we see in the next chapter, democratic social knowledge would also face significant challenges in addressing racial conflict as well.

5

"The Struggle Is Bound to Take in the Negro"

Race and Democratic Social Knowledge

Our democracy asserts that the people are fighting for the time when all men shall be brothers and the liberty of each shall be the concern of all. If this is true, the struggle is bound to take in the Negro.[1]

While the discussion of arbitration illustrated class dimensions of democratic social knowledge, the racial tensions of the early twentieth century suggest that race was one of the most significant stumbling blocks for democratic social knowledge. At the turn of the century, African American migration to Chicago had markedly increased, even though this moment was ten years before the Great Migration, which would double the city's black population.[2] The changing racial makeup of the city brought white and black residents into interaction with one another in new ways—as economic associates and competitors, neighbors, political participants, and, most important for this study, reform allies. Just as Chicago residents had experienced a drifting apart along cultural and class lines, so the growth of the black population, coupled with persistent white racism in white popular culture and social science literature that characterized blacks as lazy, immoral, biologically inferior, and prone to commit rape against white women, exacerbated racial tensions. In the face of such demographic changes

1. The epigraph to this chapter is drawn from Ida Wells-Barnett, "Our Country's Lynching Record," *Survey* (February 1, 1913): 573–74, reprinted in Mildred I. Thompson, *Ida B. Wells-Barnett: An Exploratory Study of an American Black Woman, 1893–1930* (Brooklyn, NY: Carlson, 1990), 280.

2. James R. Grossman, *Land of Hope: Chicago, Black Southerners, and the Great Migration* (Chicago: University of Chicago Press, 1989); William M. Tuttle Jr., *Race Riot: Chicago in the Red Summer of 1919* (New York: Athenaeum, 1970), 74–107; Allan Spear, *Black Chicago: The Making of a Negro Ghetto, 1890–1920,* 129–46 (Chicago: University of Chicago Press, 1967); St. Clair Drake, *Churches and Voluntary Associations in the Chicago Negro Community* (Chicago: Works Progress Administration, 1940); St. Clair Drake and Horace R. Cayton, *Black Metropolis: A Study of Negro Life in a Northern City,* vol. 1 (New York: Harcourt, Brace, 1945).

and cultural attitudes, African American antilynching activist and Chicago resident Ida Wells noted that any struggle that claimed the goals of universal brotherhood and liberty for "our democracy" was "bound to take in the Negro." This chapter examines the variety of ways that reformers—both black and white—sought to bring black/white race relations into the debate over democratic social knowledge.

In the preceding chapters I have explored various strands of democratic social knowledge—experiential, proximate, interactive, aesthetic, and sympathetic. As we have seen, a cultural dialogue about liberal republicanism ran through reformers' efforts. This dialogue sometimes offered alternative visions of social responsibility and the state and at other times served to inhibit imaginative social change. In this chapter we further expand our conception of democratic social knowledge to understand it as the ability to exercise agency in shaping cultural images and ideas across social sectors and in a variety of forms; indeed, as we saw in chapter 1, elite businessmen exercised this type of cultural power to shape social knowledge. In that chapter we also learned that this social knowledge was frequently exclusionary, particularly of African Americans. Indeed, we should recall that at the mass meeting called to address Chicago's social problems, William Stead silenced the lone African American man who sought to speak.

In this chapter we turn our attention to efforts to bring African American perspectives into the cultural struggle over democratic social knowledge. We will see this played out not just in the narrative strategies of reformers like Ida Wells-Barnett and in politics of interracial reform at the Frederick Douglass Center but also in the planning and execution of one of the city's earliest public exhibits on African Americans, the Illinois (National) Half-century Anniversary of Negro Freedom, an exhibition celebrating emancipation.

Against the backdrop of growing racism, the authority and power to shape cultural representations of African Americans was a critical factor in influencing democratic social knowledge. The stakes were high as new media forms, particularly photography and motion pictures, could appropriate personal stories to manipulate viewers' sympathies or fears. Their ability to shape popular ideas and evoke sympathy—to bring distant parties imaginatively together—made public exhibitions and displays an important site of democratic social knowledge. Such visual forms of social knowledge were important in countering reform literature and social investigations that linked urban vice and social pathology to emerging northern black ghettos. Not only did African Americans and a handful of white social scientists challenge such images by emphasizing environment over biology, but African American reform leaders also asserted the importance of explaining racial experiences and shaping popular images of African Americans whether through literature, the press, photography and public display, or personal decorum. As they asserted themselves as cultural brokers of racial images and knowledge, they help us understand inclusion, cultural agency, and the ability to define the parameters of political subjectivity as important aspects of democratic social knowledge.

Akin to the daily practices emphasized by Jane Addams and Hull House residents and to the mutually respectful workplace relationships sought through conciliation and arbitration, the strands of democratic social knowledge discussed in this chapter emphasize democracy as a social relationship, in which equality and mutual respect should prevail over racial prejudice. In his discussion of the Chicago NAACP, historian Christopher Reed emphasizes that a significant trial facing the early founders of the organization was to "develop a mutual sense of *trust*, based on cooperative, altruistic interaction. This relationship was thought to be achievable if the two races could overcome a *distrust* rooted in suspicions emanating from the legacy of slavery along with existing racism."[3] As Celia Parker Woolley, a white Progressive Era reformer, explained, "mutual knowledge must precede sympathy and sympathy must precede any attempts to minimize race friction and economics and other handicaps on the Negro."[4]

By emphasizing democracy as a social relationship, this chapter does not intend to overlook the importance of African Americans' political protest and advocacy as a means to ensure legal equality; rather, Woolley neatly captured the expectations of African Americans and their white allies that the strategies of democratic social knowledge they employed would ultimately bridge racial conflict and help bring full civic and political inclusion. Indeed, as we recall from the mass meeting that gave rise to the CFC, race was wholly unbridgeable. In that context, preventing a "fatal drifting apart" along racial lines demanded multiple strategies—activist social science, proximate interaction, and cultural agency—all with the goal of challenging racist social knowledge and upsetting racial hierarchy and segregation. Against this backdrop, efforts to prevent segregated schools, which I touch on in the chapter's conclusion, took on important democratic meaning not just as a means to ensure educational opportunity but also in terms of opportunities to promote daily interaction across racial lines. As we see, the limited successes of African Americans and their white allies to forge an *integrated* democratic social knowledge were unable to stem the tide of growing segregationist attitudes in the city. Such failures raise questions about whether democratic social knowledge could reconcile all differences and whether race would ultimately prove an unbridgeable divide.

3. Christopher Robert Reed, *The Chicago NAACP and the Rise of Black Professional Leadership, 1910–1966* (Bloomington: Indiana University Press, 1997), 4.

4. Frederick Douglass Center, Fall Calendar, 1907. Anita McCormick Blaine Papers, State Historical Society of Wisconsin, Madison, Wisconsin.

The Chicago Setting

African Americans in Chicago enjoyed a measure of equality unknown to their southern counterparts. Throughout the middle decades of the century, African Americans accounted for a very small percentage of the city's population and were geographically dispersed throughout the wards: Between 1850 and 1880 the percentage of African Americans in the wider population hovered around 1 percent, and, while most lived on the south side of the city, nineteen of thirty-five wards had an African American population of at least 0.5 percent, and only two wards had an African American population of more than 10 percent.[5] During these years, race relations were open and fluid, and African Americans made advances in legal rights. In 1870 black men gained the right to vote in Illinois, and schools were formally desegregated in 1874. Furthermore, Illinois protected African American rights in its own Civil Rights Act of 1885, which outlawed segregation in all public places.[6] During this period the economic, political, and social progress of African Americans in the city seemed predicated less on race consciousness and separation than on integration. Newspaper editor and attorney Ferdinand Barnett, future husband of Ida B. Wells, thus counseled: "As a race let us forget the past so far as we can, and unite with other men upon issues liberal, essential, and not dependent upon color of skin or texture of hair for its [sic] gravamen."[7] He articulated faith in the liberal American political promise that commitment to universal individual rights would bring about a colorblind society.[8]

However, even as African Americans gained legal rights and their numbers in the city grew, white racists mobilized, making racial relations more precarious and suggesting that actions of the autonomous individual of liberal theory were insufficient to overcome racial barriers to political and civic inclusion.[9] By the 1890s, Chicago race relations were in the midst of major transitions. The same year that Addams opened Hull House to address class and ethnic divisions, an 1889 editorial in the *Chicago Herald* illustrated a deepening racial divide. The author warned that "Our colored brother may rest assured that he will not make matters any better for him by attempting to crowd himself into places where he knows his presence is not desired. Invoking the law to enable him to do so will

5. Spear, *Black Chicago*, 11–15.

6. Elizabeth Dale, " 'Social Equality Does Not Exist among Themselves, nor among Us': *Baylies vs. Curry* and Civil Rights in Chicago, 1888," *American Historical Review* 102 (April 1997): 311–39.

7. Quoted in Spear, *Black Chicago*, 53.

8. This view characterized Radical Republicans in the wake of the Civil War; see Carol Horton, "Liberal Equality and the Civic Subject," in *The Liberal Tradition in American Politics: Reassessing the Legacy of American Liberalism*, ed. David F. Ericson and Louisa Bertch Green, 115–36, especially 118–25 (New York: Routledge).

9. Horton, "Liberal Equality and the Civic Subject," 123–24.

only increase prejudice that is now very strong. It will make no friends but serve to create many enemies."[10] Thus, while African Americans made legal gains, social conventions continued to discourage integration.

The construction of the ghetto throughout the 1890s and after the turn of the century testified to the deepening racial division. By 1910 the outlines of the city's "Black Belt" would be visible on the southwest side as the population of African Americans in the city rose to 44,103 out of a population of 2 million.[11] Ten years later, in 1920, the black population jumped to 109,000. Until World War I, when industries became more integrated, whites were likely to meet blacks only as servants in hotels, restaurants, or elevators, as more than half the African American population worked in the service sector as janitors and laundresses or in other menial jobs.[12] Jane Addams observed, "Not only in the South, but everywhere in America, a strong race antagonism is asserting itself, which has modes of lawlessness and insolence. The contemptuous attitude of the so-called superior race toward the inferior results in a social segregation of each race."[13] African Americans confronted a hardening of the racial line, apparent in economic isolation and exclusion, and a growing geographical segregation that concerned white and black reformers alike.

Several cultural factors across the United States contributed to a backdrop of racial antagonism. Northern and southern whites built the basis of reconciliation around memories of the Civil War that cast it as a regrettable moment in U.S. history.[14] In the process, they erased slavery and African American visions of emancipation and freedom from national narratives. Against northern indifference, southern state governments imposed Jim Crow laws and disfranchised African Americans. Meanwhile, northern businessmen welcomed black strikebreakers during the last decades of the nineteenth century, fueling racial antagonism between working-class whites and blacks. As the U.S. government embarked on an imperialist course, Americans divided over the wisdom of incorporating darker peoples into its population. Over the course of the nineteenth century, "a constellation of religious, historical, and biological theories positing the natural inferiority of persons of African descent [came] to be embraced as time-honored truths by white Americans."[15]

The rise of positivistic social science at the beginning of the twentieth

10. *Chicago Herald*, September 16, 1889.
11. Spear, *Black Chicago*.
12. Grossman, *Land of Hope*, 128.
13. Jane Addams, quoted in Reed, *Chicago NAACP*, 9.
14. David Blight, *Race and Reunion: The Civil War in American Memory* (Cambridge, MA: Belknap Press of Harvard University Press, 2001).
15. E. Frances White, *Dark Continent of Our Bodies: Black Feminism and the Politics of Respectability* (Philadelphia: Temple University Press, 2001).

century meant that much more was at stake as social scientific knowledge was used for a biological basis of the management of populations assumed to be inferior. At the grassroots level, racist whites mobilized to prevent African Americans from voting and moving into white neighborhoods and, in the case of the Ku Klux Klan, to terrorize blacks. In Chicago, white residents worked with realtors on the edge of the Black Belt and organized the Community Property Owners' Protective Association and the Hyde Park and Kenwood Property Owners' Association to keep the neighborhood white.[16] Such actions served to solidify a white identity predicated on racial hierarchy.[17]

Indeed, in the hands of white racists, social science methods brought the weight of scientific authority to racial hierarchy and segregation.[18] Analysis of census data showing the decline in the black birthrate and the higher death rates, for instance, were interpreted by white southern social scientists as biological determinism: Blacks were inherently physically inferior. In racist minds, the disproportionate number of African Americans convicted of crimes seemed proof that blacks were mentally and morally inferior. Popular sociology suggested that natural antipathy existed between the races, causing friction that could become violent when whites felt social pressure from blacks.[19] These "natural laws of race development" proved an obstacle to blacks' civic inclusion.[20] Buttressed by conservative interpretations of social Darwinism, more extreme racists in the South entertained ideas of deportation or looked forward to eventual extermination.

At the opening of the twentieth century, white southerners largely controlled the production of racial knowledge; narratives of black men as rapists, of black women as immoral, and of the entire race as lazy and criminalized abounded throughout the South and were widely disseminated in the North. Antilynching activist Ida Wells explained that southern whites owned "the telegraph wires, newspapers, and all other communication with the outside world. They write

16. Reed, *Chicago NAACP*, 62; Robin F. Bachin, *Building the South Side: Urban Space and Civic Culture in Chicago, 1890–1919* (Chicago: University of Chicago Press, 2004), 251–52. White owners argued that they were not racist but merely wanted to maintain their property values.

17. White, *Dark Continent of Our Bodies*, 81–116.

18. Mia Bay, " 'The World Was Thinking Wrong about Race': The Philadelphia Negro and Nineteenth-century Science," in *W. E. B. DuBois, Race, and the City: The Philadelphia Negro and Its Legacy*, ed. Michael B. Katz and Thomas J. Sugrue, 41–59 (Philadelphia: University of Pennsylvania Press, 1998). The Atlanta University Studies, sponsored by W. E. B. DuBois, were envisioned as an instrument of changing racial knowledge. David Turley, "Black Social Science and Black Politics in the Understanding of the South: DuBois, the Atlanta University Studies, and the Crisis, 1897–1920," in *Race and Class in the American South since 1890*, ed. Melvyn Stokes and Rick Halpern, especially 141–42 (Providence, RI: Berg, 1994).

19. John H. Stanfield, *Philanthropy and Jim Crow in American Social Science* (Westport, CT: Greenwood, 1985), 8.

20. Bay, "The World Was Thinking Wrong about Race," 44.

the reports which justify lynching by painting the Negro as black as possible, and those reports are accepted by the press associations and the world without question or investigation."[21] Typical of the tone of such reports, an *Atlantic Monthly* article described African American men as "incapable of adopting the white man's moral code, of assimilating the white man's moral sentiments, of striving toward the white man's moral ideals. . . . They are, in brief, an uncivilized, semi-savage people, living in a civilization to which they are unequal, partaking to a limited degree of its benefits, performing in no degree its duties."[22] African Americans were depicted as immoral and unable to perform the duties of American citizenship, especially productive labor and political participation.

Though the North could not escape the fact that race was a "national burden which the whole nation must sympathetically bear," many philanthropists limited their efforts to donating to southern black educational institutions like Tuskegee, for "the people of the South represent the direct remedial agent," and to supporting the research that largely perpetuated Booker T. Washington's version of educational accommodation.[23] Consequently, the dominant social sciences and press tended to legitimize popular prejudice and to excuse white neglect of structural problems in black communities both in the North and the South.

Changes in Chicago race relations exemplified the growing attitude that blacks were a southern "problem" best controlled by segregation. Southern racist narratives describing African American men as dangerous rapists followed black migrants north and circulated in Chicago. Beginning with an 1894 strike in the meatpacking industry, Chicago employers had begun to recruit southern black men as strikebreakers, thus using economic competition to racially divide workers and diminish the effectiveness of unions.[24] Though workers recognized this tactic, they did not always rise above the racial animosity it sought to create. During the 1905 Teamsters' strike, the CFL's *Daily Labor Bulletin* played upon white prejudices by suggesting the extent to which popular racial constructions in the white labor community inflamed racial prejudice and widened the gulf

21. Wells, "The Reason Why the Colored Man Is Not in the World's Fair," in *The Selected Works of Ida B. Wells-Barnett* (New York: Oxford University Press, 1991), 75.

22. Quincy Ewing, "The Heart of the Race Problem," *Atlantic Monthly* 103 (March 1909): 389. Also Gail Bederman, *Manliness and Civilization: A Cultural History of Gender and Race in the United States, 1880–1917* (Chicago: University of Chicago Press, 1995), 49.

23. Frank W. Blackman, Review of *Studies in the American Race Problem* by Alfred H. Stone, *American Journal of Sociology* 14 (July 1909): 837, quoted in Stanfield, *Philanthropy and Jim Crow*, 25. Also see James Anderson, *The Education of Blacks in the South, 1860–1935* (Chapel Hill: University of North Carolina Press, 1988), on support for philanthropic support for Tuskegee and similar institutions.

24. Tuttle, *Race Riot*, 112–52; Grossman, *Land of Hope*; James R. Barrett, *Work and Community in the Jungle: Chicago's Packinghouse Workers, 1894–1922* (Urbana, IL: University of Illinois Press, 1987).

between blacks and whites.[25] Remarking on the character of the strikebreakers, the paper wrote, "as you are undoubtedly aware the class of [black] men who are continuously loafing at this time of year are men who are not anxious to work, and who brought down the wrath of the people of the southern cities upon the negro." Echoing lynching rationalizations, the paper went on, "Men of this stamp have outraged every law of decency in their southern homes, and we believe that we are speaking the truth when we say the women and children of Chicago will not allow men of this character to visit their homes to deliver parcels or merchandise from these department stores."[26] Playing on perceptions of blacks as lazy and dangerous—characterizations very similar to those that many CFC members had pinned on unemployed relief recipients—such depictions tended to widen the psychological distance between the races. As the twentieth century began, reformers confronted deepening racism that was legitimized by both white social scientists and popular culture.

At the same time that Chicago's racial divide deepened, the growing African American population developed a network that made possible coordinated efforts for racial advocacy. While the growing black south side brought the problems of segregation and vice into greater relief, there also developed a visible and vibrant African American cultural and commercial center.[27] Numerous women's clubs, a YMCA, Ida Wells-Barnett's Negro Fellowship League, a settlement that focused on helping black men find housing and jobs, the NAACP, and the Urban League all served to help orient African American migrants to their new city. Indeed, "for many African Americans in Chicago, especially the new migrants just making their way from the South in the first decades of the twentieth century, civic pride and community identity were found . . . in the emerging commercial leisure district centered on State Street," which stood in the heart of the city's Black Belt.[28] In the jazz clubs and dance halls on the south side, African Americans and whites found ways to transcend racial differences in the relaxed atmosphere of these leisure and commercial spaces.[29] These opportunities for forging African American identities, as well as alliances across race, propelled blacks into the public sphere and ultimately Chicago politics in new ways.

25. David R. Roediger, *The Wages of Whiteness: Race and the Making of the American Working Class* (London: Verso, 1991).

26. *Daily Labor Bulletin*, May 26, 1905. As Georg Leidenberg explains, the Teamsters' strike left an important legacy for race relations in Chicago. It divided the labor movement along racial lines, linked African Americans to strikebreaking in the white laborer's imagination, and left many African Americans distrustful of labor unions. Leidenberg, "Working-class Progressivism and the Politics of Transportation in Chicago, 1895–1907" (PhD diss., University of North Carolina, Chapel Hill, 1995), 177–80.

27. Bachin, *Building the South Side*, 250–97.

28. Ibid., 247–48.

29. Ibid., 268–83.

The reformers' multifaceted approach to racial marginalization might best be described as a "Chicago view of race relations" that serves as a corrective to the dichotomy historians have imposed between the assimilationist strategies of Booker T. Washington and the immediatist protest strategies of W. E. B. Dubois.[30] Chicagoans' strategies undergirded a number of interracial and race-based activities in the city and were often interwoven in the same projects. Women's clubs, for example, sought to meet the black community's needs for social services by operating homes such as the Louise Juvenile Home for dependent and orphaned boys, the Phyllis Wheatley Home for single working girls, the Amanda Smith Home for dependent and orphaned girls, and the Home for the Aged and Infirm Colored People. These institutions signaled a self-help strategy but at the same time laid the foundation for protest advocacy, and indeed many of the same women used their knowledge of structural discrimination, observed through their reform activities, to protest injustice and seek state support of their activities. African Americans believed that they would be accepted by whites as equals once they proved their ability to advance "black progress" in their communities and personal behavior.[31] Such beliefs served as a catalyst for reform efforts ranging from mission work to community development and social services as critical to improving condition for blacks, presenting a positive image to whites and securing racial equality.

The racism that Chicago African Americans faced at the turn of the century was shared by other black communities across the nation, and black leaders challenged it in a number of ways by drawing from emerging social science traditions and asserting cultural agency. On the intellectual terrain, W. E. B. Dubois, along with others, developed a social science literature to counter the speculative scientific racism of whites. DuBois's now famous investigations in Philadelphia and in the Atlanta University Studies sought to insert race into a broader American social science agenda, and he worked with other black intellectuals to offer alternative paradigms of "racial progress." Less well known is DuBois's photographic archive displayed at the 1900 Paris Exposition, which offered alternative visions of African Americans, depicting them as refined, elegant members of the American middle class.[32]

30. Mary Jo Deegan, ed., *The New Woman of Color: The Collected Writings of Fannie Barrier Williams, 1893–1918* (DeKalb: Northern Illinois University Press, 2002), lv.

31. Reed, *Chicago NAACP*, 15. For additional discussion of African American reform, see Arvarh E. Strickland, *History of the Chicago Urban League* (Champaign: University of Illinois Press, 1966).

32. W. E. B. DuBois, *Philadelphia Negro: A Social Study* (Philadelphia: Published for the University, 1899). See *Proceedings of the National Negro Conference, 1909, New York, May 31 and June 1*, for a compilation of scientific and social scientific papers responding to scientific racism; Mia Bay, *The White Image in the Black Mind: African American Ideas about White People, 1830–1925* (New York: Oxford University Press, 2000); Shawn Michelle Smith, *Photography on the Color Line: W. E. B. DuBois, Race, and Visual Culture* (Durham, NC: Duke University Press, 2004). Smith's insightful

However, his academic credentials and institutional affiliations were an unusual resource for producing legitimate social knowledge.[33] Since graduate study, academic positions, and bureaucratic jobs were not widely available to African Americans, activist intellectuals forged alternative means to produce and disseminate racial knowledge. Participation in race reform within churches, community social service organizations, and clubs provided several black Chicagoans the opportunity for inquiry and reflections on the economic, social, political, and gendered dimensions of the African American urban experience.[34] These arenas lent themselves to a democratic social knowledge rooted in the proximate, personal experiences that activism facilitated. For example, in Chicago a number of articles published locally and nationally contributed to a body of sociological and popular knowledge about African Americans generally and race and power in particular. In an article titled "The Negro in Times of Industrial Unrest," Richard R. Wright Jr. of Chicago's Trinity Mission for African Americans described the manner in which the economic limitations placed on blacks led to industrial violence.[35] Fannie Barrier Williams, an activist and author whose works covered topics ranging from African American religion, women's clubs, employment, education, and interracial cooperation, used her position within reform activities to assess the black community's networks of support. For both Wright and Williams, their firsthand knowledge of the connections between structural and personal problems posed by racial segregation and discrimination was built on their experiences in and proximity to reform activities.[36] Similarly confronting racist ideologies, leaders in the African

book on the way visual culture made and remade racial identities argues that DuBois's display offered a counterarchive that challenged "a long legacy of racist taxonomy, intervening in turn-of-the-century 'race science' by offering competing visual evidence," 2.

33. See Bay, *White Image in the Black Mind*, for a discussion of DuBois's efforts to replace ethnology and Christian monogenism as the bases of racial theories. DuBois's argument for a thorough social scientific analysis of race can be found in W. E. Burghardt Du Bois, "The Study of Negro Problems," *Annals of the American Academy of Political and Social Science* (January 1898): 1–23.

34. Deegan, ed., *New Woman of Color*, and Mary Jo Deegan, ed., *Women in Sociology: A Bio-bibliographical Sourcebook* (New York: Greenwood, 1991).

35. Like union leaders, Wright noted that blacks often served as strikebreakers, but he dispelled myths that they made up a large proportion of scabs. More important, he suggested that strikebreaking was an important means for African Americans to gain access to jobs that that were usually unavailable to them. Indeed, blacks entered the meatpacking industry in large numbers only after serving as strikebreakers. His assessment illustrated how blacks' economic isolation ultimately contributed to industrial violence. R. R. Wright Jr., "The Negro in Times of Industrial Unrest," *Charities* 15, no. 1 (October 7, 1905): 69–73. See also James R. Barrett, *Work and Community in the Jungle: Chicago's Packinghouse Workers, 1894–1922* (Urbana: University of Illinois Press, 1987), 187–224, for a discussion of race relations among workers in the stockyards, particularly efforts of the Stockyards Labor Council to encourage organization among blacks and interracial cooperation.

36. The work of these early African American social scientists pointed out that migration coupled with economic interdependency would make separation of the races an increasingly difficult prospect. Stanfield, *Philanthropy and Jim Crow*, 27. This recognition helped encourage reform

American women's club movement, such as Ida Wells-Barnett, Fannie Barrier Williams, and Mary Church Terrell, asserted a politics of respectability that emphasized the importance of displaying appropriate behavior and decorum in public spaces. Strategies of self-help and political advocacy existed side by side as African American communities in cities throughout the North and South built institutions that served the needs of poor people, orphans, and elderly people, educated their children, challenged unjust laws, and built local branches of the National Association of Colored Women, the National Negro Business League, the NAACP, and the Urban League.[37]

Together these strategies combined forms of social science, self-representation, and politics to combat racism and build interracial connections. As African Americans combated racism, the line between social knowledge and the popular image of the black body was frequently blurred. As historian Evelyn Brooks Higgenbotham has written, African American reformers "spoke as if ever-cognizant of the gaze of white America, which in panoptic fashion focused perpetually upon each and every black person."[38] Reformers believed that images of blacks encountered in the media and in public put a premium on control over the black body and behavior. Black cultural authority over racial representation and displays of African American respectability were thus contestatory forms: They challenged a racist social knowledge that positioned all African Americans as inferior.[39]

The reformers countered racist images—of monstrous lynching victims, black criminals, depraved and drunken freed men, and lascivious black women appearing frequently in popular media, particularly in photographs and the new motion pictures—by asserting alternative constructions of African Americans as respectable, patriotic, and sharing common humanity and American (middle-class) cultural values. The struggle over cultural representations of African Americans was thus tied to democratic social knowledge, as African American reformers sought inclusion and authority in shaping racial narratives. The stakes for their reform efforts were very high, and they employed multiple strategies—a combination of activist social science, a framework of proximate and embodied

---

strategies that promoted racial interaction.

37. Glenda Elizabeth Gilmore, *Gender and Jim Crow: Women and the Politics of White Supremacy in North Carolina, 1896–1920* (Chapel Hill: University of North Carolina Press, 1996); Deegan, *New Woman of Color;* Anne Meis Knupfer, *Toward a Tenderer Humanity and a Nobler Womanhood: African American Women's Clubs in Turn-of-the-Century Chicago* (New York: New York University Press, 1996).

38. Quoted in White, *Dark Continent of Our Bodies.*

39. Similarly, Robin D. G. Kelley has argued that African Americans dressed up after work to present a "public challenge to the dominant stereotype of the black body, and reinforce a sense of dignity that was perpetually being assaulted." Robin D. G. Kelley, *Race Rebels: Culture, Politics, and the Black Working Class* (New York: Free Press, 1996), 169.

epistemology, sympathetic identification, and interracial cooperation—with the goal of overturning racial prejudice and legitimizing themselves and their political inclusion in the democratic polity.

In sum, racist images of blacks circulated among whites as a form of social knowledge justifying racial hierarchy that marginalized African Americans' economic, political, and social status. As African American reformers challenged such images by presenting themselves as sympathetic figures in an unjust, racist system and claiming their progress and inherent rights, they drew from a number of strands of democratic social knowledge, including, as we see in the next section, sympathetic understanding fostered through an embodied epistemology.

Sympathetic Imagination and Embodied Epistemology: Social Knowledge in the Antilynching Essays of Ida Wells

If race was the problem of the twentieth century, as W. E. B DuBois proclaimed in *The Souls of Black Folk,* then the lynching of blacks embodied the worst of that problem. It egregiously flouted the rule of law, upon which American revolutionaries had hung their hopes for democracy, and in so doing cast African Americans outside of the body politic, even "beyond the pale of human sympathy."[40] While lynching was ostensibly a southern problem, Ida Wells reminded white Americans, northerners and southerners alike, that it was a national problem that implicated all citizens in murder. Her antilynching campaign exemplifies several strands of democratic social knowledge—narrative strategies of sympathetic and embodied epistemology most prominently, though they also drew from an activist social science, proximate epistemology, and personal experience—as a means to claim authority and collapse the boundaries between black and white, North and South. This section begins by exploring those strategies, paying particular attention to Wells's complex role as a mediator as she used an embodied and sympathetic framework of democratic social knowledge to challenge racist social narratives about lynching. We find that these frameworks were wrought with tensions and contradictions, complicating our understanding of these strategies as a basis for democratic social knowledge. It finishes by exploring the political implications of her strategies, which balanced tenuously between claiming the human rights of a universal subject while simultaneously emphasizing that any critique of the U.S. political system must pay careful attention to the particular collective experiences and needs of African Americans. To overcome the tendency to position African Americans as "beyond the pale

40. Ida B. Wells, *A Red Record,* reprinted in *Selected Works of Ida B. Wells-Barnett,* 144.

of human sympathy," Wells's antilynching narratives were a means to foster an imaginative connection, a sympathetic understanding between black and white Americans, and a call for social and political activism.[41]

The details of Ida Wells's biography and her entry into a public life of anti-lynching work and race reform are well known; these place her among a number of female activists who used sociology outside of the academy to critique American society.[42] After her marriage to Ferdinand Barnett in 1895, Wells moved to Chicago and became a prominent member of the city's reform community, organizing the first African American woman's club, advocating for equal suffrage for women and blacks, and opening a settlement and employment bureau for African American men. Born a slave in Mississippi, Wells worked as a journalist in Memphis when the lynching of three friends changed her life forever, exiling her to the North and launching her on a nationwide antilynching campaign. Before this incident, Wells admitted she had been inclined to believe southern apologists who argued that lynching was an act of moral and manly outrage for the crime of female rape. Such an excuse drew its justification from domestic ideology and southern codes of chivalry, which described white women as virtuous and men as the physical and economic protectors of that virtue. After carefully examining lynchings throughout the South and the charges in each case, Wells concluded otherwise. Between 1882 and 1891 more than seven hundred African Americans had been lynched. Yet only one-third of these victims were charged with rape.[43] She pointed out the hypocrisy of the claim that lynching punished rape; building on her personal experience in Memphis, she showed that lynching was a weapon of racial terror to maintain white economic and political supremacy.[44]

41. Ibid.

42. Biographies of Wells include Patricia Ann Schechter, *Ida B. Wells-Barnett and American Reform, 1880–1930* (Chapel Hill: University of North Carolina Press, 2001); Linda O. McMurry, *To Keep the Waters Troubled: The Life of Ida B. Wells* (New York: Oxford University Press, 1998); Mildred I. Thompson, *Ida B. Wells-Barnett: An Exploratory Study of an American Black Woman, 1893–1930*. Autobiographical information is available in Miriam DeCosta-Willis, *The Memphis Diary of Ida B. Wells* (Boston: Beacon, 1995), and Alfreda M. Duster, ed., *Crusade for Justice: The Autobiography of Ida B. Wells* (Chicago: University of Chicago Press, 1970).

43. Wells, "Reason Why," 75–76.

44. Wells was the first to offer this insight into lynching. Other early studies of lynching include James Elbert Cutler, *Lynch-Law: An Investigation into the History of Lynching in the United States* (New York: Longmans, Green, 1905), and National Association for the Advancement of Colored People, *Thirty Years of Lynching in the United States, 1889–1918* (New York: National Association for the Advancement of Colored People, 1919). More recent works include Trudier Harris, *Exorcising Blackness: Historical and Literary Lynching and Burning Rituals* (Bloomington: Indiana University Press, 1984); W. Fitzhugh Brundage, *Lynching in the New South: Georgia and Virginia, 1880–1930* (Urbana: University of Illinois Press, 1993); Stewart E. Tolnay and E. M. Beck, *A Festival of Violence: An Analysis of Southern Lynchings, 1882–1930* (Urbana: University of Illinois Press, 1995); Sandra Gunning, *Race, Rape, and Lynching: The Red Record of American Literature, 1890–1912* (New York: Oxford University Press, 1996); Christopher Waldrep, *The Many Faces of Judge Lynch: Extralegal*

In her antilynching work, Wells claimed the authority of social science, using empirical methods to challenge white southerners' rationalizations about lynching. Though Wells was not a trained sociologist or practicing academic, hers was the first investigation of lynching based on statistical data, and she placed her work in the context of sociological debates.[45] "I take the statistics of lynching," she stated in an explanation of her method, giving the numbers of persons lynched, place, and categorization of alleged crimes.[46] She began A Red Record, her most thorough analysis of lynching, by noting the importance of antilynching sentiment to "the student of American sociology."[47] Carefully drawing on reports from the Chicago Tribune, Wells emphasized that her lists and tables of lynching statistics were "the result of compilations made by white men, or reports sent over the civilized world by white men in the South." In the spirit of muckraking journalism, Wells offered her statistics as "a contribution to truth, an array of facts," which had the moral power to "stimulate this great American Republic to demand that justice be done though the heavens fall."[48] Wells hoped that such statistics would mobilize public action, much as the women at Hull House had believed that sweatshop statistics might. Drawing on terms usually used to depict industrial strife and labor unions, Wells described lynching as "a system of anarchy and outlawry." It undermined American politics and law, much as conservative commentators had argued the Pullman Strike had. Indeed, Wells's use of terms like "anarchy" and "outlawry," as well as her statistics and appeal to facts, paralleled the strategies of elites who used social science to reinforce their position on the cultural battlefield. In this case, Wells met white America on that same cultural terrain and used its tactics to chart out an entirely new argument.

Using social science helped Wells maintain her respectability, though she had to be careful about how she positioned herself as she took on the role of a translator between what she hoped was a sympathetic northern white audience, southern white racism, and southern blacks' experiences. The strategy of drawing from white newspapers protected her "from the charge of exaggeration."[49] It

Violence and Punishment in America (New York: Palgrave Macmillan, 2002); Jacquelyn Dowd Hall, Revolt against Chivalry: Jessie Daniel Ames and the Women's Campaign against Lynching (New York: Columbia University Press, 1993); Hazel V. Carby, "On the Threshold of Woman's Era": Lynching, Empire, and Sexuality in Black Feminist Theory," Critical Inquiry 12, no. 1 (1985): 262–77.

45. Mary Jo Deegan has argued that Wells practiced a form of sociology despite her lack of academic credentials. Deegan, Women in Sociology; see also Deegan's discussion of female and African American traditions of sociology in New Woman of Color, xxxvii–xl.

46. Duster, Crusade for Justice, 136.

47. Wells, Red Record, 140.

48. Ida B.Wells, Southern Horrors and Other Writings: The Anti-Lynching Campaign of Ida B. Wells, 1892–1900, edited, with an introduction, by Jacqueline Jones Royster (Boston: Bedford Books, 1997), 14.

49. Ibid., 150.

also allowed her to respectably distance herself from the monstrous act of lynching. Still she employed a framework of democratic social knowledge that privileged experience, proximity, and sympathetic identification built on narrative. Claiming firsthand knowledge as an African American, a resident of the South, and a friend of Memphis lynching victims, Wells used proximity and personal experience to position herself as an authoritative speaker. Frederick Douglass lent his authority to her testimony. Deferring to Wells on the subject of lynching, he remarked in a letter published with her first pamphlet, "I have spoken, but my word is feeble in comparison." Alluding to her friends' lynching and threats to her own life, he legitimized Wells's message further: "You give us what you know and testify from actual knowledge."[50] This tactic privileged personal experience and proximity as a source of knowledge, much like that which Addams claimed for immigrants and women and for herself as translator. Indeed, claiming her proximity to lynching victims, Wells positioned herself both for northern and southern audiences as a translator of the lynching problem. Her black skin also visibly connected her with the lynching victims, lending her authority as she spoke and wrote for black and white audiences even as she maintained her respectability by distancing herself from the violence as she drew her text from white newspapers. Carefully negotiating proximity and distance, Wells removed the veil separating North and South and encouraged intervention from the North.[51]

Nevertheless, an activist social science was not enough. Statistics were often limited in their efficacy, as "the detached style and rigid form of scientific discourse not only establish distance between observer and subject, but also estrange the subject from those with whom the observer declares allegiance of perception."[52] In other words, statistics can depersonalize the human dimensions of social problems by making it difficult to identify with victims. Even those sympathetic to Wells's message then might have been unmoved. They might simply have remained detached and thus unable to muster moral outrage sufficient to warrant action. Indeed, the very act of lynching marked the victim's body as radically Other, and images of lynching might also have served to render the black body incomprehensible and unidentifiable to the white

50. Quoted in Wells, *On Lynchings*, 15. For further discussion of the tradition of African American personal experience as a corrective to racist social knowledge, see V. P. Franklin, *Living Our Stories, Telling Our Truths: Autobiography and the Making of the African American Intellectual Tradition* (New York: Scribner, 1995).

51. While still in the South, Wells was convinced that the silence of northerners "was because they did not know the facts, and had accepted the southern white man's reason for lynching and burning human beings." Duster, *Crusade for Justice*, 77.

52. Ericka M. Miller, *The Other Reconstruction: Where Violence and Womanhood Meet in the Writings of Wells-Barnett, Grimke, and Larsen* (New York: Garland, 2000), 34.

viewer, obliterating any claims of interracial social bonds.[53] Photographs of the dreadfully embodied black male lynching victim, "enabled members of the mob to seize whiteness," distancing themselves from African Americans.[54] Though Wells repeatedly argued that the dissemination of lynching statistics would revolutionize public sentiment in opposition to the crime, the weight of prejudice and white manipulation of racial discourse continued to place the black person "beyond the pale of human sympathy." Indeed, as her concern here suggests, it was whites' very sense of alienation from African Americans that allowed for the violence in the first place.

So Wells had to go beyond claims of firsthand knowledge and the use of social science facts. Using tactics designed to evoke sympathy and jar the imagination, Wells encouraged whites to see African Americans as sentient people much like themselves. Most northerners only imagined lynching, with help from depictions and narrations in white newspapers and literature.[55] Wells responded in kind, using her narrative accounts to manipulate sensibilities and make the reader aware of the common physical characteristics and values that whites and blacks shared. She sought to accomplish this through two tactics, one calling upon a framework of embodied knowledge and the other pointing out the similar cultural universe and social traits blacks and whites shared in order to evoke sympathy and political solidarity rather than horror and racial difference. Wells's tactics were complex and potentially very risky: She reread the dominant white images for counterhegemonic meanings, reinvesting the black body with personhood.[56]

Evoking an embodied epistemological framework, she highlighted the torture and physical pain of the lynching victims and made black victims recognizable as people similar to whites by emphasizing the importance of family to the lynching victims and describing African Americans' economic rationality and

53. For a discussion of the problems of a racialized gaze and the role of lynching spectacles and photographs in forging racial identities, see Smith, *Photography on the Color Line*, 113–45. Ironically, racial difference frequently has to be manufactured and policed—as Nazi Germany marked Jews by forcing them to wear gold stars, for example. Lynching served a similar cultural function, as thousands of lynchings during the Progressive Era and beyond created a visual archive of monstrous and mutilated black bodies and whites standing nearby, as though offering testament of radical racial differences.

54. Smith, *Photography on the Color Line*, 141.

55. Bederman, *Manliness and Civilization*, 47.

56. Shawn Smith argues that DuBois's display of African Americans at the Paris Exposition was also meant to reinvest the black body with a middle-class respectability. Wells's method was a bit different, however. She drew from lynching images and texts themselves, rereading them for alternative meanings. Such an interpretative move was important since it kept the victims at the center and refused whites the opportunity to justify their actions against "savages"; it also disallowed blacks the ability to dismiss the victims as "brutes" who were not representative of the race as a whole. Wells instead focused on them as human beings with rights, emotions, and reason.

habits of hard work. Wells's stories humanized the victims, using their names, telling of their circumstances and their families, describing their states of mind before death—their fear, disbelief, and hope. While white reports dwelled on the bestial nature of blacks, she emphasized the victims' pain and suffering by drawing on an embodied epistemology. For example, she relates the horribly violent death of Henry Smith, accused of murdering a young girl in Paris, Texas. He was fastened to a platform, and for fifty minutes, the child's father, brother, and uncles "thrust hot irons into his quivering flesh. It was horrible," the newspaper reported, "the man dying by slow torture in the midst of smoke from his own burning flesh. . . . After burning the feet and legs, the hot irons—plenty of fresh ones being at hand—were rolled up and down Smith's stomach, back, and arms. Then the eyes were burned out and irons were thrust down his throat."[57] In drawing readers into the lurid details of lynching, Wells's narratives evoke an embodied knowledge rooted in common physical experiences. Though few people suffered what Henry Smith did, most experienced fear and pain. At a visceral level, they imagine his suffering and recognize him as a fellow human being, one who responds to torture as they would. As the philosopher Maurice Hamington has suggested, embodied knowledge puts the readers into relationship with the imagined Other (here the black lynching victim) and invites them to take a moral position—and political action—against such practices.[58] Here, embodied knowledge has the potential to forge a democratic solidarity mobilized against torture and physical suffering.

Wells repeated this strategy throughout her essays, placing side by side numerous brutal accounts of lynching to preserve her reputation as a respectable woman in a culture that prevented women from openly discussing violence and sex and largely disregarded the testimony of African Americans.[59] She masterfully wove together vivid lynching descriptions with her own commentary, punctuating both with photos and drawings of the mangled bodies of victims, to cause shock, horror, and disgust in her readers. Presenting dramatic accounts of mob activity, her essays invited the readers into the lynching scene, making them witnesses—if not both a participant and a victim. Her work, then, stepped beyond the mere presentation of facts, and it did more than rhetorically manipulate the boundaries of white discourses of civilization, gender, and race. It appealed to human sympathy as a basis for democratic social knowledge and moral truth, inviting a response of moral action based on embodied knowledge.[60]

57. Ibid., 167–68.
58. Maurice Hamington, *Embodied Care: Jane Addams, Maurice Merleau-Ponty, and Feminist Ethics* (Urbana: University of Illinois Press, 2004), especially 61–88.
59. Bederman, *Manliness and Civilization*, 63–64.
60. Bederman has suggested that Wells "wasn't trying to depict lynching's horrible cruelty, because she didn't believe white Americans would *care* that lynching was cruel, no matter how eloquent her denunciations" (ibid., 63). But one wonders why, then, if Wells did not believe whites

The tactic of describing in detail the physical suffering of lynching victims was reminiscent of the abolitionists' strategies. Slave narratives and books relating graphic accounts of the brutality of slavery, particularly on the family, had been popular reading among antebellum white northerners and served to mobilize readers against slavery.[61] These descriptions established African Americans as "fully sentient and ardent in their desires for freedom, love, family; this contrast made their brutalization the more horrific."[62] Such narratives were significant as "fellow feeling for those in pain gave new scope to arguments for the rights of the person that were innovative in both substance and style."[63] The evolution of rights consciousness in the nineteenth century thus extended an ethos of nonviolent punishment, even of criminals. By drawing attention to the way that lynching brutalized the victim, Wells drew parallels to the experience of blacks under slavery. Both abolitionists and postbellum reformers fighting against lynching emphasized that civic inclusion was an embodied experience and, in a society haunted by slavery, required special protection from the state.

Wells used other discourses to evoke sympathetic identification between whites and blacks. Her descriptions of the gender attributes of black men and women, for example, called to mind the domestic ideology that was familiar to white, middle-class Americans. Illustrating the difficulties black women faced in protecting their sexual purity and virtuous character, she implicitly claimed these traits for them. She noted also that many of the male victims of lynchings were husbands and fathers, who, like their white counterparts, espoused their role as family providers and were trying to achieve economic security. Her friend Thomas Moss, a Memphis lynching victim, was an excellent example, having succeeded in business and provided a good home for his family. She tells of the family of Hamp Biscoe, a "hard-working, thrifty farmer" according to black and white neighbors, who was driven to insanity by the harassment of a white neighbor. Biscoe, his wife, who was nursing a baby and pregnant with another child, and his thirteen year-old son, were all shot during a dispute over a debt. The murder of this entire family seemed proof that whites disregarded

---

would be moved, she spent so much time on the scenes themselves. According to Bederman's reasoning, Wells's presentation of the facts would have been enough. I suggest that Wells did indeed hope to mobilize sentiment through the style, tone, and language of her essays. See also Miller, *Other Reconstruction*, especially chapters 1 and 2.

61. Shirley Samuels, "Introduction"; Karen Sanchez-Eppler, "Bodily Bonds: The Interacting Rhetorics of Feminism and Abolition"; Harryette Mullen, "Runaway Tongue: Resistant Orality in *Uncle Tom's Cabin, Our Nig, Incidents in the Life of a Slave Girl*, and *Beloved*," all in Shirley Samuels, ed., *The Culture of Sentiment: Race, Gender, and Sentimentality in Nineteenth-century America* (New York: Oxford University Press, 1992); Elizabeth Clark, " 'The Sacred Rights of the Weak': Pain, Sympathy, and the Culture of Individual Rights in Antebellum America," *Journal of American History* 82, no. 2 (March 1995): 463–93.

62. Clark, "Sacred Rights of the Weak," 470.

63. Ibid., 487.

the sanctity of the black family. Moreover, she tells of men like Roselius Julian, who were hunted for trying to defend their wives from attacks by whites. When a white judge cruelly insulted his wife, Julian killed the man in retaliation. Wells compared his extreme action to that of white males who exercised the same code of chivalry against black men. Wells emphasized that his violence was not evidence of depravity but "an act of a Negro [who dared] to defend his home."[64] African Americans' acceptance of middle-class gender norms and the primacy of the home and economic security undermined stereotypes of black women as promiscuous and black families as disorderly and dysfunctional, and it made the same claim to the right to protect the home that white men exercised. In Wells's formulation of lynching, patriarchal white power, not African American behavior, disrupted black families.

In light of the potential of lynching and its popular images to forge white identity and community, thus securing white supremacy, Wells's antilynching texts were an important form of alternative cultural representation of race. The details about the individual victim and his family made him concrete rather than an anonymous black body who embodied the guilt and shame of the entire race and was rendered as monstrous.[65] By naming the victims, giving them identities, and placing them into families and social networks, Wells demystified the monstrous body, sexualizing them not as rapists but as proper family men.[66] Her narratives, like those of Jane Addams, invite the readers to recognize their similarities with the victim and to understand the injustice and horror of lynching.

From Christian, sociological, and political standpoints, the brutalization that lynching wrought was extraordinarily dangerous for witnesses and, by extension, the nation. The Social Gospel was built upon sympathy. To follow the Golden Rule of loving one's neighbor as oneself, one must be able to exchange selves with the other and to collapse the psychological barriers of difference and see the other as fundamentally like oneself. Furthermore, at the time that Wells wrote, Adam Smith's *Theory of Moral Sentiments*, which emphasized sympathy as the bond that held the individual and society together, was enjoying a revival among sociologists, and "sympathy described by Smith as the capacity to identify imaginatively with the sufferings of another person, became the principle

---

64. Wells, *On Lynchings*, 171–72.

65. See Judith Halberstam, *Skin Shows: Gothic Horror and the Technology of Monsters* (Durham, NC: Duke University Press, 1995), 77–85, for a discussion of the rendering of race as monstrous Other in the Gothic imagination of the late nineteenth century.

66. Catherine Holland has argued that, in the wake of the Fourteenth Amendment, which introduced "male" into the Constitution for the first time and thus implicitly gendered both citizenship and the political imagination of the body politic by equating black men and white men, lynching served to emasculate black men, thus casting them outside the boundaries of citizenship. See Holland, *The Body Politic: Foundings, Citizenship, and Difference in the American Political Imagination* (New York: Routledge, 2001), 155–56.

by which a generation of sociologists sought to explain the relations between the individual and others."[67] By pointing out that "scenes of unusual brutality failed to have any visible effect upon the humane sentiments of the people of our land," she implicitly challenged American sociologists to include race in their research agendas and consider the damaging effects lynching had on individual psyches and the practice of democracy.[68] Jane Addams agreed. Sharing with Wells the idea of lynching as a ritual drama, she argued it "runs a certain risk of brutalizing each spectator, of shaking his belief in law and order, of sowing seed for future violence."[69] Here, then, was a dark side of proximity: witnessing monstrous acts like murder or even less jarring images of violence—poverty, abuse, humiliation—threatened to normalize them and enforce human differences rather than commonalities.[70]

Because lynching brutalized people it also threatened the American political experiment to use reason, law, and universal suffrage for orderly and peaceful social life. Repeatedly Wells's stories depicted lynch mobs that reveled in the spectacle of violence. In Paris, Texas, for example, "local papers issued bulletins detailing the preparations, the schoolchildren had been given a holiday to see a man burned alive, and the railroads ran excursions and brought people of the surrounding country to witness the event."[71] The fact that thousands of people watched the lynching proved that the violence undermined human sensibilities and fellow feeling. In Memphis, a mob watching the mutilation and hanging of Lee Walker did not find "the ghastly sight . . . trying to the nerves." Rather "the crowd looked on with complaisance if not real pleasure." A report of the Paris, Texas, lynching underscored this point. The witness recalled that "No one was himself" when the torture began. "Every man, woman and child in that awful

---

67. Ruth Leys, "Mead's Voices: Imitation as Foundation; or the Struggle against Mimesis," in *Modernist Impulses in the Human Sciences, 1870–1930,* ed. Dorothy Ross, 210–35 (Baltimore: Johns Hopkins University Press, 1994).

68. Wells, *Red Record,* 140. The subject of lynching did appear in the sociology textbook of Albion Small. He offered it as an example of the force of social psychology to overcome individual morality. Though this analysis is a hopeful effort along the lines Wells suggested, he later offered the standard white excuse that it is "aroused by a crime of unusual atrocity" (342). Albion Small, *An Introduction to the Study of Society* (New York: American Book, 1895), 308. For a more recent sociological analysis that discusses the dehumanization of African Americans as a factor in lynchings, see Tolnay and Beck, *Festival of Violence,* 23.

69. Addams, "Respect for Law," 26. In contrast to Addams and other Progressive Era reformers who maintained the benevolence of human nature, Harris argues in *Exorcising Blackness* that lynching was in fact an outgrowth of human nature, thus challenging the notion that human nature was sympathetic. See p. 14 in particular. Those writing at the time, however, rarely wrote of it in such a fashion. The practice was abhorrent precisely because it degraded human nature by teaching violence.

70. Lois Ann Lorentzen and Jennifer Turpin, eds., *Women and War Reader* (New York: New York University Press, 1998).

71. Duster, *Crusade for Justice,* 84.

crowd was worked up to a greater frenzy than that which actuated Smith's horrible crime. The people were capable of any new atrocity now, and as Smith's yells became more and more frequent, it was difficult to hold the crowd back, so anxious were the savages to participate in the sickening tortures."[72]

In the context of prevailing domestic discourse, the presence of women and children seemed especially appalling. While traveling through Texas a year later, Laura Dainty-Pelham, an associate of Hull House, met an innkeeper who "kept talking about [the lynching] as if it were something to be proud of." Her eight-year-old daughter interrupted the mother and proudly announced, "I saw them burn the nigger, didn't I Mamma?" The mother complacently affirmed, "Yes, darling, you saw them burn the nigger."[73] A minister who witnessed the lynching recalled that the children "became as frantic as the grown people and struggled forward to obtain places of advantage." When he shouted, "For God's sake . . . send the children home," the crowd responded, "No, no . . . let them learn a lesson," the lesson of white supremacy and brutality.[74]

By calling attention in her essays to the inhumane and uncontrollable mobs, Wells illustrated the delicate balance between self-government and tyranny of the passions, suggesting a parallel to mobs of violent strikers that filled the imaginations of middle-class white northerners.[75] Lynching threatened to undo the assumption of the Revolutionary Era and the Constitution that reason and law could ensure peaceful social and political relations. It was dangerous precisely because it was a public ritual in which the passions subverted law and reason, both on a personal and national level. It also revealed an antidemocratic tendency. Addams suggested that "the method of deterring crime by horrible punishment has been tried many times and that it particularly distinguishes the dealing with those crimes which a so-called lower class has committed against its superior." Such methods are elitist, as they are "founded upon a contempt for the inferior class—a belief that they cannot be appealed to by reason and fair dealing, but must be treated upon the animal plane, bullied and terrorized."

72. Wells, *Southern Horrors*, 170.

73. Duster, *Crusade for Justice*, 85.

74. Wells, *Red Record*, 170. Brundage, *Lynching in the New South*, 1–2. Booker T. Washington offered a similar critique of the dangerous lessons lynching offered to young people. Washington, "A Protest against Lynching," *Birmingham Age-Herald*, February 29, 1904, and letter to the editor, *Montgomery Advertiser*, December 30, 1910, both reprinted in *African American Political Thought, 1890–1930: Washington, DuBois, Garvey, and Randolph*, ed. Cary D. Wintz (Armonk, NY: M. E. Sharp, 1996).

Witnessing such brutal acts did indeed affect children. Following several lynchings in Salisbury, North Carolina, a white boy put a noose around his six-year-old playmate's neck and left him dangling from a beam. The boys reported that they had been playing a game they called "Salisbury." Gilmore, *Gender and Jim Crow*, 144–46.

75. For a discussion of lynching mobs as orderly and ritualistic as opposed to uncontrolled, see Brundage, *Lynching in the New South*, 40.

She links lynchings with southerners' attempts to hold on to an "essentially aristocratic attitude." Such an outlook "is particularly discernible when the lower class evinces a tendency toward democratic development, toward asserting their human claim as such, when they assert their rights rather than ask for privileges."[76]

Wells's lynching critique shared an epistemological framework with those of the Chicago reformers she later met. Wells drew from personal experience as a source of authority, and she blended them with empirical methods of social science to reach her conclusions. She also used narrative strategies to build sympathetic identification.[77] Like workers who claimed their personal experience in the workplace as a location for special knowledge about the production process and conditions of unemployment, Wells likewise offered the experiences of blacks under southern patriarchy to expose another side of lynching, one that challenged her audience to reconstruct knowledge about race that described "all black people as lewd, lecherous, and unsuitable to socialization *because of* their blackness."[78] Her use of these methods brilliantly exposed the potential of a democratic social knowledge that drew simultaneously from social science, affective narratives, and personal experience. Like Addams, Chicago's workers and many who supported the arbitration of labor disputes, she illustrated the dangers that misunderstanding and ignorance of other people's lives posed to democratic social reform and political life. In order for liberal rights to overcome racial divisions and inequitable administration of law, Wells suggested that whites needed to recognize African Americans as worthy of human sympathy.[79]

In her antilynching work Wells spoke both to blacks and whites in order to redefine the boundaries of the democratic polity. By abandoning the South and ladylike quiet, she remapped the limits that white social science and Victorian conventions imposed on African Americans and white women. Whereas economic and social pressures on southern blacks encouraged them to stay put and remain subordinate, Wells boldly encouraged them to seize America's economic and political promises by migrating out of the South. And like other race reformers, she extended the definition of U.S. citizenship to include African Americans. Demonstrating her strong faith in Enlightenment conceptions of natural rights doctrine and Revolutionary War–era promises to protect those rights, Wells's strategy of evoking sympathy had a political purpose that challenged white Americans to witness their common physical humanity with blacks and thus see them as fellow citizens with legal rights.

---

76. Jane Addams and Ida B. Wells, in Bettina Aptheker, ed., *Lynching and Rape: An Exchange of Views* (New York: American Institute for Marxist Studies, 1977).

77. Miller, *Other Reconstruction*, 1–55.

78. Ibid., 32.

79. On a similar point, see Tolnay and Beck, *Festival of Violence*, 23, 28.

While claiming the human rights of the universal subject, Wells simultane-ously challenged a liberal republicanism that dismissed gender or race as irrel-evant political categories.[80] Her gendered analysis of lynching revealed numerous cases where black women were raped with little or no impunity to the white perpetrators, and she pointed out that several alleged instances of rape were actually consensual sexual relations. Indeed, she offered several examples of white women who had initiated relationships with black men, challenging both domestic discourse that posited white women as passionless and racial stereo-types that black men were lustful savages.[81] She indicated that white women were also victims of these codes. For example, a Memphis woman indicted for miscegenation chose to renounce her racial identity altogether. "She swore in court that she was *not* a white woman."[82]

Furthermore, in a particularly disturbing example of white men's control over women, the lover of a black Kansas man was forced to accuse him of rape and ignite the fire that burned him alive. Though they were known to have been involved for more than a year, threats and fears of violence to herself compelled her to cause his death.[83] She observed that "it is their [white women's] misfor-tune that the chivalrous white men of that section . . . should shield themselves by their cowardly and infamously false excuse."[84] White women's bodies were thus the means white men used to protect their political and economic power over blacks.

Addams also pointed out the tendency of men to use protection as the trope of and excuse for control over women's bodies. Both suggested that such argu-ments served to maintain patriarchal practices that undermined all women's independence.[85] Her analysis was the basis for a potential alliance between whites and African Americans regardless of class as it exposed the patriarchal

80. Wells's effort to navigate between this tension of universality and particularity anticipates the ideas of late twentieth-century theorists like Chantel Mouffe, who argue that a radical and plural democracy can be built on an ethicopolitical consensus of values while maintaining the variety of political identities born of varying collective experiences. These identities can serve as the basis for radical democratic solidarity as they can identify oppression from multiple vantage points and espe-cially when they converge to promote liberty and equality for all. See Mouffe, "Feminism, Citizen-ship, and Radical Democratic Politics," in *Feminists Theorize the Political*, ed. Judith Butler and Joan W. Scott, eds., 369–84 (New York: Routledge, 1992).

81. Ida B. Wells, *On Lynchings: Southern Horrors* [1892], *A Red Record* [1895], *Mob Rule in New Orleans* [1900] (New York: Arno Press and the *New York Times*, 1969), 145. Mary Frances Berry, "Judging Morality: Sexual Behavior and Legal Consequences in the Late Nineteenth-century South," *Journal of American History* 78, no. 3 (1991): 835–56.

82. Peggy Pascoe suggests that, given the history of court decisions in miscegenation cases, this tactic was generally the best defense against the charge. See "Miscegenation Law, Court Cases, and Ide-ologies of 'Race' in Twentieth-century America," *Journal of American History* 83, no. 1 (1996): 44–69.

83. Ibid., 24.

84. Ibid., 147.

85. Jane Addams and Ida B. Wells, *Lynching and Rape*.

and racial boundaries of sexuality; it potentially drew all women together on the basis of their mutual sexual repression.[86] Wells's analysis of lynching emphasized the particularity of experience to critique racism's interwoven strands of political community, economics, and sexuality; it used the lens of particular racial experience to claim universal rights.

Wells thus maintained that race must be taken as a serous political category. By shocking her readers into imagining and identifying with the bodily pain of the African American victims, she challenged them to create a new outlook on race, morality, and citizenship. The mangled bodies of the lynching victims became a location of knowledge about the need for political recognition of the particular collective experiences of racial and gender minorities, just as had the "dwarfed and ill-fed" victims of industrial capitalism.[87] While white reports dwelled on the bestial nature of blacks, she emphasized the pain and suffering of the lynching victims, just as *Hull-House Maps & Papers* had emphasized the physical effects of industrialism. Her democratic social knowledge highlighted the fact that a political culture that ignored differences of embodied experience and its particular racial dimensions had consequently failed to protect African Americans and white women.[88] Democratic social knowledge that included African American experience ultimately contributed to an attack on the dominant liberal discourse that had rejected race as a distinct category of analysis.

86. Carby, *Reconstructing Womanhood*, 41–47. As Sandra Gunning and Ericka Miller have argued in slightly different guises, by reinserting both African American women and white women into the national lynching narrative, as both victims and active agents in their sexual identities, Wells reconfigured liberal narratives about women and political agency. Miller in particular suggests that the lynching narrative depends upon the silence of white women and that black and white women maintained different visions of empowerment. Still, Wells envisioned an interracial effort along gendered lines to overcome lynching.

87. In this respect, Wells's writings shared important aspects of the literary sentimentalism she grew up reading and the increasingly popular genre of realism. Though her essays do not portray the tender heroines and teary-eyed deathbed scenes associated with nineteenth-century sentimental fiction, they are designed to play upon the emotions in a similar fashion in order to help readers identify with black victims. Such works inspired sentimental fiction to expose the brutal conditions of slavery; the unprecedented success of *Uncle Tom's Cabin* suggests the significant impact this genre had on the moral imagination of the nation. See also Gregg D. Crane, *Race, Citizenship, and Law in American Literature* (New York: Cambridge University Press, 2002).

88. Wells thus worked within a tradition of "black republicanism." As Carol Horton has articulated, black republicanism "represented a reworking of the key themes of eighteenth-century republican discourse in light of the historical experience of African Americans. In particular, this position emphasized both the embeddedness of the individual in the community and the connection between civil rights and economic independence." In light of racism, black republicanism maintained that in the case of newly freed people, civic inclusion required measures that addressed the nature of blacks' particular experience. Thus liberal assumptions about the justice of the free market and the irrelevance of racial categories was turned upside down. Horton, "Liberal Equality and the Civic Subject: Identity and Citizenship in Reconstruction America," in *The Liberal Tradition in American Politics: Reassessing the Legacy of American Liberalism*, ed. David F. Ericson and Louisa Bertch Green, 115–36, especially 132–36 (New York: Routledge, 1999).

Instead, some African Americans' conception of liberal citizenship and their activism was built "in large part upon a long history of the exploitation of their labor. . . . In recognizing the social and historical importance of group difference, black republicanism made a positive claim on American society, holding that, in the case of the freed people, civic inclusion necessitated particular measures [such as an activist, protective state] that addressed the specific nature of the group experience."[89] Like other race reformers in the post–Civil War era, Wells's antilynching work and civic reforms encouraged racially conscious activism and sought state protection.

Proximate Social Science and Cultural Agency: Exhibitions and Cinema

Publicists like Wells were convinced that African American access to media of all types—print and visual—was necessary to combat racism and to contribute to a more inclusive democratic social knowledge.[90] Since the mid-nineteenth century, the power of the visual media to produce knowledge expanded as museums opened; as photography became more advanced, it lent itself to growing archives and popular images; exhibitions and world's fairs like that in Chicago in 1893 attracted millions of visitors; and the burgeoning film industry captured the attention of city residents across the United States. Indeed, this growing visual culture was critical in shaping social knowledge since images "lend shape to histories and personal stories, often providing the material evidence on which claims of truth are based."[91] Cameras were "considered at one with other modern scientific instruments—namely, the microscope, thermometer, and telegraph, with their strong claims on 'truth,' 'reality,' and empirical verifiability," and so early movies "were even more formidable in popularizing and reifying America's politics of white racial supremacy."[92]

89. Ibid., 132–36.

90. As historian Mia Bay has argued, educated African Americans, confronted with ever more demeaning theories about their origins and capabilities, "fought for access to print culture and sought to vindicate their race by creating alternative readings of race that celebrated the humanity and historical achievements of black people." Bay, *White Image in the Black Mind*, 154. Elizabeth McHenry, *Forgotten Readers: Recovering the Lost History of African American Literary Societies* (Durham, NC: Duke University Press, 2002), especially chapter 2, "Spreading the Word: The Cultural Work of the Black Press."

91. Marita Sturken, *Tangled Memories: The Vietnam War, the AIDS Epidemic, and the Politics of Remembering* (Berkeley: University of California Press, 1997), 20.

92. Anna Everett, *Returning the Gaze: A Genealogy of Black Film Criticism, 1909–1949* (Durham, NC: Duke University Press, 2001), 13. See also Smith, *Photography on the Color Line*. The importance of these forms affirms the importance of the visual, for as Joan Scott argues, "Knowledge is gained through vision; vision is a direct, unmediated apprehension of the world or transparent objects. . . . Seeing is the origin of knowing" ("Experience," 24, in Butler and Scott, eds., *Feminists Theorize the*

Thus new media like film served to posit a racist social knowledge. In this milieu, African Americans struggled to exercise cultural agency in visual representations of themselves, both in the arenas of knowledge and education, such as exhibitions, and in spaces of mass culture, such as film.[93] African Americans' efforts at display, whether through personal decorum in public spaces or formal exhibitions, used the black body as a text to assert an alternative narrative of racial progress and respectability. Such efforts were more urgent with the advent of films like *Birth of a Nation*, which had the power to reach untold thousands of audiences with its visually stunning and manipulative racist message.[94]

This section focuses on two examples of the visual dimensions of democratic social knowledge in asserting cultural agency: the Illinois National Half-century Exhibition, celebrating the fiftieth anniversary of emancipation with a public exhibition and the outcry against the Chicago showing of *Birth of a Nation*. In both cases we see how African American activists asserted agency in cultural representations of themselves to promote an alternative narrative to that of racial inferiority. They stressed instead African American progress, evidenced in respectable behavior and advancements in the arts, business, and professions. These examples suggest that struggles over cultural representation were indeed struggles over democratic social knowledge, as visual images served to enforce or challenge popularly accepted conceptions about race. In particular, they indicated a struggle for control over representations of the black body; African Americans, who frequently lacked access to other forms of cultural capital, have instead used the body as a "canvas of representation."[95] But it was more than this. Race is grounded *in* the body; it is the terrain of struggle. Blacks needed to display a respectable, disciplined body to undermine racist taxonomies that depicted them as animalistic, primitive, and sexualized.

In addition to Wells's antilynching works and the interracial socialization of the Frederick Douglass Center discussed in the following section, the examples

---

Political, 24, 22–40).

93. Photography developed in tandem with the rise of positivism, which involved the belief that "empirical truths can be established through visual evidence." Maria Sturken and Lisa Cartwright, *Practices of Looking: An Introduction to Visual Culture* (New York: Oxford University Press, 2001), 16. Photography served to racially inscribe visual taxonomy, as Shawn Smith has demonstrated. Each of these examples suggests an emphasis on imagery and objects to illustrate knowledge about race, or, as Smith puts it, "visual culture was fundamental not only to racist classification but also to racial reinscription and the reconstruction of racial knowledge in the nineteenth and early twentieth centuries."

94. *Birth of a Nation* was only one of the overtly racist films circulating in 1915. For example, Paramount made *The Nigger*, which played throughout the United States. Thomas Cripps, "The Reaction of the Negro to the Motion Picture *Birth of a Nation*," *Historian* 25, no. 3 (1962–1963): 344–62.

95. Stuart Hall, "What Is This 'Black' in Black Popular Culture?" in *Representing Blackness: Issues in Film and Video,* ed. Valerie Smith, 123–34 (New Brunswick, NJ: Rutgers University Press, 1997).

in this section illustrate how the black body acted as a location for a transgressive social knowledge about racial hierarchy. African American reformers' attention to the black body as a canvas of representation in which their behavior and public displays of themselves were performances that demonstrated their success, respectability, inventive and entrepreneurial spirit, and high-quality intellectual and cultural productions acted as both a claim to full civic inclusion and to inclusion in the process of democratic social knowledge in order to undermine the social scientific and popularly ordained white supremacy that structured American society.

African Americans' struggle for cultural agency and its connections to their political status in the city were evident in the 1893 World's Fair as African American leaders in Chicago and across the nation demanded that President Benjamin Harrison recognize their advancement and contributions as a race by awarding them representation on the planning committee. They were disappointed when Harrison appointed an all-white board of directors.[96] Ultimately, little exhibit space was allotted to African Americans, a fact that angered Ida Wells, Ferdinand Barnett, and Douglass and prompted them to publish a pamphlet, "The Reason Why the Colored Man Is Not in the World's Fair." The pamphlet described African American advances in the twenty-five years since slavery and scathingly reported continued discrimination and violence against the race. Designed to disprove the notion that "the Negro was fit only for a 'hewer of wood and a drawer of water' and that he could not be educated," it emphasized the rapid educational gains of freed slaves.[97] When the fair's leaders offered to set aside a special "Colored American Day," they were infuriated and suggested a boycott, believing their absence would clearly send a message to the world that African Americans would not endure any hint of segregation.

Douglass initially opposed the idea of a Colored American Day but later changed his mind, arguing that even with its limitations, it was too important an opportunity to be missed. African Americans turned out in great numbers on August 25 to enjoy the fair. Their decorum and Douglass's poignant, rousing speech celebrating black accomplishments served to challenge narratives about racial inferiority and savagery. Historian Christopher Reed has eloquently demonstrated the richness of African American involvement in the fair and cautioned against seeing Colored American Day as the primary concern for African

96. In the end a lone black man from Missouri was appointed to the board as an alternate delegate from that state. African American women who sought inclusion fared little better, as their requests for representation on the Board of Lady Managers were denied. Eventually Berthe Honore Palmer, the chair of that board, did assent to a paid office position for an African American woman to secure space for and collect African American exhibits and to communicate matters of interest to other members of the race. Reed, *Chicago NAACP*, 22–30.

97. J. Garland Penn, "The Progress of the Afro-American since Emancipation," in "Reason Why," 92–99; F. L. Barnett, in ibid., 118.

Americans at the fair.[98] Certainly African Americans differed over whether the race's accomplishments should be represented in separate exhibits or included with white exhibits and whether they should participate in Colored American Day. However, Reed rightly argues that such differences should not cloud our ability to see the extent to which blacks seized the opportunity to present alternative narratives—ones they constructed—about African American contributions to national progress since slavery and to the race's respectability. Their emphasis on education and the professions also made clear African Americans' contributions as cultural and economic participants in the community and, as such, required their inclusion in democratic social knowledge.

In 1913 African American leaders seized another opportunity to exercise cultural agency in creating images of racial progress. With the fiftieth anniversary of the end of the Civil War looming, African American leaders such as George Ellis, a former member of the U.S. delegation to Liberia and prominent local attorney, worked with Chicago politicians to lobby the state legislature for an appropriation to celebrate the anniversary of emancipation with a public exhibition.[99] In June the state legislature approved a bill establishing a state commission to plan for the Illinois (National) Half-century Anniversary of Negro Freedom, popularly known as the Lincoln Jubilee. With a goal to educate whites and blacks about African American progress since Emancipation, the exhibition was an exemplar of democratic social knowledge in two ways: It offered an alternative narrative about African Americans, emphasizing their progress in industry, education, the arts, and intellectual life, and it drew from representatives of both the white and black communities in Chicago to embark upon a collective process of creating an exhibit that encouraged interracial understanding and cooperation.

In the two decades between the 1893 World's Fair and 1913, when planning began for the Lincoln Jubilee, much had changed in the African American community. The population in Chicago grew by more than 25 percent, the contours of the Black Belt, as the southside ghetto was called, were solidified, and institutional culture had expanded tremendously. During these years, African Americans built their own charitable and political organizations to help provide

98. Reed's interpretation of Chicago's African American community is an important corrective to earlier works that tended to divide Chicago's black leadership between those favorable to Booker T. Washington and those who opposed him. Reed argues that this view oversimplifies the complexity with which race leaders borrowed from a variety of ideologies and strategies to promote the material, civil, and political progress of the race in the city.

99. George Ellis to Medill McCormick, n.d., Irene McCoy Gaines Papers, Box 1, Folder 1–3, Chicago Historical Society. Supporters also worked to have Ellis appointed to the commission. See letter to J. Hamilton Lewis, June 23, 1913, in ibid. Both R. R. Jackson, an African American state legislator from Chicago's south side, and Medill McCormick were instrumental in helping to secure support for the commission.

the much-needed social services that most white institutions denied blacks.[100] A professional middle class of attorneys, doctors, dentists, and journalists emerged as leaders of the community. With the establishment of the *Defender* in 1910, the city boasted two black newspapers that reached African Americans across the nation. The Republican vote in the Second Ward became important to the party's citywide success, ensuring that black voters and black Republican leaders were courted by white politicians. Despite the mounting racial tensions in industry and some southside schools, African Americans enjoyed more freedoms and sense of community identity than in most other places in the United States. It was in the midst of this vital Chicago black community, with its nationally known and connected leadership, that plans began for the Half-century Exposition.

The celebratory exhibit, like exhibitions in museums, expositions, and world's fairs, was a popular form of producing knowledge. Such displays offered new ways of knowing built around a visually oriented epistemology. American museums during this period reflected an "object-based epistemology" built on the assumption that "objects could tell stories to untrained observers." As visitors walked through the exhibits they might stop and ponder an object, look thoughtfully at the next object or image, and read the materials or, in the case of the world's fairs, the tables of statistics or photographs that accompanied it. Visitors could thus make their own meaning through a process of a "deliberate, self-reflective act of symbolic interpretation," as objects were "directly connected with ideas and with knowledge."[101]

Moreover, especially for our purposes here, public displays were popular ways of reinforcing social narratives of racial belonging and hierarchy. As in the case of lynching photographs, such visual epistemology might act to produce distance and detachment. As viewers looked at anthropological exhibits through the eyes of imperialist conquerors, seeing natives in traditional dress and surroundings, they might indeed see justification of a racist knowledge that proclaimed a hierarchy of civilizations and races.[102] But this need not be the case. Public exhibits, like that of the Lincoln Jubilee, might serve an altogether

100. See, for example, Knupfer, *Toward a Tenderer Humanity;* Reed, *Chicago NAACP;* Spear, *Black Chicago.* Knupfer, for example, found more than 150 woman's clubs in Chicago, many of them devoted to philanthropic work.

101. Steven Conn, *Museums and American Intellectual Life, 1876–1926* (Chicago: University of Chicago Press, 1998), 14. See also Flora E. S. Kaplan, ed., *Museums and the Making of "Ourselves": The Role of Objects in National Identity* (London: Leicester University Press, 1994), and Eilean Hooper-Greenhill, *Museums and the Shaping of Knowledge* (New York: Routledge, 1992).

102. Robert Rydell, *All the World's a Fair: Visions of Empire at American International Expositions, 1876–1916* (Chicago: University of Chicago Press, 1984); Maria Grever and Berteke Waaldijk, *Transforming the Public Sphere: The Dutch National Exhibition of Women's Labor in 1898* (Durham, NC: Duke University Press, 2004).

different purpose by building an alternative knowledge about African American progress that disrupted the predominant racist narrative of black people's inferiority and criminality. Against the backdrop of reunion between northern and southern whites, brought about by the erasure of blacks' contributions to the nation, to the war, and to American ideals of freedom, Chicagoans' efforts to create an alternative narrative were an important exercise of inclusive democratic social knowledge.[103]

The commission was chaired by Samuel Fallows, a white minister, founding member of the Civic Federation, and long-time participant in Chicago reform efforts, with African American minister Archibald Carey and leader Thomas Wallace Swann serving as the primary organizers. Mayor William Hale Thompson appointed a citizen's committee from Chicago composed of numerous white civic elites and prominent reformers.[104] Expectations for the exhibition ran high as the commission invited participants from every state and from foreign countries, as well.

The Progressive Era was a period of world's fairs and expositions; public display and celebration served educational and epistemological goals by teaching visitors about new inventions, new agricultural and industrial practices, cultural ideas, and racial hierarchies through the medium of public displays and material culture. In a similar vein, the fiftieth-anniversary celebrations of emancipation used these methods, but in contrast to using them to enforce racist, imperialistic logic, they sought to disrupt narratives of biological, essentialist racism. Instead, celebrations like the Half-century Anniversary synthesized "progress and celebratory black remembrance, making grand appeals to public memory as social reform."[105] The Half-century Celebration Commission believed, for example, "that the general idea underlying its work could be best conserved by gathering the fruits of the Freedmen everywhere and by comparative analysis this unequaled visible demonstration of universal, progressive effort, would act as an impetus to spur the Illinois Negro forward to still greater industry and achievement."[106] Signing on to modern Enlightenment ideals of universality and progress, the commission also implied that blacks could demonstrate their ability to participate on those terms by mobilizing an alternative social knowledge generated through "comparative analysis" and "visible demonstration."

103. See Blight, *Race and Reunion*, for a discussion of the multiple ways white northerners and southerners ultimately erased black memories and hopes for freedom as they went about the business of reconciling.

104. *Official Program, National Half-century Anniversary Exposition and the Lincoln Jubilee.* The list of appointees includes prominent men and women such as A. A. McCormick, Julius Rosenwald, J. Ogden Armour, and Grace Wilbur Trout.

105. Blight, *Race and Reunion*, 375.

106. *Fiftieth Anniversary of Emancipation of Negroes*, 16.

Following the example of the world's fairs and expositions, the commission included a number of departments that focused on religion, education, military and naval affairs, industry, social progress, fraternal organizations, and athletics. Each department solicited materials and performances for exhibition. By the time it opened at the coliseum in downtown Chicago, the exposition included displays from women's clubs, inventors, schools from across the country, and colleges such as Tuskegee and Wilberforce. It also used material culture to connect African American history to both African history and American history. An extensive Liberian exhibit brought the history and culture of Africa to the exposition, while items such as Lincoln's deathbed, the table on which Robert E. Lee signed the South's surrender at Appomattox, and chairs from Lincoln's box at Ford theater connected American history and black history.[107]

Should the visitor miss this interpretation, a Historical Tableau and Pageant of Negro History and Progress in fourteen acts directly connected African and American history and celebrated the wisdom, resilience, and promise of blacks.[108] Beginning with the creation and moving through Egyptian and Ethiopian history, the pageant juxtaposed Christian, European, and American history, showing Dutch slave traders breaking up religious and marriage rites, the "mournful" middle passage, the role of blacks in Revolutionary America and, later, black and white abolitionists. Depicting the potential of African Americans, the pageant linked education in Chicago public schools and middle-class home entertainment with a slide of the Supreme Court "Knocking Out the Grandfather Clauses" in southern state constitutions. The final act returned to Africa, where Ethiopia was shown rejecting the "Spirit of War" and accepting the Bible from the "Spirit of Peace." Interwoven in this fashion, the pageant drove home the interconnections between African and American history by depicting western commerce for disrupting families and religion in Africa, while pointing to the domesticity and Christianity of modern blacks.

The exposition also sponsored several congresses for the discussion of current research and public endeavors. Using a social scientific framework, the commission gathered survey data "to call the attention of the people and the country to what the Negro has accomplished in art, literature, science, wealth, industry and thrift in his fifty years of freedom" in order that "these facts might be properly established, and their success and achievements fittingly set forth."[109]

---

107. Unfortunately, little evidence remains of the exhibit itself. In addition to the report (*Fiftieth Anniversary of Emancipation of Negroes*) and a few articles in the *Broad Ax* and the *Defender*, only the *Catalogue of the Liberian Exhibit, Official Program*, and the *Lincoln Jubilee Album, 50th Anniversary of Our Emancipation* remain. All are available at the Chicago Historical Society.

108. The outline of the pageant appears in the *Official Program, National Half-century Anniversary Exposition and Lincoln Jubilee*.

109. *Chicago Broad Ax*, May 15, 1915.

Though little visual evidence remains of the celebration, the first annual report catalogued statistics gathered that surely accompanied the exhibits. Paired with objects—inventions, artwork (including paintings and photography), musical performances, and live demonstrations of woodworkers and dry goods production—these statistics and the displays they accompanied were meant to produce new knowledge about the progress of African American life since Emancipation and a new narrative about American democracy as inclusive of blacks.

Displays of African American progress countered pervasive scientific and popular racism. Similar to Wells's antilynching works, the commissioners emphasized blacks' and whites' common humanity. Rejecting biological determinism that enforced racial hierarchy, the commission drew attention to historical circumstances that explained racial differences: "This accurate, scientific collation vindicates the lessons of history. It is unmistakable proof that all mankind possesses the same fundamental human traits, and the same innate capacities. The development of special or peculiar talents depends upon cultural environment, and history shows us that the changes improve from year to year and century to century."[110]

The commission also drew from an experiential and proximate epistemology to explain its method of demonstrating African American success: "[Participants] will show the actual advances of these people verified by every day evidences in shop and field, in home and office, in the kitchen and the schoolroom. The energy and power of such . . . activity can thus be embodied into intelligent information and manifold willing efforts."[111] Juxtaposed with predominant racial narratives, the exhibit makes clear that "[t]he wisdom gained by ordinary experience shows how few people who talk about the 'Progress of the Negro' have comparatively reliable knowledge gained from personal study and actual information of the subject."[112]

The exhibit designers and commissioners seemed to have an agenda that conferred African American agency and status and invited critical reflection—and social action—from white visitors. Editorializing that "[t]oo long has [sic] many of the questions affecting our people been juggled by men and women but poorly prepared to defend us," the Broad Ax reported that "[l]uckily the exhaustive program [on literature and Negro authors meeting at the exhibition] which covers a wide range of subjects will embody almost all if not all of the very abstruse problems affecting us, and will be scholarly handled by our own great writers and distinguished citizens."[113] Another reporter from the Broad Ax described a demonstration of boys from a southern school engaged in "scientific industrial construction" and sixteen girls turning dry goods. We might recognize in such

110. *Fiftieth Anniversary of Emancipation of Negroes*, 21.
111. Ibid., 18.
112. Ibid.
113. *Chicago Broad Ax*, August 21, 1915.

demonstrations an accomodationist display, showing the docile, productive capabilities of African Americans. However, the reporter finds instead a story of progress in which the evidence, embodied in the boys and girls and their products and viewed personally, challenges white racism: "The children are doing more by their public demonstrations to tell the story of deliverance than any thing else I could say. [What] they are teaching the observer daily, is greater than could be expressed by voice or organ."[114] The author here points to an embodied form of social knowledge in which the actions and respectable comportment visible in the black bodies assume the role of educating the white spectator.

Such displays opened up new possibilities for American democracy. Before the exposition opened, the governor explained that the exhibition would make greater knowledge of African Americans available to whites and thus diminish racism, which worked to prevent African American inclusion in political life: "Governor Deneen had emphasized in a public address, the educational value of the Half-Century Exposition idea, to allay race prejudice, growing out of a widespread unfamiliarity with the Negro's general social Progress."[115] The project thus united intellectual and affective goals by forging a democratic social knowledge that drew upon activist social science, proximate epistemology, and interaction. The goal was ultimately, as the commission trumpeted, " 'A LESSON IN SIMPLE AMERICAN DEMOCRACY!'" Democracy here meant cooperative interaction, and the commission explained that "the exposition had provided many occasions when the workers for human uplift were brought together." In particular, "the Educational Congress and the International Interracial gathering was an opportunity . . . to meet together, to study together, and to work together for the upreach and outreach of human kind."[116]

The connection between democratic social knowledge and democratic practice across racial lines was well summed up in the commission's report and is worth quoting at some length:

> The aim of this exposition was not to show the prowess of one race over the other. Far from it. The ideal of unity and co-operation will be all pervasive. The first thing to do is not to emphasize differences, and to formulate platforms, but to come together in a spirit of human brotherhood and to work for those things about which there exists [sic] no differences of opinion. Moreover, there is nothing that begets suspicion and distrust so much as ignorance. We are always dubious about the people we do not know, especially if we have been trained in a traditional belief that they hold wrong

114. Ibid.
115. *Fiftieth Anniversary of Emancipation of Negroes*, 8.
116. Ibid., 21–22.

views. This inevitably means failure to understand each other, and inability to appreciate the different points of view. Many of our present economic, social and racial differences are due to pure ignorance. There remain, of course, the real and valid differences, but the only way in which these can be appreciated and reconciled is by a better understanding of one another.[117]

In the context of a nation obsessed with racial hierarchy and in the process of forging northern and southern reconciliation, the commission offered a vision of interracial cooperation, not of the competitive "prowess of one race over another." Just as Wells had emphasized African Americans' common humanity with whites, so the commission focused on "human brotherhood" and refused to dwell on differences. Reflecting a democratic social knowledge that emphasized mutual relationships to overcome "suspicion and distrust," the commission emphasized that the exposition was a step toward each race's understanding the other. As the commission framed it, democratic social relations were based on equality between the races, mutual understanding and knowledge, and ultimately, appreciation and recognition.

The commission's vision required white and black interaction, but implicitly it aimed at whites; in so doing it recognized the disparity of power between the two races. In a similar vein, the *Broad Ax* concluded its comments on the demonstrations of industrial work by emphasizing that "the Negroes from the various states have brought the story home to you my White brother, my White sister[;] are you magnanimous enough to hear it by the eye of the soul at first hand?" The language here emphasized the appeal not just to the intellect but also to the soul, the symbolic moral center. More significant, however, it underscored the power differentials between the races. Indeed, despite the racial pride the Half-century Exposition encouraged, its primary goal was to reach white visitors by changing their minds as well as their hearts and effecting a transformation that would enable democracy. Pleading for white support, the commission's report exclaimed, "this exposition will fail utterly if you do not attend, you are the ones to see what the Lord has wrought. 'Tis for you," the language emphasizing just how important white participation was for the success of the exposition—and indeed for the democratic nation.[118] Similarly, in an address at the exhibition, George Ellis, former Liberian ambassador and one of the exhibition organizers, appealed to white audience members to "rejoice with us, not so much that the Negro was liberated, as that the whole nation,—white and black— was suddenly moved measurably forward for all the races of men on the highway of social progress and civic freedom."[119]

117. Ibid.
118. *Chicago Broad Ax*, August 28, 1915.
119. George Ellis, "Chicago Democracy and the Negro," 1, in Irene McCoy Gaines Papers,

Unfortunately it is nearly impossible to know how many of the visitors were white and how they responded to the exposition.[120] The only hint we have is from an article in the white *Chicago Evening Post* of August 24, 1915. The editor affirmed the commission's success in creating a narrative of African American progress and even strikes an apologetic tone in recognizing how these gains have come despite white racism: "Substantial evidence of the Negro genius in art, in education, in literature and in industry is to be found in the exhibits. It has been a hard and wearisome struggle against prejudice and injustice that has reached this stage of encouraging achievement." But the reporter does not end there. Affirming the promise of American democracy, he observes that "it is gratifying to reflect that, in spite of much wrong that has been done the Negro in the past, in America the opportunity has been given for a progress so remarkable. And there is promise for the future in this Coliseum display." Turning the burden of overcoming the racism back on African American economic advancement, he celebrates that "the race problem is working out to its own adjustment, as the Negro finds in the cultivation of hand and brain the salvation of himself and his people from the ills sequential to the era of slavery."

These efforts to present an alternative image of African American progress were fraught with urgency as D. W. Griffith's film, *Birth of a Nation*, opened in Chicago earlier that summer. African American responses to the movie suggest the importance they placed on exercising agency over public representations of the race, particularly as new forms of media like motion pictures captured the attention of audiences throughout the country. The NAACP denounced the film as a conspiracy: "Every resource of a magnificent new art has been employed with an undeniable attempt to picture Negroes in the worst possible light."[121] As *Birth of a Nation* illustrated, new media like films were powerful ways to shape popular knowledge. Since "debates over what counts as cultural memory are also debates about who gets to participate in creating national meaning," exhibitions such as the Lincoln Jubilee and films such as *Birth of a Nation* were similarly important aspects of democratic social knowledge.[122]

In collaboration with Thomas Dixon, the author of *The Clansman*, on which *Birth of a Nation* was based, Griffith created the film as a history of the story of the Civil War and Reconstruction Era South and as a depiction of how the Ku Klux Klan saved the entire nation from the grasp of cunning and arrogant

---

Chicago Historical Society, Box 1, Folder 1–4.

120. Estimates of the number of visitors varied from 100,000 reported by the *Broad Ax,* September 18, 1915, to 862,000, reported by the *Fiftieth Anniversary of Emancipation of Negroes,* 18. Given that the population of African Americans in the city numbered approximately 45,000 in 1915, a significant number of whites, as well as blacks, must have visited the exhibition.

121. NAACP, *Sixth Annual Report* (n.p., 1915), 11.

122. Sturken, *Tangled Memories,* 12.

northern politicians (in the form of character Austin Stoneman, a thinly veiled Thaddeus Stevens) who sought to establish political and social equality between blacks and whites. The most infamous scene in the movie portrays the symbolic rape and murder of Flora Cameron by Gus, a former family slave. The Ku Klux Klan, led by Flora's brother, rides out to exact revenge, engaging in its own symbolic castration and lynching of Gus. Much like Addams and Wells did in their narrative essays, the film presented personal stories to illustrate larger political points—primarily that the Civil War was a tragic moment in the nation's history but that reunification enacted through the triumph of the Klan's vision of white supremacy would bring about the true birth of the nation. Film historian Michael Rogin has pointed to Griffith's success in drawing on the personal story: "[H]e wanted, like other middle-class progressives, to get closer to life without falling into chaos."[123] The film's appropriation of personal stories to elicit sympathetic responses marked a cultural shift in the balance of power between the portrayal of experience as depicted in older media forms like newspapers, abolitionist literature, slave narratives, autobiographies, lectures, and essays and the new media's visual representations.

Audience responses to *Birth of a Nation* illustrated the power of film's visual display to elicit emotional responses, with the goal of shaping viewers' impressions, beliefs, and political consciousness; in this respect, movies were potent tools for shaping social knowledge.[124] As Dixon himself explained, film impersonates reality.[125] Griffith purposefully gave the movie a documentary feel by describing several events as historical fact and using the endorsement of the film by historian-turned-president Woodrow Wilson to corroborate the story he told. He quoted the president in advertisements: "It is like writing history with lightning . . . and my only regret is that it is all so terribly true."[126] Dorothea Dix, a member of the cultural elite, described the film as "history vitalized" and urged readers to "go see it, for it will make a better American of you."[127] As historians and film critics have demonstrated, then, the film substantiated a racist narrative that contributed to the formation of white supremacy as a political identity.[128]

123. Michael Rogin, "'The Sword Became a Flashing Vision': D. W. Griffith's *The Birth of a Nation*," *Representations* 9 (1985): 150–95, 158.

124. On the way that films serve as a powerful medium of political socialization, see Terry Christensen, *Reel Politics: American Political Movies from* Birth of a Nation *to* Platoon (New York: Basil Blackwell, 1987); David Platt, *Celluloid Power: Social Film Criticism from* The Birth of a Nation *to* Judgment at Nuremberg (Metuchen, NJ: Scarecrow Press, 1992).

125. Rogin, "Sword Became a Flashing Vision," 185.

126. Ibid., 151. See also Marilyn Fabe, *Closely Watched Films: An Introduction to the Art of Narrative Film Technique* (Berkeley: University of California Press, 2004).

127. Quoted in Rogin, "Sword Became a Flashing Vision."

128. See, for example, Stanley Corkin, *Realism and the Birth of the Modern United States: Cinema, Literature, and Culture* (Athens: University of Georgia Press, 1996), especially chapter 6, "D. W. Griffith's *The Birth of a Nation*: Positivist History as a Compositional Method," 133–60; Christensen,

For these reasons, Jane Addams denounced the film "as an appeal to race prejudice" and a "most subtle form of untruth." Like Addams, Percy Hammond, the drama critic for the *Chicago Tribune*, was critical of the way the film blurred fact and fiction. Both Addams and Hammond were particularly concerned that Griffith used distortions of the past and of African Americans to play upon sympathy and build support for southern apologists. Addams pointed out that the representation of the Ku Klux Klan was designed "to stir [the audience's] sympathy" and "[was] full of danger."[129] Hammond noted that the crowd "cheered the Stars and Bars, and it was not moved by the Stars and Stripes." He credited Griffith as an "authority on the beat of the human heart; he feels to an atom what retards and what accelerates the rhythm of that susceptible organ."[130] In recognizing the interconnection between the audience's physical and emotional responses and the movie's distortions of the truth, Addams and Hammond both highlighted the ability of the new media form to manipulate emotions in new ways by contributing to a dangerous potential to confuse another's opinion for reliable knowledge; film was a powerful new tool to forge a racist brand of social knowledge, one that both excluded African Americans from its creation and depicted them as biologically and socially inferior to whites. The use of such media pointed out one of the dangers of a sympathetic social knowledge. It could be used to create unity (in this case white racial unity) at the exclusion and violent repression of the Other (blacks).[131]

In light of the new media's ability to manipulate its audiences and reach many more viewers from all segments of society, African Americans recognized the high stakes in their efforts to present alternatives to the racist narratives circulating among the white media.[132] Across the country, the fledgling NAACP tried to resist Griffith's power to manipulate the white audience and forge a racist interpretation of the past to justify racial segregation and hierarchy in the present. Its leaders tried to shut the movie down in Los Angeles, Boston, and New York and called for boycotts and picketing outside of movie theaters. In Chicago, African

Reel Politics; Rogin, "Sword Became a Flashing Vision."

129. *New York Post,* March 13, 1915.

130. *Chicago Tribune,* June 13, 1915. See also *Chicago Defender,* June 19, 1915.

131. This is indeed one of the enduring political problems of the new forms of media. See, for example, Walter Lippmann, *Public Opinion* (New York: Harcourt, Brace, 1922), on the way politicians might manipulate the media. Also Philip Ethington, "The Metropolis and Multicultural Ethics: Direct Democracy versus Deliberative Democracy in the Progressive Era," in *Progressivism and the New Democracy,* ed. Sidney M. Milkis and Jerome M. Mileur, 192–225 (Amherst: University of Massachusetts Press, 1999). For an example of this issue in another place and time, see Lessie Jo Frazier, *Salt in the Sand* (Durham: Duke University Press, 2007).

132. For discussion about the dilemmas posed by the consumer orientation of the modern liberal marketplace of ideas and the tensions inherent between free speech and racist or hate speech, see David S. Allen, *Democracy, Inc.: The Press and Law in the Corporate Rationalization of the Public Sphere* (Urbana: University of Illinois Press, 2005), 37–44, 123–43.

American leaders and some white reformers had tried to prevent the movie from opening in the city. They lobbied Mayor William Hale Thompson, who had won his office with the help of the predominantly black Second Ward, to keep the movie from opening in the city.[133]

State legislator R. R. Jackson, an African American from Chicago, proposed a bill "to prohibit acts tending to incite ill feeling or prejudice or to ridicule or disparage others on account of race."[134] Recognizing the importance of public representation, the bill specifically outlawed "any lithograph, drawing, picture, play, drama, or sketch, that tends to incite race riot, prejudice, hatred or antagonism, or to subject any individual, race, or people to public ridicule, scorn or contempt" and prevented the exhibition of any depiction of lynching or unlawful hanging "based on the theory that presentation of such pictures tends to race hatred and to rioting."[135] Jackson's bill overwhelmingly passed the Illinois house but lost in the state senate by one vote.[136]

Mayor Thompson was unable to keep a promise to prevent the movie from opening in the city, and it premiered in Chicago on May 3. A contributing editor of the Chicago Defender saw the film and suggested African Americans offer a corrective. In his review of the film, he "recite[d] facts about 'The Real Birth of a Nation,'" a story that paid particular attention to the treatment of black slaves and the progress of African Americans, suggesting that Griffith's film might be more appropriately named "THE REJUVENATOR of the MEMORY of a CRIME."[137] The response of African Americans and their white reform allies across the nation drew attention to the importance of the struggle over cultural representations of race and the necessity of including multiple perspectives, particularly from the marginalized groups themselves.[138]

Jackson's legislative initiative illustrates the connections between public representation and politics. Coming as they did amid increasing racial tensions and northern and southern reconciliation efforts that erased African American aspirations and experiences from public memory, the Fiftieth Anniversary of Emancipation and the fight to ban Birth of a Nation were important means of presenting alternative social narratives about race and progress. As African Americans and their white allies fought to prevent degrading images of African Americans, reformers used an activist and experiential framework to challenge a racist social knowledge that justified segregation and racial hierarchy; their

133. For Thompson's public position on the film, see Chicago Defender, May 1, May 22, 1915; May 29, 1915.

134. Ibid., March 13, 1915.

135. Ibid.; Broad Ax, May 22, 1915.

136. Chicago Defender, June 26, 1915.

137. Ibid., June 12, 1915.

138. For other examples, see Michel-Rolph Trouillot, Silencing the Past: Power and the Production of History (Boston: Beacon, 1995).

efforts emphasized the importance of including African American perspectives in the development of a democratic social knowledge. They also sought to provide white Americans with a greater knowledge about black accomplishments, while at the same time forging political subjectivity built on collective experiences and affective, sympathetic ties formed in the arenas of social reform. Thus we can see in the work of the Frederick Douglass Center an interracial settlement, the epistemological and political significance of bringing the races together to forge cooperation and mutual understanding. It was an arena through which to break down racial ignorance and prejudice by creating new knowledge and political possibilities that simultaneously held in tension the universality of liberal republicanism and the experiences of particular collectivities—in this case racial experience.

The Frederick Douglass Center and Interracial Cooperation

Founded by Celia Parker Woolley in 1905, the interracial Frederick Douglass Center (FDC) social settlement exemplified the intersection of democratic social knowledge and racial cooperation. Like Hull House, it engaged in activist social science and fostered experiential, proximate epistemology across race rather than across class or ethnicity. Though Chicago's black community had established a number of settlements by 1905, when the settlement opened, the FDC was unique in its purpose of encouraging social interaction among middle-class blacks and whites.[139] Fannie Barrier Williams, a prominent African American reformer in Chicago, emphasized the importance of such interracial work since "the average white American knows the Negro only as he sees him on the street or engaged in some employment that does not permit of association. As this average American sees but little of the Negro and knows but little of him, he is at liberty to form any kind of erroneous opinion about him."[140] Assuming that distance and ignorance fostered prejudice, Woolley and her allies turned to proximate knowledge and mutuality to overcome it.

This section further explores both the possibilities and limitations of democratic social knowledge as it played out in the arena of race reform. As we saw in the previous section, new technologies could manipulate sympathies by offering means to both challenge racial hierarchies and mobilize support for exclusion and violent repression. Indeed, this was the problem Wells had faced

139. For information on other black settlements, see Knupfer, *Toward a Tenderer Humanity*, and Elizabeth Lasch-Quinn, *Black Neighbors: Race and the Limits of Reform in the American Settlement House Movement, 1890–1945* (Chapel Hill: University of North Carolina Press, 1993).

140. "The Negro and Public Opinion," *Voice of the Negro* 1, no. 1 (1904): 31–32, reprinted in Mary Jo Deegan, ed., *New Woman of Color,* 87–89.

in her antilynching campaign as well. Here again, we see that emancipatory gestures of sympathetic understanding and proximate, experiential knowledge do not necessarily address deeply implicated assumptions about race that shape power relationships between blacks and whites. The section thus recognizes the promises of democratic social knowledge in the work of the Frederick Douglass Center, while also thinking critically about its limitations.

A member of the white cultural elite of the city, Woolley was born into an abolitionist family in Michigan. She grew up steeped in racial egalitarianism and liberal Christianity.[141] In 1876 she moved with her husband to Chicago, where she became a Unitarian minister active in local reform. She served as the president of the Chicago Woman's Club in the 1890s and brought formal desegregation to the club when she sponsored her friend Fannie Barrier Williams for membership.[142] By the turn of the century, Woolley actively took up race reform. She approached Wells with her idea for an interracial settlement, and Wells raised subscriptions for operating expenses and played a significant role in its activities and fund raising.

The FDC's location on the border of "an entirely respectable though not an aristocratic" white neighborhood, and the south-side black belt physically illustrated its challenge to the human geography and social inequality of the city.[143] Like Hull House, it was a step toward fusing the public and private, as Woolley and her husband lived upstairs, while the downstairs rooms and parlors served as public meeting areas. In this respect it was particularly challenging to customs of white respectability that frowned on social interaction between blacks and whites. Offering an "opportunity for wholesome contact between those like-minded, irrespective of color," the center provided a location from which to attack stereotypes that suggested all blacks were morally suspect. In her opening address, Woolley outlined the dual goals of the center: to break down barriers between the white and black middle class by bringing them into contact with each other and to address the needs of Chicago's poorer blacks.[144] The FDC positioned Woolley and her activist friends Wells and Williams as mediators between whites and blacks, middle and working classes.

141. For biographical information on Woolley, see Koby Lee-Forman, "The Simple Love of Truth: The Racial Justice Activism of Celia Parker Woolley" (PhD diss., Northwestern University, 1995).

142. Mary Jo Deegan discusses Fannie Barrier Williams in her introduction to *A New Woman of Color.*

143. This location was a compromise. When Woolley had tried to rent a building farther north on Wabash in a predominantly white area, wealthy whites in the neighborhood blocked her actions. With the help of supporters who raised money for a down payment and expenses, Woolley purchased and renovated a building and then, in settlement house fashion, left her comfortable home and moved into it. See Lee-Forman, "Simple Love of Truth," 253–57; McMurry, *To Keep the Waters Troubled,* 273–77; Schechter, *Ida B. Wells-Barnett and American Reform,* 184–86.

144. Celia Parker Woolley, *Unity* 49 (May 4, 1905): 55.

As Hull House had done fifteen years earlier when it brought middle-class women to live in the city's ethnic working-class areas, the center raised curiosity and fear. When Woolley invited a mixed-race group of twelve African Americans and seven whites to her home to outline the project and work up a plan of action, one newspaper declared the interracial "luncheon" a "striking innovation, a startling if not a revolutionary thing to do."[145] Aware of these public sentiments and the threat they posed to white respectability, the members carefully minimized the radical implications of the club. Williams claimed that the FDC's purpose was to do "whatever can be done in a sane, rational, and just manner to check the conditions that make for a wider separation of the races in their non-social relations."[146] However, the FDC did promote socializing between blacks and whites. Their fund-raising events included integrated dinner dances and theater productions. White fears about such social mingling reinforced the need for a place that would act as a mediator of white public opinion about race. Each white member might be "a committee of one to do away with this cruel spirit of generalization against the negro."[147] The center's goals shared much with Jane Addams's version of mutuality and experience in that firsthand experience of interracial cooperation would provide a basis for new social knowledge.

The center contributed to a paradigm of democratic social knowledge in several ways. In addition to offering educational activities—a kindergarten, boys' arts-and-crafts club, girls' sewing class, classes for adults in manual training, cooking, and dressmaking—it also served as an arena for deliberation and political activism. In order to undermine racist perceptions of African Americans as inherently inferior, the center promoted the idea that African Americans had made impressive progress since the days of slavery. The leadership sought to demonstrate that blacks could be responsible participants in urban life while it simultaneously worked to raise African American interest in civic affairs.[148]

A year after the center opened, Williams wrote that "it is the purpose of the Douglass Center to make as much as possible of this effort to arouse a new interest among the colored people of the city to get in at the beginning [of the civil service and charter movements] and as far as possible be a part of the working force in the formation of these new conditions in our civil life."[149] In 1906 the FDC's Women's Club sponsored discussions on "The Ideals of Citizenship" and

145. *Unity* 48 (November 3, 1904): 53–54.

146. Fannie Barrier Williams, "The Frederick Douglass Centre: A Question of Social Betterment and Not of Social Equality," *Voice of the Negro* 1, no. 12 (1904): 601–4; reprinted in Deegan, ed., *New Woman of Color.*

147. Woolley, quoted in Lee-Forman, "Simple Love of Truth," 263.

148. Ibid.

149. Fannie Barrier Williams, "New Method of Dealing with the Race Problem," in Deegan, ed., *New Woman of Color,* 132.

"Shall the New Charter Grant Municipal Suffrage to Women?"[150] Such topics point to African Americans' shared efforts with white reformers to invigorate Chicago's political life. In the context of uncertain boundaries and even growing hostility to African Americans in the city, the efforts of people like Wells, Williams, and Woolley sought to crystallize African American political consciousness and squarely situate it in reform debate.

The settlement also hosted dances, political discussions, and reading groups that attracted both African American and white participants.[151] As literary historian Elizabeth McHenry has suggested, African American reading groups provided important arenas in which participants created educational and cultural opportunities for participation in a democratic deliberation.[152] In this regard, the interracial nature of the FDC's reading groups is especially striking, as they offered opportunities for both whites and blacks to exercise *together* the deliberative skills needed for democratic practice.

In settlement house tradition the center offered public lectures and discussions on local reform issues, the purpose of which was both education and the transformation of racial logic. Sanitation, neighborhood improvement, and civics were typical topics. Following the Child Welfare Exhibit held at the Chicago Coliseum, the FDC sponsored a conference on settlements and children. These educational activities were similar to efforts begun at Hull House and carried on by the Civic Federation ward committees. But the interracial composition of the FDC's audiences was significant. Since most whites had a dubious opinion of blacks as worthy civic participants, bringing African Americans into discussions surrounding vital urban questions challenged these attitudes.

The FDC's strategies for overcoming ideas about race were reminiscent of those used by Wells in the antilynching campaign and in the Half-century Exposition; all of them sought to point out similarities between blacks and whites. Such concern about framing similarities and downplaying differences suggest a deeply embedded logic that recognized race as a relational category. The problem of racism was not that blacks were biologically inferior but that they were perceived as different, as "Other." The reformers' efforts to demonstrate blacks as similar to whites was an important distinction in an intellectual and popular culture concerned with providing a scientific rationalization for racial hierarchy. At the same time, this strategy reveals its own inherent racial logic: The effort was always to show that blacks were like whites, not the other way around. Recognizing this, we are left with the sense that these strategies did not ultimately challenge an important aspect of white power—one that positioned

---

150. Knupfer, *Toward a Tenderer Humanity,* 51.

151. Notices about Frederick Douglass Center activities (and other black club activities) appeared regularly in the *Broad Ax* and *Chicago Defender.*

152. McHenry, *Forgotten Readers,* 19.

it as the universal good to which black people must stake a claim and prove their similarity.

However, given the historical context in which these reformers operated, their efforts to provide a place where blacks and whites could come together was vitally important, particularly since places like the FDC offered an arena in which to discuss difficult questions of race that were frequently absent from public debate. Indeed, the center took on the subject of race directly. After completing a research trip through the region, Jenkins Lloyd Jones, a Unitarian minister and friend of Woolley, delivered a lecture series titled "Sermons from the South." In addition, the center hosted several speakers on civic life and racial issues. The center's willingness to explore the problem of race in an interracial public forum challenged the silence English reformer William Stead had imposed on public discussion of race in Chicago a decade earlier; it responded to Wells's and Addams's admonishment that the subject was indeed a nationwide issue that demanded attention from white northerners, as well as African Americans.

The FDC also used an activist social science that contributed to citywide knowledge about Black Belt conditions. Because few statistics were known about Chicago's black community, it created a social statistics committee that sought "to gather information about the colored people in Chicago and establish a scientific basis of inquiry and helpfulness."[153] Its work was useful to the wider Chicago community. For example, the Board of County Visitors called on the FDC for assistance when it wanted to know what services were available for African American children. In response, Woolley gathered detailed information on the number of African American children served by local institutions, the attitude toward extending services for black children, and the nature of racial interaction that took place in the social settings.[154] Throughout its existence, the center also hosted several University of Chicago sociology students studying Chicago's African American community. In addition, it worked closely with the Juvenile Protective League, an activist social science organization growing out of Chicago's female reform community, as it investigated Black Belt playgrounds and amusements and worked to improve these recreational facilities serving African American children.[155]

Woolley and Ida Wells-Barnett also organized the interracial Frederick Douglass Center Women's Club. During its first year, the club enrolled seventy women, a third of whom were white.[156] The FDC Women's Club was part of a

---

153. Williams, "Frederick Douglass Centre," 115.

154. In a similar vein, see Louise DeKoven Bowen, *The Colored People of Chicago: An Investigation Made for the Juvenile Protection Associations by A. P. Drucker, Sophia Boaz, A. L. Harris, Miriam Schaffner* (Chicago: Rogers and Hall, 1913).

155. *Chicago Defender*, September 23, 1911.

156. Williams, "New Method of Dealing with the Race Problem," 502–5.

growing interracial cooperation among women and was similar to the cross-class and multiethnic Hull House Women's Club. White Chicago women were much ahead of white men in confronting racial matters as they worked together to assert a maternalist agenda emphasizing the importance of protecting children and the home. In contrast, there were no integrated men's clubs in the 1890s.[157] These interracial endeavors were under way even before the FDC opened. In the late 1890s Mary Redfield Plummer, a prominent white clubwoman, approached Wells with an invitation for the Ida B. Wells Club to join a new integrated organization of women's clubs in Cook County.[158] Wells also worked with an interracial group to protest lynching.

Interracial women's activities served as cultural mediators that supported black women's respectability and civic participation, but they also exposed the complex and fragile intersection of race and class that reformers like Wells and Woolley had to navigate in drawing on a democratic social knowledge that privileged proximity and experience. Interracial clubs made possible a closer interaction between the races, just as social settlements brought together immigrants and native born, middle and lower classes. Such proximity challenged prejudice by offering an experiential basis for social knowledge and planting what race reformers hoped would be the seeds of affective, sympathetic bonds between the races. Once established, these bonds might take root and flower into collective political action toward social justice.[159]

The domestic feminism of these clubs further provided a rationale for alliance and integration between black and white women's clubs and was important to black women's reform strategies. Because white society had repeatedly denied black women the psychological and physical protection afforded by middle-class female respectability, integration was an expedient for claiming such privilege and power. Through activities and organizations that emphasized their feminine and domestic fitness, African American women drew on an experiential and proximate logic by challenging white women who worked with them to recognize their commonalities and shared social agendas.

The FDC's twin goals of interracial cooperation and racial uplift posed an important dilemma of class and race evident in the epistemological strategies of proximity and the cultural representation of respectability. Several historians have recently argued that African American elites consciously attempted to

---

157. Maureen Flanagan, *Seeing with Their Hearts: Chicago Women and the Vision of the Good City, 1871–1933* (Princeton, NJ: Princeton University Press, 2002), 207.

158. On learning of Wells's actions, the president of the club criticized what she took as Wells's assumption of power. See Duster, *Crusade for Justice*, 272–74.

159. For discussion of the importance of sympathy and affective bonds—and their problematic role—in creating political subjectivity and the nation itself, see Frazier, *Salt in the Sand*. Also Jeff Goodwin, James M. Jasper, and Francesca Polletta, eds., *Passionate Politics: Emotions and Social Movements* (Chicago University of Chicago Press, 2001).

ally themselves with middle-class whites in order to reshape racist perceptions of a singular and inferior African American community.[160] In doing so, they distanced themselves from working-class blacks. For example, Fannie Barrier Williams, writing on the black community in Chicago, decried "the huddling together of the good and the bad, compelling the decent element of the colored people to witness the brazen display of vice of all kinds in front of their homes and in the faces of their children." These were "trying conditions under which to remain socially clean and respectable."[161] Her description sets apart "decent" blacks and their moral struggles in the face of dangers posed by contact with the "bad" element. As race leaders emphasized the differences among African Americans, they shared with middle-class whites a language of respectability rooted in family and patriarchal gender relations, evident in FDC programs that served to assert a black middle-class identity and ensure that racial reform would continue from that important social base.[162] Their strategies threatened to erase working-class African Americans from view. By putting forth an alternative narrative of blackness, one cleaved by the axis of class, they implicitly delegitimized working-class experiences. The center's emphasis on a cautious socialization between middle-class members of the two races thus seemed to come at the expense of poorer African Americans. The emphasis on respectability ironically ran the danger of contributing to a liberal republican discourse on worthiness, which undergirded a logic of discrimination and racism.[163]

This "politics of respectability" black middle-class reformers employed, however, was more complex. It did indeed emphasize middle-class domestic manners and morals to supplant negative ideas about race, but it also included the belief that all black women (and men) possessed dignity and honor and were worthy of respect.[164] It provided the basis for critiques of structural problems in African

160. Kevin Gaines, *Uplifting the Race: Black Leadership, Politics, and Culture in the Twentieth Century* (Chapel Hill: University of North Carolina Press, 1996); Deborah Gray White, "The Cost of Club Work, the Price of Black Feminism," in *Visible Women: New Essays on American Activism*, ed. Nancy Hewitt and Suzanne Lebsock, 247–69 (Urbana: University of Illinois Press, 1993).

161. Williams, "Social Bond in the "Black Belt of Chicago," *Charities* 15 (October 7, 1905): 40.

162. Gaines, *Uplifting the Race*, 5; Higgenbotham, quoted in White, *Dark Continent of Our Bodies*, 185–229. In *Gender and Jim Crow*, Glenda Gilmore seeks to recover the southern African American middle class and their political and reform activities. McMurry argues that in Chicago an older African American elite was threatened by new migrants from the South. See p. 288 in particular. See also Smith, *Photography on the Color Line*.

163. Linda Gordon, *Pitied but Not Entitled: Single Mothers and the History of Welfare, 1890–1935* (New York: Free Press, 1994); Nancy Fraser and Linda Gordon, "A Genealogy of Dependency: Tracing a Keyword of the U.S. Welfare State," *Signs* 19, no. 2 (1994): 309–36; Jill Quadagno, *The Color of Welfare: How Racism Undermined the War on Poverty* (New York: Oxford University Press, 1994). Sanford F. Schram, Joe Soss, and Richard C. Fording, eds., *Race and the Politics of Welfare Reform* (Ann Arbor: University of Michigan Press, 2003).

164. Evelyn Brooks Higginbotham argues that within the black Baptist women's movement the politics of respectability assumed that all black women possessed dignity and honor and were worthy

American communities, problems that were not biologically determined. As Williams put it, "the colored people have lost in the last ten years nearly every occupation of which they once had almost a monopoly. . . . [A]ny group that can be systematically deprived of one occupation after another becomes an easy victim to all kinds of injustice. When they can be reduced to a point to be pitied, they will cease to be respected."[165] The emphasis on self-presentation and middle-class respectability thus also encouraged cross-class political efforts among African Americans to change social and economic conditions as they joined forces to protest unjust legislation, work for social services, and organize mutual aid networks. Whites like Woolley who worked with African Americans seemed focused more on incorporating the perspectives and protecting the rights of *middle-class* blacks like those they had come to know personally. In other words, they foregrounded the issues that they recognized as affecting blacks *and* whites. Very few white reformers worked to make available the social services that were so desperately needed by non-middle-class blacks. Consequently, this focus remained the exclusive work of black men's and women's clubs. Middle-class African American reformers understood such efforts in political, not just philanthropic, terms, maintaining mutual efforts across class to assert black political power and a race-based political project. What some historians have suggested was an elitist tendency was thus much more complicated.

The FDC's interracial strategy was also more politically charged than critics of black middle-class reformers have suggested. Though very little evidence remains about how visitors understood their participation in the settlement, given the radical philosophy of racial egalitarianism of the center, any participation must have entailed some thought and commitment, especially for

---

of respect; this set it apart from the National Association of Colored Women, which was often more elitist in its attitudes toward lower-class blacks. Nonetheless, she argues that the politics of respectability had classist and assimilationist tendencies in that it consciously drew from white discourses of domesticity and was often used for purposes of uplift among lower-class African American women. Kevin Gaines has advanced a similar argument, suggesting that black men and women used white domestic norms as a form of self-help to prove their worthiness for U.S. citizenship. He takes his argument a step farther by suggesting that the employment of a politics of respectability served to divide blacks and reinforce negative attitudes toward lower-class African Americans. Both seem to assume that domesticity was a "white" construct. Yet Higgenbotham herself suggests that black women drew from their own religious values in addition to "white" norms in constructing their view of respectability. The discussions offered by Higgenbotham and Gaines suggest that a clearer articulation of the sources of African Americans' gender and domestic ideologies would be useful. See Higgenbotham, quoted in White, *Dark Continent of Our Bodies*, especially 185–231; Gaines, *Uplifting the Race*. See also Glenda Gilmore, *Gender and Jim Crow* (Chapel Hill: University of North Carolina Press, 1996), and White, "Cost of Club Work"; Gunning, *Race, Rape, and Lynching*, 78–79. For a thoughtful contemporary discussion of black respectability that connects it with gender and sexuality and sees it as an always complicated, occasionally problematic construct, see White, *Dark Continent of Our Bodies*.

165. Fannie Barrier Williams, "Social Bonds in the Black Belt of Chicago: Negro Organizations and the New Spirit Pervading Them," *Charities* 15 (October, 15, 1905): 44.

middle-class whites and blacks. For white women who put their respectability in jeopardy simply by interacting with blacks on a basis of equality, actions such as going to dances, reading groups, and the settlement's women's club meetings were particularly courageous steps toward interracial solidarity. African American leaders likewise risked their credibility among the masses who might remain suspicious of philanthropic whites. Indeed, similar to the tensions we saw in the previous discussion of Ida Wells and lynching, their transgressions of cultural norms were assertions of political agency that required delicacy.

The Frederick Douglass Center remained open until Woolley's death in 1918, when its facilities were given to the Chicago Urban League.[166] During her nearly fifteen years of leadership, Woolley accomplished a significant feat: She and African American leaders like Williams, with whom she worked, created a space where blacks and whites came together not only to pursue reform goals but to socialize as well. Such socialization was an important means for African Americans to combat white supremacist portrayals of themselves. As in the struggle over cultural representations of African Americans in lynching, film, and the Half-century Exhibition, reformers used public displays of the black body and African American behavior, as well as interracial socialization like that at the FDC, as a text to create a new narrative about black respectability and progress and a new vision of American political community that included African Americans as fully equal.

This version of democratic social knowledge was thus built on their position as cultural agents in creating public perceptions of race that were inclusive and emphasized the similarities between races and on sympathetic understanding and personal interaction between whites and blacks as a way to provide experiences that break down prejudice. Overcoming racial mistrust was a gradual process that required careful and repeated interracial effort on both sides of the color line. Though the interracial cooperation of African Americans and whites in the 1900s and 1910s enjoyed limited success, it planted the seeds for future interracial reform, particularly in the Chicago NAACP, which fully blossomed after World War II.[167]

Possibilities and Limitations of Democratic Social Knowledge

In each of these examples we see African Americans and their white allies employing facets of democratic social knowledge that included struggles over

166. Arvah Strickland, *History of the Chicago Urban League* (Urbana: University of Illinois Press, 1966).

167. Reed, *Chicago NAACP*, 4.

the representation of race. We also see the possibilities of interracial cooperation to create opportunities for democratic social relations to develop across what was, in the early twentieth century, a deepening racial divide. These examples illustrate that a politics of presentation and respectability—as well as arenas in which to exercise rationality and deliberation and build relationships based on mutual respect—were important aspects of democratic social knowledge. Their importance was enhanced by a growing cultural and economic orientation toward consumption and public display; representation, the gaze, and mutual recognition—seeing the Other in oneself—took on added meaning as a basis for sympathetic identification and a catalyst for collective action.

Commitments of whites like Woolley, the power of cultural critiques like that of Wells, the appeal of the Half-century Exposition were important examples of the possibilities of overcoming the racial divide that served both to challenge dominant racial narratives and to forge interracial reform. Their efforts also highlighted what would prove to be one of the most challenging aspects of twentieth-century political and cultural life: walking the tenuous line between the universal political subject, which in nineteenth-century Chicago had been cast in liberal republican terms, and the particular collective experiences of groups. This tension was reflected in the effort to build new political subjectivities around knowledge of and sympathetic identification with people across race.[168]

However, the possibilities of democratic social knowledge to bridge the racial divide also encountered limitations that raise some important questions about its efficacy to serve as a basis for political connections and activism. Sympathetic identification, an embodied epistemological framework, mutual understanding, and interaction required whites to confront their own prejudice, to be reflective about their practices, and to be willing to suspend their own habits of mind and carefully listen to the Other. Democratic social knowledge could offer only an alternative praxis; individuals ultimately had to be willing to listen, to see differently, and to change deeply rooted habits of mind and behaviors. In this respect, the power of democratic social knowledge—its potential to serve both affective and intellectual purposes—was also a significant limitation. Its affective qualities proved at times unable to erode the subjective nature of racism, and, indeed, films like *Birth of a Nation* could actually use sympathetic techniques to entrench a racist social knowledge that gave shape to political mobilization; as its many critics and historians have noted, the film had significant cultural and political consequences as it revitalized the modern Klan in the South.

168. For a discussion of the variety of ways African Americans constructed political subjectivity and the tensions between the need to see political subjectivity as both universal and attendant to particular collective experiences, see Kelley, *Race Rebels;* Holland, *Body Politic;* Sharon Patricia Holland, *Raising the Dead: Readings on Death and (Black) Subjectivity* (Durham, NC: Duke University Press, 2000).

Two examples, both involving Ida Wells-Barnett, exemplify the limitations of sympathy, embodied knowledge, and particularly claims to firsthand experience to create an inclusive democratic social knowledge. Wells found her middle-class, white women's club allies unwilling to acknowledge her statistical work and her personal experiences. For example, following the Atlanta riot of 1906, J. Max Barber, editor of the Atlanta-based *Voice,* spoke at the Frederick Douglass Center Women's Club. He had been run out of the city following the riot and described the details of the event and his own exile from Atlanta. After hearing the harrowing story, Mary Redfield Plummer replied, " 'I do not know what we can do or say about this terrible affair, but there is one thing I can say and that is to urge all of you to drive the criminals out from among you.' "[169]

Wells confronted Plummer afterward and inquired how she could ignore the evidence of racial oppression and terrorism that Barber presented. Plummer responded that black men committed 10 percent of all crimes in Chicago and "anyway every white woman that I know in the South has told me that she is afraid to walk out after dark." Wells reminded her, "I have told you of my experiences and investigations so often, Mrs. Plummer; I thought you knew the situation and that those charges are false." Plummer laughed in response. "My dear, your mouth is no more a prayer book than that of any other of my friends who have talked with me about this subject."[170]

When confronted with two firsthand accounts of racial dynamics of the South—her southern friend's account of her fear of black men and Wells's experience and social scientific investigations into lynching—Plummer sided with her personal friend. Sympathetic understanding, proximity, and personal experience were potential weapons against prejudice and misunderstanding.[171] But such a basis for democratic social knowledge would not necessarily transform everyone, even those involved in its process. Subjective aspects of individual and social experiences, values, and beliefs—all dimensions of social knowledge—in this case served to entrench rather than root out prejudice. Indeed, Plummer's position illustrates late twentieth-century feminist critiques that experience as an unquestioned form of evidence can obscure the ability to understand the cultural values, hierarchies, and frameworks shaping it.[172]

Later experience with the National American Woman Suffrage Association (NAWSA) reinforced the limitations of an embodied framework of knowledge as a basis for promoting interracial understanding. When, in 1913, the Illinois

---

169. Duster, *Crusade for Justice,* 283–84.

170. Ibid. For further discussion of the ways that white women helped maintain the lynching/ rape myth and stereotypes of African Americans, see Miller, *Other Reconstruction,* 42–47, and Angela Y. Davis, *Women, Race & Class* (New York: Vintage, 1983).

171. Duster, *Crusade for Justice,* 285.

172. Scott, "Experience," in *Feminists Theorize the Political,* 22–40.

Federation of Women's clubs sent an integrated group to represent the state in a walk on Washington, DC, the national office requested that their black delegates walk at the end of the parade with black women from other states.[173] When Wells expressed her determination to march with the Illinois women, another member retorted, "'if I were a colored woman, I should be willing to march with the other women of my race.'" Wells told her pointedly, "'there is a difference . . . which you probably do not see.'" This exchange suggests the broad epistemological gap between white and black women at that moment and a limit to sympathetic, embodied knowledge in closing that gap; despite their shared sex, white women did not share the same embodied experience as their African American counterparts. Having never experienced racism, they did not understand what Wells did and that physical segregation was a badge of inferiority.

Wells stood her ground. " 'Either I go with you or not at all. I am not taking this stand because I personally wish for recognition. I am doing it for the future benefit of my whole race.' "[174] Again in this case, white clubwomen's reactions highlight a limitation in the strategy of embodied experience as a basis for mutual understanding; it was successful only to the extent that both parties were able to carefully listen to, imagine, and respond to the other. However, there were no guarantees that it was a firm enough basis on which to build political action.

Schools, Race, and Democratic Social Knowledge

As the twentieth century unfolded, the possibilities and limitations of interracial reform—and those of democratic social knowledge—became more visible. Interracial cooperation expanded throughout the 1910s with the goal of alleviating the problems of discrimination and segregation that African Americans faced in the city. The Woman's City Club worked with African American women's clubs to address matters of housing, education, and recreation. Connecting this work to the well-being of Chicago, Mary McDowell, head of the University Settlement in Chicago's packinghouse district, explained, "Civic patriotism demands that for the welfare of the city as a whole, race prejudice must be lost in a constructive program to provide proper housing, full recreational privileges and increased educational opportunities [f]or all where they are now lacking."[175]

John L. Fitzpatrick, president of the Chicago Federation of Labor, accepted

173. Duster, *Crusade for Justice*, 345–47; Rosalyn Terborg-Penn, *African American Women in the Struggle for the Vote, 1850–1920* (Bloomington: Indiana University Press, 1998), 122–23; Wanda Hendricks, *Gender, Race, and Politics in the Midwest: Black Club Women in Illinois* (Bloomington: Indiana University Press, 1998).

174. Duster, *Crusade for Justice*, 347.

175. *Women's City Club Bulletin* 8 (February 1920): 4, in University of Illinois–Chicago Department of Special Collections, Women's City Club Papers, Box 2, Folder 12.

an appointment to the Negro Workers Advisory Committee of Cook County, which was created to "study, plan, and devise methods of coping with the very serious problem of Negro labor."[176] Recognizing that the end of World War I had brought unemployment for many African Americans, the U.S. Department of Labor commissioned these committees to help local areas address the problems of unemployment and racial animosity that surfaced after the war. Building on a foundation of interracial cooperation, the NAACP opened a local branch in Chicago. Although these were fragile and halting efforts, they planted the seeds for the further growth of race reform.

In other ways, however, racial tensions mounted as the 1920s approached. Housing in the Black Belt became more expensive and more difficult to find as African Americans were prevented from moving into other neighborhoods. Despite the efforts of Fitzpatrick and African American leaders who sought to help migrants adjust to new jobs, racial tension remained in the packinghouses and other large industries, and indeed African Americans were overly represented in less desirable and less remunerative jobs. These factors contributed to the infamous Chicago race riot of 1919, in which thirty-eight people were killed and more than five hundred were injured. The riot exposed the limits of cross-race solidarity and foreshadowed the challenges of forging interracial cooperation outside of leisure spaces in the decades to come.

This racial drifting apart was evident not just in the cataclysmic race riot of 1919, which served to highlight the extent of racial tension not only in housing, the workplace, and public spaces but in the schools as well. The segregation of Chicago's schools boded ill for democratic social and political practice. Throughout the 1910s, administrators generally supported black teachers and integrated classrooms.[177] At a school near the Black Belt, Raymond Elementary, the principal explained, "When one treats these dear little children, both black and white, with tenderness and makes no difference between them . . . they both lose their prejudice."[178] The principal at Wendell Phillips High School rebuffed a group of students complaining about the school's first African American teacher. The teacher was "a cultured man," he told the students. "Go in there and forget the color, and see if you can get the subject matter."[179]

Both individual educational investigators and members of the Commission on Race Relations, formed in the wake of the 1919 race riot, visited schools but

176. Forrester Washington to John L. Fitzpatrick, January 25, 1919, Chicago Federation of Labor Papers, Box 7, Folder, January 22–31, 1919, Chicago Historical Society.

177. Michael Homel, *Down from Equality: Black Chicagoans and Public Schools, 1920–1941* (Urbana: University of Illinois Press, 1984).

178. *Chicago Defender*, November 12, 1910.

179. Chicago Commission on Race Relations, *The Negro in Chicago: A Study of Race Relations and a Race Riot* (Chicago: University of Chicago Press, 1922), 252–53.

found little trace of color consciousness.[180] These integrated schools, where white, African American, immigrant, middle- and working-class children mixed freely in integrated classrooms and playgrounds, were important places in which to practice democratic social relationships. As African American clubwoman and early sociologist of Chicago's black community Fannie Barrier Williams observed in an article on "impartial schools," "Is there a democratic spirit that, for the time being at least, makes the child of the alley equal to the child of the avenue?" She answered her own question with an "emphatic yes."[181] George Ellis likewise praised Chicago's democratic spirit, connecting it with education: "[I]n Chicago we are actualizing the true American ideals of equality more than other large cities, with the children of all races attending together the common and higher schools."[182]

Nevertheless, racial tensions mounted as the 1910s unfolded. Indeed, as early as 1905, during the Teamsters' strike, white children joined their parents in attacking black strikebreakers. White children also attacked African American children who moved into their schools. White parents began to petition the school board for transfers out of schools where African Americans constituted a noticeable minority.[183] Parents of white students at Wendell Phillips High School on the south side were particularly alarmed to find that black and white students were dancing together in the school's social room. Administrators responded by segregating the room. While African American parents urged their children to boycott the segregated social room, Celia Parker Woolley and Marion Talbot, dean of women at the University of Chicago, spoke out against the policy. Talbot spoke to the heart of the importance of schools as a place to encourage proximity, experience, and understanding across differences: "Our public school certainly is an agency for fostering sympathy and democracy which must not be allowed to fail the community." Woolley argued that "the color line has no more place in the social gatherings of the school than in the classroom or laboratory." Segregation was unacceptable since it "sets at naught the fundamental principles on which our public school was based."[184]

However, these sentiments were increasingly a minority among white Chicagoans. In 1918 Max Loeb, a businessman and member of the school board, sent a letter to black Chicagoans urging segregated schools and enraging its recipients. "How best can the Race antagonisms be avoided which often spring up when the two races are brought into close juxtaposition? . . . Do you think it wiser,

180. "John Farren School, Chicago," *Journal of Education* 73 (February 2, 1911): 119; Chicago Commission on Race Relations, *Negro in Chicago.*
181. *New York Age,* April 5, 1906.
182. Ellis, "Democracy and the Negro," 3.
183. On the segregation of Chicago schools, see Homel, *Down from Equality.*
184. Quoted in ibid., 16.

when there is a large Colored population, to have separate schools for white and Colored children? If the separation came at the desire and upon the initiative of the Colored people, would the sympathetic understanding of Colored by whites, and vice versa, be heightened, or would such a separation increase prejudice and antagonism?"[185] Though his question seems open ended, he goes on to ask how a separation movement, if "it is wise, be begun?"[186] Here then was a twisted version of democratic social knowledge—distance rather than proximity, separation rather than interracial cooperation—that might foster the sympathetic understanding necessary for democracy. It was the same logic, however, that Woodrow Wilson used to justify the legal segregation of government employees. White women had been "forced unnecessarily to sit at desks with colored men," his son-in-law Secretary of the Treasury William G. McAdoo explained, and this "proximity created 'friction.'"[187]

This was a position neither African American leaders nor their white allies had accepted throughout the 1910s as they watched racial tensions mount. In the wake of the riot, however, they were a minority. Despite their best efforts, Chicago's schools drifted toward segregation.[188] One white parent summed up the growing sentiment among many of her race: "It is all wrong for colored children and white children to be in school together. There should be separate schools, because the two races of children are as different in everything as in their color."[189] Another called for the "complete segregation of the races . . . two entirely distinct and separate castes." The rise of segregated schools boded ill for the proponents of democratic social knowledge, who had sought to find commonalities and believed that racial differences were reconcilable. Indeed, along with race riots, Jim Crow and other practices of racism helped lay the groundwork for what would, in the 1920s, become a full-scale indictment of participatory democracy. As democratic theorist and journalist Walter Lippmann put it in his 1922 book *Public Opinion*, "the failure of self-governing people to transcend their casual experience and their prejudice, by inventing, creating, and organizing a machinery of knowledge" threatened democracy itself.[190]

185. *Chicago Defender*, August 17, 1918.
186. Ibid.
187. Quoted in Rogin, "Sword Became a Flashing Vision," 155.
188. Chicago Commission on Race Relations, *Negro in Chicago*. As Robin Bachin has suggested, the commission was an example of activist social science. Its members drew on social science methods to inform public policy. Its interracial composition was an important recognition of the necessity of integrated efforts to prevent future violence. Its methods and language drew from the emerging Chicago school of sociology, which sought to determine the environmental causes of urban problems. Bachin, *Building the South Side*, 299–302. Nonetheless, the commission's report was only advisory and was fairly conservative in tone.
189. *Chicago Tribune*, August 6, 1919; *Daily News*, August 5, 1919.
190. Walter Lippmann, *Public Opinion* (New York: Free Press, 1965), 230.

Conclusion

Despite the best efforts of African Americans and their white allies, Chicago's schools and neighborhoods became more segregated than they had been when the century began. In light of the persistence of racist sentiments, it is tempting to see the failure of democratic social knowledge to bring significant advances in democratic practices. The limitations of democratic social knowledge to off-set growing white racism suggested that, while it could be a valuable means of reform, it was insufficient by itself.

Thus reformers like Wells-Barnett turned to the political arena, promoting racial solidarity to influence politics. Wells used the Negro Fellowship League (NFL), the settlement she established in 1911, as a base.[191] Though she and other African American leaders worked with white politicians, in the black commu-nity they emphasized the importance of pursuing a racial agenda. Calling upon government to represent and protect their rights as a disadvantaged group in the polity, these black reformers contributed to the notion of a pluralist critique of state sovereignty that emerged following World War I. Pluralism posited that society was composed of antagonistic groups that are united by common inter-ests and require the state to serve as an arbiter that maintains justice and stabil-ity.[192] Their strategy proved its value when, in 1904, Edward Green was elected to the state legislature from Chicago's south side. He was instrumental in passing a bill designed to suppress mob violence.[193] The law was tested when a black man was lynched on November 11, 1909, in a town located in the extreme southern portion of the state. Under the provisions of the law, the sheriff was removed from office.[194] Tough laws backed by black political mobilization helped secure African Americans' rights.

Wells increased her efforts to obtain women's suffrage and mobilize Chi-cago's black voters. Like most black women supporting suffrage, she viewed it as a means to secure political and legal recognition of African American con-cerns.[195] In 1910 she had started the Women's Second Ward Republican Club,

191. The settlement maintained a reading room, offered temporary lodging, and ran an employ-ment service. Situated in the middle of the vice district, the NFL catered specifically to migrants, workers, and the morally suspect—those the FDC tended to neglect. The NFL was decidedly differ-ent from the FDC or even Hull House in that it promoted racial solidarity rather than interracialism. McMurry, *To Keep the Waters Troubled*, 289.

192. Robert Westbrook, *John Dewey and American Democracy* (Ithaca, NY: Cornell University Press, 1991), 245–49.

193. The statute punished those who incited lynchings and provided that aggrieved parties could sue for damages against the city and county in which lynchings occurred. Furthermore, any lynching would warrant removal of the sheriff from office for failure to fulfill his duties.

194. Ida B. Wells-Barnett, "How Enfranchisement Stops Lynching," *Original Rights* (June 1910): 42–53, reprinted in Thompson, *Ida B. Wells-Barnett*.

195. Glenda Gilmore, *Gender and Jim Crow*; Hazel Carby, *Reconstructing Womanhood*; Rosalyn

which sought "to assist the men in getting better laws for the race and having representation in everything which tends to the uplift of the city and its government."[196] After women gained the vote in state and local elections in 1913, Wells organized the Alpha Suffrage Club. This was an interracial endeavor, but the main focus was on the political education of black women. Like Civic Federation ward organizations, it distributed lists of candidates, made recommendations, circulated directories of voting locations, and instructed women in how to use the voting machine.

The club also sponsored speakers, and candidates frequently appeared to outline their platforms. But the ultimate purpose of the Alpha Suffrage Club was to secure a place "to study political and civic questions for themselves" so that the women might then prove "strong enough to help elect some conscientious race man as alderman."[197] Indeed, once black women gained the vote, they were a deciding factor in electing an African American alderman from the heavily black Second Ward. Their door-to-door canvassing paid off when Oscar DePriest, the Republican candidate, was elected to the city council over three white men. The ward's African American women were credited with giving DePriest his victory, and in 1915 African Americans helped elect William Hale Thompson as mayor.[198] In return, the newly elected mayor of Chicago became a political ally of African Americans, so much so that he even became known as "the negro mayor."

These political successes certainly did not herald the end of racial oppression in the city or the state. Only a few years later, in 1917, East St. Louis, Illinois experienced a bloody race riot, and on June 30, 1919, Wells wrote an editorial to the Chicago Tribune, foreshadowing the Chicago race riot three weeks later.[199] However, they illustrated that methods of democratic social knowledge were insufficient without political mobilization. Political solidarity had to transcend class differences among blacks, a fact that Wells recognized when she opened her Negro Fellowship League and welcomed gamblers and unemployed black men, men for whom the FDC had no programs.

The contrast between the Frederick Douglass Center, dedicated to breaking

Terborg-Penn, "Ida B. Wells-Barnett and the Alpha Suffrage Club of Chicago," in One Woman, One Vote: Rediscovering the Woman Suffrage Movement, ed. Marjorie Spruill Wheeler, 263–76 (Troutdale, OR: New Sage, 1995).

196. Broad Ax, April 9, 1912.

197. Ibid., November 15, 1913, quoted in Knupfer, Toward a Tenderer Humanity, 52.

198. Wanda Hendricks, "'Vote for the Advantage of Ourselves and Our Race': The Election of the First Black Alderman in Chicago," Illinois State Historical Journal 87 (1994): 171–84, and Hendricks, Gender, Race, and Politics in the Midwest.

199. Wells's editorial, although dated June 30, 1919, actually appeared in the Chicago Tribune on July 7, 1919. For information about the riot see Tuttle, Race Riot; Chicago Commission on Race Relations, Negro in Chicago.

down racial barriers by forging social relationships with whites, and the Negro Fellowship League, with its emphasis on black racial solidarity, reveals one of the central tensions within interracial politics and ultimately one of the challenges for democratic social knowledge: the tensions between a politics that sought to transcend a particular group identity and one that fostered it as the anchor of a political strategy. Of course, it would be an oversimplification to suggest that either of these organizations and the black community in general relied solely on a single strategy. Rather, the two settlements, along with the other efforts at racial reform discussed in this chapter, point to the challenges of forging democratic relationships and politics that both recognized and engaged differences and transcended them.

Using proximity and mutuality to promote social relationships across race, the FDC implicitly encouraged a color-blind society whose politics encouraged sympathetic understanding while downplaying racial difference. Such a position demanded that government protect the rights of the individual political actor, expecting the state to protect procedural justice—the right to vote, due process, trial by jury—for all equally. Thus, black and white race reformers joined together in organizations like the FDC and the NAACP to rally for a racially blind liberal state. By encouraging mutuality and sympathy, democratic social knowledge would ideally overcome racism and discrimination that spread from personal prejudices into public life and political policy and that threatened the realization of liberal democracy.

But as Ida Wells knew from her experiences and indeed as we see in the creation of segregated schools, dependence on mutuality and sympathy was not enough; the NFL thus used an additional tactic to secure the same end. It encouraged a politics of racial solidarity—one fostered by African Americans' particular collective (as opposed to individual) experiences of racism—and responded with a racially conscious political subjectivity. Experiential knowledge in this case served to challenge Chicago's liberal republican framework in two ways. First, the overarching commonality in blacks' experience pointed to the deeply entrenched practice of *institutional* racism and challenged the widely accepted notion of equal opportunity that undergirded the liberal republicanism in which so many of Chicago's white civic elites believed. Careful attention to racial experience, coupled with activist social science, indicated that racism foreclosed the free market's ability to sort out the worthy from the unworthy. It opened up the question of whether the state needed policies that were conscious of distinct groups to secure the equality of opportunity and justice promised by liberal democracy and to ensure that the polity was truly inclusive.[200] Second,

---

200. Jeff Madrick, "Inequality and Democracy," in *The Fight Is for Democracy: Winning the War of Ideas in America and the World*, ed. George Packer, 241–64 (New York: Perennial, 2003).

the politics of racial solidarity threatened the ideal of the autonomous political actor that anchored liberal political theory. Democratic social knowledge shaped by the particular set of experiences, which African Americans labeled as similar and thus collective, offered a different basis for political subjectivity—group politics in which individual political autonomy was attained by forging collective subjectivities and projects.

Like the reformers at Hull House and in arbitration debates discussed in previous chapters, racial leaders used the particular collective experiences of blacks to articulate not just new social knowledge but new political subjectivities as well, both built around group identities. As we see in the final chapter, civic elites who composed the CFC were increasingly uncomfortable with this new style of politics based on a collective subjectivity, as they believed it hastened the fatal drifting apart they so feared. The tensions played out in Chicago's charter campaign—tensions over a vision of the state as embodying a broader spectrum of the democratic polity and its needs and of politics as recognizing the particular collective experiences of groups—suggest that the struggles over democratic social knowledge ultimately affected the arena of formal politics. This is where we now turn.

6

"Drawn on Rational and Scientific Lines"

The Fate of Democratic Social Knowledge

We are all seeking to get constitutional reform; we desire the best, safest, and speediest method; to find this the subject should be studied as a scientific or objective question is studied. To "take sides" for the mere sake of holding to a prior impression or opinion or of working up a fight and having something to "champion" is mischievous and undignified.[1]

During the Progressive Era, Chicago was a city in flux, searching for ways to prevent a fatal drifting apart along class, race, ethnic, and gender lines. It was a wide-open moment of crisis when economic transformation threatened permanent class conflict, urbanization and immigration brought social alienation, and racial and gender hierarchy and disfranchisement challenged the universalist claims of liberal democracy. As we have seen, the Chicago reformers responded creatively. What emerged from their efforts was the outline of a democratic social knowledge whose methods privileged proximity, sympathetic understanding, experience, interaction, and the value of multiple perspectives in framing social problems and solutions. Democratic social knowledge seemed a hopeful means to stem the political and ultimately epistemological divide modernity posed for this most modern of nineteenth-century U.S. cities and, in the process, to redefine democracy as praxis of mutuality, respect, proximate interaction, sympathetic understanding, and social action. As we will see shortly, conflicts over democratic social knowledge ultimately erupted into the arena of formal politics, when Chicagoans sought to create a new city charter. In the charter campaign we see a struggle over politics as the site of application for "scientific

1. The epigraph to this chapter is drawn from E. Allen Frost, Robert McCurdy, and Harry S. Mecartney, *Chicago and the Constitution: Report to the Civic Federation of Chicago* (Chicago: Barnard and Miller Printers, 1902), 7.

or objective" knowledge and as the arena in which the "opinions" of special interests are cast as "mischievous and undignified." It exposes the impact that epistemological conflicts had for the practice of formal politics.

The previous chapters have introduced a number of historical actors, often treated disparately by historians, who offered a range of approaches to democratic social knowledge. The civic elites who comprised the majority of the Civic Federation sought to bring a variety of groups into conversation with one another, though its members struggled with negotiating between a deeply entrenched liberal republicanism and a more open-ended vision of democratic social knowledge that included conversations between experts, elites, and representatives from labor and ethnic communities. At Hull House, Jane Addams and her fellow residents laid the foundation for a democratic social knowledge in their rich array of settlement activities and ultimately created an activist social science that wed community participation, social science expertise, and political activism into new demands upon the state. Allying with labor leaders, white middle-class elites outlined a foundation for labor conciliation and arbitration that responded to the hostility and violence of labor strikes like that at the Pullman Carworks. They ultimately served to position the state as an arbiter of last resort in cases of irreconcilable economic claims.

Moreover, in the face of growing racial animosity, African Americans claimed cultural agency as they sought to introduce their perspectives about race into the marketplace of ideas. They and their white allies challenged racist social knowledge through a variety of strategies ranging from proximity, embodiment, and visual culture, although—like the white female reformers and unions—they also turned to politics and the state to arbitrate their political rights. In the sum of these efforts we see the outlines of a democratic social knowledge operating at the local level and giving flesh to a commitment to the inclusion of a wide array of perspectives in framing social explanations and cultural meanings and in asserting claims upon the state.

The struggles over democratic social knowledge told in this book laid bare significant matters born of the cultural, political, and ideological conjunctures of intellectual reorientation, class formation, and economic and family transformations that stressed the nineteenth-century boundaries of patriarchy and liberalism, race and politics. Ultimately, the reformers' struggles over democratic social knowledge raised important questions about democracy and expertise, about power and the democratic polity, about the responsibilities and limits of the state, and about the foundations of justice, questions that reformers confronted directly, though in the long run their ability to respond successfully to them were mixed.

In the attempt to reconcile democracy and expertise, the reformers' efforts to incorporate local, experiential knowledge with social science expertise were significant. Perhaps the most successful example of this marriage came in the work of the Hull House women, who used an activist social knowledge to inform a new direction for the state, one that served as a proponent of social justice, not just a defense of liberal property rights. The Frederick Douglass Club also served as a location in which to wed social scientific studies of the African American community with local investigators familiar with and attentive to the experiences of the members of that group. The Civic Federation of Chicago brought together different segments of the community with social scientists, engineers, and medical experts to work toward a fuller understanding of the problems of urban infrastructure and health and the challenges of political corruption. Even conciliation, arbitration, and trade agreements were ways for unions and management to collectively frame workers' knowledge of industrial problems, as we saw in the Congress on Arbitration and Conciliation and complaints against Pullman's managers in the aftermath of the strike. In each of these examples, reformers sought to legitimate a wide range of perspectives, and in so doing, they raised the epistemological—and political—status of the groups that had frequently been marginalized outside of the political system.

In seeking to legitimate frameworks of local knowledge, the reformers also recognized the status claims of unions, women, immigrants, and African Americans and thus attempted to widen the democratic polity.[2] They viewed the particular collective experiences of different groups as resources both for understanding social problems and forging public solutions—for creating democratic social knowledge through a process of deliberation and experimentation. African Americans illustrated this point most persistently, as reformers like Ida Wells and Fannie Barrier Williams pointed out how racism had structured the African American experience. Examining American democracy and the liberal tradition from the perspective of African Americans' experiences suggested the limits of a liberal republican narrative that promised equal opportunity, privileged the autonomous political actor, and looked suspiciously at group identities and politics. These points were further evident in workers' experiences under new forms of industrial capitalism and scientific management. At Hull House, moreover, the experiences of the women and ethnic working classes that came together demonstrated the limits of the industrial wage system to distribute resources in a manner that adequately provided a living.[3] For women, immigrants, workers,

2. In discussing the categories of unions, women, immigrants, and African Americans, I do not mean to treat them monolithically. Indeed, identities of race, ethnicity, and class were fluid during this period, with political actors claiming and/or being marked by one or several simultaneously. See, for example, Mae Ngai, "The Architecture of Race in American Immigration Law: A Reexamination of the Immigration Act of 1924," *Journal of American History* 86, no. 1 (1999): 67–92.

3. Women's activists and labor unionists were not the only ones arguing this point. As Nancy Cohen has argued, social scientists, particularly economists, were divided over this issue for decades, and it remained for many the most pressing social problem of the industrial era. Cohen, *The*

and African Americans, their membership in collective groups proved effective in translating their experiences into politically recognizable social claims. In so doing they further challenged the vision of justice promulgated by liberal republicanism, a vision that seemed to them too abstract and too connected to the liberal market. Instead, they used their experiences to point out injustices or to offer a new logic of justice based on needs or social claims.[4] However, although liberal republicanism's insistence on the justice of the free market and the necessity of laissez-faire faced bitter attacks, it was resilient, leading some reformers to imagine that some conflicts might indeed be irreconcilable if left in the realm of voluntary action.[5] Despite the emphasis on a process of democratic social knowledge that encouraged mutuality, respect, and sympathetic understanding, clashes between visions of rights, responsibilities, and justice—conflicts that were deeply rooted in epistemological differences—ultimately led these different sectors to seek protection from a state that no longer simply defended private property but had to arbitrate social justice as well.

Although deliberative processes and social relationships that built mutuality, respect, sympathetic understanding, and trust were critical in forging democratic social knowledge, in the end they proved insufficient in themselves to address the liberal democratic dilemmas of freedom, rights, and power wrought by equal, yet irreconcilable, claims of democracy and expertise. Nonetheless, the reformers' insistence that these dispositions were essential for democratic equality, which they encouraged in wide-ranging efforts such as the neighborliness of social settlements and labor arbitration, suggested their commitment to a conception of democracy apart from the procedural practices of voting. They insisted that the challenges of pluralism and differences required a democratic praxis that brought together dispositions, social action, and politics. The impulses of sympathetic understanding, mutuality, interaction, and deliberation beneath the struggle over democratic social knowledge affected political life and fostered civic engagement with pressing public matters. Indeed, politics was an arena in which competing social meanings, explanations of problems, and ideas

---

Reconstruction of American Liberalism, 1865–1914 (Chapel Hill: University of North Carolina Press, 2002).

4. Nancy Fraser, Unruly Practices: Power, Discourse, and Gender in Contemporary Social Theory (Minneapolis: University of Minnesota Press, 1989); Nancy Fraser and Axel Honneth, Redistribution or Recognition?: A Political-philosophical Exchange, trans. Joel Golb, James Ingram, and Christiane Wilke (London: Verso, 2003).

5. Mary O. Furner, "The Republican Tradition and the New Liberalism: Social Investigation, State Building, and Social Learning in the Gilded Age," in The State and Social Investigation in Britain and the United States, ed. Michael J. Lacey and Mary O. Furner, 171–242 (New York: Woodrow Wilson Center Press and Cambridge University Press, 1993). Furner discusses two potential strands of new liberalism, voluntarism and democratic collectivism, arguing that American political traditions led to a voluntaristic framework as the basis for state policy making, despite the support for the latter among some social scientists and labor leaders.

for solutions were negotiated as various groups espousing diverse visions sought legitimacy. Democratic praxis thus promoted arenas for public deliberation where democratic social knowledge would be translated into political visions—and where competing epistemologies lay deeply beneath public debate.

If we follow our historical actors once more, this time to the political table as they sat down to (or were excluded from) negotiations over a new city charter, we see that the struggle over democratic social knowledge was, in some measure, successful in the short term but largely lost in the larger picture of the twentieth century. Though most players in Chicago's public life believed that the city needed a new charter, the process was contentious and ultimately failed to secure it. Women's cross-class, interethnic groups of settlement houses, labor unions, and clubs mobilized into an anticharter coalition that opposed their former allies in the Civic Federation and worked successfully to defeat the charter.[6] The story of the charter campaign suggests that those union members, women, and ethnic groups vying for recognition and political inclusion were able to use the political stage to advance their reform agendas.[7] But these were only short-term victories. In the long run, their successes were mixed, leaving their inheritors to wrestle with unresolved questions about democratic society. As we pause briefly to consider the charter campaign we will see how the battle over the charter illuminates issues raised in other chapters and speaks to the possibilities and limitations of democratic praxis today.

The Charter Campaign

Charters establish cities as legal entities and give shape to local government; they arrange social, economic, and political relationships in the city. Charters thus reflect an understanding of social responsibilities, state functions, and individual and corporate rights. As such, a charter is much more than a blueprint for local government; it is also an expression of a negotiated social knowledge among citizens in constituting themselves as a polity.

6. Maureen Flanagan, *Seeing with Their Hearts: Chicago Women and the Vision of the Good City, 1871–1933* (Princeton, NJ: Princeton University Press, 2002), 79–80.

7. Maureen Flanagan, *Charter Reform in Chicago* (Carbondale: Southern Illinois University Press, 1987), and Thomas Pegram, *Partisans and Progressives: Private Interest and Public Policy in Illinois, 1870–1922* (Urbana: University of Illinois Press, 1992), provide the most thorough accounts of the charter campaign. These books have been useful in pointing me to several sources connected to the charter. Though I draw from their basic narratives of the charter campaign in the discussion that follows, my emphasis is different. Without disagreeing entirely with their interpretation, I argue that the charter campaign helps us understand how the various questions about democratic social knowledge explored in the previous chapters were played out in the formal political arena. In contrast, Flanagan argues that the charter campaign was one of competing visions of urban government, and Pegram describes it as an example of how partisanship overshadowed progressive reform.

Like most major cities during the era, Chicago had outgrown its 1870 charter and badly needed a new one to more effectively govern a metropolis then exceeding two million people. Though the need for municipal services rose with the population, the city was burdened with an inadequate and cumbersome arrangement in governing bodies and taxing powers due to state incorporation of provisions that strictly defined municipal structures and revenue collections and left matters regarding public utilities, franchises, and municipal ownership to be decided in the state legislature.[8] As early as 1896, the Civic Federation of Chicago (CFC) explored ways to secure a new charter, and when the opportunity arose in 1906, it spearheaded a convention that brought together representatives from around the city.[9] Delegates considered a number of measures, among them new taxing and administrative functions, home rule measures that would free the city from extensive oversight by the state legislature, election procedures including primary and referendum laws, school board powers, women's suffrage, and municipal ownership.

One of the issues of the charter campaign as a case study of democratic social knowledge was the role of expertise in democracy. While democratic social knowledge offered an alternative framework to emerging social scientific expertise, one that sought to merge distanced and neutral expertise with grassroots proximate experiences and local knowledge, the businessmen of the CFC and its allies in the charter campaign privileged social scientific and political expertise shorn of its connection to popular deliberation. The CFC explained its preferred methods in 1902 as it spearheaded the process of constitutional change. "Debate, even by the best lawyers and thinkers," announced a CFC pamphlet, "is not enough. It is a valuable method when preceded by painstaking investigation, by the methodical collection of data and items of experience, by suggested drafts in pursuance thereof, and by printed arguments covering the natural scope of the subject."[10] Merritt Starr, a member of the businessmen's Union League Club, suggested to CFC president B. E. Sunny that the new charter be "drawn on rational and scientific lines and [that it] utilize to the upmost [*sic*] all of the lessons of experience and embodying no rash experiments which have no justification in experience at their back."[11] A CFC committee urged that any constitutional changes be approached

8. Flanagan, *Charter Reform in Chicago,* 23–27; Pegram, *Partisans and Progressives;* Civic Federation of Chicago, *Second Annual Report;* letter from Joint Committee on Constitutional Revision, February 1899, in Anita McCormick Blaine Papers, Wisconsin State Historical Society, Box 182, Folder "Civic Federation of Chicago, 1898–1900," Madison, Wisconsin.

9. *Report of the Legislative Committee of the Civic Federation,* n.d., 6, Chicago Historical Society; "A Great and Better Chicago: How to Get It," 1899, Chicago Historical Society.

10. *Chicago and the Constitution,* 17–18.

11. Merritt Starr to B. E. Sunny, April 14, 1904, Civic Federation Papers, Box No. 3, Chicago Historical Society. Maureen Flanagan, in *Charter Reform in Chicago,* cites Starr to show how elites in the city sought to dominate the process of writing a new charter. My point here is different as I

"as a scientific or objective question is studied," which increasingly meant from the standpoint of an all-knowing, distanced investigator, not from deliberation among participants with a multitude of positions. Indeed, the committee urged that, "if in handling such grave and important matters we can get rid of banquet opinions and mass meeting skill, not the least of our burdens will be rolled away."[12] In preparation for writing a new charter, the CFC built up a library on municipal and state politics, solicited the experiences of civic organizations in other cities, and drew upon the expertise of social scientists.[13] During the ensuing convention, Charles Merriam and Ernest Freund, political scientists at the University of Chicago, were the most prominent members of the convention, as delegates called upon them to verify the wisdom and legality of the charter as it unfolded. Striking in this process is the rejection of the mass meeting and coordinated discussions among different sectors of the population—democratic tools that had been so valuable in forming the CFC in the first place and in gaining support for its most successful reform endeavors, such as civil service and the repeal of particularly loathsome public franchises.

Coupled with a rejection of the participatory interaction of open meetings and public forums, the CFC's call for study and expertise indicated a new orientation toward politics as one of administration and regulation. The charter that was finally drawn up reflected this orientation. Despite widespread interest in municipal ownership of public utilities and transportation, the charter called for a regulatory body instead.[14] Recommendations for the school board included maintaining its appointive and unpaid status and expanding the superintendent's powers.[15] It also demanded home rule powers, which meant locally centralized governmental authority, more rational city administration, and expanded power over public finances, not the power for residents to vote on socially charged issues like the regulation of drinking establishments, which unions and ethnic societies demanded. The emphasis on administration certainly

---

emphasize that Starr's letter is part of a larger framework supporting a culture of expertise.

12. *Chicago and the Constitution*, 13.

13. CFC Minutes, May 20, 1897, Chicago Historical Society, Civic Federation of Chicago Papers, Box 1; C. C. Willard to Municipal Voters' League, January 3, 1906, in Citizen's Association of Chicago, Box 6, Folder 4, Chicago Historical Society; also "List of Titles on Municipal Government with Special Reference to City Charters," in City Club Papers, Box 20, Folder 2. Daniel T. Rodgers discusses the trans-Atlantic community of discourse that developed around these municipal and political issues in his book *Atlantic Crossings: Social Politics in a Progressive Age* (Cambridge, MA: Belknap Press of Harvard University Press, 1998).

14. Georg Leidenberger discusses support for municipal ownership in "Working-class Progressivism and the Politics of Transportation in Chicago, 1895–1907" (PhD diss., University of North Carolina, Chapel Hill, 1995), 113–64.

15. Julia Wrigley, *Class Politics and Public Schools* (New Brunswick, NJ: Rutgers University Press, 1982); David Hogan, *Class and Reform: School and Society in Chicago, 1880–1930* (Philadelphia: Temple University Press, 1985).

responded to a real need to reorganize Chicago's ineffective and outdated governing structure. However, it also reflected a trend among political scientists who emphasized the practical study of administration and politics as separate from the study of the state.[16] The shift won the political scientists, people like Merriam, for example, allies among reformers and civic elites and helped them to secure the status of their discipline in reform debates that emerged during the Progressive Era. Merriam in particular worked to establish ways for technical experts to serve society, though he was committed to democratic politics and cautioned repeatedly that social scientists should never control decision making.[17] In the best of worlds, the emphasis on administration—freed from partisan wrangling—left politics potentially as an arena to guide policy, particularly if voters could exercise the initiative and referendum. But it also threatened to insulate the experts and secure their power—or at least make them vulnerable to such public perceptions.[18] While the emphasis on administration and regulation by experts did not of itself foreclose the possibility of forging a democratic social knowledge from deliberations between experts and city residents, like those in the Working People's Social Science Club, for example, in the particular case of the CFC it did indicate its growing suspicion of democratic politics as a process of interaction among a number of groups.

16. At the time, political scientists sought to stake out their professional territory by moving their discipline away from a Hegelian framework of the "State" and the art of statecraft and toward a more practical study of "politics" and "administration." The new approach promised to make the discipline more empirical and win them allies among municipal reformers. Daniel T. Rodgers, *Contested Truths: Keywords in American Politics since Independence* (New York: Basic Books, 1987). For an example, see Woodrow Wilson, "The Study of Administration," *Political Science Quarterly* 2, no. 2 (June 1887): 197–222. This approach also obscured the role women played in restructuring the state since most of their work was done outside of formal "politics" or "administration." Helene Silverberg, "'A Government of Men': Gender, the City, and the New Science of Politics," in *Gender and American Social Science: The Formative Years*, ed. Helene Silverberg, 166 (Princeton, NJ: Princeton University Press, 1998). Also Camilla Stivers, *Bureau Men, Settlement Women: Constructing Public Administration in the Progressive Era* (Lawrence: University of Kansas Press, 2000).

17. Mark Smith, *Social Science in the Crucible: The American Debate over Objectivity and Purpose, 1918–1941* (Durham, NC: Duke University Press, 1994), 100. Smith's discussion of Merriam's efforts in the 1920s and 1930s to establish the Social Science Research Council and the Public Administration Clearing House and his role on the National Planning Board during the New Deal sheds light on the difficulty social scientists faced in walking the frequently blurred line between modern democratic and technocratic society. He points out the tension between value-neutral knowledge, which did not engage normative concerns, and a purposive approach, which insisted on preconceived goals for social science and the social scientist's personal role in determining those goals.

18. This has been one of the complaints leveled against the state transformation of the Progressive Era and beyond and served as an explanation for the decline in voter participation. Robert Wachbroit, "The Changing Role of Expertise," in *Civil Society, Democracy, and Civic Renewal*, ed. Robert K. Fullinwider, 355–74 (Lanham, MD: Rowman and Littlefield, 1999). Also Michael McGerr, *The Decline of Popular Politics: The American North, 1865–1928* (New York: Oxford University Press, 1986), and *A Fierce Discontent: The Rise and Fall of the Progressive Movement in America, 1870–1920* (New York: Free Press, 2003).

◭

However, Chicago's female reformers, ethnic societies, and workers had a different vision of the democratic polity, one that both expanded the political community by securing women's suffrage and put more direct governing power in voters' hands. The marginal political position women confronted mediated their other class and race concerns during the charter campaign since, without the vote, women had to work through men to get their perspectives into public debate. Women from across the class and ethnic spectrum joined in the charter debate.[19] They sought full recognition and legitimacy through the suffrage. The Chicago Political Equality League (CPEL), founded in 1894 to "'promote the study of political science and government'" and to "'foster and extend the political rights and privileges of women,'" joined with members of the Illinois Equal Suffrage Association, the Chicago Women's Trade Union League, the Chicago Teachers Federation, and settlement house residents and their immigrant neighbors to include women's suffrage in the charter debate.[20] A coalition of leaders representing one hundred women's organizations attempted to meet with the charter convention members even before the official deliberations began so that they might shape the direction of the suffrage debate.[21] Suffrage rights were particularly important since women's political visions, unlike those of elite businessmen who were seeking to build municipal government "on the same general principles that prevail[ed] in the management of business enterprises," focused instead on restructuring city government and institutions to help provide for the common welfare.[22] Women reformers based their visions

19. Flanagan, *Seeing with Their Hearts,* 76. Their hopes for the charter seemed realistic enough. As early as 1899, the CFC had turned to Chicago's elite women and appealed to their "high standard of American citizenship" to solicit money for the charter campaign. Letter from Thomas J. Finney to "Dear Madam," March 4, 1899, in Anita McCormick Blaine Papers, Box 82, "Civic Federation of Chicago, 1898–1900."

20. Flanagan, *Seeing with Their Hearts,* 74, from Chicago Political Equality League, "By-laws," in *First Annual Report* (1895–1896). The following discussion of women's efforts to insert themselves into the charter debate draws from Flanagan, *Seeing with Their Hearts,* 74–77. The women's cooperation illustrates that, unlike in other cities, Chicago's suffrage movement was a cross-class, interethnic endeavor. For comparison with other cities divided by class and ethnicity, see James J. Connolly, *The Triumph of Ethnic Progressivism: Urban Political Culture in Boston, 1900–1925* (Cambridge, MA: Harvard University Press, 1998); Philip J. Ethington, *The Public City: The Political Construction of Urban Life in San Francisco, 1850–1900* (New York: Cambridge University Press, 1994).

21. Chicago Woman's Club Minutes, February 27,1907, report of the Political Equality League.

22. Flanagan, *Seeing with Their Hearts,* 78, 74. The original quotation is from A. C. Bartlett, June 18, 1906, to Catherine Waugh McCulloch, in McCulloch Collection, Arthur and Elizabeth Schlesinger Library, Microfilm Reel 1. On the importance of suffrage for Chicago women to pursue their own political agendas, see, for example, Grace Wilber Trout, "Early League History," Chicago Political Equality Yearbook, 1911, 58–62, in the League of Women Voters of Chicago, Folder 61, Chicago Political Equality League Yearbooks, 1909–1916. In her article Trout equates the lack of political

on the democratic social knowledge emanating from places like social settlements and clubs. Though they had succeeded in working through husbands, male voluntary associations, and unions, they needed the vote to bring it to bear on public life.

As did women, union representatives espoused a vision of democracy less concerned with a politics of administration than a politics that put more power in voters' hands. Their vision of the democratic polity was more expansive, and they refused to accept a framework of expertise that eliminated their voices. We saw such examples in chapter 2 in the matter of reform and again in chapter 4 on arbitration. In the charter campaign, the unionists again staked out this position; they sought to strengthen their role in local government by restructuring public school administration.

J. J. Linehan, a convention delegate from the CFL and former CFC founder, proposed to replace the appointed board with an elected school board whose members would be paid. Under his plan, the superintendent would be subordinate to the board.[23] Such measures would allow workers to serve the city and give them more voice in school governance. In contrast, the Merchants Club petitioned the convention to reorganize Chicago schools on a "rational and businesslike basis," and indeed, charter provisions reduced the size of the school board, maintained its appointive membership, reinforced the supremacy of the superintendent, and rejected the idea of paying board members.[24] The CFL responded through its own petition that if such measures were adopted it would "'resist by every honorable means any attempt of any and all interests and influences to take away the control of the Chicago school system from the people of Chicago.'"[25] Not easily acquiescing to the emerging power of educational experts, the workers asserted their demands for a prominent voice in public education.[26]

---

power with the inferior status of women. She also emphasizes that the CPEL sought to investigate questions that "directly and indirectly affect woman and her environment and that "it would be hard to find any great question that doesn't." In framing women's concerns in this way, she emphasizes not that women had a separate political agenda from men but that they offered an additional vantage point onto political issues.

23. Pegram, *Partisans and Progressives*, 104. Julia Wrigley, *Class Politics and Public Schools: Chicago, 1900–1950* (New Brunswick, NJ: Rutgers University Press, 1982).

24. The Merchant's Club letter to the Charter Convention was reprinted in *The Public*, November 19, 1906, available in Chicago Teachers' Federation Papers, Box 39, Folder 2, Chicago Historical Society. Pegram, *Partisans and Progressives*, 104; Flanagan, *Charter Reform in Chicago*, 79. These provisions closely followed the recommendations of the proposed Harper law of 1899, which had met resistance from city teachers and the working classes.

25. Chicago Charter Convention, *Proceedings*, December 20, 1906, 561.

26. Working-class efforts to maintain their input on schooling matters dated back to the 1880s and 1890s. Workers fought the attempts of business elites and educational experts to scale back arts education in the schools and resisted a narrowed version of vocational education that they feared would limit opportunities for the children of Chicago's working classes. In a report on the proposed

As Linehan explained to the charter convention, the workers' participation in educational decision making was a significant way of confirming their political legitimacy: " '[T]he great civic pride which brings a millionaire who has no children . . . into the mayor's office every year endeavoring to get an appointment on the school board is not any more worthy of recognition than the pride of the workmen, who supply all the children and all the money for the maintenance of the public institutions of this city.' "[27] Linehan's argument struck at the core of an emerging administrative Progressivism that heralded businessmen and educational experts as the best source of leadership. His reasoning was similar to that of workers during the depression of 1893, when workers had suggested that their contributions to city building rendered the wider community responsible to aid them in economic downturns and they demanded public jobs programs. In this case, Linehan argued that the workers' contributions of human and economic resources to public schools were a resource that merited their inclusion in educational matters.

Demands for autonomy and increased access to political decision making were common threads weaving together workers' involvement in the charter campaign, but they also believed home rule meant more direct popular decision making in crucial areas affecting city residents. In the area of administration, for example, they urged the convention to provide the city council with full powers to assess, levy, and collect taxes for municipal purposes; as a check on abuses to those powers, they included a mandatory popular referendum on revenue matters. Furthermore, delegate J. J. Linehan attacked efforts to lengthen aldermanic terms from two to four years since this would decrease popular representation. The people might change their minds within two years, he argued, or they might desire to use elections to send a message to the aldermen or mayor.[28] Linehan had been a founding member of the CFC but had increasingly distanced himself from the organization in the wake of its failure to mediate the Pullman Strike and its growing affinity with conservative business interests. Linehan now found himself at odds with most CFC members as he expressed serious reservations about the way the charter took shape, arguing on behalf of his constituents who believed it did not go far enough to extend power to local citizens.

Indeed, Chicago laborers particularly sought political mechanisms such as

---

charter, the CFL was wary that the school system would become "'a cog in the capitalist machine so that the children may reach manhood's estate, content in a condition of abject servitude.'" Quoted in Flanagan, *Charter Reform in Chicago,* 118. See also Legislative Committee of the Chicago Federation of Labor, "A Report on Public School Fads" [ca. 1902], Chicago Historical Society. For working-class protests against the loss of power in Chicago schools, see Wrigley, *Class Politics and Public Schools;* David Tyack, *The One Best System: A History of American Urban Education* (Cambridge, MA: Harvard University Press, 1974); Hogan, *Class and Reform.*

27. Charter Convention, *Proceedings,* December 21, 1906, 623.
28. Charter Convention, *Proceedings,* December 11, 1906, 242–46.

the referendum, initiative, and direct primary as a way to further popular control over the city council.[29] Their position marked what would become a hotly contested debate over direct democracy in the ensuing two decades.[30] The supporters of such measures understood them as the difference between a "true" democracy, in which ultimate sovereignty rested in the hands of the people, and representative democracy, which was not, in their minds, actual democracy. The CFL argued that extending political power offered the electorate greater occasion for political education and autonomy. The *Union Labor Advocate* supported a statewide bill granting the initiative and referendum because of "the wholesome effect it would have on the whole people to have removed the sense of dependence, which the people now feel, on the will or whim or possible honesty of one or a few men who often seek and secure office only because of the temptations to betray the public these offices now make possible because of the people's helplessness."[31]

Unions thus linked such political prerogatives to an independent, moral, and active self, the proof of which lay in its attack on political and economic injustice. They saw the administrative functions of government not as an arena separate from them but as subject to them. These efforts to concretize popular democracy in the charter provisions echoed ideas on government and

29. The wide popularity of these electoral reforms was evident in two general elections of 1902 and 1904 in which a majority of Chicagoans voiced their support for these measures. Flanagan, *Charter Reform in Chicago*, 74; *Union Labor Advocate* 3, no. 7 (March 1903); Chicago Federation of Labor Minutes, September 18, 1904.

30. For discussion of the initiative, referendum, and recall, see Delos F. Wilcox, *Government by All the People or the Initiative, the Referendum, and the Recall as Instruments of Democracy* (New York: Macmillan, 1912); William Bennet Munro, ed., *The Initiative, Referendum, and Recall* (New York: Appleton, 1915); Ellis Paxson Oberholtzer, *The Referendum in America Together with Some Chapters on the Initiative and the Recall* (New York: Charles Scribner's Sons, 1911); Hermann Lieb, *The Initiative and Referendum* (Chicago: H. Lieb Jr., 1902); William Horace Brown, "The Popular Initiative as a Method of Legislation and Political Control," *American Journal of Sociology* 10, no. 6 (May 1905): 713–49; Theodore Roosevelt, "The Right of the People to Rule" (Washington, DC: Government Printing Office, 1912). A helpful list of contemporary writings is found in Hermann H. B. Meyer, *Select List of References on the Initiative, Referendum, and Recall* (Washington, DC: Government Printing Office, 1912). For a more recent discussion on direct democracy, see Steven L. Piott, *Giving Voters a Voice: The Origins of the Initiative and Referendum in America* (Columbia: University of Missouri Press, 2003); Thomas E. Cronin, *Direct Democracy: The Politics of Initiative, Referendum, and Recall* (Cambridge, MA: Harvard University Press, 1989); Pegram, *Partisans and Progressives;* Johnston, *Radical Middle Class.* Elizabeth Sanders, *Roots of Reform: Farmers, Workers, and the American State, 1877–1917* (Chicago: University of Chicago Press, 1999), 388, discusses the importance of the mechanisms of direct democracy for farmer and worker movements in the Gilded Age and Progressive Era.

31. *Union Labor Advocate* 3, no. 7 (March 1903): 2–3. Jonathan Bourne Jr. expressed a similar sentiment in "Functions of the Initiative, Referendum, and Recall," in *The Initiative, Referendum, and Recall* (Philadelphia: American Academy of Political and Social Science, 1912), 3–16. He argues that one of the functions of the initiative and referendum is to "educate and develop the people." See especially pp. 6–9.

democratic participation that had surfaced during the Pullman Strike (chapter 4), when strikers had criticized their employer for undermining the political freedom necessary for full citizenship. A lack of political power and the moral duties it demanded left residents dependent and humiliatingly childlike.[32] In the face of a trend toward expertise and administration in political life, their position pointed to the educational and moral value of participatory democracy.

Chicago's ethnic communities likewise articulated a vision of democratic politics that posited home rule as a means to recognize residents' autonomy. Represented at the convention by only a few prosperous ethnic businessmen, thousands of Chicago's Germans, Bohemians, Poles, Swedes, Danes, and Italians joined together to form the United Societies for Local Self-Government. They sought extensive home rule powers in order to protect activities that were dimensions of cultural interaction and public life.[33] Along with the unions, the United Societies believed home rule meant more popular decision making in areas affecting city residents such as public schooling, utilities and transportation, and regulation of drinking establishments. Confident of the popularity of its views, the United Societies told the convention, "we believe that we reflect the sentiment of four-fifths of the voters of our city on this subject.... We demand home rule on this question and believe the city council can be trusted to so regulate both matters as to satisfy the true religious sentiments and wants of the large majority of our citizens."[34]

Women's cross-class, interethnic groups of women's clubs, settlement houses, and labor unions mobilized into an anticharter coalition that worked feverishly to defeat the charter.[35] After appointing a special committee to evaluate the charter, the CFL attacked it because it did not provide sufficient democratic measures; pointing out that the charter failed to provide for the local referendum, the committee argued that the charter offered "nothing that will give the people better control of their own affairs ... nothing to preserve the liberties of the people against the encroachments of concentrated wealth and plutocratic greed."[36] The United Societies shared this view, arguing that a ward-redistricting

---

32. Judith Shklar, *American Citizenship: The Quest for Inclusion* (Cambridge, MA: Harvard University Press, 1991).

33. Paul Kleppner, *The Cross of Culture: A Social Analysis of Midwestern Politics, 1850–1900* (New York: Free Press, 1970); John D. Buenker, *Urban Liberalism and Progressive Reform* (New York: Norton, 1978, ca. 1973).

34. Letter to Milton J. Foreman from Fritz Glogauer, Nicholas Michels, and A. Landa, in "Bulletin Published by the United Societies for Local Self-Government," vol. 1, no. 2, December 20, 1906, Chicago Historical Society.

35. Flanagan, *Seeing with Their Hearts*, 79–80.

36. Chicago Federation of Labor Minutes, July 21, 1907. John Fitzpatrick visited other unions to encourage them to defeat the charter. See Chicago Typographical Union No. 16 Minutes, August 25, 1907, Chicago Historical Society.

plan included in the charter favored wealthier neighborhoods and "deprived the workingman of his vote."[37]

While women's organizations, the United Societies, and the CFL were all certainly disappointed that the charter did not provide for their particular interests, their disaffection went deeper; the charter did not address the questions of justice that had emerged in public discussion over the past twenty years. Their visions of justice were expansive, extending to social, political, and economic matters: protection and well-being of children; economic security; voice in workplace decision making and in city affairs. They understood justice as a social construction that was determined by the polity. Thus democratic political mechanisms that widely distributed power were critical. Suspicious that market-mediated justice privileged the city's elite, ethnic leaders and unionists attacked the charter provisions for revenue and taxation. The CFL argued that the revenue and taxation measures benefited only the " 'predatory, tax-dodging, labor baiting interests.' "[38] Other critics suggested that "the kings of Packington, convicted of a thousand offenses against the public from whom they derive their revenue, are near the head of the list of tax-dodgers."[39] Suggesting the extent to which they sought to redefine the purposes and use of the state, the CFL argued that the taxation plan "deprived the masses for the benefit of the few because what really was needed was a scheme to compel all to pay their fair share." In this argument, "fair" did not mean that all should pay the same amount; it meant instead that those who had more should pay more to support the city. Likewise during the Pullman Strike, workers had rejected a notion of justice that guaranteed a return on investment to capitalists by cutting wages. Such principles may have been justified by an older liberal political economy, workers suggested, but they hardly recognized the rights of labor and the social needs of city residents.

Such notions of justice had not rested on a priori principles of the justice of the liberal market. They drew instead from a variety of frameworks—domesticity, labor solidarity, social Christianity. These alternative logics encouraged mutuality, sympathy, and relationships over a strict notion of fairness. Consequently, workers and their female reform allies followed a different democratic logic that linked rights and duties in a socialized rather than an individualistic understanding of society.[40] Their democracy did not locate political authority

37. Quoted in Flanagan, *Charter Reform in Chicago*, 134.
38. Chicago Federation of Labor Minutes, July 21, 1907.
39. *American*, July 5, 1907; Flanagan, *Charter Reform in Chicago*, 120.
40. On Chicago labor and the new liberalism, see Richard Schneirov, *Labor and Urban Politics: Class Conflict and the Origins of Modern Liberalism in Chicago, 1864–97* (Urbana: University of Illinois Press, 1998). For a discussion of variations of new liberalism, see Mary O. Furner, "The Republican Tradition and the New Liberalism: Social Investigation, State Building, and Social Learning in the Gilded Age," in *The State and Social Investigation in Britain and the United States*, ed. Michael

in professional elites or administrators alone but situated it also in an active democratic public life. Articulated by Chicago's working classes and their union representatives, women's organizations, ethnic societies, and African American associations, such ideas had grown out of their experiences—in the home, as members of families, and within the economic system. These formed the basis of their knowledge about society and the foundation of their visions of social reform. Though they often invoked a language of liberal rights, it served a strategic function to win them access to a public hearing in a political culture oriented in that direction.[41]

However, the CFC and other charter supporters dismissed their opponents' viewpoints, thus undermining their legitimacy. Mayor Busse encouraged Chicagoans to vote for the charter because "the best thought of the best citizenship in this community approves the Charter. It is demanded by the press, the pulpit, the commercial and industrial interests."[42] Such comments placed workers, women, immigrants, and other opponents outside of Chicago's liberal republican political community by rendering them irrational and incapable of participating in reasoned (i.e., expert) political debate. Indeed, the day before the referendum, the *Chicago Tribune* ran a front-page cartoon picturing a hand casting a ballot of support for the charter; across the hand was labeled "Progressive Citizen." The CFC further denounced criticism of the charter as "uttered by persons of unsafe theories and principles."[43] Positioning the CFL, the immigrants of the United Societies, and the women of more than one hundred reform organizations as "unsafe" persons, the CFC attempted to draw the boundaries around the legitimate democratic polity ever more narrowly.

It was such renderings of themselves as dangerous, incompetent, and irrational that had been at the root of efforts by workers, immigrants, women, and African Americans to forge new versions of democratic polity that would win them legitimacy as rational participants in public life. They invoked their contributions to urban life—as intelligent and diligent workers, eager citizens, and faithful, compassionate mothers and responsible fathers—casting themselves as authoritative political actors in a culture that described citizenship in terms of economic and familial roles. Furthermore, in contrast to attempts to depersonalize justice, they provided concrete ways to debate the principles of justice and

J. Lacey and Mary O. Furner, 171–241 (Washington, DC: Woodrow Wilson Center Press and Cambridge University Press, 1993); also Cohen, *Reconstruction of American Liberalism, 1865–1914*, on the role of social scientists in articulating and implementing the new liberalism.

41. As Eldon Eisenach has shown, rights language often reappeared in progressive rhetoric, but it was "firmly tied to its positive origins within the framework of social duty." See Eisenach, *Lost Promise of Progressivism* (Lawrence: University Press of Kansas, 1994), 193.

42. *Chicago Inter-Ocean*, September 14, 1907; Flanagan, *Charter Reform in Chicago*, 134.

43. Civic Federation of Chicago, *New Charter Convention*, 2. For discussion of this cartoon, see Flanagan, *Charter Reform in Chicago*, 117.

prod the public to find "newer manifestations of government, in which personal welfare is considered a legitimate object."[44]

Their social organizations and the civic interactions they orchestrated were attempts to bring a spectrum of interests into greater identification with one another along these lines. Their efforts to appear as worthy participants in public life also challenged the political significance of the autonomous liberal individual and social scientific expertise as the sole basis of social knowledge. Instead they demanded recognition of their collective experiences—expressed as opposing visions of democracy and justice—as legitimate sources of social ideas and critiques of prevailing gender, economic, and racial principles. They thus reflected politics as a means to negotiate democratic social knowledge.

But the exclusion of women and substantial numbers of workers from the convention and the final version of the charter itself seemed to mark the failure of democratic politics to account for these groups' collective experiences. Fritz Glogauer, editor of the German-language *Abendpost,* indicated as much at one of the United Societies' gatherings, noting that "we were not considered in [the charter's] planning."[45] A United Societies pamphlet argued that the new charter did not extend much home rule control over "taxation, public utilities, the education system and all concerns which immediately touch the welfare of our Societies and the personal rights and freedoms of the people of Chicago," and similar charges emanated from the Democratic Party.[46]

Glogauer further explained his organization's opposition to the charter: "They insolently rejected our two amendments and now we are also using our rights to reject the bill." Highlighting their weariness of being cast outside of the political community despite the labor they contributed to building the city, he noted that immigrants were "thoroughly tired of being regarded as hangers-on. In their own opinion they are not an inferior, unchained mob, but full-fledged citizens, who have as much a share in the progress of the city as the natives have had, and hence insist that they receive the consideration due them." He went on, "the immigrant voters, who with their immediate descendants by far make up the majority, will not accept a city charter which was drafted by the 'upper classes' to promote their own interests only."[47] Ethnic residents, like workers, sought recognition for themselves as valuable members of the city. Insulted that civic elites and the state government had slighted their claims, they vehemently

44. Jane Addams, *Newer Ideals of Peace* (Chautauqua, NY: Chautauqua Press, 1907), 15.

45. *Abendpost,* September 16, 1907, quoted in Pegram, *Partisans and Progressives,* 117.

46. United Societies for Local Self-Government, "Seven Reasons to Vote against the Charter," quoted in Flanagan, *Charter Reform in Chicago,* 115; "Reasons Why the Proposed Charter Should Be Defeated, issued by the Democratic Central Committee of Cook County," Charles Merriam Papers, Box 72, Folder 10, Department of Special Collections, Joseph Regenstein Library, University of Chicago.

47. Quoted in Pegram, *Partisans and Progressives,* 117.

opposed the charter. Together women's organizations, the CFL, the United Societies, and the Democratic Party defeated the charter.

The charter convention reconvened in subsequent years and sent another draft to the state legislature in 1909. When that one also failed, Chicago residents tried again in 1914, but ultimately the city would be forced to wait until 1974 for a new charter.[48] The failure to pass the charter in the early part of the century left many businessmen of the Civic Federation not only disillusioned with what they perceived as their fellow Chicagoans' ignorance and selfish interests but also suspicious of the democratic process itself. The defeat signaled to them the way particular interests undermined the CFC's goal of forging a nonpartisan politics characterized by efficient and effective administration of the city. They found it "regrettable that factional interests and prejudices should have been so aroused" as to defeat the proposed charter and "make subsequent efforts of the New Charter convention equally unsuccessful."[49] For them, the failure of charter reform was symptomatic of the dangerous tendencies of a subjective social knowledge to irreparably divide the city. Indeed, one historian of the charter campaign has suggested that "the flawed attempt to reform Chicago government pointed not back to the civic culture of city-republics but rather ahead to the racial antipathy, bureaucratic jumble, and political misrule of urban America in the twentieth century."[50] In other words, the failure of the charter campaign, some argue, is a window onto both the difficulties of government in which experts remained largely outside policy debates and the problems created by inefficient political machines dominated by special-interest groups.[51]

The CFC looked on the failed charter with deep regret. The loss seemed to signal the emergence of a divisive interest-group politics. Indicators of this new style of politics appeared shortly after the charter ferment, in the 1910 campaign for aldermen in the Second Ward. Located in the southside Black Belt, the ward was home to the largest concentration of African Americans in the city, and black residents had grown dissatisfied with the lack of racial representation in

48. Flanagan, *Charter Reform in Chicago*, 136–47.

49. Civic Federation of Chicago, "Biennial Meeting and Report of the Executive Committee" (Chicago, 1909).

50. Pegram, *Partisans and Progressives*, 90.

51. Kenneth Finegold, *Experts and Politicians: Reform Challenges to Machine Politics in New York, Cleveland, and Chicago* (Princeton, NJ: Princeton University Press, 1995). This interpretation suffers from a vision of one interpretation of democratic realism—that the liberal democracy that privileged expertise by the 1950s is what ought to be. Thus Chicago's failure to conform to this model is a sign of the problems of democracy. For a critique of this democratic realism, see Robert B. Westbrook, *John Dewey and American Democracy* (Ithaca, NY: Cornell University Press, 1991), 545.

the Republican party organization. In response, Edward H. Wright, an African American lawyer, ran as an independent. The black press summarized the issue at the heart of the campaign. "Do You Want a Colored Alderman?" the paper asked. If so, the *Defender* urged that "true citizens" would ignore all other considerations in order to "fight for the common cause, a Negro in City Council."[52]

African Americans had to rally together not as party members or as independent voters but "for the sake of the race of which you are a part, of which your fathers, mothers, sisters and children are members." Though Wright lost this race, it set the stage for concerted efforts by African Americans to join forces in electing Oscar DePriest in 1915.[53] In that election, black women also emphasized the importance of voting for a "race man." The kind of identity politics built around interests and needs that such rhetoric fostered was exactly what the CFC had feared.

However, throughout the process of writing the charter, the CFC had not taken seriously women, workers, and ethnic groups it initially believed it could bring together.[54] As it spearheaded the charter convention, the CFC refused again to engage a process of forming democratic social knowledge that accounted for particular experiences. Ignoring these groups, many businessmen and professionals who composed the CFC could not recognize their own interests in the maintenance of liberal republicanism; in so doing, they claimed their own experience and interests as universal and, tying them to an emerging social science, framed them as neutral. The CFC failed to confront the power dynamics of urban life, which the CFL, the United Societies, and women had raised during the charter convention and campaign. Ironically, though the CFC had originally set out to encourage civic cooperation as a way to bridge distinct interests among Chicagoans, its leadership in the charter campaign ultimately isolated the organization from these other groups, helping to strengthen their separate interests and agendas and further encouraging them to unite in new political coalitions that put the CFC on the defensive.

This defensive position found expression in attacks on the extension of the mechanisms of direct democracy and an embrace of a corporate liberalism that sought an alliance of businessmen and experts in government agencies. For

---

52. *Chicago Defender*, April 2, 1910; January 29, 1910. Wanda Hendricks, "'Vote for the Advantage of Ourselves and Our Race': The Election of the First Black Alderman in Chicago," *Illinois Historical Journal* 3, no. 87 (1994): 171–84.

53. Hendricks describes the significant role women played in DePriest's election and notes that the strategy of rallying African American voters around the racial identity of candidates served to realign Chicago politics in the election of William Hale Thompson as mayor in 1915. Wanda A. Hendricks, *Gender, Race, and Politics in the Midwest: Black Club Women in Illinois* (Bloomington: Indiana University Press, 1998).

54. Perhaps part of the reason the organization failed to bring together a diverse body of city residents in the charter campaign was that its own membership had changed. By the late 1890s many women and workers had left the organization.

the CFC, democracy, the logic of economic development supported by liberal republicanism, and expertise went hand in hand.[55] In the future, the organization would work closely with the Bureau of Public Efficiency, merging its activities with those of the agency for a brief period in the 1910s and officially in 1932.[56] By the middle decades of the twentieth century, the CFC described its members as experts on municipal fiscal policies, taxes, and budgets.[57]

In the years following the charter defeat, struggles over democratic political practices continued to shape Chicago's local politics as the CFC turned further away from the democratic visions of Chicago's unions, women's groups, and ethnic societies. Instead it embraced an elitist vision of expertise while opposing the expansion of democratic reforms such as the initiative and referendum. Both of these legislative tools, along with the recall, held politicians accountable by allowing voters to bypass unresponsive legislators. Reformers campaigned for them in the 1910s and early 1920s, believing them a way to cure the problems of political corruption. But the CFC rejected the referendum and other such measures, arguing that they were "not progress, but a return to 'town meeting' and 'mob rule,' the rock on which early popular government was wrecked." This position reflected the sentiments of members who feared the power of particular, subjective interests and believed that "that there is a large percentage of the unthinking part of the population that would always be ready to vote on anything that would change the existing conditions" and that "the people themselves need . . . restraint."[58] Even as early as 1905, William Brown, then the secretary of the CFC, cautioned against the power that direct legislation would give to labor unions and the masses and argued that "a despotism of democracy, with its ignorance and

55. Letter from CFC to IMA, June 8, 1906, in Illinois Manufacturers Association Papers, Box 1, Folder 10, Chicago Historical Society.

56. The Bureau of Public Efficiency was founded to maintain watch over the "systems of accounting in the eight local governments of Chicago." *Chicago Tribune*, June 8, 1910.

57. Civic Federation of Chicago, Miscellaneous Pamphlets, Chicago Historical Society. The Civic Federation of Chicago Papers at the University of Illinois–Chicago, Special Collections, also contain a number of reports linking the CFC to fiscal efficiency.

58. Chicago Charter Convention, *Proceedings*, March 1, 1907, 173–79. In 1911 the CFC circulated a petition, signed by the executives of companies such as Pullman and Commonwealth Edison and banking interests, that opposed the initiative and referendum. They presented it to Progressive Republicans, who were angered at the suggestion that it be included as part of the party platform. Paul Steinbrecher, chair of the state campaign committee, publicly reminded the CFC that "the citizens of Illinois have voted nearly five to one in favor of the initiative, referendum, and recall." *Chicago Tribune*, December 29, 1911. For a time, the matter of the initiative and referendum divided Chicago's "highbrows" as the *Chicago Journal* reported on March 19, 1912. The article reported that the CFC sent out a letter to political candidates urging them not to pledge their support for the reform measures to any voluntary organization. For discussion of the issue in the 1920s, see Citizen's Committee for Popular Representation, "Limitation of Representation in the General Assembly of Illinois; an argument against the proposal pending before the Constitutional Convention" (Chicago, 1922).

class-hatred, as continually exhibited in industrial turmoils, is the worst kind of despotism."[59]

The starkest articulation of this sentiment appeared in a pamphlet the CFC published in 1911. Titled "The Referendum Long Ago," it drew on the crucifixion of Jesus Christ as a lesson about the dangers of the political mechanism.[60] In the CFC pamphlet, Pontius Pilate appears as a bureaucratic expert who was "imbued with a sense of justice and knowledge of the law." Though Pilate could find no fault with Jesus, "he put the matter up to the surging mob that surrounded the helpless and inoffensive prisoner." The result, of course, was the death of Christ. By drawing such ominous parallels, the federation suggested that the salvation of the city depended upon management by experts. To the CFC, the most attractive vision of democratic politics by the 1910s ultimately appeared as a kind of deference to expertise and bureaucratic professionalism.[61]

Having lost during the charter campaign, the CFC had little tolerance for a democratic social knowledge as it played out in the arena of formal politics. This position was a shift away from the original intent of the federation. Initially it had sought to bring a variety of groups together for a communal pursuit of social knowledge that would reinvigorate democratic participation. In so doing, it had hoped to act as a mediator for groups that had little knowledge of and contact with one another. As was evident in its campaign for the civil service law and in CFC ward committees, formal politics had proved a useful means to accomplish this goal. Such activities suggested a democratic hope that civic participation could provide the basis for overcoming the city's divisions. Even so, the organization had struggled with its aspirations to serve as a medium of acquaintance and sympathy and its tendencies to support Chicago's older liberal republican tradition of market rationality. These tensions reached their limits by the time of the charter campaign and its aftermath, where we see that the civic elites and businessmen of the CFC implicitly aligned their own interests with those of experts. Their conception of "expert" and of a universal political subject remained unmarked by categories of race, class, gender, or ethnicity. The CFC members no longer recognized its opponents' ideas and experiences as legitimate contributions to Chicago's public life. Instead, the CFC saw these claims as special interests that threatened to divide the city still further.

59. William Horace Brown, "The Popular Initiative," 741. Brown's article gives an accounting of the history of the referendum in Illinois and the work of the Referendum League, a reform organization endorsed by individuals and organizations like Jane Addams, the Chicago Federation of Labor, and the City Women's Club.

60. Civic Federation of Chicago Collection, Box 3, "Scrapbook Containing Circular Letters Sent Out from Time to Time," reprinted from *Cincinnati Enquirer*, April 19, 1911.

61. For an argument similar to that presented by the CFC, see Rome G. Brown, "The Judicial Recall—A Fallacy Repugnant to Constitutional Government," in *The Initiative, Referendum, and Recall* (Philadelphia: American Academy of Political and Social Science, 1912), 239–77.

However, the failure of the charter campaign also signaled a different reorientation of political culture, one in which the boundaries of special interests and identities were not as rigid or divisive as the CFC portrayed them and in which democratic political solidarity was more possible than the CFC believed. Within their associations, Chicago's women, workers, and immigrants exercised political voices with a new sense of purpose. Their collective experiences first provided them a basis for understanding the multiple ways that the prevailing terms of liberal republicanism inscribed in the city's institutions, social practices, and culture acted to limit them; these collective experiences formed the foundation for their activism and helped them to unite in defeating the charter. Thus we see simultaneously the way that a struggle over democratic social knowledge ultimately played out in the arena of formal politics and debates over political knowledge—that is, knowledge of how to make government work. Desire for the implementation of a framework of democratic social knowledge in formal politics—particularly inclusive deliberation—animated and mobilized opposition.

At the same time, the elites failed to embrace it as a model for framing political institutions. In this light, the failure of charter reform appears not as the dissolution of the polity into divisive public interests but as the rejection of the political vision the charter offered and, more important, a rejection of the civic hierarchies that the CFC had tried to solidify. Framing their political subjectivities less in terms of liberal individualism than in terms of collective experiences of oppression and different visions of the public good, these groups sought to find autonomy, individual fulfillment, and equality through collective political solidarity. In defeating the charter, they demonstrated both their desire for and the power of participatory democracy.

The Fate of Democratic Social Knowledge

By the 1920s another vision of democracy had emerged, one that built on the sentiments found in the CFC during the charter campaign. It privileged the rule of technocrats and business elites and was captured in the ideas of those whom we now recognize as democratic realists. Distrustful of what they saw as irrational political behavior and questioning the practicality and even the value of participatory politics, democratic realists like Walter Lippmann posited a democratic theory that relied on leadership by a technocratic body of social science experts. This rule by elites was democratic in that, from time to time, the electorate indirectly influenced politics by voting on whether to maintain the rule of those same elites. Focusing on social stability, the democratic realists were, as historian Robert Westbrook has explained, "willing to sacrifice a large measure of self-government."[62] By the 1950s, democratic realism was deeply entrenched in both the social sciences and liberal democratic political circles.

Repackaged versions of liberal republicanism helped secure this transformation, thus proving its resilience in the long run. Elite support buttressed liberal republicanism as it adapted to new historical circumstances. Indeed, its adaptability was apparent in the years during and after World War I. The alliances such as those Chicago's civic elites forged with workers and other reformers proved temporarily helpful in stemming more radical experiments in democratic collectivism, as they sought to solve social problems through an associationist approach, in which voluntary organizations like the CFC and its child, the National Civic Federation (NCF), rather than the state negotiated competing interests.[63] But the NCF, which brought together social scientists and policy advocates with business and labor leaders, enjoyed only limited successes in the 1910s. Emphasizing mutual education and peaceful settlement of labor conflict, its voluntarist approach was subsumed by the urgent needs of World War I, which opened up an opportunity for the state to emerge as the central mediator. During the war, the federal government could claim that unions' and businessmen's interests were subordinate to the interest of the state in prosecuting the war.

Under the rubric of the war effort, the federal government's War Labor Board adopted an interventionist policy, by which it hoped to ensure that it enjoyed the support of both labor and business.[64] During the war the state emerged as the arbiter of economic justice by focusing on a living wage for workers. In those days, unions spoke optimistically of industrial democracy, and Chicago Federation of Labor president John Fitzgerald even campaigned on such a platform. Ultimately, however, the Great War turned the struggle over democratic social knowledge into one that the state used to secure a "corporate liberalism" that legitimized its connection to the business elite and an increasingly powerful

---

62. See Westbrook, *John Dewey and American Democracy*, 543–46, for a discussion of democratic theory in the 1950s. See also 280–86 and 293–97 for a discussion of democratic realism in the 1920s and Walter Lippmann's critique in particular. For a similar critique of Lippmann, see James Hoopes, *Community Denied: The Wrong Turn of Pragmatic Liberalism* (Ithaca, NY: Cornell University Press, 1998), 100–23.

63. Mary O. Furner, "The Republican Tradition and the New Liberalism: Social Investigation, State Building, and Social Learning in the Gilded Age," 171–242; Marguerite Green, "The National Civic Federation and the American Labor Movement, 1900–1925" (PhD diss., Catholic University of America, 1956); Christopher Cyphers, *The National Civic Federation and the Making of a New Liberalism, 1900–1915* (Westport, CT: Praeger, 2002).

64. Valerie Jean Conner, *The National War Labor Board: Stability, Social Justice, and the Voluntary State in World War I* (Chapel Hill: University of North Carolina Press, 1983); Alan Dawley, *Struggles for Justice: Social Responsibility and the Liberal State* (Cambridge, MA: Harvard University Press, 1991), 172–217; Shelton Stromquist, *Reinventing "The People": The Progressive Movement, the Class Problem, and the Origins of Modern Liberalism* (Urbana: University of Illinois Press, 2005).

cadre of social science technocrats.[65] Because the business elites were able to ally themselves with the government at all levels, they secured their own and their agents' important places on regulatory bureaus as Republicans, and Democratic politicians, along with their reform allies, went about building the apparatus of the modern administrative, welfare state in the 1920s, 1930s, and beyond.

In Chicago this trend was foreshadowed in the early 1900s as the neoclassical liberal Illinois Manufacturers Association (IMA) worked with the Civic Federation to protect the interests of business both *from* the state and *with* the help of the state.[66] Initially organized to dismantle the Sweatshop Law and maturing during the open-shop campaign in 1904–1905, the IMA soon recognized the benefits of some state regulation and worked with legislators to shape policy. It joined forces with the National Association of Managers (NAM), an organization that negotiated between neoclassical and corporate liberalism to work toward an associationist approach to regulation that ensured the protection of their interests, indeed arguing that a healthy free market served the interests of all.[67] Government, employers' associations like NAM, and the American Federation of Labor soon found themselves under the sway of the same logic of capitalist economic growth, identifying each of their interests as identical. Of course this had been Pullman's and his generation's logic, albeit as a reason to reject unions and arbitration. The IMA and NAM similarly resisted arbitration and state intervention as long as possible.[68]

By midcentury, social scientists were closely connected to the federal government as both employees and advisors, and intellectual trends within the social sciences served to promote a developmentalist logic of progress that privileged capitalist economic growth and the political agenda of the state.[69] Such a logic

65. Dawley, *Struggles for Justice;* James Weinstein, *The Corporate Ideal in the Liberal State* (Boston: Beacon, 1968).

66. See, for example, Illinois Manufacturing Association Papers, Chicago Historical Society, Annual Report, Charles A. Plamondon, president, December 10, 1900; annual report of Charles H. Deere, president, January 7, 1903; letter from Civic Federation, April 13, 1906, requesting the IMA to attend a fund-raiser for candidates for municipal judgeships, Box 1, Folder 10; "A Legislative Program to Restore Business Freedom and Confidence," January 5, 1917, Illinois Manufacturing Association Papers, Box 180, Folder 8, Chicago Historical Society; "Defects of and Objections to State Insurance," 1919, Illinois Manufacturing Association Papers, Box 180, Folder 8, Chicago Historical Society. For ways in which the IMA used state regulation to promote its members' business interests, see IMA Bulletin, May 1902, which discusses IMA support for a state antitrust law that would limit monopoly and thus drive shipping costs down.

67. Albert K. Steigerwalt, *The National Association of Manufacturers 1895–1914: A Study in Business Leadership* (Grand Rapids: Bureau of Business Research, University of Michigan, 1964).

68. The Wagner Act (1935) finally ensured federal mandates for union recognition, collective bargaining, and arbitration. For an interpretation of the Wagner Act's (negative) impact on unions over the course of the twentieth century, see David Brody, *Labor Embattled: History, Power, Rights* (Champaign: University of Illinois Press, 2005).

69. We see this interplay both in modernization theory and the emergence of the three worlds system. As Carl Pletsch has argued, the "first," "second," and "third" world model as a way of study-

reinforced business, government, and labor interests as identical in promoting economic security and the health of consumer society through the advancement of big business.[70] The state pursued knowledge that it would then use to promote economic development.[71] With certain aspects of liberal republicanism— individualism, rational economic behavior, laissez-faire, the moral discipline of work, the justice of the free market—recast with developmentalist logic (or by the late 1980s as neoliberalism), it helped maintain a close alliance between the business elite, government bureaucrats, and technocratic experts throughout the twentieth century.

Moreover, the resilience of strands of liberal republicanism within business and social science theory has shaped the way we think about politics and talk about social welfare. Today, as in the 1890s, narratives of economic opportunity that "naturalize" (i.e., make inevitable and commonsensical) the market as a mediator of justice tend to foreclose discussions of other ways to allocate resources.[72] A moral language of individualism and hard work still conflates worthiness and respectability with economic success, as it did during the 1893 depression and debates over poor relief. Similarly, the identification of market growth with the public good has served to naturalize the interests of business while positing other collective groups, such as workers, African Americans, and

ing societies mutually reinforced capitalist growth and the United States' agenda for international politics. The three worlds system was naturalized within social scientific and political circles, where the "first world" was seen as lacking any ideology precisely because it followed that of capitalist representative democracies. More important for my purposes, it also demonstrates how political and economic imperatives were tightly connected to a particular kind of "objective" scientistic social knowledge production that figured some nations and their populations as more "rational" and "modern," buttressing classical liberal ideas about Economic Man and his behaviors. The effect on the American social sciences was profound, Pletsch argues, since ultimately it left unquestioned a "model of society constituted of autonomous individuals, each motivated by the same underlying characteristic, namely selfishness" (580). We can thus see how deeply implicated social scientists and the state were in maintaining a social knowledge that supported a certain economic system. Carl Pletsch, "The Three Worlds, or the Division of Social Scientific Labor, Circa 1950–1975," *Comparative Studies in Society and History* 23, no. 4 (October 1981): 565–90.

70. This is the logic behind the popular slogan "What's Good for General Motors Is Good for America." On the iteration of this developmentalist logic, see Lizabeth Cohen, *A Consumers' Republic: The Politics of Mass Consumption in Postwar America* (New York: Knopf, 2003). Bill Fletcher Jr., "Labor's Renewal? Listening to the 1920s and the 1930s," *Labor: Studies in Working-class History of the Americas* 1, no. 3 (Fall 2004): 13–18. Alicia R. Schmidt Camacho, "Migrant Subjects: Race, Labor, and Insurgency in the Mexico-U.S. Borderlands" (PhD diss., Stanford University, 2000, 225–37), and Maria Josefina Saldaña-Portillo, *The Revolutionary Imagination in the Americas and the Age of Development* (Durham, NC: Duke University Press, 2003) discuss the emergence of this developmentalist logic in post–World War II relations of globalization and its impact on transnational labor movements.

71. See, for example, Lacey and Furner, eds., *State and Social Investigation in Britain and the United States;* Smith, *Social Science in the Crucible;* Pletsch, "The Three Worlds."

72. See, for example, David S. Allen, *Democracy, Inc.: The Press and Law in the Corporate Rationalization of the Public Sphere* (Champaign: University of Illinois Press, 2005).

women, as "special interests," thus relegating their claims as subordinate to the interest of those who equate their position with national interests.

This was not at all the understanding of democracy most Chicago reformers who appeared in this book envisioned. Rather, they sought to bring the experiences and perspectives of different groups together to forge a democratic social knowledge that would enrich public discussion of social and economic concerns—not leave them primarily to bureaucratic social scientists, business interests, and the state. The fate of democratic social knowledge was thus at the mercy of liberal republicanism and its variants in the twentieth century. The question that I take up in the epilogue is whether any vestiges of democratic social knowledge survive into the present.

Conclusion

In the charter campaign and beyond, as well as the other reform debates in this book, we see a reworking of Chicago's—and the nation's—political culture; thus it is a fitting place to end this story of democratic social knowledge. The charter campaign and the debates over popular politics that followed illustrate how struggles over democratic social knowledge ultimately affected the arena of formal politics. The civic harmony Chicago's civic elites had believed possible in liberal republicanism was embattled (permanently, the CFC feared), and a fatal drifting apart now seemed inevitable. Framing the charter's opponents as special interests, CFC members and other civic elites differentiated them from their own interest, which they cast as universal and the basis for civic health. Linking themselves to reason and expertise, these elites identified political knowledge as their province. Concerned with expert and efficient management of public life, they welcomed the emergence of a democratic realism that privileged the policy-making power of technocrats. It gave them a new foundation on which to build their elitist vision of democratic representation. This formulation represented one variety of democracy emerging from the Progressive Era.

The pluralism evidenced in Chicago's reform debates and culminating in the charter campaign and the election of Oscar Depriest, the African American alderman elected by voters mobilized around racial interests, pointed to another form of democratic politics solidified during this period: interest-group politics in which the state served as moderator and occasionally, as some arbitration and civil rights advocates hoped, took sides to protect the interests of marginalized groups. Indeed, given their lack of power and even, in the case of women and African Americans, access to the formal political arena during the Progressive Era, appeals to the state were an important tactic to counterbalance the power of the elites and white racism. Though it made CFC members uncomfortable, this interest-group model was not inherently at odds with democratic realism. From the perspective of democratic realists, it merely served as a way, and a more convenient way perhaps, to mobilize voters for periodic elections.

From the vantage points both of political reformers who were concerned that the party system had led to corruption and of groups who had been excluded from electoral politics—women and African Americans in particular—interest-group politics marked a more expansive democracy. Influencing elected officials through a number of channels like lobbying and voter education campaigns and through the organizing efforts of popular associations, interest-group politics expanded the public voices and power of groups and sought to link policy outcomes to citizens' concerns. Such pluralism helped reframe the political autonomy of the individual (white male) voter in terms of the group: Individual political actors exercised power by harnessing their vote to the interests of like-minded groups.

Over the course of the twentieth century, as collective experiences framed through the lenses of race, gender, ethnicity, class, sexual orientation, and so on became the basis of political action, this pluralistic model of interest-group politics has become conflated with identity politics. Even at the founding of the CFC, the organization had headed in this direction as it sought members representing "women," "labor," "business," "education," and "religion." With its attention to the collective experiences of groups, the framework of democratic social knowledge undoubtedly contributed to identity politics, which today has become synonymous with political divisiveness. This was certainly an ironic outcome for Chicago reformers, for it was precisely this "fatal drifting apart" that reformers had hoped to prevent.

Yet democratic social knowledge also contained the seeds of a democracy different from that offered by democratic realism or a model of pluralistic interest groups. Built on democratic praxis emphasizing deliberation, mutuality, and shared experiences across identity lines, this vision of politics required ways of building social relationships that mediated multiple experiences and diverse forms of knowledge. Participatory democracy built on such terms meant creating arenas, processes, and relationships necessary to building habits of mind that fostered inclusive politics, just as they fostered inclusive democratic social knowledge.

Together the political and social reform debates explored in this book exposed the deep roots of conflicts over the nature of liberal democracy, conflicts that became some of our most significant challenges to democracy during the twentieth century. As the members of the CFC learned, the expansion of the public sphere and the extension of political rights to both minorities and women introduced a plethora of claims and needs—social, economic, and political—into the public sphere. As these groups sought legitimacy and claimed their equal rights and status, they posed a dilemma: how to reconcile what a logic of liberalism could recognize as equal rights and interests without a resort to illiberal and undemocratic use of power. The CFC's solution to this dilemma—to turn to management by technocratic elites and bureaucratic experts, who operated without much interaction with the broader public—provided one response attractive to Progressives and their descendants. Though not necessarily at odds with democratic realism, interest-group pluralism, like that which coalesced in the charter opposition, pointed to yet another model. Yet the reform efforts contributing to democratic social knowledge offered a different vision of democracy, one that was built on proximity, mutuality, activist social science, and sympathetic understanding and that sought a political framework for collective and particular experiences deliberated in public.

By the end of the charter campaign, then, and well into the twentieth century, democratic social knowledge as a framework for reform failed to solve decisively the crisis of liberal republicanism that had ignited Chicago's reform community in the 1890s. Its failure left significant questions about democracy unresolved, thus laying the groundwork for a liberal democracy that bore more similarity to the democratic realism of Walter Lippmann than the participatory democracy of Jane Addams, activist and theorist Mary Parker Follett, or philosopher John Dewey, whose version of democracy was rooted in a framework that I have described as democratic social knowledge.[73] Such democracy was not limited to the procedures of electoral politics. Rather, many of the Chicago reformers herein viewed democracy as pervading all aspects of life. Self-government was a critical aspect of self-realization; thus they privileged the *process* of participatory democracy over the democratic realists' concern for social stability.[74] Their ideas seemed wholly subsumed in the mid-twentieth century by a liberal democracy that privileged the role of technocratic and social scientific experts in framing political policy. This direction had important consequences for the United States over the course of the twentieth century.

73. There were important differences in the details of each of their ideas. For example, Follett's democratic theory blended pragmatism and idealism and took issue with Dewey's notion that citizens could live outside politics. James Hoopes, *Community Denied: The Wrong Turn of Pragmatic Liberalism* (Ithaca, NY: Cornell University Press, 1998), especially 156–57; Kevin Mattson, *Creating a Democratic Public: The Struggle for Urban Participatory Democracy during the Progressive Era* (University Park: Pennsylvania State University Press), 87–104; Westbrook, *John Dewey and American Democracy*; Victoria Bissell Brown, *The Education of Jane Addams* (Princeton, NJ: Princeton University Press, 2004). Despite their differences, however, they all shared a commitment to participatory democracy by rejecting the democratic realism espoused by Lippmann.

74. For a discussion of this idea, see Westbrook, *John Dewey and American Democracy*, 534, and Mattson, *Creating a Democratic Republic*.

Epilogue

The essential feature of common thought is not that it is held in common but that it has been produced in common.—Mary Parker Follett, *The New State* (1918)

The seemingly pervasive hold of liberal republicanism and democratic realism over the course of the twentieth century suggests that democratic social knowledge failed to offer a viable democratic alternative. Or did it? In the hundred years since the height of Chicago's Progressive Era social reform, theories of liberal democracy that privileged a scientistic, bureaucratic expertise and downplayed the value of participatory politics have not solved the challenges of corporate capitalism and the tensions surrounding pluralist politics that emerged in the Progressive Era. Indeed, we continue to grapple with similar questions about corporate power, the role of the polity and experts in framing inquiry and policy, and the possibility of a politics that simultaneously recognizes differences and promotes democratic solidarity. Moreover, significant changes throughout the twentieth century—the Civil Rights movement and Second Wave feminism, in particular—have been brought about not by experts working within government bureaucracy and removed from the influence of the polity but by public pressure and alliances of the polity, in some cases together *with* social scientists. A populist strain of reform, dating back to farmers' and workers' movements of the late nineteenth century, has remained part of the political terrain, opposing not the state per se but the bureaucratic state and corporate power.[1] Renewed efforts to enact participatory, deliberative democracy have emerged in recent years.[2] These point to the possibility of a different kind of democratic politics,

---

1. Elizabeth Sanders, *Roots of Reform: Farmers, Workers, and the American State, 1877–1917* (Chicago: University of Chicago Press, 1999), 387–408; Robert D. Johnston, *The Radical Middle Class: Populist Democracy and the Question of Capitalism in Progressive Era Portland, Oregon* (Princeton, NJ: Princeton University Press, 2003).

2. The National Issues Forum and Study Circle Resource Centers are two examples of nationwide programs that encourage deliberative, participatory democracy. For examples of the varieties of efforts, see Ronald Hayduk and Kevin Mattson, eds., *Democracy's Moment: Reforming the American Political System for the 21st Century* (Boulder, CO: Rowman and Littlefield, 2001); Kevin Mattson, *Creating a Democratic Public: The Struggle for Urban Participatory Democracy in the Progressive Era* (University Park: Penn State Press, 1998).

one seeking a more participatory and inclusive framework reminiscent of democratic social knowledge.

In light of this history, we might rethink the story of democratic social knowledge and the moment of struggle over democracy of which it was a part. The methods of democratic social knowledge require us to pose difficult questions about the goals and nature of democracy. To what extent should the power to frame public policy reside within either the polity or a technocracy of social science elites? In what ways might the polity and social science experts work more closely together, particularly on the local level? By fostering grassroots participatory democracy, can we build the kinds of knowledge and social relationships that are important for democratic habits of mind? Does the administrative, regulatory nature of liberal democracy today adequately account for experiences and local knowledge of those affected? Might the particular and collective experiences of diverse groups help forge a democratic solidarity that opposes oppression? As the historical actors in these pages negotiated such questions in the past, they gave shape to a democratic praxis whose methods are well worth reconsidering and whose shortcomings are instructive. If we today are to imagine the possibilities for democracy's future, we might consider the lessons of Chicago's reform community more than a century ago as it wrestled with democratic social knowledge.

Recovering a framework of democratic social knowledge reveals the potential for a more participatory and transformative politics along several lines. It helps us envision an alternative both to democratic realism privileging political policy making by technocratic experts and to the challenges and limitations of pluralist liberalism, in which the state acts as arbiter for competing interest groups even as it uses a developmentalist logic to occlude corporate capital as an interest. Instead, democratic social knowledge is a method that emphasizes process, education, and dispositions as a basis for sympathetic understanding, deliberation, and mutuality—for a democratic praxis. Emerging from the early twentieth century, these features inform the methods of democratic practice today.[3] However, since democratic social knowledge frequently fell short of reformers' democratic hopes, it requires attention to its limitations before we turn to its potential.

Certainly the lessons of the charter campaign and its aftermath, both in Chicago and in the broader context of political culture over the course of the twentieth century, indicate that historical circumstances—war, the resilience of elites, a paradigm of liberal republicanism (today in the form of neoliberalism abroad and neoconservatism at home), and the emergence of a culture of expertise—militated against a framework of democratic social knowledge as a basis for politics. Indeed, even before democratic social knowledge had barely

3. Hayduk and Mattson, eds., *Democracy's Moment.*

taken root, civic elites and World War I had begun to undermine it. Some of its problems may be attributed to unforeseen historical circumstances. But as the Chicago reformers employed it, democratic social knowledge had its own inherent limitations as well. As we saw particularly in chapter 5 on interracial reform, one significant problem was the limits of sympathetic understanding both as a method of knowing and as a basis for collective politics.

Strategies of reform geared toward building sympathetic understanding did not adequately interrogate power hierarchies between parties. As we saw in the Half-century Exposition of Emancipation, Ida B. Wells's antilynching campaign, and the interracial cooperation of the Frederick Douglass Center, both white and black reformers built claims to African American equality by showing how they were like whites, thus exposing the unacknowledged, privileged position of whites, which equated their cultural characteristics and values with those of the universal subject. New media forms like film also lent themselves to more dangerous uses, as *Birth of a Nation* manipulated sympathies to foster a white racist national identity, even condoning methods of oppression and violence to do so. Such a critique of the limits of sympathetic knowledge would have to wait until the advent of black and "third world" feminism.[4]

Chapter 5 offered several examples of limitations of sympathetic and proximate understanding as a way of knowing. On the one hand, when Mary Plummer refused to accept Ida Wells-Barnett's explanations of lynchings, we saw that sympathetic understanding, claims of experiential, proximate knowledge, and even social science failed to transform subjective opinions. Despite Plummer's interactions with and sympathies for African Americans, she held fast to her personal understanding of racial problems, which, on the one hand, was built on her southern friend's own claims of proximate experience and, on the other, was framed by a widespread racism in white social science and popular culture. Many white parents, as well, rejected integrated schools, maintaining the distinctiveness of the races and the inferiority of blacks. Though such anecdotes reflect the personal limitations of the people involved, they point to the larger problem of whether democratic social knowledge can expose and overcome the subjective opinions of individuals like Plummer, who privilege one claim of proximate knowledge over another. In the face of extensive racism, sympathetic understanding *alone* proved inadequate.

The collision of opposing viewpoints, like those between Wells and Plummer,

---

4. Patricia Hill Collins, *Black Feminist Thought: Knowledge, Consciousness, and the Politics of Empowerment* (Boston: Unwin Hyman, 1990); bell hooks, *Ain't I a Woman: Black Women and Feminism* (Boston: South End Press, 1981); Chandra Talpade Mohanty, "Under Western Eyes: Feminist Scholarship and Colonial Discourses," in *Third World Women and the Politics of Feminism*, ed. Chandra Talpade Mohanty, Ann Russo, and Lourdes Torres, 51–80 (Indianapolis: Indiana University Press, 1991).

or among participants in the charter campaign pointed to another inherent limitation of democratic social knowledge: It lacked a way to navigate the delicate balance between liberal rights, power, and the open-ended processes it required. Indeed, one of the strengths of a framework of democratic social knowledge in the early twentieth century was its pluralism—it sought to legitimate viewpoints and experiences frequently overlooked or silenced. Yet we are left with the significant question of whether democratic social knowledge requires that we recognize *all* viewpoints as legitimate. We saw the conundrum it posed when black reformers demanded censorship of *Birth of a Nation*—a most undemocratic action—in order to *better forge* a democratic social knowledge that included African Americans. Democratic social knowledge, with its emphasis on mutuality, proximity, and pluralism that legitimized different experiences, had no response to these dilemmas of power and individually based liberal rights. The question it failed to adequately address is one that continually challenges political liberalism: How do we settle irreconcilable differences between equally "valid" perspectives, interests, and frameworks of knowledge?[5] Indeed, some frameworks of social knowledge—natural law or religious fundamentalism, for example—do not open themselves up to the possibilities of pluralism because they reject the idea that social knowledge is a social construction. When the methods of democratic social knowledge failed to negotiate colliding perspectives, it had no other frameworks for understanding power to help mediate differences. Furthermore, democratic social knowledge, with its commitment to process and consensus, had no way of addressing the structural advantages and disadvantages of some groups.

Ultimately, reformers who conceived of democracy in its broadest terms as everyday praxis ironically turned to the state as arbiter of social claims and differences, and they demanded that the state protect their interests. In the meantime, the pluralist politics they helped frame was separated from their insistence on democracy as everyday praxis and as habits of mind promoted through proximate relationships. Instead, democratic theory by the mid-twentieth century posited that citizen *disengagement* from policy making was desirable.[6] Here, then, we can see that the intertwining of liberal republicanism with a model of interest-group politics shorn of democratic habits has had important consequences for the way that we think about politics and political behavior. As liberal republicanism encouraged capitalist growth as the ultimate, "natural"

5. John Rawls, *Political Liberalism* (New York: Columbia University Press, 1993). Also David S. Allen, *Democracy, Inc.: The Press and Law in the Corporate Rationalization of the Public Sphere* (Champaign: University of Illinois Press, 2005).

6. Robert B. Westbrook, *John Dewey and American Democracy* (Ithaca, NY: Cornell University Press, 1991), 543–46; Edward A. Purcell Jr., *The Crisis of Democratic Theory: Scientific Naturalism and the Problem of Value* (Lexington: University Press of Kentucky, 1973).

goal for the state, it has concomitantly relegated the claims of collective groups as "special interests," thus delegitimizing the perspectives of those who challenged the individual state-citizen model of rights and claims, offered an alternative vision of social policy, or claimed a different role for the state.

The problems associated with certain aspects of democratic social knowledge or the limitations of those who practiced it should not lead us to dismiss its potential out of hand, however. We might see it instead as introducing a framework of ideas and a set of practical lessons. While unsuccessful in an earlier time and subsequently falling out of favor among political theorists and social scientists in the mid-twentieth century, democratic social knowledge still lingers in a multitude of political and local community projects and thus remains available to us as we consider the kind of democratic politics we seek.

As we reflect on the tensions between democracy and expertise, employing a framework of democratic social knowledge can serve as a way to mediate between local knowledge and expertise, where each must inform the other. As we saw in the Working People's Social Science Club at Hull House and carried out in similar endeavors in other settlements around the city, at the CFC's ward councils, and at the Hull House and Frederick Douglass women's clubs, this vision of democratic social knowledge was aided by deliberative spaces and practices and by mediators who served as translators between communities. Faltering at the time, these efforts suggest a model for democratic engagement that technocratic bureaucracy and scientific specialization diminished during the twentieth century.[7] Indeed, as the needs of an ever more complex society have become increasingly dependent upon expert knowledge, the need for such places, practices, and especially mediators has become even more acute (though these translators must recognize their cultural, economic, and political power in forging knowledge).

The efforts of the Chicago reformers help us imagine ways to address the undemocratic tendencies of positivist social science and to transform people from subjugated objects of study into active subjects in the creation of new knowledge about themselves and their communities. We see such possibilities in the methods of qualitative research and participant-observation to which Hull House contributed.[8] The legacy of the Chicago social settlements' distinct form of inquiry

7. Robert Wachbroit, "The Changing Role of Expertise in Public Deliberation," in *Civil Society, Democracy, and Civic Renewal*, ed. Robert K. Fullinwider, 355–71 (Lanham, MD: Rowman and Littlefield, 1999); Leon Fink, "Expert Advice: Progressive Intellectuals and the Unraveling of Labor Reform, 1912–1915," in *Intellectuals and Public Life: Between Radicalism and Reform*, ed. Leon Fink, Stephen T. Leonard, and Donald M. Reid, 182–213 (Ithaca, NY: Cornell University Press, 1996); Thomas L. Haskell, ed., *The Authority of Experts: Studies in History and Theory* (Bloomington: Indiana University Press, 1984); Mark Smith, *Social Science in the Crucible: The American Debate over Objectivity and Purpose, 1918–1941* (Durham, NC: Duke University Press, 1994).

8. Shannon Jackson, *Lines of Activity: Performance, Historiography, Hull-House Domesticity* (Ann

and activism has lived on in other ways as well. Studs Terkel, perhaps the greatest oral historian of the twentieth century, grew up in the neighborhood of Graham Taylor's Chicago Commons, from which he based his work in the WPA Writers' Project radio division. Myles Horton, founder of the Highlander Research and Education Center in Tennessee, drew some of his inspiration from Hull House and his conversations with Jane Addams while he was a graduate student at the University of Chicago. More popularly known as the Highlander Folk School, the Research and Education Center serves as an adult education center. Initially it trained farmers and laborers in economic justice issues and was a meeting ground for civil rights activists. It continues today to train people struggling against injustice to take leadership roles and enact democratic change.

The Chicago Area Project, founded in 1932 by Clifford Shaw, also drew from the community-organizing visions of the settlement houses. Joined by Saul Alinsky in the early 1930s, Shaw envisioned an approach to juvenile delinquency that brought neighborhood members together with delinquents to work toward collective solutions to their problems.[9] The Oregon Health Parliament brought together public policy advocates and healthcare providers with community members statewide to develop a set of principles for the healthcare system.[10] National Issues Forums and the Study Circle Resource Center also reflect the fact that elements of democratic social knowledge still circulate. Designed to bring community members together to discuss common problems of national and local concern, these programs focus on practical models of deliberation in which participants are encouraged to bring their "intuition" and "common sense" to the study of a problem. The process of deliberation helps individuals reflect on their values and opinions and recognize their unwarranted stereotypes. The focus on the common work of addressing—and making choices about—practical issues helps people very different from one another to get beyond stereotypes.[11] These

---

Arbor: University of Michigan Press, 2000).

9. Benjamin Shepard, "Community as a Source for Democratic Politics," in *Democracy's Moment*, ed. Hayduk and Mattson, 109–120; Dana Cuff, "The Figure of the Neighbor: Los Angeles Past and Future," *American Quarterly* 56, no. 3 (September 2004): 559–82.

10. As Benjamin Barber observes, the Oregon Health Parliament is an example of a healthy and effective sphere of civil society. Barber, "Clansmen, Consumers, and Citizens: Three Takes on Civil Society," in *Civil Society, Democracy, and Civic Renewal*, ed. Fullwinder, 9–30. Another valuable example of the intersection of expertise and local, experiential knowledge is seen in the AIDS movement. Wachbroit, "The Changing Role of Expertise in Public Deliberation," 355–71; James Bohman, "Deliberative Democracy and Effective Social Freedom: Capabilities, Resources, and Opportunities," in *Deliberative Democracy: Essays on Reason and Politics*, ed. James Bohman and William Rehg, 321–48 (Cambridge, MA: MIT Press, 1997); James Bohman, "Participants, Observers, and Critics: Practical Knowledge, Social Perspectives, and Critical Pluralism," in *Pluralism and the Pragmatic Turn: The Transformation of Critical Theory: Essays in Honor of Thomas McCarthy*, ed. William Rehg and James Bohman, 87–114 (Cambridge: MIT Press, 2001).

11. R. Claire Snyder, "Democratic Theory and the Case for Public Deliberation," in *Democracy's Moment*, especially 87–89.

programs offer us models of democracy as a relational praxis that are open ended and ever changing and that promote autonomy and individuality realized through social interaction.[12] Today the growing popularity of character education in K–12 education and civic engagement in institutions of higher education (however embattled and partisan they may be) attests to a continued sensibility that healthy democracy depends on habits of mind and must rest on foundations of social action.[13]

Despite the limitations of sympathetic understanding and the challenges of located (sometimes irreconcilable) perspectives discussed above, affective ties and differences remain important aspects of democratic politics throughout our history and potential resources for today. However, they require greater historical attention, particularly as some feminist critiques of contemporary politics suggest that our political life has been impoverished by its marginalization of empathy. Theorist Judith Kegan Gardiner, for example, has suggested that the focus on (masculine) individualism has impoverished our ability to foster and mobilize empathy as a basis for politics. The effect has been to maintain traditional social divisions (i.e., class, race, and gender) since these can be "maintained more easily when most people are kept isolated and insensitive to the needs of others." Indeed, it operates against a politics built on collective experiences. Empathy, in contrast, "potentially serves equality, letting all people understand the sufferings of the oppressed and exploited and so motivating calls for social justice."[14]

Similarly, theorists and activists who promote an ethics of care suggest it offers an alternative basis for politics. Care ethics reflect certain aspects of democratic social knowledge in requiring a contextual approach to morality and assuming human connectedness.[15] Furthermore, in contrast to liberal republicanism's emphasis on the market as a mediator of justice, it takes the maintenance of relationships and human needs to be a priority. Though there are limits to affective ties such as sympathy as a basis for collective politics, both the lack of historical attention to the role of affective ties in public life and the recent attention among

12. Westbrook, *John Dewey and American Democracy*; James Livingston, *Pragmatism, Feminism, and Democracy: Rethinking the Politics of American History* (New York: Routledge, 2001).

13. There are of course multiple approaches to character education and civic engagement, each with loyal partisans. See, for example, Ann Colby et al., *Educating Citizens: Preparing America's Undergraduates for Lives of Moral and Civic Responsibility* (San Francisco: Jossey-Bass, 2003); Peter Smagorinsky, *The Discourse of Character Education: Culture Wars in the Classroom* (Mahwah, NJ: Erlbaum, 2005). My purpose here is only to point out the recent rise in interest in these subjects, both of which aim to develop a particular disposition regarded as necessary for a democracy.

14. Judith Kegan Gardiner, "Masculinity, The Teening of America, and Empathic Targeting," in *Feminisms at a Millennium*, ed. Judith A. Howard and Carolyn Allen, 248–52 (Chicago: University of Chicago Press, 2000). Quotes are from 249–50.

15. Maurice Hamington, *Embodied Care: Jane Addams, Maurice Merleau-Ponty, and Feminist Ethics* (Champaign: University of Illinois Press, 2004); Grace Clement, *Care, Autonomy, and Justice: Feminism and the Ethic of Care* (Boulder, CO: Westview, 1996).

some social theorists to the function of empathy in political mobilization suggest that we might explore more carefully what history has to teach us about the possibilities and limitations of emotion in framing democratic social knowledge and mobilizing democratic politics.[16]

Even as it is worth recovering the methods of democratic social knowledge that fostered interaction and mediated between expertise and local experience, treated difference as a resource in public life, and encouraged the democratic dispositions of mutual respect, sympathetic understanding, and trust, so too it is important to recall reformers' attempts to create deliberative spaces in which to enact these methods and practice these traits. Without widespread democratic debate and mutual engagement, however faltering they were at that moment in Chicago, productive social action across racial, class, ethnic, and gender boundaries would have been impossible. More recently, democratic theorists have looked to new arenas of deliberation—in National Issues Forums or on the Internet, for example—to foster public-spirited debate.[17] Building on a commitment to a process of democratic social knowledge in which experiences of affected groups are brought to bear, such deliberation may ultimately help foster a radical democratic politics in which differences and a range of particular collective experiences will help us to see the ways that power and knowledge serve to exclude and oppress some groups.[18]

The lessons of democratic social knowledge at its best emphasize that proximity, shared experience, and interaction are important to inspire the habits of mind that serve as the foundation of democracy. The building blocks of a rich and vibrant local participatory democracy more than a hundred years ago—the principles of democratic social knowledge—continue to animate activists today. The lives of people like my friend Annjie, whose story opens this book, continue to tell of commitments to a radical democracy that extends far beyond voting in one's self-interest.

16. Jeff Goodwin, James M. Jasper, and Francesca Poletta, eds., *Passionate Politics: Emotions and Social Movements* (Chicago: University of Chicago Press), 2001.

17. R. Claire Snyder, "Democratic Theory and the Case for Public Deliberation," and Peter Levine, "Can the Internet Rescue Democracy? Toward an On-Line Commons," in *Democracy's Moment*, ed. Hayduk and Mattson.

18. Discussion of the public sphere is found in Jürgen Habermas's classic text, *The Structural Transformation of the Public Sphere: An Inquiry into a Category of Bourgeois Society* (Cambridge, MA: MIT Press, 1994). There is of course a vast literature on how public deliberation unfolds in ways that reinforce and recreate power differentials. See, for example, Seyla Benhabib, ed., *Democracy and Difference: Contesting the Boundaries of the Political* (Princeton, NJ: Princeton University Press, 1996). My suggestion here follows that of Chantal Mouffe, who argues that, despite differences, collective identities might be forged around a radical commitment to equality for all. Seeing the multiple ways in which relations of power are constructed is an important step in such a radical democratic politics. Mouffe, "Feminism, Citizenship, and Radical Democratic Politics," in *Feminists Theorize the Political*, ed. Judith Butler and Joan W. Scott, 369–84 (New York: Routledge, 1992).

The story of democratic social knowledge told in this book suggests that we might think about democracy differently, both for the Progressive Era and for our own time—as an intersection between various frameworks of knowledge, expertise, and popular sovereignty, as a method for social action, and as public life that views difference as a resource and searches for ways to include multiple perspectives while building consensus for the common good. Such democratic praxis suggests an alternative to the narrowly conceived positivistic scientism that transformed liberal democracy during the Progressive Era. The emphasis on civic interaction and mutual social relationships, sympathetic understanding of the Other, deliberation, and cultural agency illustrate a democracy rooted in relational practices and processes. Ultimately for the Chicago reformers, the practices of democracy were educative and spilled over into formal politics, though these democrats believed that democracy was not only about procedures of voting and governance. Instead they also sought measures to encourage the formation of a democratic personality in which citizens would understand different sides, negotiate and compromise, and be able to change their minds. These skills and habits of mind were most effectively cultivated on the local level through interactions with diverse people, but they also shaped habits of mind that extended to people in distant areas.

The reformers' efforts to create democratic social knowledge that recognized and legitimized different groups' experiences and needs meant fostering a vision of democratic equality built on respect, mutuality, trust, and understanding. It meant engaging issues of difference within both civil and political life. As Addams observed in the midst of the charter campaign, "we have fallen into the Anglo-Saxon temptation of governing all people by one standard."[19] This had been the particular failing of Pullman, who was willing to sacrifice his residents' and workers' freedoms to fabricate a moral community, and of the CFC, despite its early goal to coordinate different interests. Both used social science in ways that sought conformity and control rather than egalitarian interaction. Instead, Addams suggested that reformers needed "to dissolve 'humanity' into its component parts of men, women, and children and to serve their humblest needs."[20] In the embodiment of collective differences and particularities and social needs in public debate, these reformers called for a new conception of democratic justice.[21]

It was a view of public life that threatened to finally dissolve the civic myths

19. Addams, *Newer Ideals of Peace* (New York: The Macmillan Company, 1907), 47.
20. Ibid.
21. Nancy Fraser, *Unruly Practices: Power, Discourse, and Gender in Contemporary Social Theory* (Minneapolis: University of Minnesota Press, 1989).

that had grown up with the city—of a liberal republican unity and a natural and divine justice operating through the liberal market. While the failed charter campaign did not herald a widespread end of these beliefs, it did illustrate ongoing tensions within reform thought between fear of a divisive subjectivism and a desire for a more opened-ended democracy. From her vantage point as a prominent participant in Chicago's political reforms, Jane Addams astutely observed that the extension of democracy would witness more such struggles. "The framers of the carefully prepared charters, upon which the cities are founded," Addams suggested, "did not foresee that after the universal franchise had once been granted, social needs and ideals were bound to enter in as legitimate objects of political action."[22] Continued struggle over the legitimacy of democratic social knowledge that seriously engaged the definitions of social needs and democratic ideals would indeed shape the city's, the nation's, and—as we look toward the globalization of the twenty-first century—the world's future. Indeed, in light of the global concerns and possibilities the United States faces in the twenty-first century, we might do well to consider the costs of a fatal drifting apart.

22. Addams, *Newer Ideals of Peace*, 51–52.

Select Bibliography

Newspapers, Bulletins, Periodicals, and Journals

American
American Federationist
Broad Ax
Bulletin of the Chicago Teachers Federation
Chicago Defender
Chicago Mail
Chicago Record-Herald
The Chicago Teacher and School Board Journal
Chicago Times
Chicago Tribune
The Crisis
Daily Labor Bulletin
International Seamen's Journal
Locomotive Firemen's Magazine
New York Post
Outlook
The Public
Rockford Register
Typographical Journal
Union Labor Advocate
The Women's City Club Bulletin

Manuscript Collections

Chicago Historical Society

Agnes Nestor
Chicago Teachers' Federation
Chicago Woman's Club
Chicago Federation of Labor
Chicago Federation of Labor Minutes
Chicago Trades and Labor Assembly
City Club of Chicago
Citizens' Association of Chicago
Civic Federation of Metropolitan Chicago
Commercial Club of Chicago

George and Madeleine Wallin-Sikes
Illinois Manufacturers' Association
Irene McCoy Gaines

Meadville-Lombard Theological School, Wiggin Library

Jenkin Lloyd Jones

Newberry Library, Modern Manuscripts Collection

Graham Taylor
Pullman Company Archives
Pullman Strike Scrapbooks

New York Public Library, Rare Books and Manuscripts Division

National Civic Federation

State Historical Society of Wisconsin

Henry Demarest Lloyd
Anita McCormick Blaine
Raymond Robbins

University of Chicago, Special Collections, Joseph Regenstein Library

Bessie Louise Pierce
Charles Merriam
University Presidents
William Rainey Harper
Julius Rosenwald
Ida B. Wells-Barnett

University of Illinois-Chicago, Special Collections

Jane Addams Memorial Collection
Chicago Federation of Settlements and Neighborhood Centers
Chicago Political Equality League Yearbooks
Chicago Urban League
Stuart Hecht Collection
Hull House Association Records
Hull House Collection
Juvenile Protection Association
League of Women Voters of Chicago
Catherine Waugh McCulloch
Mary Jo Deegan
Hilda Satt Polacheck
Harriet Vittum
Women's City Club of Chicago
Women's Trade Union League Scrapbooks

Microfilm Collections

Jane Addams, Swarthmore College Peace Collection
National Association for the Advancement of Colored People

Primary Sources

Materials at Chicago Historical Society

Elliot Anthony Pullman Scrapbooks, [1894?]
"Bulletin published by the United Societies for Local Self-Government" vol. 1, no. 2, December 20, 1906.
Charity Organization Society, *Annual Report of the Directors of the Charity Organization Society of Chicago,* 1886
Chicago Relief and Aid Society, *Annual Report,* 1880
Civic Federation of Chicago, Miscellaneous Pamphlets
Handbook of Chicago Charities
Legislative Committee of the Chicago Federation of Labor, "A Report on Public School Fads" [n.d. 1902?]
Manual of the Citizen's Association, 1882–83
Official Program, National Half Century Anniversary Exposition and the Lincoln Jubilee
Fiftieth Anniversary of Emancipation of Negroes
Catalogue of the Liberian Exhibit, Official Program
Lincoln Jubilee Album, 50th Anniversary of Our Emancipation
Sunset Club, *Sunset Club Yearbook*

Printed Primary Sources

Addams, Jane. "Breadgivers." *Rockford Seminary Magazine* 8 (April 1880): 110–11.
———. "Cassandra." *Essays of Class of '81, Rockford Seminary,* June 22, 1881.
———. *Democracy and Social Ethics.* New York: Macmillan, 1902.
———. *The Excellent Becomes the Permanent.* New York: Macmillan Company, 1932.
———. "A Function of the Social Settlement." In *Jane Addams on Education.* Edited by Ellen Condliffe Lagemann. New York: Teachers College Press, 1985.
———. *The Long Road of Woman's Memory.* New York: Macmillan, 1916.
———. *Newer Ideals of Peace.* Chautauqua, NY: Chautauqua Press, 1907.
———. *The Second Twenty years at Hull-House: September 1909 to September 1929, with a Record of a Growing World Consciousness.* New York: Macmillan, 1930.
———. "The Settlement as a Factor in the Labor Movement." In *Hull-House Maps and Papers,* by Residents of Hull-House. New York: Crowell, 1895.
———. "Social Settlements." National Conference of Charities and Corrections *Proceedings* (1897): 344–45.
———. *Spirit of Youth and City Streets.* New York: Macmillan, 1909.
———. *Twenty Years at Hull House with Autobiographical Notes.* New York: Macmillan, 1910.
Addams, Jane, and Ida B. Wells. Lynching and Rape: An Exchange of Views. Edited by Bettina Aptheker. New York: American Institute for Marxist Studies, 1977.

Alschuler, Samuel. *In the Matter of the Arbitration of Six Questions Concerning Wages, Hours and Conditions of Labor in Certain Packing House Industries, by Agreement Submitted for Decision to a United States Administrator.* Chicago, 1918.

Annual Report of B. A. Eckhart, President, to the Members of the Illinois Manufacturers' Assn. Chicago: M. A. Fountain & Co. Printers, 1903.

Arnold, Matthew. *Culture and Anarchy: An Essay in Political and Social Criticism.* Edited with an Introduction by J. Dover Wilson. Cambridge: Cambridge University Press, 1960.

Baker, Ray Stannard. "The Civic Federation of Chicago." *Outlook* 27 (July 1895).

———. "Shop Council Plan Real Aid to Public." *The Hart, Schaffner & Marx Labor Agreement: Industrial law in the Clothing Industry.* Compiled by Earl Dean Howard. Chicago, 1920.

Barnett, George E., et. al. "Discussion of Trade Unions and Compulsory Arbitration." In *Proceedings of the Academy of Political Science. 7: Labor Disputes and Public Service Corporations,* vol. 7, no. 1 (January, 1917): 81–93.

Barton, Elmer Epictetus. *A Business Tour of Chicago.* Chicago: E. E. Barton, 1887.

The Biographical Dictionary and Portrait Gallery of Representative Men of Chicago and the World's Columbian Exposition. New York: American Biographical Publishing Co., 1892.

Bisno, Abraham. *Abraham Bisno, Union Pioneer.* Madison: University of Wisconsin Press, 1967.

Blackman, Frank W. Review of *Studies in the American Race Problem,* by Alfred H. Stone. *American Journal of Sociology* 14 (July 1909): 837.

Blanc, Madame Theresa. *The Condition of Woman in the United States.* Translated by Abby Langdon Alger. Freeport, NY, 1895. Reprint, 1972.

Bonnett, Clarence E. *Employers' Associations in the United States: A Study of Typical Associations.* New York: Macmillan Company, 1922.

Bourne, Jonathon, Jr. "Functions of the Initiative, Referendum and Recall." In *The Initiative Referendum and Recall,* 3–16. Philadelphia: American Academy of Political and Social Science, 1912.

Bowen, Louise DeKoven. *The Colored People of Chicago: An Investigation made for the Juvenile Protection Associations* by A.P. Drucker, Sophia Boaz, A.L. Harris, Miriam Schaffner. Chicago: Rogers & Hall, 1913.

Brown, Rome G. "The Judicial Recall—A Fallacy Repugnant to Constitutional Government." In *The Initiative, Referendum, and Recall.* Philadelphia: American Academy of Political and Social Science, 1912.

Brown, William Horace. "The Popular Initiative as a Method of Legislation and Political Control." *American Journal of Sociology* 10, no. 6 (May 1905): 713–749.

Bushnell, Horace. "Unconscious Influence" (1846). In *Bushnell, Sermons for the New Life,* rev. ed. New York: Charles Scribner's Sons, 1886.

Carwardine, William H. *The Pullman Strike.* Chicago: Charles H. Kerr, 1894.

Chicago Charter Convention. *Proceedings,* October 3, 1906–March 1, 1907. Chicago, 1906–1907.

Chicago Commission on Race Relations. *The Negro in Chicago: A Study of Race Relations and a Race Riot.* Chicago: University of Chicago Press, 1922.

Civic Federation of Chicago. *Analyses of Chicago market milk: a report by the Health and Sanitation Committee of the Civic Federation of Chicago.* Chicago: Civic Federation, 1904.

———. *Biennial Meeting and Report of the Executive Committee.* Chicago, 1909.

———. *Chicago Gas Trust bills: Another Attack on the People.* Chicago [1897?].

———. *Congress on Industrial Conciliation and Arbitration.* Chicago, 1895.

———. *50 Years on the Civic Front, 1893–1943: A Report on the Achievements of the Civic Federation.* Chicago: The Federation, 1943.

———. *First Annual Report.* Chicago, 1895.

———. *The New Chicago Charter : Why it Should be Adopted at the Special Election, September 17th.* Chicago, 1907.

———. Report of the Legislative committee of the Civic Federation, by William A. Giles, chairman. Chicago, 1899.

———. *The Street Railways of Chicago: Report of the Civic Federation of Chicago.* Edited by Milo Roy Maltbie, PhD Accountant's Report by Edmund F. Bard. New York, 1901.

———. *Tax facts for Illinois: Findings of the Illinois Special Tax Commission; reprinted (in part) by the Civic Federation.* Chicago: Rogers & Hall Co., Printers, [1912?].

———. *To the Civic Federation of Chicago: Preliminary Report on the Need for a New Chicago City Charter.* Chicago, 1902.

———. *The Work of the Civic Federation: Report of the Secretary, Ralph M. Easley, read at the 5th annual meeting, April 26, 1899.* Chicago: Press of Hollister Bros., 1899.

Citizen's Committee for Popular Representation. *Limitation of Representation in the General Assembly of Illinois; an argument against the proposal pending before the Constitutional Convention.* Chicago, 1922.

Cohen, Julius Henry. "A League to Enforce Industrial Peace." In *Proceedings of the Academy of Political Science, vol. VII, Labor Disputes and Public Service Corporations* 7, no. 1 (January 1917).

Commercial Club of Chicago. *Yearbook, 1908.* Chicago: Executive Committee of the Commercial Club of Chicago, 1908.

Commons, John R., ed. *Trade Unionism and Labor Problems.* Boston: Ginn and Company, 1905.

Compton, Wilson. "Wage Theories in Arbitration." In *Trade Unionism and Labor Problems.* Edited by John R. Commons. Second Series. Boston: Ginn and Company, 1921.

Cutler, James Elbert. *Lynch-Law: An Investigation into the History of Lynching in the United States.* New York: Longmans, Green, and Co., 1905.

DeCosta-Willis, Miriam, ed. *The Memphis Diary of Ida B. Wells.* Boston: Beacon Press, 1995.

Dewey, John. *Democracy and Education: An Introduction to the Philosophy of Education.* New York: MacMillan, 1916; New York: The Free Press, 1966.

———. *The Public and Its Problems.* New York: Henry Holt and Company, 1927.

———. "The School as Social Center." In *100 Years at Hull-House.* Edited by Mary Lynn McCree Bryan and Allen F. Davis. Bloomington, IN: Indiana University Press, 1990.

Doty, Mrs. Duane. *The Town of Pullman: Its Growth with Brief Accounts of Its Industries.* Rev. ed. Chicago: Pullman Civic Organization, 1974.

Draper, Andrew. "Common School Problems of Chicago." Address delivered at a citizens meeting under the auspices of the Commission of One Hundred of the Civic Federation of Chicago, December 1, 1900.

Dreiser, Theodore. "Life Stories of Successful Men, No. 12." *Success* 1 (December 8, 1898): 7–8.

DuBois, W. E. B. *Philadelphia Negro: A Social Study.* Philadelphia, 1899.

———. "The Study of Negro Problems." *Annals of the American Academy of Political and Social Science* (January, 1898): 1–23.

Duster, Alfreda M., ed. *Crusade for Justice: The Autobiography of Ida B. Wells.* Chicago: University of Chicago Press, 1970.

Ely, Richard T. "Pullman: A Social Study." *Harper's Monthly* 70 (1885).

Ewing, Quincy. "The Heart of the Race Problem." *Atlantic Monthly* 103 (March 1909): 389.

First Annual Report of the State Board of Arbitration of Illinois. Springfield, IL, 1896.

Fish, Carl. *The Civil Service and Patronage.* New York: Longmans, Green, and Co., 1905.

Fourth Annual Report of the State Board of Arbitration of Illinois. Springfield, IL, 1899.

Frank, Henrietta Greenebaum, and Amalie Hofer Jerome. *Annals of the Chicago Woman's Club for the First Forty Years of Its Organization 1876–1916.* Chicago, 1916.

Frost, E. Allen, Robert McCurdy, and Harry S. McCartney. *Chicago and the Constitution: Report to the Civic Federation of Chicago.* Chicago: Barnard & Miller Printers, 1902.

Gage, Lyman. *Memoirs of Lyman Gage.* New York, 1937.

Henderson, C. R. "Business Men and Social Theorists." *American Journal of Sociology* 1 (January, 1896): 385–97.

Haley, Margaret. "Comments on the New Education Bill." *CTF Bulletin,* January 23, 1903, 1.

———. "Why Teachers Should Organize." National Education Organization. *Addresses and Proceedings* (1904): 145–52.

Handbook of the National Association of Steam and Hot Water Fitters and Helpers (1892).

Harrison, Carter. *Stormy Years: The Autobiography of Carter H. Harrison, Five Times Mayor of Chicago.* New York: Bobbs-Merrill, Co., 1935.

U. S. Congress. House. Committee on Education and Labor, *National Arbitration Tribunal Hearings.* 58th Congress, April 7, 1904.

"Hull-House." *New England Magazine* (July 1898): 550.

Hull-House Maps and Papers: A Presentation of Nationalities and Wages in a Congested District of Chicago, together with comments and essays on problems growing out of the social conditions, by residents of Hull-House, a social settlement at 335 South Halsted Street, Chicago, Ill. New York: T. Y. Crowell & Co., 1895.

"John Farren School, Chicago." *Journal of Education* 73 (February 2, 1911), 119.

Krauskopf, Joseph. "Necessity of Industrial Arbitration." In *The Annals of the American Academy of Political and Social Science; Settlement of Labor Disputes* 36, no. 2 (September 1910): 57–66.

Florence Kelley, "Need Our Working Women Despair?" *The International Review* 13 (Nov. 1882): 517–27.

Kolb, John Harrison. "Arbitration in the Chicago Street Car Controversy of 1912." PhD diss., University of Chicago, 1913.

Lieb, Hermann. *The Initiative and Referendum.* Chicago: H. Lieb, Jr. & Co., 1902.

Lippmann, Walter. *Public Opinion.* New York: Harcourt, Brace, 1922.

Lloyd, Henry Demarest. "No Mean City." In *Mazzini and Other Essays.* Edited by Jane Addams and Anne Withington. New York: Doubleday, Page, & Co., 1910.

Lowell, Josephine Shaw. "The Arbitration of Labor Disputes." *Locomotive Firemen's Magazine* 23, no. 2 (August 1897): 114.

David McCabe, "Federal Intervention in Labor Disputes under the Erdman, Newlands and Adamson Acts." In *Proceedings of the Academy of Political Science,* vol. VII, *Labor Disputes and Public Service Corporations* 7, no. 1 (January, 1917): 94–107.

MacVeagh, Franklin, "A Programme of Municipal Reform." *American Journal of Sociology* 1, no. 5 (March 1896): 551–63.

Meyer, Hermann H. B. *Select List of References on the Initiative, Referendum, and Recall.* Washington: Government Printing Office, 1912.

Munro, William Bennet, ed. *The Initiative , Referendum, and Recall.* New York: D. Appleton & Co., 1915.

National Association for the Advancement of Colored People. *Thirty Years of Lynching in the United States, 1889–1918.* New York: National Association for the Advancement of Colored People, 1919.

National War Labor Board. "Before the War Labor Board, Transcripts of Proceedings in Chicago Vicinity, 1918–1919." Twelve volumes.

Oberholtzer, Ellis Paxson. *The Referendum in America Together with some Chapters on the Initiative and the Recall.* New York: Charles Scribner's Sons, 1911.

Penn, J. Garland. "The Progress of the Afro-American Since Emancipation." In *The Reason Why.* 1893. Reprinted in *Selected Works of Ida B. Wells-Barnett.* Compiled with an introduction by Trudier Harris. New York: Oxford University Press, 1991.

Peters, John P., ed. *Labor and Capital: A Discussion of the Relations of Employer and Employed.* New York: G. P. Putnam's Sons, 1902.

Polacheck, Hilda Satt. *I Came a Stranger: The Story of a Hull-House Girl.* Urbana: University of Illinois Press, 1991.

Proceedings of the General Managers' Association of Chicago, Chicago, June 25, 1894–July 14, 1894. Chicago: Knight, Leonard and Company Press, 1894.

Proceedings of the National Negro Conference, 1909, New York, May 31 and June. New York, 1909.

Rauschenbusch, Walter. *Christianity and the Social Crisis.* New York: Macmillan, 1907.

Roosevelt, Theodore. "The Right of the People to Rule." Washington, DC: Government Printing Office, 1912.

Ruskin, John. *Art and Life: A Ruskin Anthology.* New York: J. B. Alden, 1900.

Small, Albion. "The Organic Concept of Society." *Annals of the American Academy* 5, no. 5 (1894): 740–46.

———. "Private Business as a Public Trust." *American Journal of Sociology* 1, no. 2 (September 1895): 276–89.

———. "The Relation of Sociology to Political Economy." *Journal of Political Economy* 3 (1894–95): 169–84.

———. "Scholarship and Social Agitation." *American Journal of Sociology* 1, no. 5 (March 1896): 564–82.

Small, Albion, and George E. Vincent. *An Introduction to the Study of Society.* New York, 1894.

Snowden, Clifford L. "The Armour Institute of Technology." *New England Magazine* 16 (May 1897): 371.

State Board of Arbitration. *Views of Arbitration as Means of Settling Labor Disputes.* Rochester, NY: Union & Advertiser's Company's Printers, 1886.

Sumner, William Graham. *Folkways: A Study of the Sociological Importance of Usages, Manners, Customs, Mores, and Morals.* Boston: Ginn and Co., 1906.

———. *What the Social Classes Owe Each Other.* New York: Harper, 1883.

The Statistical History of the United States from Colonial Times to the Present. Stamford, CT: Fairfield Publishing, Inc., 1965.

Stead, William T. *If Christ Came to Chicago.* Chicago: Laird & Lee, 1894.

Strong, Josiah. "Are the Interests of Employer and Employed Mutual, and, if so, How can this Mutuality of Interests be Made Effective." In *Labor and Capital: A Discussion of the Relations of Employer and Employed.* Edited by John P. Peters. New York: G. P. Putnam's Sons, 1902.

Taylor, Fredrick Winslow. *The Principles of Scientific Management.* New York: Harper, 1911.

Taylor, Graham. *Pioneering on Social Frontiers.* Chicago: University of Chicago Press, 1930.

U.S. Congress. *Final Report of the Industrial Commission on the Industrial Commission on the Relations and Conditions of Capital and Labor Employed in Manufactures and General Business Including Testimony with Review,* vol. 7. Washington, DC: Government Printing Office 1901; Westport, CT: Greenwood Press.

———. *Report of the Industrial Commission of the Chicago Labor Disputes of 1900, with Especial Reference to the Disputes in the Building and Machinery Trades,* vol. 8. Washington: Government Printing Office, 1901; Westport, CT: Greenwood Press.

———. *Reports of the Industrial Commission on Labor Organizations, Labor Disputes, and Arbitration, and on Railway Labor,* vol. 17. Washington, DC: Government Printing Office, 1901.

———. *Final Report of the Industrial Commission on the Industrial Commission on the Relations and Conditions of Capital and Labor Employed in Manufactures and General Business Including Testimony with Review,* vol. 19. Washington, DC: Government Printing Office, 1901; Westport CT: Greenwood Press.

U. S. Department of Labor Bureau of Labor Statistics. *Mediation and Arbitration Laws of the United States.* Washington, DC: Government Printing Office, 1913, 17–19

United States Strike Commission. *Report on the Chicago Strike of June–July, 1894.* Washington, DC: United States Strike Commission, 1895.

Washington, Booker T., *Montgomery Advertiser,* December 30, 1910. Reprinted in *African American Political Thought, 1890–1930: Washington, DuBois, Garvey, and Randolph.* Edited by Cary D. Armonk Wintz. New York: M.E. Sharp, 1996.

———. "A Protest against Lynching." In the *Birmingham Age-Herald,* February 29, 1904. Reprinted in *African American Political Thought, 1890–1930: Washington, DuBois, Garvey, and Randolph.* Edited by Cary D. Armonk Wintz. New York: M.E. Sharp, 1996.

Weeden, William B. "Arbitration and its Relation to Strikes." Boston: Press of Geo. H. Ellis, 1887.

Weeks, Joseph D. "Labor Differences and Their Settlement: A Plea for Arbitration and Conciliation." *Economic Tracts,* No. 20. New York: The Society for Political Education, 1886.

Wells-Barnett, Ida B. "How Enfranchisement Stops Lynching." *Original Rights Magazine* (June 1910): 42–53. Reprinted in Mildred I. Thompson, *Ida B. Wells-Barnett: An Exploratory Study of an American Black Woman, 1893–1930.* Brooklyn, NY: Carlson Publishing, Inc., 1990.

———. *On Lynchings: Southern Horrors [1892], A Red Record [1895] Mob Rule in New Orleans [1900].* New York: Arno Press and the *New York Times,* 1969.

"Our Country's Lynching Record." Survey (February 1, 1913): 573–74. Reprinted in Mildred I. Thompson, *Ida B. Wells-Barnett: An Exploratory Study of an American Black Woman, 1893–1930.* Brooklyn, NY: Carlson Publishing, Inc., 1990.

———. *Selected Works of Ida B. Wells-Barnett.* New York: Oxford University Press, 1991.

Wilcox, Delos F. *Government by All the People or the Initiative, the Referendum and the Recall as Instruments of Democracy.* New York: The MacMillan Co., 1912.

Williams, Fannie Barrier. "The Frederick Douglass Centre: A Question of Social Betterment and Not of Social Equality." *Voice of the Negro* 1, no. 12 (1904): 601–4. Reprinted in *The New Woman of Color: The Collected Writings of Fannie Barrier Williams, 1893–1918.* Edited by Mary Jo Deegan. DeKalb: Northern Illinois University Press, 2002.

———. "A New Method of Dealing with the Race Problem." *Voice of the Negro* 3, no. 7 (1906): 502–5. Reprinted in *The New Woman of Color: The Collected Writings of Fannie Barrier Williams, 1893–1918.* Edited by Mary Jo Deegan. DeKalb: Northern Illinois University Press, 2002

———. "Social Bonds in the Black Belt of Chicago: Negro Organizations and the New Spirit Pervading Them." *Charities* 15 (October, 15, 1905): 44. Reprinted in *The New Woman of Color: The Collected Writings of Fannie Barrier Williams, 1893–1918.* Edited by Mary Jo Deegan. DeKalb: Northern Illinois University Press, 2002.

Williams, J. E., Sidney Hillman, Earl Dean Howard. *The Hart Schaffner & Marx Labor Agreement, Being a Compilation and Codification of the Agreements of 1911, 1913 and 1916 and decisions rendered by the Board of Arbitration.* Chicago, 1916.

Winslow, Charles H. *Collective Agreements in the Men's Clothing Industry.* U.S. Department of Labor, Bureau of Labor Statistics. Washington, DC: Government Printing Office, 1916.

Woolley, Celia Parker. *Unity* (4 May 1905): 5.

———. *Unity* (3 November 1904): 53–54.

Wood, David Ward, ed. *Chicago and Its Distinguished Citizens or the Progress of Forty Years.* Chicago: Milton George and Co., 1881.

Wood, Henry. *The Political Economy of Natural Law.* Boston: Lee and Shepard Publishers, 1894.

Wright, Carroll. *Industrial Conciliation and Arbitration.* Boston: Rand, Abery, & Co., 1881.

Wright, Jr., R. R. "The Negro in Times of Industrial Unrest." *Charities* 15, no. 1 (October 7, 1905): 69–73.

Secondary Sources

Adelman, William J. "The Road to Fort Sheridan." In *Haymarket Scrapbook.* Edited by David Roediger. Chicago: C. H. Kerr Publishing Company, 1986.

Agnew, Jean-Christophe. *Worlds Apart: The Market and the Theater in Anglo-American Thought, 1550–1750.* New York: Cambridge University Press.

Akin, William E. "Arbitration and Labor Conflict: The Middle Class Panacea, 1886–1900." *The Historian* 29, no. 4 (August 1967): 565–83.

Allen, David S. *Democracy, Inc.: The Press and Law in the Corporate Rationalization of the Public Sphere.* Urbana: University of Illinois Press, 2005.

Anderson, Benedict. *Imagined Communities: Reflections on the Origin and Spread of Nationalism.* London: Verso, 1991.

Anderson, James. *The Education of Blacks in the South, 1860–1935.* Chapel Hill: The University of North Carolina Press, 1988.

Aron, Cindy Sondik. *Ladies and Gentlemen of the Civil Service: Middle Class Workers in Victorian America.* New York: Oxford University Press, 1987.

Bachin, Robin F. *Building the South Side: Urban Space and Civic Culture in Chicago, 1890–1919.* Chicago: University of Chicago Press, 2004.

Barber, Benjamin. "Clansmen, Consumers, and Citizens: Three Takes on Civil Society." In *Civil Society, Democracy, and Civic Renewal.* Edited by Robert K. Fullinwider. Lanham, MD: Rowman & Littlefield, Publishers, 1999.

Barnes, Elizabeth. *States of Sympathy: Seduction and Democracy in the American Novel.* New York: Columbia University Press, 1997.

Barrett, James R. *Work and Community in the Jungle: Chicago's Packinghouse Workers, 1894–1922.* Urbana, IL: University of Illinois Press, 1987.

Bay, Mia. *The White Image in the Black Mind: African-American Ideas about White People, 1830–1925.* New York: Oxford University Press, 2000.

———. "'The World Was Thinking Wrong about Race': The *Philadelphia Negro* and Nineteenth-Century Science." In *W. E. B. Dubois, Race, and the City: The Philadelphia Negro and Its Legacy.* Edited by Michael B. Katz and Thomas J. Sugrue. Philadelphia: University of Pennsylvania Press, 1998.

Beckert, Sven. "Propertied of a Different Kind: Bourgeoisie and Lower Middle-Class in the Nineteenth Century United States." In *The Middling Sorts: Explorations in the History of the American Middle Class.* Edited by Burton Bledstein and Robert D. Johnston. New York: Routledge, 2001.

Bederman, Gail. *Manliness and Civilization: A Cultural History of Gender and Race in the United States, 1880–1917.* Chicago: University of Chicago Press, 1995.

Bender, Daniel E. *Sweated Work, Weak Bodies: Anti-Sweatshop Campaigns and Languages of Labor.* New Brunswick: Rutgers University Press, 2004.

Bender, Thomas, ed. *The Antislavery Debate: Capitalism and Abolitionism as a Problem in Historical Interpretation.* Berkeley: University of California Press, 1992.

———. *Intellect and Public Life: Essays on the Social History of Academic Intellectuals in the United States.* Baltimore: The Johns Hopkins University Press, 1992.

Benhabib, Seyla, ed. *Democracy and Difference: Contesting the Boundaries of the Political.* Princeton: Princeton University Press, 1996.

Berger, Peter L., and Thomas Luckmann. *The Social Construction of Reality: A Treatise in the Sociology of Knowledge.* New York: Doubleday & Co, Inc., 1966.

Berry, Mary Frances. "Judging Morality: Sexual Behavior and Legal Consequences in the Late Nineteenth-Century South." *Journal of American History* 78, no. 3 (December 1993): 835–56.

Bingham, Truman Cicero. "The Chicago Federation of Labor." MA thesis, University of Chicago, 1924.

Bizjack, Jack. "The Trade and Labor Assembly of Chicago." MA thesis, University of Chicago, 1969.

Blake, Casey Nelson. *Beloved Community: The Cultural Criticism of Randolph Bourne, Van Wyck Brooks, Waldo Frank, and Lewis Mumford.* Chapel Hill: University of North Carolina Press, 1991.

Bledstein, Burton J. *The Culture of Professionalism: The Middle Class and the Development of Higher Education.* New York: Norton, 1976.

———. "Introduction: Storytellers to the Middle Class." In *The Middling Sorts: Explorations in the History of the American Middle Class.* Edited by Burton Bledstein and Robert D. Johnston. New York: Routledge, 2001.

Blight, David. *Race and Reunion: The Civil War in American Memory.* Cambridge, MA: Belknap Press of Harvard University Press, 2001.

Blumin, Stuart. *The Emergence of the Middle Class: Social Experience in the American City, 1760–1900.* New York: Cambridge University Press, 1989.

Bohman, James. "Deliberative Democracy and Effective Social Freedom: Capabilities, Resources, and Opportunities." In *Deliberative Democracy: Essays on Reason and Politics.* Edited by James Bohman and William Rehg. Cambridge: MIT Press, 1997.

———. "Participants, Observers, and Critics: Practical Knowledge, Social Perspectives, and Critical Pluralism." In P*luralism and the Pragmatic Turn: The Transformation of Critical Theory: Essays in Honor of Thomas McCarthy.* Edited by William Rehg and James Bohman. Cambridge: MIT Press, 2001.

Bordin, Ruth. *Women and Temperance: The Quest for Power and Liberty, 1873–1900.* Philadelphia: Temple University Press, 1981.

Borus, Daniel H. *Writing Realism: Howells, James, and Norris in the Mass Market.* Chapel Hill: University of North Carolina Press, 1989.

Boydston, Jeanne. "To Earn Her Daily Bread: Housework and Antebellum Working-Class Subsistence." In *Unequal Sisters: A Multi-Cultural Reader in U.S. Women's History.* New York: Routledge, 1994.

Boyer, Paul. *Urban Masses and Moral Order in America, 1820–1920.* Cambridge, MA: Harvard University Press.

Brody, David. *Labor Embattled: History, Power, Rights.* Champaign: University of Illinois Press, 2005.

Brown, Victoria Bissell. "Advocate for Democracy: Jane Addams and the Pullman Strike." In *The Pullman Strike and the Crisis of the 1890s: Essays on Labor and Politics.* Edited by Richard Schneirov, Shelton Stromquist, and Nick Salvatore. Urbana: University of Illinois Press, 1999.

———. *The Education of Jane Addams.* Philadelphia: University of Pennsylvania Press, 2004.

———. "Introduction." In *Jane Addams, Twenty Years at Hull-House.* Edited by Victoria Bissell Brown. Boston: Bedford/St. Martin's, 1999.

Brundage, W. Fitzhugh. *Lynching in the New South: Georgia and Virginia, 1880–1930.* Urbana: University of Illinois Press, 1993.

Buder, Stanley. *Pullman: An Experiment in Industrial Order and Community Planning, 1880–1930.* New York: Oxford University Press, 1967.

Buenker, John D. *Urban Liberalism and Progressive Reform.* New York: Norton, 1973.

Buenker, John D., John C. Burnham, and Robert M. Crunden. *Progressivism.* Cambridge: Harvard University Press, 1977.

Bulmer, Martin, Kevin Bales, and Kathryn Kish Sklar, eds. *The Social Survey in Historical Perspective, 1880–1940.* Cambridge: Cambridge University Press, 1991.

Burg, Douglas F. *Chicago's White City of 1893.* Lexington, KY: University of Kentucky Press, 1976.

Burke, Peter. *A Social History of Knowledge: From Gutenberg to Diderot.* Malden, MA: Blackwell, 2000.

Burnham, Robert A. "The Boss Becomes a Manager: Executive Authority and City Charter Reform, 1880–1929." In *Making Sense of the City: Local Government, Civic Culture, and Community Life in Urban America.* Edited by Robert B. Fairbanks and Patricia Mooney-Melvin, eds. Columbus: The Ohio State University Press, 2001.

Burstein, Andrew. *Sentimental Democracy: The Evolution of America's Romantic Self-Image.* New York: Hill and Wang, 1999.

Camacho, Alicia R. Schmidt. "Migrant Subjects: Race, Labor and Insurgency in the Mexico-U.S. Borderlands." PhD diss., Stanford University, 2000.

Carby, Hazel V. "'On the Threshold of Woman's Era': Lynching, Empire, and Sexuality in Black Feminist Theory." *Critical Inquiry* 12, no. 1 (1985): 262–77.

———. Reconstructing Womanhood: *The Emergence of the Afro-American Woman Novelist.* New York: Oxford University Press, 1987.

Carson, Mina. *Settlement Folk: Social Thought and the American Settlement Movement, 1885–1930.* Chicago: University of Chicago Press, 1990.

Christensen, Terry. *Reel Politics: American Political Movies from Birth of a Nation to Platoon.* New York: Basil Blackwell, 1987.

Clarke, Elizabeth. "'Sacred Rights of the Weak': Pain, Sympathy, and the Culture of Individual Rights in Antebellum America." *Journal of American History* 82, no. 2 (March 1995): 463–93.

Clemens, Elisabeth. *The People's Lobby: Organizational Innovation and the Rise of Interest Group Politics in the United States, 1890–1925.* Chicago: University of Chicago Press, 1997.

Clement, Grace. *Care, Autonomy, and Justice: Feminism and the Ethic of Care.* Boulder, CO: Westview, 1996.

Cohen, Andrew Wender. *The Racketeer's Progress: Chicago and the Struggle for the Modern American Economy, 1900–1940.* New York: Cambridge University Press, 2004.

Cohen, Lizabeth. *A Consumer's Republic: The Politics of Mass Consumption in Postwar America.* New York: Knopf, 2003.

———. Making a New Deal: *Industrial Workers in Chicago, 1919–1939.* Cambridge: Cambridge University Press, 1990.

Cohen, Nancy. *The Reconstruction of American Liberalism, 1865–1914.* Chapel Hill: University of North Carolina Press, 2002.

Colby, Anne, et al. *Educating Citizens: Preparing America's Undergraduates for Lives of Moral and Civic Responsibility.* San Francisco: Jossey-Bass, 2003.

Coleman, Peter J. "'Strikes are War! War is Hell!': American Responses to the Compulsory Arbitration of Labor Disputes, 1890–1920." *Wisconsin Magazine of History* (1987): 187–210.

Collins, Patricia Hill. *Black Feminist Thought: Knowledge, Consciousness, and the Politics of Empowerment.* Boston: Unwin Hyman, 1990.

Conn, Steven. *Museums and American Intellectual Life, 1876–1926.* Chicago: University of Chicago Press, 1998.

Connolly, James J. *The Triumph of Ethnic Progressivism: Urban Political Culture in Boston, 1900–1925.* Cambridge, MA: Harvard University Press, 1998.

Conner, Valerie Jean. *The National War Labor Board: Stability, Social Justice, and the Voluntary State in World War I.* Chapel Hill: University of North Carolina Press, 1983.

Corkin, Stanley. *Realism and the Birth of the Modern United States: Cinema, Literature, and Culture.* Athens, GA: The University of Georgia Press, 1996.

Cott, Nancy. *The Bonds of Womanhood: "Woman's Sphere" in New England, 1780–1835.* New Haven : Yale University Press, 1977.

Crane, Gregg D. *Race, Citizenship, and the Law in American Literature.* Cambridge: Cambridge University Press, 2002.

Cripps, Thomas. "The Reaction of the Negro to the Motion Picture Birth of a Nation." *The Historian* 25, no. 3 (1962–63): 344–62.

Crunden, Robert M. *Ministers of Reform: The Progressives' Achievement in American Civilization, 1889–1920.* New York: Basic Books, 1982.

Cuff, Dana. "The Figure of the Neighbor: Los Angeles Past and Future." *American Quarterly* 56, no. 3 (September 2004): 559–82.

Curti, Merle. "Jane Addams and Human Nature." *Journal of the History of Ideas* 22 (April–June 1961): 240–53.

Cronin, Thomas E. *Direct Democracy: The Politics of Initiative, Referendum, and Recall.* Cambridge, MA: Harvard University Press, 1989.

Cronon, William. *Nature's Metropolis: Chicago and the Great West.* New York: W.W. Norton, 1991.

Cyphers, Christopher J. *The National Civic Federation and the Making of a New Liberalism, 1900–1915.* Westport, CT: Praeger, 2002.

Dale, Elizabeth. "'Social Equality Does Not Exist among Themselves, nor among Us': *Baylies vs. Curry* and Civil Rights in Chicago, 1888." *American Historical Review* 102 (April 1997): 311–39.

Davis, Allen F. *American Heroine: The Life and Legend of Jane Addams.* New York: Oxford University Press, 1973.

———. *Spearheads of Reform: The Social Settlements and the Progressive Movement.* New York: Oxford University Press, 1967.

Davis, Angela Y. *Women, Race & Class.* New York: Vintage, 1983.

Dawley, Alan. *Struggles for Justice: Social Responsibility and the Liberal State.* Cambridge, MA: Harvard University Press, 1991.

Deegan, Mary Jo. *The New Woman of Color: The Collected Writings of Fannie Barrier Williams, 1893–1918.* DeKalb: Northern Illinois University Press, 2002.

———, ed. *Women in Sociology: A Bio-Bibliographical Sourcebook.* New York: Greenwood Press, 1991.

Derber, Milton. *The American Idea of Industrial Democracy, 1865–1965.* Urbana, IL: University of Illinois Press, 1970.

Deutsch, Sarah. "Learning to Talk More like a Man: Boston Women's Class-Bridging Organizations, 1870–1940." *American Historical Review* 97 (1992): 379–404.

Dimock, Wai Chee. *Residues of Justice: Literature, Law, Philosophy.* Berkeley: University of California Press, 1996.

Diggins, Patrick. *The Promise of Pragmatism: Modernism and the Crisis of Knowledge and Authority.* Chicago: University of Chicago Press, 1994.

Diner, Steven J. *A City and Its Universities: Public Policy in Chicago 1892–1919.* Chapel Hill: University of North Carolina Press, 1980.

Donohue, Kathleen G. *Freedom from Want: American Liberalism and the Idea of the Consumer.* Baltimore: Johns Hopkins University Press, 2005.

Dorfman, Joseph. *The Economic Mind in American Civilization.* New York: Viking, 1949.

Dorsey, Bruce. *Reforming Men & Women: Gender in the Antebellum City.* Ithaca: Cornell University Press, 2002.

Drake, St. Clair. *Churches and Voluntary Associations in the Chicago Negro Community.* Chicago: Works Progress Administration, 1940.

Drake, St. Clair, and Horace R. Cayton. *Black Metropolis: A Study of Negro Life in a Northern City.* Vol. I. New York: Harcourt, Brace and Company, 1945.

Duis, Perry. "Whose City?: Public and Private Places in Nineteenth-Century Chicago." *Chicago History* 12 (March 1983): 2–23.

Einhorn, Robin L. *Property Rules: Political Economy in Chicago, 1832–1877.* Chicago: University of Chicago Press, 1991.

Eisenach, Eldon J. *The Lost Promise of Progressivism.* Lawrence: University of Kansas Press, 1994.

Elshtain, Jean Bethke. *Jane Addams and the Dream of American Democracy.* New York: Basic Books, 2002.

Enstad, Nan. *Ladies of Labor, Girls of Adventure: Working Women, Popular Culture, and Labor Politics at the Turn of the Twentieth Century.* New York: Columbia University Press, 1999.

Ethington, Philip. "The Metropolis and Multicultural Ethics: Direct Democracy versus Deliberative Democracy in the Progressive Era." In *Progressivism and the New Democracy.* Edited by Sidney M. Milkis and Jerome M. Mileur. Amherst: University of Massachusetts Press, 1999.

———. *The Public City: The Political Construction of Urban Life in San Francisco, 1850–1900.* New York: Cambridge University Press, 1994.

Everett, Anna. *Returning the Gaze: A Genealogy of Black Film Criticism, 1909–1949.* Durham: Duke University Press, 2001.

Fabe, Marilyn. *Closely Watched Films: An Introduction to the Art of Narrative Film Technique.* Berkeley: University of California Press, 2004.

Fabian, Ann Vincent. *Card Sharps, Dream Books, and Bucket Shops.* Ithaca: Cornell University Press, 1990.

Farrell, James. *Beloved Lady: A History of Jane Addams' Ideas on Reform and Peace.* Baltimore: Johns Hopkins University Press, 1967.

Feffer, Andrew. *The Chicago Pragmatists and American Progressivism.* Ithaca: Cornell University Press, 1993.

Finegold, Kenneth. *Experts and Politicians: Reform Challenges to Machine Politics in New York, Cleveland, and Chicago.* Princeton: Princeton University Press, 1995.

Fink, Leon. "Expert Advice: Progressive Intellectuals and the Unraveling of Labor Reform, 1912–1915." In *Intellectuals and Public Life: Between Radicalism and Reform.* Edited by Leon Fink, Stephen T. Leonard, and Donald M. Reid. Ithaca: Cornell University Press, 1996.

Fischer, Marilyn. "Jane Addams's Critique of Capitalism as Patriarchal." In *Feminist Interpretations of John Dewey*. Edited by Charlene Haddock Seigfried. University Park, PA: Pennsylvania State University Press, 2002.

Fisher, Philip. *Hard Facts: Setting and Form in the American Novel*. New York: Oxford University Press, 1985.

Fitzpatrick, Ellen. *Endless Crusade: Women Social Scientists and Progressive Reform*. New York: Oxford University Press, 1990.

Flanagan, Maureen. *Charter Reform in Chicago*. Carbondale, IL: Southern Illinois University Press, 1987.

———. "The City Profitable, the City Livable: Environmental Policy, Gender and Power in Chicago in the 1910s." *Journal of Urban History* 22, no. 2 (1996): 163–90.

———. *Seeing with Their Hearts: Chicago Women and the Vision of the Good City, 1871–1933*. Princeton: Princeton University Press, 2002.

Fletcher, Bill, Jr. "Labor's Renewal? Listening to the 1920s and the 1930s." *Labor: Studies in Working-Class History of the Americas* 1, no. 3 (Fall 2004): 13–18.

Foner, Eric. *Free Soil, Free Labor, Free Men: The Ideology of the Republican Party before the Civil War*. New York : Oxford University Press, 1970.

———. *Reconstruction: America's Unfinished Journey*. New York : Harper & Row, 1988.

Forbath, William E. *Law and the Shaping of the American Labor Movement*. Cambridge, MA: Harvard University Press, 1991.

Foucault, Michel. *The Archeology of Knowledge*. Translated by A. M. Sheridan Smith. New York: Pantheon Books, 1972.

———. *Power/Knowledge: Selected Interview and Other Writings, 1972–1977*. Edited and Translated by Colin Gordon. New York: Pantheon Books, 1980.

Franklin, V. P. *Living Our Stories, Telling Our Truths: Autobiography and the Making of the African-American Intellectual Tradition*. New York: Scribner, 1995.

Fraser, Nancy. *Unruly Practices: Power, Discourse, and Gender in Contemporary Social Theory*. Minneapolis: University of Minnesota Press, 1989.

Fraser, Nancy, and Linda Gordon. "A Genealogy of Dependency: Tracing a Keyword of the U.S. Welfare State." *Signs* 19, no. 2 (1994): 309–36.

Fraser, Nancy, and Axel Honneth. *Redistribution or Recognition?: A Political-Philosophical Exchange*. Translated by Joel Golb, James Ingram, and Christiane Wilke. London: Verso, 2003.

Frazier, Lessie Jo. *Salt in the Sand*. Durham, NC: Duke University Press, 2007.

Fuhrman, Ellsworth R. *The Sociology of Knowledge in America, 1883–1915*. Charlottesville, VA: University Press of Virginia, 1980.

Fullinwider, Robert K. *Civil Society, Democracy, and Civic Renewal*. Lanham, MD: Rowman & Littlefield, Publishers, 1999.

Furner, Mary O. *Advocacy and Objectivity: A Crisis in the Professionalization of American Social Science, 1865–1905*. Lexington: University Press of Kentucky, 1975.

———. "Knowing Capitalism: Public Investigation of the Labor Question in the Long Progressive Era." In *The State and Economic Knowledge: The American and British Experiences*. Edited by Mary O. Furner and Barry Supple. New York: Cambridge University Press, 1990.

———. "The Republican Tradition and the New Liberalism: Social Investigation, State Building, and Social Learning in the Gilded Age." In *The State and Social Investigation in Britain and the United States*. Edited by Michael J. Lacey and Mary O. Furner. Cambridge: Woodrow Wilson Center Press and Cambridge University Press, 1993.

Furner, Mary O., and Michael J. Lacy. "Social Investigation, Social Knowledge, and the State: An Introduction." In *The State and Social Investigation in Britain and the United States*. Edited by Mary O. Furner and Michael Lacey. Washington, DC: Woodrow Wilson Center Press and Cambridge University Press, 1993.

Gaines, Kevin. *Uplifting the Race: Black Leadership, Politics, and Culture in the Twentieth Century*. Chapel Hill: University of North Carolina Press, 1996.

Gardiner, Judith Kegan. "Masculinity, The Teening of America, and Empathic Targeting." In *Feminisms at a Millennium*. Edited by Judith A. Howard and Carolyn Allen. Chicago: University of Chicago Press, 2000.

Geertz, Clifford. *The Interpretation of Cultures*. New York: Basic Books, 1973.

———. *Local Knowledge: Further Essays in Interpretive Anthropology*. New York: Basic Books, 1983.

Gere, Anne Ruggles. *Intimate Practices: Literacy and Cultural Work in U.S. Women's Clubs, 1880–1920*. Urbana, IL: University of Illinois Press, 1997.

Gilbert, James. *Perfect Cities: Chicago's Utopias of 1893*. Chicago: University of Chicago Press, 1991.

Gilmore, Glenda. *Gender and Jim Crow: Women and the Politics of White Supremacy in North Carolina, 1896–1920*. Chapel Hill: University of North Carolina Press, 1996.

Ginger, Ray. *Altgeld's America: The Lincoln Ideal versus Changing Realities*. Chicago: Quadrangle Books, 1958.

Glenn, Evelyn Nakano. *Unequal Freedom: How Race and Gender Shaped American Citizenship and Labor*. Cambridge: Harvard University Press, 2002.

Glickman, Lawrence B. *A Living Wage: American Workers and the Making of Consumer Society*. Ithaca: Cornell University Press, 1997.

Goodwin, Jeff, James M. Jasper, and Francesca Polletta, eds. *Passionate Politics: Emotions and Social Movements*. Chicago University of Chicago Press, 2001.

Goodwyn, Lawrence. *Democratic Promise: The Populist Moment in America*. New York: Oxford University Press, 1976.

Gordon, Linda. *Pitied but not Entitled: Single Mothers and the History of Welfare, 1890–1935*. New York: Free Press, 1994.

———, ed. *Women, the State, and Welfare*. Madison: University of Wisconsin Press, 1990.

Gramsci, Antonio. *Selections from the Prison Notebooks of Antonio Gramsci*. Edited and translated by Quintin Hoare and Geoffrey Nowell Smith. New York: International Publishers, 1972.

Green, Marguerite. "The National Civic Federation and the American Labor Movement, 1900–1925." PhD diss., Catholic University of America, 1956.

Grever, Maria, and Berteke Waaldijk. *Transforming the Public Sphere: The Dutch National Exhibition of Women's Labor in 1898*. Durham, NC: Duke University Press, 2004.

Grossman, James R. *Land of Hope: Chicago, Black Southerners, and the Great Migration*. Chicago: University of Chicago Press, 1989.

Guglielmo, Thomas A. *White on Arrival: Italians, Race, Color, and Power in Chicago, 1890–1945.* New York: Oxford University Press, 2003.

Gunning, Sandra. *Race, Rape, and Lynching: The Red Record of American Literature, 1890–1912.* New York: Oxford University Press, 1996.

Gutman, Herbert. "The Failure of the Movement by the Unemployed for Public Works in 1873." *Political Science Quarterly* 80, no. 2 (1965): 254–76.

Habermas, Jürgen. *The Structural Transformation of the Public Sphere: An Inquiry into a Category of Bourgeois Society.* Cambridge, MA: MIT Press, 1994.

———. *Theory of Communicative Action: Reason and Rationalization of Society.* Translated by Thomas McCarthy. Boston: Beacon Press, 1981.

Halberstam, Judith. *Skin Shows: Gothic Horror and the Technology of Monsters.* Durham, NC: Duke University Press, 1995.

Hall, Jacquelyn Dowd. *Revolt against Chivalry: Jessie Daniel Ames and the Women's Campaign against Lynching.* New York: Columbia University Press, 1993.

Hall, Stuart. "What is this 'Black' in Black Popular Culture." In *Representing Blackness: Issues in Film and Video.* Edited by Valerie Smith. New Brunswick, NJ: Rutgers University Press, 1997.

Hamington, Maurice. *Embodied Care: Jane Addams, Maurice Merleau-Ponty, and Feminist Ethics.* Urbana, IL: University of Illinois Press, 2004.

Hapke, Laura. *Labor's Text: The Worker in American Fiction.* New Brunswick, NJ: Rutgers University Press, 2001.

———. *Sweatshop: The History of an American Ideal.* New Brunswick: Rutgers University Press, 2004.

Harris, Howell John. *Bloodless Victories: The Rise and Fall of the Open Shop in the Philadelphia Metal Trades, 1890–1940.* New York: Cambridge University Press, 2000.

———. "The Making of a 'Business Community,' 1880–1930: Definitions and Ingredients of a Collective Identity." In *Federalism, Citizenship, and Collective Identities in U.S. History.* Edited by Cornelius A. van Minnen and Sylvia L. Hilton. Amsterdam: Vu University Press, 2000.

Harris, Trudier. *Exorcising Blackness: Historical and Literary Lynching and Burning Rituals.* Bloomington: Indiana University Press, 1984.

Harvey, David. *Consciousness and the Urban Experience: Studies in the History and Theory of Capitalist Urbanization.* Baltimore: Johns Hopkins University Press, 1985.

Haskell, Thomas. *The Emergence of Professional Social Science: The American Social Science Association and the Nineteenth Century Crisis of Authority.* Urbana, IL: University of Illinois Press, 1977.

———, ed. *The Authority of Experts: Studies in History and Theory.* Bloomington, IN: Indiana University Press, 1984.

Hays, Samuel. "The Politics of Reform in Municipal Government in the Progressive Era." *Pacific Northwest Quarterly* 55 (1964): 157–69.

———. *The Response to Industrialism, 1885–1914.* 2nd ed. Chicago: University of Chicago Press, 1995.

Hecht, Stuart Joel. "Hull-House Theatre: An Analytical and Evaluative History." PhD diss., Northwestern University, 1984.

Hendricks, Wanda. *Gender, Race, and Politics in the Midwest: Black Club Women in Illinois.* Bloomington: Indiana University Press, 1998.

————. "'Vote for the Advantage of Ourselves and Our Race': The Election of the First Black Alderman in Chicago." *Illinois State Historical Journal* 87 (1994): 171–84.

Hirschman, Albert. *The Passions and the Interests: Political Arguments for Capitalism Before Its Triumph.* Princeton: Princeton University Press, 1977.

Hayduk, Ronald, and Kevin Mattson, eds. *Democracy's Moment: Reforming the American Political System for the 21st Century.* New York: Rowman and Littlefield Publishers, Inc., 2002.

Hofstadter, Richard. *The Age of Reform, from Bryan to F. D. R.* New York: Vintage Books, 1955.

Hogan, David. *Class and Reform: School and Society in Chicago, 1880–1930.* Philadelphia: University of Pennsylvania Press, 1985.

Holland, Catherine. *The Body Politic: Foundings, Citizenship, and Difference in the American Political Imagination.* New York: Routledge, 2001.

Holli, Melvin. *Reform in Detroit: Hazen S. Pingree and Urban Politics.* New York: Oxford University Press, 1969.

Hollinger David. *In the American Province: Studies in the History and Historiography of Ideas.* Bloomington, IN: Indiana University Press, 1985.

————. "The Knower and the Artificer, with Postscript 1993." In *Modernist Impulses in the Human Sciences.* Edited by Dorothy Ross. Baltimore: Johns Hopkins University Press, 1999.

Holland, Sharon Patricia. *Raising the Dead: Readings on Death and (Black) Subjectivity.* Durham, NC: Duke University Press, 2000.

Homel, Michael. *Down from Equality: Black Chicagoans and the Public Schools, 1920–41.* Urbana: University of Illinois Press, 1984.

hooks, bell. *Ain't I a Woman: Black Women and Feminism.* Boston: South End Press, 1981.

Hooper-Greenhill, Eilean. *Museums and the Shaping of Knowledge.* New York: Routledge, 1992.

Hoopes, James. *Community Denied: The Wrong Turn of Pragmatic Liberalism.* Ithaca: Cornell University Press, 1998.

Horowitz, Helen Lefkowitz. *Culture and the City: Cultural Philanthropy in Chicago from the 1880s to 1917.* Chicago: University of Chicago Press, 1976.

————. "Hull-House as Women's Space." *Chicago History* (December 1983): 40–55.

Horowitz, Morton J. *The Transformation of American Law, 1870–1960: The Crisis of Legal Orthodoxy.* New York: Oxford University Press, 1977.

Horton, Carol. "Liberal Equality and the Civic Subject: Identity and Citizenship in Reconstruction America." In *The Liberal Tradition in America: Reassessing the Legacy of American Liberalism.* Edited by David F. Ericson and Louisa Bertch Green. New York: Routledge, 1999.

Hummel, Ralph P. "Stories Managers Tell: Why They Are as Valid as Science." In *Democracy, Bureaucracy, and the Study of Administration.* Edited by Camilla Stivers. Boulder, CO: Westview Press, 2001.

Ingraham, Patricia Wallace. *The Foundation of Merit: Public Service in American Democracy.* Baltimore: The Johns Hopkins University Press, 1995.

Jackson, Shannon. *Lines of Activity: Performance, Historiography, Hull-House Domesticity.* Ann Arbor: The University of Michigan Press, 2000.

Johnston, Robert D. "Conclusion: Historians and the Middle Class." In *The Middling Sorts: Explorations in the History of the American Middle Class.* Edited by Burton J. Bledstein and Robert D. Johnston. New York: Routledge, 2001.

———. *The Radical Middle Class: Populist Democracy and the Question of Capitalism in Progressive Era Portland, Oregon.* Princeton, NJ: Princeton University Press, 2003.

———. "Re-Democratizing the Progressive Era: The Politics of Progressive Era Political Historiography." *Journal of the Gilded Age and Progressive Era* 1, no. 1 (2002): 68–92.

Joslin, Katherine. *Jane Addams, a Writer's Life.* Champaign: University of Illinois Press, 2004.

Kaplan, Amy. *The Social Construction of American Realism.* Chicago: University of Chicago Press, 1988.

Kaplan, Flora E. S., ed. *Museums and the Making of "Ourselves": The Role of Objects in National Identity.* London: Leicester University Press, 1994.

Kelley, Robin D. G. *Race Rebels: Culture, Politics, and the Black Working-Class.* New York: Free Press, 1996.

Kleppner, Paul. *The Cross of Culture: A Social Analysis of Midwestern Politics, 1850–1900.* New York: Free Press, 1970.

Kloppenberg, James T. *Uncertain Victory: Social Democracy and Progressivism in European and American Thought, 1870–1920.* New York: Oxford University, 1986.

———. "The Virtues of Liberalism: Christianity, Republicanism, and Ethics in Early American Political Discourse." *Journal of American History* 71 (1987): 9–33.

Knight, Louise W. "Biography's Window on Social Change: Benevolence and Justice in Jane Addams's 'A Modern Lear.'" *Journal of Women's History* 9, no. 1 (Spring 1997): 111–38.

———. *Citizen: Jane Addams and the Struggle for Democracy.* Chicago: University of Chicago Press, 2005.

Knupfer, Anne Meis. *Reform and Resistance: Gender, Delinquency, and America's First Juvenile Court.* New York: Routledge, 2001.

———. *Toward a Tenderer Humanity and a Nobler Womanhood: African American Women's Clubs in Turn-of-the-Century Chicago.* New York: New York University Press, 1996.

Kraut, Alan M. *The Huddled Masses: The Immigrant in American Society, 1880–1921.* Arlington Heights, IL, 1982.

Lambert, Josiah Bartlett. *"If the Workers Took a Notion": The Right to Strike and American Political Development.* Ithaca: Cornell University Press, 2005.

Laqueur, Thomas W. "The Humanitarian Narrative." In *The New Cultural History.* Edited by Lynn Hunt. Berkeley: University of California Press, 1989.

Lasch, Christopher. *The New Radicalism in America, 1889–1963: The Intellectual as a Social Type.* New York: Knopf, 1965.

———, ed. *The Social Thought of Jane Addams.* New York: Bobbs-Merrill, 1965.

Lasch-Quinn, Elizabeth. *Black Neighbors: Race and the Limits of Reform in the American Settlement House Movement, 1890–1945.* Chapel Hill: University of North Carolina Press, 1993.

Lears, T. J. Jackson. *No Place of Grace: Antimodernism and the Transformation of American Culture, 1880–1920.* Chicago: University of Chicago Press, 1981.

———. *Something for Nothing: Luck in America.* New York: Penguin Books, 2003.

————. "'What if History were Gambler?'" In *Moral Problems in American Life: New Perspectives on Cultural History.* Edited by Karen Halttunen and Lewis Perry. Ithaca: Cornell University Press, 1998.

Lee-Forman, Koby. "The Simple Love of Truth: The Racial Justice Activism of Celia Parker Woolley." PhD diss., Northwestern University, 1995.

Leidenberg, Georg. "Working-Class Progressivism and the Politics of Transportation in Chicago, 1895–1907." PhD diss., University of North Carolina-Chapel Hill, 1995.

Levine, Daniel. *Jane Addams and the Liberal Tradition.* Madison: The State Historical Society of Wisconsin, 1971.

————. *Varieties of Reform Thought.* Madison: The State Historical Society of Wisconsin, 1964.

Levine, Lawrence. *High Brow/Low Brow: The Emergence of Cultural Hierarchy in America.* Cambridge, MA: Harvard University Press, 1988.

Levine, Peter. "Can the Internet Rescue Democracy? Toward an On-Line Commons." In *Democracy's Moment: Reforming the American Political System for the 21st Century.* Edited by Ronald Hayduk and Kevin Mattson. New York: Rowman and Littlefield Publishers, Inc, 2002.

Leys, Ruth. "Mead's Voices: Imitation as Foundation; or the Struggle against Mimesis." In *Modernist Impulses in the Human Sciences, 1870–1930.* Edited by Dorothy Ross. Baltimore: Johns Hopkins University Press, 1994.

Lichtenstein, Nelson, and Howell John Harris, eds. *Industrial Democracy in America: The Ambiguous Promise.* New York: Woodrow Wilson Center Press and Cambridge University Press, 1993.

Livingston, James. *Pragmatism and the Political Economy of Cultural Revolution, 1850–1940.* Chapel Hill: University of North Carolina Press, 1994.

Lorentzen, Lois Ann, and Jennifer Turpin, eds. *Women and War Reader.* New York: New York University Press, 1998.

Lustig, R. Jeffrey. *Corporate Liberalism: The Origins of Modern American Political Theory, 1890–1920.* Berkeley, CA: University of California Press, 1982.

Madrick, Jeff. "Inequality and Democracy." In *The Fight is for Democracy: Winning the War of Ideas in America and the World.* New York: Perennial, 2003.

Marks, David. "Polishing the Gem of the Prairie: The Evolution of Civic Reform Consciousness in Chicago, 1874–1900." PhD diss., University of Wisconsin, 1975.

Marshall, David. *The Surprising Effects of Sympathy: Marivaux, Diderot, Rousseau, and Mary Shelley.* Chicago: University of Chicago Press, 1988.

Mattson, Kevin. *Creating a Democratic Public: The Struggle for Urban Participatory Democracy during the Progressive Era.* University Park, PA: The Pennsylvania State University Press, 1998.

Mayer, John Albert. "Private Charity in Chicago from 1871–1915." PhD diss., University of Minnesota, 1978.

McCarthy, Kathleen D. *Noblesse Oblige: Charity and Cultural Philanthropy in Chicago, 1849–1929.* Chicago: University of Chicago Press, 1982.

McCarthy, Michael. "Businessmen and Professionals in Municipal Reform: The Chicago Experience, 1887–1920." In *The Age of Urban Reform: New Perspectives on the Progressive Era.* Edited by Michael H. Ebner and Eugene M. Tobin. Port Washington, NY: Kennikat Press, 1977.

McCartin, Joseph Anthony. *Labor's Great War: The Struggle for Industrial Democracy and the Origins of Modern American Labor Relations, 1912–1921*. Chapel Hill: University of North Carolina Press, 1997.

McCormick, Richard L. "The Discovery That Business Corrupts Politics: A Reappraisal of the Origins of Progressivism." *American Historical Review* 86, no. 2 (1981): 247–74

McCoy, Drew R. *The Elusive Republic: Political Economy in Jeffersonian America*. Chapel Hill: University of North Carolina Press, 1980.

McGerr, Michael. *The Decline of Popular Politics: The American North, 1865–1928*. New York: Oxford University Press, 1986.

———. *A Fierce Discontent: The Rise and Fall of the Progressive Movement in America, 1870–1920*. New York: Free Press, 2003.

McHenry, Elizabeth. *Forgotten Readers: Recovering the Lost History of African American Literary Societies*. Durham: Duke University Press, 2002.

McMurry, Linda O. *To Keep the Waters Troubled: The Life of Ida B. Wells*. New York: Oxford University Press, 1998.

Meacham, Standish. *Toynbee Hall and Social Reform, 1880–1914: The Search for Community*. New Haven: Yale University Press, 1987.

Melosi, Martin V. *The Sanitary City: Urban Infrastructure in America from Colonial Times to the Present*. Baltimore: The Johns Hopkins University Press, 2000.

Melucci, Alberto. "Social Movements and the Democratization of Everyday Life." In *Civil Society and the State: New European Perspectives*. Edited by John Keane. London: Verso 1988.

Melvin, Patricia Mooney. *The Organic City: Urban Definition & Community Organization*. Lexington, KY: University Press of Kentucky, 1987.

Meyerowitz, Joanne. *Women Adrift: Independent Wage Earners in Chicago, 1880–1930*. Chicago: University of Chicago Press, 1987.

Miller, Donald L. *City of the Century: The Epic of Chicago and the Making of America*. New York: Simon & Schuster, 1996.

Miller, Ericka M. *The Other Reconstruction: Where Violence and Womanhood Meet in the Writings of Wells-Barnett, Grimke, and Larsen*. New York: Garland Publishers, 2000.

Miller, Zane L. *Boss Cox's Cincinnati: Urban Politics in the Progressive Era*. Columbus: The Ohio State University Press, 1968.

Mirola, William Andrew. "Fighting in the Pews and Fighting in the Streets: Protestantism, Consciousness, and the Eight-Hour Movement in Chicago, 1867–1912." PhD diss., Indiana University, 1995.

Mohanty, Chandra Talpade. "Under Westhern Eyes: Feminist Scholarship and Colonial Discourses." In *Third World Women and the Politics of Feminism*. Edited by Chandra Talpade Mohanty, Ann Russo, and Lourdes Torres. Indianapolis: Indiana University Press, 1991.

Moorhead, James. "Between Progress and Apocalypse: A Reassessment of Millennialism in American Religious Thought." *Journal of American History* 71 (December 1984): 524–40.

Mouffe, Chantal. "Feminism, Citizenship, and Radical Democratic Politics." In *Feminists Theorize the Political*. Edited by Judith Butler and Joan W. Scott. New York: Routledge, 1992.

Mosher, Frederick C. *Democracy and the Public Service.* New York: Oxford University Press, 1982.

Montgomery, David. *The Fall of the House of Labor: The Workplace, the State, and American Labor Activism, 1865–1925.* Cambridge, MA: Harvard University Press, 1987.

Mullen, Harryette. "Runaway Tongue: Resistant Orality in Uncle Tom's Cabin, Our Nig, Incidents in the Life of a Slave Girl, and Beloved." In *The Culture of Sentiment: Race, Gender, and Sentimentality in Nineteenth-Century America.* Edited by Shirley Samuels. New York: Oxford University Press, 1992.

Muncy, Robyn. *Creating a Female Dominion in American Reform, 1890–1935.* New York: Oxford University Press, 1991.

Nackenoff, Carol. "Gendered Citizenship: Alternative Narratives of Political Incorporation in the United States, 1875–1925." In *The Liberal Tradition in American Politics: Reassessing the Legacy of American Liberalism.* Edited by David F. Ericson and Louisa Bertch Green. New York: Routledge, 1999.

Nelson, Bruce. *Beyond the Martyrs: A Social History of Chicago's Anarchists, 1870–1900.* New Brunswick: Rutgers University Press, 1988.

Ngai, Mae. "The Architecture of Race in American Immigration Law: A Reexamination of the Immigration Act of 1924." *Journal of American History* 86, no. 1 (June 1999): 67–92.

Norton, Anne. *Alternative Americas: A Reading of Antebellum Political Culture.* Chicago University of Chicago Press, 1986.

Notable American Women. Cambridge, MA: Belknap Press of Harvard University Press, 1971.

Novak, William J. *The People's Welfare: Law and Regulation in Nineteenth-Century America.* Chapel Hill: University of North Carolina Press, 1996.

Oleson, Alexandra, and John Voss. *The Organization of Knowledge in Modern America.* Baltimore: Johns Hopkins University Press, 1979.

Painter, Nell Irvin. *Standing at Armageddon.* New York: W.W. Norton, 1987.

Pascoe, Peggy. "Miscegenation Law, Court Cases, and Ideologies of 'Race' in Twentieth-Century America." *Journal of American History* 83, no. 1 (1996): 44–69.

Payne, Elizabeth Anne. *Reform, Labor, and Feminism: Margaret Dreier Robins and the Women's Trade Union League.* Urbana, IL: University of Illinois Press, 1989.

Pauly, John J. "The City Builders: Chicago Businessmen and Their Changing Ethos." PhD diss., University of Illinois at Urbana-Champaign, 1979.

Pegram, Thomas. *Partisans and Progressives: Private Interest and Public Policy in Illinois, 1870–1922.* Urbana, IL: University of Illinois Press, 1992.

Pierce, Bessie Louis. *A History of Chicago vol. III, The Rise of a Modern City, 1871–1893.* New York: Alfred A. Knopf, 1947.

Piott, Steven L. *Giving Voters a Voice: The Origins of the Initiative and Referendum in America.* Columbia: University of Missouri Press, 2003.

Platt, David. *Celluloid Power: Social Film Criticism from The Birth of a Nation to Judgment at Nuremberg.* Netuchen, NJ: The Scarecrow Press, 1992.

Pleck, Elizabeth. *Domestic Tyranny: The making of Social Policy against Family Violence from Colonial Times to the Present.* New York: Oxford University Press, 1987.

Pletsch, Carl. "The Three Worlds, or the Division of Social Scientific Labor, circa 1950–1975." *Comparative Studies in Society and History* 23, no. 4 (October, 1981): 565–90.

Poole, Ernest. *Giants Gone: Men Who Made Chicago.* New York: McGraw-Hill, 1943.

Purcell, Edward A., Jr. *The Crisis of Democratic Theory: Scientific Naturalism and the Problem of Value.* Lexington: University Press of Kentucky, 1973.

Quadagno, Jill. *The Color of Welfare: How Racism Undermined the War on Poverty.* New York: Oxford University Press, 1994.

Rawls, John. *Political Liberalism.* New York: Columbia University Press, 1993.

Reed, Christopher Robert. *The Chicago NAACP and the Rise of Black Professional Leadership, 1910–1966.* Bloomington, IN: Indiana University Press, 1997.

Rieff, Janice L. "A Modern Lear and His Daughters: Gender in the Model Town of Pullman." In *The Pullman Strike and the Crisis of the 1890s: Essays on Labor and Politics.* Edited by Richard Schneirov, Shelton Stromquist, and Nick Salvatore. Urbana: University of Illinois Press, 1999.

Roberts, Sidney I. "Businessmen in Revolt: Chicago, 1874–1900." PhD diss., Northwestern University, 1960.

———. "The Municipal Voters' League and Chicago's Boodlers." *Journal of the Illinois State Historical Society* 53, no. 2 (June 1960): 117–48.

———. "Portrait of a Robber Baron," *Business History Review* 35, no. 3 (Autumn 1961): 344–71.

Rodgers, Daniel T. *Atlantic Crossing: Social Politics in a Progressive Age.* Cambridge, MA: The Belknap Press of Harvard University Press, 1998.

———. *Contested Truths: Keywords in American Politics since Independence.* New York: Basic Books, Inc., 1987.

———. "In Search of Progressivism." *Reviews in American History* 10, no. 4 (December 1982): 113–32.

Roediger, David R. *Wages of Whiteness: Race and the Making of the American Working Class.* London: Verso, 1991.

———, ed. *Haymarket Scrapbook.* Chicago: C. H. Kerr Publishing Company, 1986.

Rogin, Michael. "'The Sword Became a Flashing Vision': D.W. Griffith's *The Birth of a Nation.*" *Representations* 9 (1985): 150–95.

Rosenzweig, Roy. *Eight Hours for What We Will.* New York: Cambridge University Press, 1985.

Ross, Dorothy. "Gendered Social Knowledge: Domestic Discourse, Jane Addams, and the Possibilities of Social Science." In *Gender and American Social Science.* Edited by Helene Silverberg. Princeton, NJ: Princeton University Press, 1998.

———. "Historical Consciousness in Nineteenth Century America." *American Historical Review* 89 (October 1984): 909–28.

———. "Liberalism." In *A Companion to American Thought.* Edited by Richard Wightman Fox and James T. Kloppenberg. Malden, MA: Blackwell Publishers, 1995.

———. *The Origins of American Social Science.* New York: Cambridge University Press, 1991.

Rothman, David J. *The Discovery of the Asylum: Social Order and Disorder in the New Republic.* Boston: Little, Brown, 1971: 1990.

Rueben, Julie. *The Making of the Modern University: Intellectual Transformation and the Marginalization of Morality.* Chicago: University of Chicago Press, 1996.

Rydell, Robert. *All the World's a Fair: Visions of Empire at American International Expositions, 1876–1916.* Chicago: University of Chicago Press, 1984.

Saldaña-Portillo, Maria Josefina. *The Revolutionary Imagination in the Americas and the Age of Development.* Durham, NC: Duke University Press, 2003.

Salvatore, Nick. *Eugene V. Debs: Citizen and Socialist.* Urbana: University of Illinois Press, 1982.

Samuels, Shirley, ed. *The Culture of Sentiment: Race, Gender and Sentimentality in Nineteenth Century America.* New York: Oxford University Press, 1992.

Sanchez-Eppler, Karen. "Bodily Bonds: The Interacting Rhetorics of Feminism and Abolition." In *The Culture of Sentiment: Race, Gender, and Sentimentality in Nineteenth-century America.* Edited by Shirley Samuels. New York: Oxford University Press, 1992.

Sanders, Elisabeth. *Roots of Reform: Farmers, Workers, and the American State, 1877–1917.* Chicago: University of Chicago Press, 1999.

Sawislak, Karen. *Smoldering City: Chicagoans and the Great Fire, 1871–1874.* Chicago: University of Chicago Press, 1995.

Schechter, Patricia Ann. *Ida B. Wells-Barnett and American Reform, 1880–1930.* Chapel Hill: University of North Carolina Press, 2001.

Schiesl, Martin. *Politics of Efficiency: Municipal Administration and Reform in America, 1800–1920.* Berkeley: University of California Press, 1977.

Schmidt, Mary R. "Grout: Alternative Kinds of Knowledge and Why They Are Ignored." In *Democracy, Bureaucracy, and the Study of Administration.* Edited by Camilla Stivers. Boulder, CO: Westview Press, 2001.

Schneirov, Richard. *Labor and Urban Politics: Class Conflict and the Origins of Modern Liberalism in Chicago, 1864–1897.* Urbana: University of Illinois Press, 1998.

Schneirov, Richard, Shelton Stromquist, and Nick Salvatore, eds. *The Pullman Strike and the Crisis of the 1890s: Essays on Labor and Politics.* Urbana: University of Illinois Press, 1999.

Schneirov, Richard, and Thomas J. Suhrbur. *Union Brotherhood, Union Town: The History of the Carpenters' Union of Chicago, 1863–1987.* Carbondale: Southern Illinois University Press, 1988.

Schram, Sanford F., Joe Soss, and Richard C. Fording, eds. *Race and the Politics of Welfare Reform.* Ann Arbor: University of Michigan Press, 2003.

Scott, Anne Firor. *Natural Allies: Women's Associations in American History.* Urbana: University of Illinois Press, 1991.

Scott, Joan Wallach. *Gender and the Politics of History.* New York: Columbia University Press, 1988.

———. "The Evidence of Experience." *Critical Inquiry* 17 (Summer 1991): 773–97.

———. "Experience." In *Feminists Theorize the Political.* Edited by Judith Butler and Joan W. Scott, 22–40. New York: Routledge, 1992.

Seigfried, Charlene Haddock. "Introduction" to Jane Addams, *Democracy and Social Ethics.* Urbana: University of Illinois Press, 2002.

———. *Pragmatism and Feminism: Reweaving the Social Fabric.* Chicago: University of Chicago Press, 1996.

Sennett, Richard. *The Fall of Public Man.* New York: Vintage Books, 1977.

Shepard, Benjamin. "Community as a Source for Democratic Politics." In *Democracy's Moment: Reforming the American Political System for the 21st Century.* Edited by Ronald Hayduk and Kevin Mattson. New York: Rowman and Littlefield Publishers, Inc., 2002.

Sherrick, Rebecca. "Private Visions, Public Lives: The Hull-House Women in the Progressive Era." PhD diss., Northwestern University, 1980.

Shi, David E. *Facing Facts: Realism in American Thought and Culture, 1850–1920.* New York: Oxford University Press, 1995.

Shklar, Judith. *American Citizenship: The Quest for Inclusion.* Cambridge, MA: Harvard University Press, 1991.

Shpak-Lissak, Rivka. *Pluralism and Progressives: Hull-House and the New Immigrants, 1890–1919.* Chicago: University of Chicago Press, 1989.

Silver, Regene Henriette Spero. "Jane Addams: Peace, Justice, Gender, 1860–1918." PhD diss., University of Pennsylvania, 1990.

Silverberg, Helene. "'A Government of Men': Gender, the City and the New Science of Politics." In *Gender and American Social Science: The Formative Years.* Edited by Helene Silverberg. Princeton, NJ: Princeton University Press, 1998.

Sklansky, Jeff. *The Soul's Economy: Market Society and Selfhood in American Thought, 1820–1920.* Chapel Hill: University of North Carolina Press, 2002.

Sklar, Kathryn Kish. "Hull House in the 1890s: A Community of Women Reformers." *Signs* 10, no. 4 (1985): 658–77.

———. "Hull-House Maps and Papers: Social Science as Women's Work in the 1890s." In *Gender and American Social Science.* Edited by Helene Silverberg. Princeton, NJ: Princeton University Press, 1998.

———. *Florence Kelley and the Nation's Work: The Rise of Women's Political Culture, 1830–1900.* New Haven: Yale University Press, 1995.

———. "'Some of Us Who Deal with the Social Fabric': Jane Addams Blends Peace and Social Justice, 1907–1919." *Journal of the Gilded Age and the Progressive Era* 2, no. 1 (2003): 80–96.

Skocpol, Theda. *Protecting Soldiers and Mothers: The Political Origins of Social Policy in the United States.* Cambridge: Harvard University Press, 1992.

Skolnik, Richard. "1895—A Test for Municipal Nonpartisanship in New York City." In *Essays in the History of New York City: A Memorial to Sidney Pomerantz.* Edited by Irwin Yellowitz. Port Washington, NY: Kennikat Press, 1978.

Smagorinsky, Peter. *The Discourse of Character Education: Culture Wars in the Classroom.* Mahwah, NJ: L. Erlbaum Associates, 2005.

Smith, Adam. *The Theory of Moral Sentiments.* Edited by D. D. Raphael and A. L. Macfie. Oxford: Clarendon Press, 1976.

Smith, Carl. *Urban Disorder and the Shape of Belief: The Great Chicago Fire, the Haymarket Bomb, and the Model Town of Pullman.* Chicago: University of Chicago, 1995.

Smith, Karen Ruth. "'Pain into Sympathy': Ethical Realism and the Conversion of Feeling in Eliot, Tolstoy, and Stowe." PhD diss., University of Michigan, 1992.

Smith, Mark. *Social Science in the Crucible: The American Debate over Objectivity and Purpose, 1918–1941.* Durham, NC: Duke University Press, 1994.

Smith, Nina B. "'This Bleak Situation': The Founding of Fort Sheridan, Illinois." *Journal of the Illinois State Historical Society* 80, no. 1 (Spring 1987).

Smith, Rogers. *Civic Ideals: Conflicting Visions of Citizenship in U.S. History.* New Haven: Yale University Press, 1997.

Smith, Shawn Michelle. *Photography on the Color Line: W.E.B DuBois, Race, and Visual Culture.* Durham: Duke University Press, 2004.

Snyder, R. Claire. "Democratic Theory and the Case for Public Deliberation." In Ronald Hayduk and Kevin Mattson, eds. *Democracy's Moment: Reforming the American Political System for the 21st Century.* New York: Rowman and Littlefield Publishers, Inc, 2002.

Solomon, Barbara. *In the Company of Educated Women: A History of Women and Higher Education in America.* New Haven: Yale University Press, 1985.

Somers, Margaret R., and Gloria D. Gibson. "Reclaiming the 'Other': Narrative and the Social Constitution of Identity." In *Social Theory and the Politics of Identity.* Edited by Craig Calhoun. Cambridge, MA: Blackwell, 1994.

Spear, Allan. *Black Chicago: The Making of a Negro Ghetto, 1890–1920.* Chicago: University of Chicago Press, 1967.

Staley, Alvah Eugene, "A History of the Illinois Federation of Labor." PhD diss., University of Chicago, 1928.

Stanfield, John H. *Philanthropy and Jim Crow in American Social Science.* Westport, CT: Greenwood Press, 1985.

Stanley, Amy Dru. "Beggars Can't be Choosers: Compulsion and Contract in Postbellum America." *Journal of American History* 78 (March 1992): 1265–93.

___ . "Conjugal Bonds and Wage Labor: Rights of Contract in the Age of Emancipation." *Journal of American History* 75 (September 1988): 471–500.

Steigerwalt, Albert K. *The National Association of Manufacturers 1895–1914: A Study in Business Leadership.* Grand Rapids: Bureau of Business Research, University of Michigan, 1964.

Stein, Leon, ed. *The Pullman Strike and American Labor: From Conspiracy to Collective Bargaining.* New York: Arno, 1969.

Stivers, Camilla. *Bureau Men, Settlement Women: Constructing Public Administration in the Progressive Era.* Lawrence: University of Kansas Press, 2000.

Strickland, Arvarh E. *History of the Chicago Urban League.* Urbana: University of Illinois Press, 1966.

Stromquist, Shelton. "The Crisis of 1894 and the Legacies of Producerism." In *The Pullman Strike and the Crisis of the 1890s: Essays on Labor and Politics.* Edited by Richard Schneirov, Shelton Stromquist, and Nick Salvatore. Urbana: University of Illinois Press, 1999.

———. *Reinventing "The People": The Progressive Movement, the Class Problem, and the Origins of Modern Liberalism.* Urbana: University of Illinois Press, 2005.

Sturken, Marita. *Tangled Memories: The Vietnam War, the AIDS Epidemic, and the Politics of Remembering.* Berkeley: University of California Press, 1997.

Sturken, Marita, and Lisa Cartwright. *Practices of Looking: An Introduction to Visual Culture.* New York: Oxford University Press, 2001.

Tarr, Joel. *A Study in Boss Politics: William Lorimer of Chicago.* Urbana, IL: University of Illinois Press, 1971.

Tax, Meredith. *The Rising of the Women: Feminist Solidarity and Class Conflict, 1880–1917.* New York: Monthly Review Press, 1980.

Terborg-Penn, Rosalyn. *African American Women in the Struggle for the Vote, 1850–1920.* Bloomington, IN: Indiana University Press, 1998.

———. "Ida B. Wells-Barnett and the Alpha Suffrage Club of Chicago." In *One Woman,*

One Vote: Rediscovering the Woman Suffrage Movement. Edited by Marjorie Spruill Wheeler. Troutdale, OR: New Sage Press, 1995.

Thelen, David P. *The New Citizenship: Origins of Progressivism in Wisconsin, 1885–1900.* Columbia: University of Missouri Press, 1972.

Thomas, John L. *Alternative America: Henry George, Edward Bellamy, Henry Demarest Lloyd and the Adversary Tradition.* Cambridge, MA: Belknap Press, 1983.

Thompson, Mildred I. *Ida B. Wells-Barnett: An Exploratory Study of an American Black Woman, 1893–1930.* Brooklyn, NY: Carlson Publishing, 1990.

Tolnay, Stewart E., and E. M. Beck. *A Festival of Violence: An Analysis of Southern Lynchings, 1882–1930.* Urbana: University of Illinois Press, 1995.

Trachtenberg, Alan. *The Incorporation of America: Culture and Society in the Gilded Age.* New York: Hill and Wang, 1982.

Trouillot, Michel-Rolph. *Silencing the Past: Power and the Production of History.* Boston: Beacon Press, 1995.

Turley, David. "Black Social Science and Black Politics in the Understanding of the South: Dubois, the Atlanta University Studies and The Crisis, 1897–1920." In *Race and Class in the American South since 1890.* Edited by Melvyn Stokes and Rick Halpern. Providence: Berg, 1994.

Tuttle, William M., Jr. *Race Riot: Chicago in the Red Summer of 1919.* New York: Athenaeum, 1970.

Tyack, David. *The One Best System: A History of American Urban Education.* Cambridge, MA: Harvard University Press, 1974.

Wachbroit, Robert. "The Changing Role of Expertise." In *Civil Society, Democracy, and Civic Renewal.* Edited by Robert K. Fullinwider. Boulder, CO: Rowman & Littlefield, Publishers, 1999.

Wade, Louise C. *Graham Taylor: Pioneer for Social Justice, 1851–1938.* Chicago: University of Chicago Press, 1964.

Waldrep, Christopher. *The Many Faces of Judge Lynch: Extralegal Violence and Punishment in America.* New York: Palgrave Macmillan, 2002.

Weber, Arnold R., ed., *The Structure of Collective Bargaining: Studies in Business, Problems and Perspectives; proceedings of a seminar sponsored by Graduate School of Business, University of Chicago and the McKinsey Foundation.* Glencoe, IL: The Free Press of Glencoe, Inc., 1961.

Weinstein, James. *The Corporate Idea in the Liberal State, 1900–1918.* Boston: Beacon Press, 1968.

Westbrook, Robert. *John Dewey and American Democracy.* Ithaca: Cornell University Press, 1991.

White, Deborah Gray. "The Cost of Club Work, the Price of Black Feminism." In *Visible Women: New Essays on American Activism.* Edited by Nancy Hewitt and Suzanne Lebsock. Urbana: University of Illinois Press, 1993.

White, E. Frances. *Dark Continent of Our Bodies: Black Feminism and the Politics of Respectability.* Philadelphia: Temple University Press, 2001.

White, Morton. *Social Thought in America: The Revolt against Formalism.* Boston: Beacon Hill Press, 1959.

Wiebe, Robert. *The Search for Order, 1877–1920.* New York: Hill & Wang, 1967.

Wilentz, Sean. *Chants Democratic: New York City and the Rise of the American Working Class.* New York: Oxford University Press, 1984.

Williams, Raymond. *Culture and Society.* New York: Columbia University Press, 1983.

Wright, Gwendolyn. *Moralism and the Model Home: Domestic Architecture and Cultural Conflict in Chicago, 1873–1913.* Chicago: University of Chicago Press, 1980.

Wrigley, Julia. *Class Politics and Public Schools: Chicago, 1900–1950.* New Brunswick, NJ: Rutgers University Press, 1982.

Yellin, Jean Fagan, and John C. Van Horne, eds. *The Abolitionist Sisterhood: Women's Political Culture in Antebellum America.* Ithaca: Cornell University Press, 1994.

Index

Addams, Jane, 1, 6, 8 17, 46, 49; "Bread-givers," 94–95; "Cassandra," 95–96; and Civic Federation, 46, 62, 85; *Democracy and Social Ethics,* 123; as family mediator, 92n15; influence of father, 91n13; and liberalism, 87n3; and lynching, 202n69, 205; narrative writing style, 123–29; and participatory democracy, 91n11; and religion, 94n22; social work, contributions to, 90, 90n9; *Twenty Years at Hull-House,* 92n13, 98n37; views of democracy 107, 107n68, 130–31, 275–76; youth 91–96. *See also* Hull-House; pragmatism

African Americans, 10; and alternative social knowledge, 207n90; in Chicago, 186–94; cultural agency, 8, 185, 193, 207–21; and domestic ideology, 200–201; and interracial reform, 7, 27, 221–27; middle class, 227n164; reformers, 190–193; as strikebreakers, 189–90, 190n26 192n35. *See also* lynching; segregation; social knowledge and race; social science and race; Ida B. Wells-Barnett; Fannie Barrier Williams

anti-gambling campaign, 77–81

anti-lynching. *See* Ida B.Wells-Barnett

arbitration. *See* labor arbitration

Armour, Philip, 33–34

Bachin, Robin, 8n14, 24, 24n49, 235n188

Birth of a Nation, 217–220

Brown, Victoria Bissell, 91n11; on Jane Addams and democracy, 112n89, 149n56

charter reform, 6–8, 28, 244; and democratic social knowledge, 244n7; female

reformers, 248; home rule, 250–52; provisions of, 246; workers' visions, 249–50; *See also* Civic Federation of Chicago; United Societies for Local Self-Government

Chicago, economic development, 3, 32, 45, 137n12, 171n143; city government, 3, 37; class conflict 12, 39; immigration 3, 32; population growth, 32; race relations, 45

Chicago Federation of Labor, 189; attacks on charter, 249, 251, 253–54, 261

Chicago Teachers' Federation, 72, 248

Chicago Woman's Club, 1, 53, 54n27, 73; and gendered social knowledge, 61n49; support for Hull House, 97

Citizen's Association, 40, 51

civic elites, 5, 9; charter reform, 255, 259, 260, 264; and labor arbitration, 136; and laissez-faire, 37, 83, 153, 264; and liberal republicanism, 32, 81–82, 139, 144, 172; social views of, 33–34; views of poverty, 38

Civic Federation of Chicago, 5–6, 17; Board of Conciliation, 133, 152; and charter campaign, 245–47; direct democracy, opposition to, 258n8; Industrial committee, 53; and interest-group politics, 256–57; and labor arbitration, 136, 145, 168–69, 177–78; and membership, 47, 50, 257n54; and poor relief, 74–77; and social knowledge, 47, 55–61

civil service, 67–68, 67n77, 81–82

classical political economy, 3, 5, 7, 9, 28; and growth of Chicago, 30–32; 142; as natural law, 39–40, 77, 81–82, 84, 126, 130, 135, 148–49

Urban Life and Urban Landscape
Zane L. Miller, Series Editor

The series examines the history of urban life and the development of the urban landscape through works that place social, economic, and political issues in the intellectual
and cultural context of their times.

*Reading London: Urban Speculation and Imaginative Government in Eighteenth-Century
Literature*
Erik Bond

Lake Effects: A History of Urban Policy Making in Cleveland, 1825–1929
Ronald R. Weiner

High Stakes: Big Time Sports and Downtown Redevelopment
Timothy Jon Curry, Kent Schwirian, and Rachael A. Woldoff

Suburban Steel: The Magnificent Failure of the Lustron Corporation, 1945–1951
Douglas Knerr

New York City: An Outsider's Inside View
Mario Maffi

Merchant of Illusion: James Rouse, America's Salesman of the Businessman's Utopia
Nicholas Dagen Bloom

The Failure of Planning: Permitting Sprawl in San Diego Suburbs, 1970–1999
Richard Hogan

Faith and Action: A History of the Catholic Archdiocese of Cincinnati, 1821–1996
Roger Fortin

Regionalism and Reform: Art and Class Formation in Antebellum Cincinnati
Wendy Jean Katz

*Making Sense of the City: Local Government, Civic Culture, and Community Life in
Urban America*
Edited by Robert B. Fairbanks and Patricia Mooney-Melvin

Suburban Alchemy: 1960s New Towns and the Transformation of the American Dream
Nicholas Dagen Bloom

Visions of Place: The City, Neighborhoods, Suburbs, and Cincinnati's Clifton, 1850–2000
Zane L. Miller

A Right to Representation: Proportional Election Systems for the Twenty-First Century
Kathleen L. Barber